Governance and Economic Development

NEW THINKING IN POLITICAL ECONOMY

Series Editor: Peter J. Boettke
George Mason University, USA

New Thinking in Political Economy aims to encourage scholarship in the intersection of the disciplines of politics, philosophy and economics. It has the ambitious purpose of reinvigorating political economy as a progressive force for understanding social and economic change.

The series is an important forum for the publication of new work analysing the social world from a multidisciplinary perspective. With increased specialization (and professionalization) within universities, interdisciplinary work has become increasingly uncommon. Indeed, during the 20th century, the process of disciplinary specialization reduced the intersection between economics, philosophy and politics and impoverished our understanding of society. Modern economics in particular has become increasingly mathematical and largely ignores the role of institutions and the contribution of moral philosophy and politics.

New Thinking in Political Economy will stimulate new work that combines technical knowledge provided by the 'dismal science' and the wisdom gleaned from the serious study of the 'worldly philosophy'. The series will reinvigorate our understanding of the social world by encouraging a multidisciplinary approach to the challenges confronting society in the new century.

Recent titles in the series include:

Governance and Economic Development

A Comparative Institutional Approach

Joachim Ahrens
University of Göttingen, Germany

NEW THINKING IN POLITICAL ECONOMY

Edward Elgar
Cheltenham, UK • Northampton, MA, USA

Published by
Edward Elgar Publishing Limited
Glensanda House
Montpellier Parade
Cheltenham
Glos GL50 1UA
UK

Edward Elgar Publishing, Inc.
136 West Street
Suite 202
Northampton
Massachusetts 01060
USA

A catalogue record for this book
is available from the British Library

Library of Congress Cataloguing in Publication Data
Ahrens, Joachim, 1963–
    Governance and economic development: a comparative institutional approach/ Joachim Ahrens.
       p. cm. — (New thinking in political economy)
    Includes bibliographical references and index.
       1. Corporate governance—Developing countries. 2. Corporate governance—Europe, Eastern. 3. Corporate governance—East Asia. 4. Industrial policy—Developing countries. 5. Industrial policy—Europe, Eastern. 6. Industrial policy—East Asia. 7. Developing countries—Economic conditions. 8. Europe, Eastern—Economic conditions—1989– 9. East Asia—Economic conditions. 10. Post-communism—Europe, Eastern. 11. Economic development. I. Title. II. Series.

HD2741 .A45 2002
338.7—dc21

2002020229

ISBN 1 84064 960 7

Printed and bound in Great Britain by MPG Books Ltd, Bodmin, Cornwall

Contents

Figures, Tables, and Boxes

Figures

Tables

Boxes

Appendices

Abbreviations and Acronyms

ADB	Asian Development Bank
BERI	Business Environmental Risk Intelligence
BJP	Bharatiya Janata Party (India)
CCP	Chinese Communist Party
CDF	Comprehensive Development Framework
CEE	Central and Eastern Europe
CIS	Commonwealth of Independent States
DIW	Deutsches Institut für Wirtschaftsforschung
EBRD	European Bank for Reconstruction and Development
EC	European Communities
EU	European Union
FDI	Foreign Direct Investment
FRG	Federal Republic of Germany
GATT	General Agreement on Tariffs and Trade
GDP	Gross Domestic Product
GDR	German Democratic Republic
GNP	Gross National Product
HPAEs	High-Performing Asian Economies[*]
HRD	Human Resource Development
IAS	Indian Administrative Service
ICRG	International Country Risk Guide
ILO	International Labour Organization
IMF	International Monetary Fund
LAC	Latin America and the Caribbean
LDCs	Less Developed Countries
MDBs	Multilateral Development Banks
MEGS	Market-Enhancing Governance Structure(s)
MITI	Ministry of Trade and Industry (Japan)
MPF	Market-Preserving Federalism
NATO	North Atlantic Treaty Organization
NGO	Non-Governmental Organization
NICs	Newly Industrialized Countries

---

[*]   In this study, the HPAEs include Hong Kong, Indonesia, Malaysia, Singapore, South Korea, Taiwan, and Thailand.

NIE	New Institutional Economics
NIR	National Institutional Review
NPE	New Political Economy
NWC	National Wages Council (Singapore)
OECD	Organization for Economic Co-operation and Development
PMPF	Participatory Market-Preserving Federalism
PSCs	Post-Socialist Countries
PSEs	Public-Sector Enterprises (India)
R&D	Research and Development
SOE	State-Owned Enterprise
SSA	Sub-Saharan Africa
TVEs	Township-Village Enterprises
UF	United Front (political party, India)
UNDP	United Nations Development Programme
US	United States (of America)
USAID	United States Agency for International Development
USSR	Union of Socialist Soviet Republics
WBI	World Bank Institute
WTO	World Trade Organization

Preface

This study outlines a theory of governance and applies it to key problems relating to the implementation of economic reforms in less developed countries and economies in transition. It examines more comprehensively than earlier studies of the political economy of policy reform the interplay of economic and political institutions and the nature of institutional change. The specification of the meaning of governance and how it influences the incentives of policy makers and economic agents is the basis of much of the analysis.

Failures in policy reform, poor public sector management, over-centralization, rent-seeking, corruption, and internal conflict are viewed as systematic, though not exclusive, instances of institutional failure. The analysis looks for ways of crafting effective governance structures which provide appropriate incentive systems to cope with such failures.

The ideas presented here are based on a comparative institutional approach. It is institutional because it seeks to provide explanations which go beyond the standard assumptions of economic analysis to the patterns of formal rules and informal constraints underlying an economy and a polity. It is comparative because it addresses concrete variations in policy and institutional reform across contemporary and historical cases.

The analysis essentially pursues four objectives: (1) scrutinizing the explanatory power of the New Institutional Economics and the New Political Economy for development and transition economics; (2) exploring the importance of institutions for sustainable policy reforms; (3) identifying the institutional conditions for the design and implementation of effective policy reforms which are suitable to overcome underdevelopment and poverty, and (4) providing new theoretical explanations of the state's role in sustainable economic development and policy conclusions which may guide political leaders through the complicated terrain of policy making. With its main focus on the relations between the economy and the polity, this study seeks to explore the impact of the dialectic interaction between political and economic forces on economic development. By applying the principles of institutional analysis to the problems of development and transition economics, its aim is to contribute to the theories of institutional change, comparative institutional economics, and comparative economic systems.

The main objective is to elaborate a suitable way of dealing with the issues. Hence, first of all, the study seeks to develop the theoretical foundation for an understanding of why and how governance matters for economic development. Subsequently, based on the conceptual underpinning of a market-enhancing governance structure, which serves as a reference model, the practice of governance and its impact on the quality of policy making are explored in a systematic way. Although the primary message of the book is aimed at economists, I believe that the arguments will be equally interesting to a wider audience including political scientists and sociologists. Therefore, I have tried to keep the technical economic terminology at a minimum and to make the argument clear to the noneconomist.

This study was greatly inspired by the works of several scholars on the role of institutions and the state in economic development. In particular, it has accumulated a significant intellectual debt *vis-à-vis* the works of Pranab Bardhan, Peter Evans, Douglass North, Mancur Olson, Yingyi Qian, Dani Rodrik, Hilton Root, Barry Weingast, and Oliver Williamson.

Numerous persons have been helpful during the process of research and writing. I am particularly grateful for discussions with Bruce Bueno de Mesquita, Joel Hellman, Niels Hermes, Herman Hoen, Ingolf Kaspar, Urooj Malik, Martin Meurers, Helga Müller, Uwe Mummert, Rajat Nag, Douglass North, Sunita Parikh, Hilton Root, Henry Rowen, Dagmar Sakowsky, Wiemer Salverda, Paul Streeten, Barry Weingast, and Oliver Williamson and for the encouragement and criticism they provided. Moreover, I owe special debts to Helmut Kuhn, Hermann Sautter, and Jürgen Bloech, with whom I have discussed many of the ideas developed herein and who commented extensively on several drafts of this study. Of course, these persons are in no way to be held responsible for any error, omission, or wrong conclusion. For that, the author alone is to blame. Last but not least, I greatly appreciate Peter Boettke's support and his offer to include the book in his series *New Thinking in Political Economy*.

The main ideas on governance and the role of the state in economic development were formulated during a very rewarding and enjoyable research stay at the Department of Economics at the University of California/Berkeley and the Hoover Institution in Stanford. Financial support from the Deutsche Forschungsgemeinschaft and the German American Fulbright Commission made this research possible.

This book is dedicated to my wife Karin and my son Simon in gratitude for their patience, support, and encouragement. It is they who are well aware of the opportunity costs.

Joachim Ahrens,
Göttingen, February 2002

1. Introduction: market, state, and economic development

In the last two decades, the developing world has experienced two events of lasting significance. First, external shocks, particularly the debt crisis at the beginning of the 1980s, hit the less developed countries (LDCs) and contributed (along with underlying policy weaknesses) to economic stagnation, a decline in real per capita income, and macroeconomic instabilities. Numerous countries in Latin America, Asia, and Africa responded to these shocks by abandoning their state-led development strategies mainly based on import-substitution policies and embarking on market-oriented economic policies emphasizing privatization and external liberalization. By the end of the 1980s, even the post-socialist countries (PSCs) of Eastern Europe and some socialist countries in Asia had jumped on the bandwagon of market-oriented policy reform in the course of their systemic transformation. The challenge of economic policy reform, however, has become even more complicated in many countries due to a second epochal event. Beginning in southern Europe in the mid-1970s, a widespread trend emerged of moving away from authoritarian rule toward democratization. This process of political transition accelerated in the 1980s and the 1990s, encompassing Asian countries such as South Korea, Taiwan, the Philippines, Thailand, Pakistan, and Turkey. What Huntington (1991) called the *Third Wave of Democratization* has eventually become a global phenomenon, even including the countries of Central and Eastern Europe and several successor states of the Soviet Union, and putting increasing pressure on authoritarian regimes in the Middle East and Africa (Haggard and Kaufman 1995).

The coincidence of these historical processes raises long-standing questions about the interaction between political and economic change and the political economy of policy reforms. What role have economic crises played in the twofold transition towards democratic rule and a market economy? How do the political, economic and institutional legacies of authoritarian rule affect the capacity of new democratic governments to initiate and to sustain economic policy reform? Are emerging democracies capable of managing the political challenges caused by economic crises and reform needs? Which institutional and economic conditions foster the consolidation of democracy? What kind of political institutions are conducive to formulating, implementing, and enforcing appropriate economic reforms? Does economic growth spur democratization? It is obvious to say that political, social, and economic changes are strongly interrelated. Nevertheless, social scientists still do not know enough about the conditions and mechanisms of political and socio-cultural change which will be most favorable for economic development. 'If policy makers cannot identify the functional relationships between economic and noneconomic factors and their quantitative significance, how can they determine whether to operate on economic incentives, attitudes, organizational structure, social relations, or any of the many other factors that connect economic and noneconomic change?' (Meier 1995: 579).

Since economists have usually treated politics, and until recently institutions, as exogenous, they have observed the effects of policies on economic development, but have generally not analysed the determinants of policy choices. Political scientists, sociologists, and historians, on the other hand, have considered external constraints as determinants of national policies. As a consequence, they have similarly neglected institutions and domestic political forces (Haggard 1990). However, puzzlement over these questions has recently led to substantial research efforts and a growing literature on the interaction between economy and polity in the course of development.[1] Remarkably, economists, political scientists, and sociologists have begun to focus their attention on these problems of development, often in co-edited or co-authored works yielding a considerable number of interdisciplinary studies. Moreover, this strand of research has greatly benefited from the emergence of the New Institutional Economics (NIE) and the progress made in the field of the New Political Economy (NPE) and its application to problems of economic development.[2]

As its starting point, this book takes the phenomenon of the twofold transition and the emerging consensus that economic reforms in most LDCs and PSCs will be less effective or even doomed to fail without political commitment and adjustment. It provides an economist's perspective on the political economy of policy reform, elaborates on the impact of institutions on economic development, and seeks to provide a coherent analysis of the role of the state in economic development by overcoming the alleged dichotomy of states and markets.

1.1 ECONOMIC DEVELOPMENT, POLICY REFORM, AND THE INTERACTION BETWEEN THE ECONOMY AND THE POLITY

While economic growth is usually taken as the main indicator to measure economic development, the term is basically defined in a wider sense as long-term, self-sustaining growth-cum-change. As Meier (1995: 7) puts it:

> (T)here are essential qualitative dimensions in the development process that extend beyond the growth or expansion of an economy through a simple widening process. (...) It may be defined as (...) the 'upward movement of the entire social system', or it may be interpreted as the attainment of a number of 'ideals of modernization', such as a rise in productivity, social and economic equalization, modern knowledge, improved institutions and attitudes, and a rationally coordinated system of policy measures that can remove the host of undesirable conditions in the social system that have perpetuated a state of underdevelopment.

This implies that policy reform is a critical condition of economic development. In fact, it is not only a means to overcome the burden of underdevelopment and to foster economic growth, but it represents an indispensable condition to eventually improve individuals' capabilities and to enhance their entitlements in the sense of Amartya Sen (1985).

Among the major constraints that have been identified to limit achievable rates of economic development, a low level of savings, a foreign-exchange constraint, the lack of human resource development, and neglecting the agricultural sector are of particular significance (Meier 1995: 64). But facing these constraints, an economy's ultimate success in narrowing the gap between its actual and potential rate of development critically depends on the political leadership's commitment and ability to implement and enforce appropriate policies. Inadequate quality of economic management represents, according to Meier (1995: 65), the principal constraint on the abatement of the above constraints. Similarly, Olson (1996: 19) writes that

> the large differences in per capita income across countries cannot be explained by differences in access to the world's stock of productive knowledge or to its capital markets, by differences in the ratio of population to land or natural resources, or by differences in the quality of marketable human capital or personal culture. (...) The only remaining plausible explanation is that the great differences in the wealth of nations are mainly due to differences in the quality of their institutions and economic policies.

Today, it is widely accepted that the stability of a government, the pursuit of appropriate policies and a capacity for sound public management are at the core of sustained development. Regarding the design of policy reform, a remarkable convergence of current fashions in development and transition policy has emerged, essentially based on the neoclassical paradigm of competitive markets. This new orthodoxy, highlighted in the so-called *Washington Consensus* (Williamson 1994), includes sound fiscal management, redirection of government activities towards the provision of public goods such as education, health, and infrastructure, tax reforms, competitive exchange rates, privatization and secure property rights, financial liberalization, deregulation, trade liberalization, and eliminating barriers to direct foreign investment. This consensus view basically advocates a stabilization-cum-adjustment strategy aimed at controlling inflation and generally reducing macroeconomic instability as well as changing the structure of consumption and production and increasing the flexibility and efficiency of the economy.

What is not sufficiently understood, however, is the practice of policy reform, that is the process of replacing inefficient policies with effective ones, and the way in which effective management capacities are created. Since policy makers base their decisions on political rather than on economic incentives, and dominant groups in society as well as public officials are all too often inclined to extract rents from established policies, there is a lack of incentive-compatibility of government policies and economic performance in many LDCs. What appears to be feasible politics does not necessarily turn out to be good economics. For that reason, students of economic development have been pessimistic regarding the opportunities for policy reform (Grindle and Thomas 1991). In addition, there is clear evidence that political factors often prevent authorities from realizing reform programs in LDCs which, for economic reasons, appear to provide sound prospects for accelerating growth and improving living standards (Bates and Krueger 1993). Addressing these problems requires explicit study of the political institutions related to development management. Taking the institutional structure of the political sphere into consideration implies a differentiated understanding of the political economy of policy reform.

These issues are highlighted by the experiences of the high-performing Asian economies (HPAEs),[3] which achieved substantial economic growth rates and considerable progress in areas such as public health and education during the past 40 years, whereas economic and social development rather stagnated in most LDCs.[4] This obvious contrast between success and failure in economic development raises the question of why the experiences of various countries show these vast differences. How can policy reform in developing countries be successfully pursued in order sustainably to increase the productivity of their economies and the well-being of their populations? Are there any lessons to be derived from the development concepts of more advanced economies for less successful countries?

Experiences show that institutions as well as the design of the economic order and policies are of utmost importance. This fact is encouraging insofar as it allows the conclusion that less successful countries should basically be capable of overcoming the impediments to development. This requires, however, that governments of these economies (as well as authorities of industrialized countries and international organizations) are ready to take advantage of existing options to development.

During the 1980s and particularly since the early 1990s, numerous developing countries have launched ambitious economic reforms. Although these reforms (like the transformation policies in Central and Eastern Europe) imply similarly structured stabilization-cum-adjustment programs and policy prescriptions, the achieved outcomes have differed substantially. To understand this, one central aspect of development and transformation processes must be considered more closely, namely the interdependencies of the polity and the economy. Historical experience and theoretical considerations show that emerging markets and economic reforms require an institutional foundation. Institutional reforms, however, tend to have redistributive effects on income as well as on power among various groups of society and, hence, may also require political reforms. This, in turn, raises questions concerning the balance of power in society, the legitimacy of the political leadership, the political skills of policy makers, and the management capacity of the public administration.

If political and economic institutions determine a country's development trajectory, arguments about whether and how governments, social elites, and citizens can facilitate the emergence of developmental governance structures become critically important to understanding the performance of economies over time and the process of economic development. Exploring and laying out such arguments is the purpose of this book.

1.2 THE ARGUMENTS: BEYOND THE STATE-VERSUS-MARKET DEBATE

Development economics as a separate field of research emerged only after the Second World War. In the 1950s and 1960s, the view was predominant that governments, as paternalistic, benevolent guardians, should take a leading role in initiating as well as sustaining the process of development. The principal charge assigned to the state was to foster industrialization and structural change actively by comprehensive development planning. Throughout the world, the emergence of numerous former colonies as sovereign states, anxious to overcome the exploitation, inequality, and elitism they had experienced under foreign rule, and their very low standards of living, gave rise to a political imperative for political leaders to adopt state-led nationalist development strategies. This approach was reinforced by the virtually unanimous view among academics and policy makers concerning the principles underlying development policy. Memories of the economic disasters resulting from the Great Depression and of running command economies in the industrialized countries during the war, the apparent economic success of central planning in the Soviet Union, the Keynesian revolution in macroeconomics, and the belief that market failure was the rule rather than an exception resulted in a deep suspicion of the functioning of markets. In LDCs, experiences with colonialism and external shocks during the Great Depression, when the terms of trade for primary commodities had sharply deteriorated, also went hand-in-hand with a deep distrust of the international economy. The policies undertaken to spur economic growth and development were roughly the same in the majority of LDCs. Since improving manufacturing was considered to be critical and protection essential for industrialization, import substitution policies and discrimination against agriculture became the central means to achieve modernization. In numerous countries, economic plans were introduced that pre-determined levels of savings and investment. Regarding industrial activities, major proportions of targeted increases were often to be realized through public investment and activities of parastatal enterprises in large-scale manufacturing. In addition, agricultural marketing boards were established and given monopsony and monopoly powers for output collection and input distribution, respectively (Krueger 1995).

During the 1950s and 1960s, economic growth rates increased considerably. But in hindsight economic progress could be largely explained by a favorable international environment and restored economic opportunities following the constraints of wartime needs, so that Krueger (1995: 2508) concluded that 'any economic policies that did not entirely thwart (...) investments would have generated rates of economic growth significantly above long-term trends'. And, in fact, the adverse economic effects resulting from import-substitution policies and comprehensive state intervention soon became evident. Many countries experienced severe difficulties in managing inefficient parastatal enterprises. Inward-oriented policies were generally associated with high levels of effective protection of the (nascent) domestic industry, strong discrimination against agriculture, a distorted domestic price structure, repressed financial systems, credit rationing at negative real interest rates, excessive and growth-impeding interventions in factor markets, overvalued exchange rates, and pervasive controls over private sector activities. In the course of time, productivity growth was virtually absent, and product quality was low. Adopted policies provided incentives for capital-intensive and labor-saving methods of production and hence resulted in increasing profits in the protected sector and rising industrial wages for a relatively small labor elite. This, in turn, aggravated income inequalities and contributed to a rise in unemployment. Eventually, many LDCs experienced unsustainable budget deficits, inflationary pressures, and balance of payments crises. These problems became even more severe due to the oil crises in the 1970s and the subsequent global debt crisis in the 1980s, when it eventually became evident that adopted policy mixes were not sustainable.

The sobering experience with disappointing interventionist policies induced widespread disillusionment and was the starting point of a second wave in development theorizing and politics at the beginning of the 1980s. Instead of fostering growth, governments hindered modernization and mobilization and actively contributed to large-scale inefficiencies. States did not redistribute wealth and income to the poor, but rather invited rent-seeking and opened the door for elitism and corruption. The view of a benevolent state being capable of successfully steering the process of economic development came to be rejected, and the pendulum of opinion swung away from a strong confidence in the state toward the market. In the 1980s, many LDCs were confronted with unsustainable balance of payments difficulties, high inflation, stagnating growth, and increasing unemployment. These problems resulted from poor policies, weak institutions, and unfavorable external conditions. Therefore, policy reform was considered an indispensable condition among students of economic development and policy makers alike. This view was supported by progress in research, the use of improved empirical techniques, and the availability of improved data bases, which contributed to undermining gradually the theoretical underpinnings of the old simplistic paradigm on which development economics had been based and to yielding new policy conclusions. Moreover, the success of the high-performing Asian economies (HPAEs) that realized and sustained the highest growth rates since the beginning of the 1960s, escaped the debt crisis, and achieved rapid improvement of other economic and social indicators thereby outperforming most other LDCs and sometimes even surpassing industrial economies, was essentially attributed by many economists to their reliance on free markets, export promotion, and comparably limited government control. The lessons learned from failed import-substitution policies and the experiences of the outward-oriented HPAEs convinced policy makers, academics, and international organizations that there was an alternative approach to overcoming the burden of underdevelopment and to achieving sustained growth (Klitgaard 1991 and World Bank 1993).

A major lesson learned from the failures of earlier policies and the ensuing crises was to account for the dialectic interconnectedness of different policies affecting both the macroeconomy and specific markets. Hence the multilateral financial institutions, particularly the World Bank, strengthened their efforts to systematically encourage and assist stabilization and structural adjustment in developing countries. Structural adjustment was seen as a process of market-oriented policy reform aimed at overcoming balance of payments problems, reducing inflation, and creating the conditions for a sustainable increase in per capita income. By 1979, the World Bank had already introduced structural adjustment lending in order to support reform in policies explicitly aimed at reducing current account deficits, assisting countries in bearing the costs of structural change, and encouraging the inflow of external capital. Typically, structural adjustment includes macroeconomic stabilization, liberalization, privatization, as well as deregulation.[5]

By the early 1990s, the International Monetary Fund (IMF) had provided more than 50 LDCs with loans designed to implement free-market policies, and most of these countries had also received sectoral or structural adjustment loans from the World Bank which required a retreat from state interventionism. Moreover, a number of countries such as Chile or Vietnam had initiated drastic reforms without relying on financial assistance. The new approach to policy reform represented a sharp reversal of thinking about economic development. The emphasis was now on shrinking the scope and the size of government and to trust in the efficiency of private sector activities. This induced a remarkable convergence of current fashions in development policy that has been highlighted in the so-called Washington Consensus.[6]

The New Orthodoxy assigned a new role to governments. Particularly, it required the state to withdraw from regulating and managing economic activities and to restrict itself to the classic tasks of providing law and order, a predictable and reasonable legal system, a stable macroeconomic framework, and improving health services, education systems, and physical infrastructure. State intervention in specific industries was considered to be irrelevant or even harmful and distortive for the allocation of resources. A role for government in *picking winners* or *governing the market* – as postulated by revisionists and structuralists (Amsden 1989; Wade 1990) – was categorically rejected. This view received some modification, though no contradiction, when the World Bank (1991) proposed the market-friendly view, provided a more nuanced discussion on the most adequate division of labor between market and state, and sought to overcome the disputes of the neoclassical and revisionist interpretations of the sources of rapid growth in East Asia. In its *East Asian Miracle* study, the World Bank (1993: 84) concluded 'that rapid growth is associated with effective but carefully delimited government activism'. This view attributed a limited, but effective role to governments, which 'is to ensure adequate investments in people, provision of a competitive climate for enterprise, openness to international trade, and stable macroeconomic management' (ibid.). Regarding selective government interventions in the HPAEs, the World Bank noted that fewer interventionist policy choices were more conducive to growth, although it admits that policy makers need to exploit the complementary interactions between market processes and government activities. In that sense, rethinking state activism means less government intervention in areas where markets basically work or can be made to work and more interventions in those areas in which market failures persist or markets do not exist. Another central insight is that economic policy making in the HPAEs (in contrast to numerous other LDCs which rigidly maintained unsuccessful policies) has been characterized by a high degree of pragmatic flexibility regarding governments' attempts to use different policy instruments in their pursuit of (economic) policy objectives: measures which worked effectively were retained, while those that failed were abandoned. Finally, the market-friendly approach highlights the importance of political stability and social consensus for successful reforms and emphasizes the critical role of those institutions which determine the economic order, such as legal codes, property rights, and market entry and exit regulation. Nevertheless, the World Bank continued to adhere to the New Orthodoxy despite these ramifications in its argumentation.[7]

However, the surge of the neoclassical consensus has been self-limiting. Problems in the implementation of policy reform in general and structural adjustment programs in particular, doubts about whether stabilization-cum-adjustment is sufficient to ensure sustained growth, existing coordination failures, economies of scale, and externalities in LDCs implied rethinking and redefining the role of the state in economic development once again. Since the end of the 1980s, a third wave of theorizing about economic development and thinking on the role of governments has begun to crystallize led by a revival of interest in the institutional characteristics of states (Evans 1992). This focuses on the view that economic policies can only be implemented successfully if the chosen institutional mechanism is strong, regardless of neoclassical or interventionist frameworks. The prospect of rent-seeking – the use of public power to confer unearned income on particular interests – can arise under either framework. If vested interest groups are strong enough to defeat sensible selective interventions, it follows that they may also distort markets and subvert free trade. The problems of development arise not just from misguided policies, but from institutional deficiencies that are correctable only in the long term (Wade 1990). Getting government out of development paradoxically requires a strong government capacity to create and sustain the institutions (such as labor markets, financial and capital markets, or legal frameworks to enforce contracts and protect property) that will replace it. The management of public investment in areas falling within the neoclassical reckoning (those parts of health and education where social benefits are high but private incentives are inadequate, and physical infrastructure allowing scale economies) requires institutional capacities that are as complex as those under the interventionist paradigm. Governance capacity – focusing on specific features like bureaucratic capability and the interface between government and non-government institutions, and more widely on its keystones of accountability, participation, predictability, and transparency as a means to avoid the rent-seeking that otherwise can be pervasive – has become the obverse side of good economic policy in determining development outcomes. This new line of thinking seeks to bring politics back in and to overcome the apparent dichotomy between the market and the state as two mutually exclusive mechanisms of resource allocation. The fact is that in the contemporary world, neither the minimal nor the interventionist state has ensured rapid economic growth and development. Like it or not, state involvement has been a given fact through space and time. In order to understand better the past failures and present problems of policy reform, we need to go beyond the traditional debate over the proper roles of markets and states and analyse why neither lives up to the expectations of its advocates, how the performance of both can be improved, and how private sector coordination and government activities may complement each other. Thus the pendulum has actually begun to swing back toward redefining the role of the state in economic development – and one objective of the present study is to add some impetus to the pendulum's momentum. This time, however, scholars will have to define and explain more clearly than before the relations between the state, society, and development performance.

Traditional policy-oriented approaches to analysing economic reforms and development have identified those policy mixes that are theoretically adequate and necessary for economic take-off processes. However, they do not show sufficient explanatory strength regarding the question of how these policies are initiated, implemented, and eventually sustained. The neoclassical view is ahistoric, generally neglects institutions and political processes, and regards policy making simply as a matter of making the right choice. In this view, 'wrong' policies just reflect a lack of political commitment or misguided ideas (Haggard 1990). In contrast, revisionists recognize a positive role of the state as well as the interdependencies between political and economic decisions. It is the quality of government intervention that is crucial, not its level. A strong state in the sense that it can insulate itself from vested interests and rent-seeking is able to intervene effectively in the economy. However, revisionists do not examine how a strong state evolves and fail to explain the process of policy formulation, implementation, and enforcement.

The World Bank's (1993) *East Asian Miracle* study weakens the contradictions between neoclassical and revisionist explanations and yields more differentiated insights into the East Asian development process. It identifies pragmatic and flexible policy mixes, including a set of policy measures that have been realized in all HPAEs and another set of measures varying across countries whose selection depended on country-specific institutional conditions. It also finds that government intervention had a limited usefulness depending on quality not quantity, and that this again depended on the availability of suitable institutions. But this approach is limited to analysing a subset of institutions that only included those subject to economic policy making and that determine the economic order. This reasoning not only fails to consider the political institutions that directly affect policy making but also fails to explain where the high degree of policy adaptability and the flexibility in tactical policy making have come from, how the presumably strong East Asian states have evolved, and how economic reforms have been initiated and sustained.

Therefore, the broad consensus among economists on the policy reforms, which LDCs ought to conduct to promote economic development, raises new questions. What hinders numerous developing countries from implementing the recommended policies? If those policies are pursued (more often than not under pressure of the multilateral financial organizations), why do the expected outcomes not materialize? Or regarding the HPAEs, why were interventionist policies adopted and why and how did they work effectively? How were country-specific policy mixes agreed upon in the course of political decision-making processes, how were they successfully implemented and eventually enforced? These questions need to be addressed by institutional analysis. On the one hand, they concern a country's political institutions and how these affect policy formation and bureaucratic implementation as well as the (institutional) interconnectedness between public agencies, private business, and civil society. On the other hand, they are related to economic institutions such as contract enforcement and property rights.

Recent theoretical work has taken these questions as a point of departure and has explicitly begun opening the black box of the state and focusing on political behavior and the role of institutions. This particularly holds for (1) applying the New Political Economy (NPE), which essentially encompasses the perspectives of public choice and collective choice theory, to problems of underdevelopment and (2) the New Institutional Economics (NIE) and its application to economic history and development. The former theoretical approach fits well with orthodox economic prescriptions. By applying the theoretical tools of neoclassical economics to politics, the NPE provides a positive theory of policy making and political behavior. By operationalizing and disaggregating the state, it considers the government as an endogenous variable. Neoclassical political economy has been very useful in explaining how widespread rent-seeking and corruption could emerge in LDCs and how these adversely affected economic performance and hampered the adoption of growth-enhancing policies. The NPE shows considerable strengths and contributes to understanding the failures of policy reform in rent-seeking societies, notably in Latin America.

But this approach has weaknesses regarding the basic understanding of policy making in LDCs due to its oversimplifications in modeling the state in developing countries and its assumption that politics is basically to be considered as a negative factor for successful policy reform (Grindle 1991). Moreover, the NPE implies a logical flaw: since the state is seen as the problem, its central policy conclusion is the withdrawal of government activism and the establishment of a minimal, though strong, state. This postulate is flawed for three reasons: (1) policy prescriptions paradoxically assume that the criticized state would be capable of initiating and sustaining market-oriented policies, once it is a minimalist state. This view, however, does not account for the complex set of political institutions and administrative capacities that are necessary to implement desirable adjustment programs. Hence, it remains ambiguous how a minimalist state should be able to perform its tasks. Moreover, even the rules underlying a *laissez-faire* economy are not the natural outcome of a market process, but result from active government intervention which is necessary to avoid any tampering with the rule of law; (2) the postulate of a minimal state is not consistent with the widespread rent-seeking behavior that is predicted by neoclassical economy. Why should blamed politicians and bureaucrats who behave rationally by pursuing their self-interest and extracting rents be inclined to give up their power and influence by establishing a minimal state? The NPE has not been able to advise on how this type of state is to be realized; (3) even if a minimal, though strong, state existed, it would not be sufficient to overcome the 'fundamental political dilemma of an economic system', which is that a 'government strong enough to protect property rights and enforce contracts is also strong enough to confiscate the wealth of its citizens' (Weingast 1995: 1). Emerging markets do not only require an appropriate set of economic institutions, but also a stable political foundation delimiting the capability of the state to confiscate private wealth and violate citizens' rights. Far from clear, however, are which mechanisms create a political system that makes a viable market economy a stable policy choice.

By using the tools of the NIE as well as the insights of political scientists and sociologists, these shortcomings of the NPE can be effectively addressed, notwithstanding the important and illustrative, though limited, analyses of the NPE. This is because these strands of theoretical reasoning put institutions, defined as the rules of the game comprising formal rules and informal constraints including their enforcement characteristics, at the center of their analysis (North 1990a). The view that the state remains a central variable to economic development, structural change, and the process of policy reform inevitably raises the question of state capability and capacity. As Evans (1992: 141) puts it:

> The consistent pursuit of any policies, whether they are aimed at 'getting prices right' or implanting local industry, requires the enduring institutionalization of a complex set of political machinery and, as Samuel Huntington pointed out forcefully a generation ago, such institutionalization can by no means be taken for granted.

This point of view fits well with Grindle's (1996) thesis that political leaderships and structures, while often part of the problem, are necessarily also part of the solution that will lead to creating a more effective and responsive state. Recognition of the importance of state capabilities and capacities resulting from effective and durable politico-institutional structures and informal institutions is the central element of the third wave of theorizing about the role of the state in economic development. The utopian vision of the benevolent state as the ultimate promoter of economic development, proposed by the first wave, has proved to be unrealistic, but so have the optimistic expectations regarding free markets and minimalist states, which characterize the second wave.

North (1995a) argues convincingly that the institutional and organizational structure of a country is the primary source of economic growth and development. Economic growth occurs if the political and economic institutions provide relatively low transaction costs in impersonal markets. The evolution and effects of institutions critically depend on informal constraints embodied in the belief systems of society. Institutions can neither be taken for granted nor will they come automatically into existence as a result of getting the prices right. Experience clearly indicates that efficient institutions, promoting economic growth and welfare, have been rare across space and time. Eventually, creating efficient economic institutions crucially depends on the existence of efficient political markets, because the polity specifies, implements, and enforces the formal rules of economic exchange. However, present knowledge about how to create efficient political institutions is limited.

This book aims to contribute to the third wave of development theorizing. Its main thesis can be outlined as follows: the appropriate question to ask is not how much state involvement, but what kind of state activism is conducive to economic growth and development. Effective state involvement not only requires credible commitments that political promises are actually delivered to citizens, but it crucially depends on the capacity and capability of policy makers to fit the roles which the political leadership seeks to pursue. In this regard, the governance structures underlying the process of policy making are of utmost importance. Governance, defined as the capacity of a country's institutional matrix to implement and enforce public policies and to improve private-sector coordination, affects the incentives of politicians, bureaucrats, and private economic agents alike and determines the terms of exchange among citizens and between them and government officials. Governance structures are based on both formal and informal institutions. With respect to problems of initiating, implementing, and sustaining government policies, political institutions play a dominant role because they determine how different actors are involved in political processes, what kinds of economic reforms are politically feasible, and how the behavior of individual actors is shaped. After all, the structure of political institutions shapes the interactions of individuals to determine the outcomes of public policies.

In reality, states are located somewhere along the continuum between predatory and developmental states. In order to understand the developmental impact of their governance structures it is essential to identify systematic connections between the developmental outcomes of political economies and the institutional characteristics of states. Experience indicates that governance structures are basically subject to political design as far as formal institutions are concerned. The effectiveness of governance structures in general, and political institutions in particular, however, is essentially shaped by the incentive structures they provide, resulting from the structural characteristics of states including their administrative organization and their relations to society. In contrast to predatory states, which extract wealth at the expense of society, lack the ability to prevent arbitrary political action, and rely on clientelism and favoritism, developmental states are distinguished by a politico-institutional structure and are based on rule by impersonal institutions that make policy reform a politically feasible option. The complex coordination and collective-action problems associated with policy reform may be overcome by politically-crafted self-enforcing governance structures, which reduce transaction costs and information asymmetries, stabilize expectations, and prompt political authorities to precommit themselves credibly to abide by rules and regulations and to promote sustainable economic development. Besides international competition, it is the organizational design and the incentives within the public sector and the institutions linking the public and private sector that are crucial to the developmental consequences of government activism.

Policy reform in a complex institutional structure, which itself may be subject to change, has not only an economic, but also a political and social dimension. Neglecting these may lead to theoretically efficient, but (due to non-economical obstacles to reforms) politically unfeasible propositions and eventually to what Myrdal called opportunistic ignorance (Streeten 1993). Besides the formulation of consistent reform policies, the concept of governance, based on a specific setting of political institutions, is the fundamental mechanism which decides the success of economic reforms and eventually determines a country's development path. Moreover, policy reform and high economic growth rates cannot be sustained without continuing institutional change. Therefore, effective governance needs to be interpreted as a dynamic process. New institutions will only survive and unfold their positive developmental impact if they are supported by individuals and organizations which have a stake in their survival. This requires both a high degree of incentive-compatibility of government policies and economic performance as well as the creation of flexible institutional arrangements that constitute a stable economic and political order and permit institutional change. However, the recent literature on the political economy of policy reform or on the efficacy of activist states on economic development does not provide an explanation for the emergence of either incentive-compatibility or the adaptive efficiency of institutions.

The outline of the argument can be essentially recapitulated in five points: (1) the ability to craft and adopt specifically-tailored institutional structures is as important to effective governance as the formulation of policies; (2) effective governance structures and hence developmental outcomes depend on the roles that policy makers pursue and the general character of state structure; (3) effective governance is independent of the form of government (the regime type); (4) while the initiation of economic reforms may be facilitated by the discretionary authority of elites and political institutions that insulate policy making from distributive claims of interest groups, their consolidation requires stabilized expectations regarding a new set of incentive structures and the confidence that these cannot be discretionarily altered; (5) policies need to match institutions or vice versa. Effective governance is a dynamic process that requires a constant fine-tuning and adjusting of institutions and policy solutions to changing technological, social, economic, and political environments.

1.3 RESEARCH STRATEGY

The main theme of this study is the analysis of policy reform in developing and transitional countries from an institutional perspective. The importance of incentive structures resulting from societal institutions for a country's economic development and the institutional causes of variations in economic performance have long been neglected in the standard economics literature.

If, however, the progress in economic development is closely related to institutional structures, the explanatory power of orthodox neoclassical models, which treat institutions as exogenous variables, remains limited and incomplete. Appropriate theoretical approaches ought to be capable of addressing the question of which institutions support policy reform and promote economic development, which institutions jeopardize these processes, and what are the determinants of institutional change. More specifically, this study explores the following questions: (1) How can we explain the observed differences in economic policies across space and over time? (2) Under which conditions are policy reforms likely to be initiated and sustained? (3) What are the circumstances under which policy changes may improve efficiency or reduce poverty? (4) What theoretical insights can be deduced from the experience of developing countries on the one hand and from a synopsis of the existing literature on the other hand which help to explain variations in the efficacy of policy reform across countries? (5) How can these insights systematically contribute to the improvement of policy making in LDCs and PSCs?

Until the 1980s, sociologists, political scientists, and also economists sought to explain why economic growth occurred slowly, if at all, or why policy reform did not materialize. More recently, scholars have started to focus on the political and institutional basis of development rather than underdevelopment. However, the questions and processes to be analysed are far too complex to rely on a single unified model. Instead, this book draws on different theories and a large number of now-available case studies, uses various small models, each of which addresses only parts of the underlying questions, and attempts to take advantage of these different approaches to further a coherent understanding of the political economy of policy reform. Contrasting the conventional perspective of a government–market dichotomy, this study is based on a comparative institutional approach. It is institutional because it seeks to provide explanations that go beyond the standard assumptions of economic analysis to the patterns of formal rules and informal constraints underlying an economy and a polity. It is comparative because it focuses on concrete variations in policy reform across contemporary and historical cases. Since the ways in which institutional arrangements evolve and the roles that governments play in shaping institutions are not uniform among LDCs and PSCs, comparative studies need to constitute an integral part of analysing the role of governments in economic development.

The emerging prominence of institutions and institutional change in the literature on economic history and development is based on several foundations. First, development economists and economic historians have analysed the functioning and performance of economies whose institutional arrangements and environments differed strongly from those of contemporary industrialized countries. Secondly, scholars have recognized that explanations of economic growth that neglect the demand for, and supply of, institutions and changes therein remain incomplete. Per capita output growth has clearly resulted from increases in factor accumulation. But input growth accounts only partially for overall growth. Another major source of growth is technological change, the generation and exploitation of which depends on the effectiveness of institutions (Feeny 1993).

The demand for institutional change has been basically attributed to a change in transaction costs. The theory of transaction costs suggests that existing institutional disequilibria imply profitable opportunities for institutional innovations. Institutional change will occur if the marginal transaction costs of change are lower than the expected marginal benefits of the potential new institutional arrangement. This reasoning leaves the impression that the demand for new institutions will trigger institutional change, and that new institutions will be more efficient than old ones. But there is overwhelming evidence that efficient institutions have been rare throughout history (North 1990a). Due to free-rider problems, institutional change does not necessarily occur, even if a demand for institutional change exists. If, however, private economic agents are able to implement new institutions that increase their private net benefits, this does not ensure an increase in net social benefits. Problems of collective action and the existence of externalities and coordination failures, as well as an unequal distribution of power among private agents, have typically hampered efficient institutional change. In this regard, the state may play a crucial role in the supply of institutions. In a broader context, this also holds for providing the conditions and institutions promoting technological change and for conducting market-oriented macroeconomic policies that support the functioning of economic institutions. However, political markets are usually neither perfectly competitive nor efficient. The ability of the state to promote institutional change that benefits the economy as a whole crucially depends on the institutional structure of the polity and hence the incentives faced by policy makers (an aspect usually neglected by economic analysis). Transaction costs also exist within the political apparatus and affect the relations between the electorate, business elites, and the government. The interaction of the government, legislatures, state agencies, and society is constrained by political and social institutions. Moreover, economic outcomes are not only responses to market conditions, but are also the products of these institutionalized relations (Dixit 1996 and Evans 1995). Understanding different outcomes is the objective of this study, not forcing various cases into a universal mold.

Therefore, a thorough analysis of the proper role of the state in economic development needs to overcome the oversimplified treatment of the state as a monolithic organization. Max Weber defined the state as a compulsory association that successfully claims the monopoly of the legitimate use of physical force within a specific community. Contemporary scholars usually view the state in the Weberian tradition, but attempt to amend this definition usefully by reducing the complexity of analysing what states do and what roles they perform. This book takes the recent literature on the role of states in development as a starting point. In its definition of the state, it essentially follows the perspective on the state outlined in Evans, Rueschemeyer, and Skocpol (1985) and Grindle (1996). Thus the state is seen as an organization based on a nexus of institutions for social control, authoritative policy formation and implementation, in which policy makers and social actors interact with each other and influence the path of economic, social, and political development, which in turn shapes the behavior of individuals and groups.[8]

This study views failures in policy reform, poor public sector management, rent-seeking, corruption, overcentralization, and internal conflict as systematic, though not exclusive, instances of institutional failure. It looks for ways of constructing effective governance structures which provide appropriate incentive systems to cope with such failures. No blueprint is offered, and answers to central questions can be specific to the context. The analysis of actual developments combined with theoretical considerations essentially aims at improving the understanding of the political economy of policy reform and the importance of underlying governance structures.

The subsequent analysis of policy and institutional reforms in LDCs and PSCs essentially pursues four objectives: (1) scrutinizing the explanatory power of the NIE and NPE for development and transition economics; (2) exploring the importance of political institutions for sustainable policy reforms; (3) identifying the institutional conditions for the design and implementation of effective policy reforms that are suitable to overcome underdevelopment and poverty, and (4) providing new theoretical explanations of the state's role in sustainable economic development and policy conclusions which may guide political leaders through the complicated terrain of policy making. With its main focus on the relations between the economy and the polity, this study seeks to explore the impact of the dialectic interaction between political and economic forces on economic development. By applying the principles of institutional analysis to the problems of development and transition economics, its aim is to contribute to the theories of institutional change, comparative institutional economics, and comparative economic systems.

In order to address these aspects adequately, this book is structured as follows: Part I focuses on the interrelations between policy reforms, institutions, and economic performance. It starts with a brief discussion of the economics and the political economy of policy reform in LDCs and PSCs and highlights the limits of the so-called Washington Consensus (Chapter 2). Then comes a chapter that introduces the key concepts, notions, and axioms underlying two distinct methodological approaches in economics, namely the NPE and the NIE, which are regarded as useful tools to be applied to questions relating to policy reform. The focus of Chapter 4 is on institutional change which is discussed within a demand and supply framework. Particular emphasis is put on the factors impeding the emergence of efficient institutions, the role of the state in facilitating institutional change, and the need for a secure politico-institutional foundation of policy reform.

Whereas Part I is intended to lay the theoretical foundation for an understanding of why and how institutions matter for economic development, Part II focuses on the theory and practice of governance and explores in a systematic way the impact of institutions on the quality of policy making in LDCs and PSCs. Chapter 5 provides the conceptual underpinning of a market-enhancing governance structure (MEGS) that serves as a reference model for assessing the quality of governance in practice. Subsequently, Chapter 6 discusses the empirical evidence of the impact of political and economic institutions on economic performance and applies the reference model to the assessment of the actual governance structures in both the developmental states in East Asia and a number of economies in transition in Asia and Central and Eastern Europe. On the basis of this analysis, Chapter 7 draws general conclusions in a comparative perspective. It suggests policy implications for LDCs and PSCs to improve the quality of governance through institution building, discusses how international organizations can assist these countries in doing so, and explores the opportunities and chances for a *Post-Washington Consensus* to evolve.

NOTES

1. See, for example, the books by Aoki *et al.* (1997a), Bates and Krueger (1993), Bradford (1994), Diamond and Plattner (1995), Evans (1995), Grindle and Thomas (1991), Haggard and Kaufman (1992a and 1995), Haggard and Webb (1994), Krueger (1993), Meier (1991a), Przeworski (1991), Ranis and Mahmood (1992), Weiss and Hobson (1995), Williamson (1994), World Bank (1997), as well as countless papers.
2. With regard to the application of the NIE to development problems, the studies by Clague (1997), Harriss, Hunter, and Lewis (1995), Lin and Nugent (1995), Nabli and Nugent (1989a), North (1981, 1990a, and 1995a), as well as Ostrom, Feeny and Picht (1993) deserve special mention. In the field of NPE, Krueger (1993), Meier (1991a), and Williamson (1994) have been of major importance, to name but a few.

3. The HPAEs include Hong Kong, Indonesia, Malaysia, Singapore, South Korea, Taiwan, and Thailand. When this study makes any references to Japan (which is also included in this sub-group of countries in some works in the literature; see, for example, World Bank (1993)), this will be explicitly indicated.
4. See, for example, World Bank (1990) and UNDP (1996) as well as Chapter 6, section 6.2 in this study.
5. See Corbo and Fischer (1995) and Summers and Pritchett (1993).
6. See Klitgaard (1991), Rodrik (1996), and Williamson (1994).
7. For a distinct and illustrative critique of the World Bank's *East Asian Miracle* study see Fishlow *et al.* (1994).
8. In this study, states are distinguished from administrations and regimes, but not from governments.

PART I

Policy reform, institutions, and economic
performance

2. The Washington Consensus and its limits

In the 1980s and early 1990s a remarkable convergence took place as to which policy components, broadly speaking, constituted appropriate development strategies for both less developed and transitional economies. This *New Orthodoxy* (Rodrik 1996) or *counterrevolution* (Krugman 1993) rejected the insights and policy prescriptions of the first wave of theorizing about economic development. In particular, it questioned the notion that the state needs to play an active role in guiding or directing economic development. The new policy directions recommended by the multilateral financial organizations and followed by many reforming countries reflected major lessons learned from the failures of earlier interventionist policies and the subsequent crises. First of all, new policies were required because poverty and economic stagnation in LDCs were increasingly viewed as having resulted from policy regimes that undermined the operation of markets forces. Secondly, academics, policy makers, and development agencies recognized that the dialectic interconnectedness of different policies affecting both the macroeconomy and specific markets needed to be taken explicitly into account. As a consequence, structural adjustment and reducing the role of the state in economic development were increasingly seen as indispensable preconditions for sustained growth and development. The growing consensus on the economics of policy reform was mainly based on the neoclassical paradigm of competitive markets. Since the 1980s, the neoclassical approach has become the dominant factor shaping development economics and has performed an influential intellectual role in interpreting the state and the market as rival forms of resource allocation (Dutt *et al.* 1994). Derived from neoclassical reasoning, a supposedly necessary and sufficient set of reform measures includes the following policy imperatives:[1]

- stabilization (in order to correct imbalances in the balance of payments, government budgets as well as the money supply);
- letting markets work (so that free markets can determine prices);
- getting prices right (so that prices reflect scarcity values);

- privatization (so that private property rights can exercise their beneficial effects on economic competition);
- budget rationalization (in order to rationalize governments' reduced role in economic and social development);
- integrating the domestic economy into the world economy (in order to allow exports to become an engine of growth and to take advantage of the disciplining role of international markets);
- getting institutions right (so that governments are well equipped to carry out their new roles).

These policy prescriptions, to which most mainstream development economists could generally subscribe, represented a sharp reversal of thinking about economic development. The emphasis was now on shrinking the scope and the size of government and on trusting in the efficiency of market processes and private sector activities, which were regarded as critical to fostering growth. Particularly, this New Orthodoxy required the state to withdraw from regulating and managing economic activities and to restrict itself to the classic tasks of setting appropriate macro conditions and providing public goods.

Box 2.1: Elements of the Washington Consensus

- fiscal discipline
- redirection of public expenditure priorities towards health, education, and infrastructure
- tax reform
- unified/competitive exchange rates

- secure property rights
- deregulation
- trade liberalization
- privatization
- promoting FDI
- financial liberalization

Sources: Williamson (1990 and 1994)

Moreover, economists agreed that the application of the general neoclassical principles needed to be tailored to the specific circumstances of individual countries undertaking policy reform. Depending on the initial conditions prior to reform, this concerns particularly the problems of sequencing and timing the reform process. In general, stabilization is considered a prerequisite for structural adjustment. Theoretical considerations and practical experiences also suggest that a bold stabilization-cum-adjustment program is preferable to gradual and partial reforms, which threaten to delay structural adjustment and to preserve persisting market distortions.[2] The widespread agreement on the principles of policy reform led to a remarkable convergence in the prevailing fashions in development policy and led to a set of practical policy desiderata which are usually called for at the beginning of any policy reform process (Rodrik 1996). Williamson (1990) compiled such a list of policy actions and dubbed it the *Washington Consensus* (see Box 2.1). The term is meant to indicate that it has been mainly organizations in Washington, DC that have propagated this reform program. These essentially include the Bretton Woods organizations (IMF and World Bank), the US Congress, the US Treasury, and various influential think tanks.

Based on the diagnosis that widespread government failures, including excessive government intervention and economic populism, were key factors in the economic crises of the Latin American economies in the 1980s, the Washington Consensus listed a packet of stabilization-cum-adjustment policies which were regarded as indispensable measures to address the underlying causes of economic crises effectively. It emphasized the need for prudent macroeconomic and financial policies, trade and financial liberalization, privatization of public enterprises, and deregulation of domestic markets. Implicitly, it called for a *minimal state* that refrains from intervening in the economy and focuses on sound monetary policy, secure property rights, and providing primary education, basic health care, and infrastructure. In order to recover from the debt crisis, the main priorities of most Latin American countries were to ensure macroeconomic stability and to eliminate the elements of the predominant protectionist development model, that is priorities that the consensus view regarded as indispensable for exploiting the benefits from international trade and global financial flows (Burki and Perry 1998). In the course of the 1980s and especially the 1990s, most policy prescriptions inherent in the Washington Consensus have been recommended to or imposed on (mostly in the context of IMF-led stabilization-cum-adjustment programs) numerous countries outside Latin America; notably the economies in transition in Central and Eastern Europe and the former Soviet Union, but also many economies in Africa and Asia (Kolodko 1999 and Sender 1999). At that time, it was not only John Williamson (1993) who thought that his list of policy prescriptions is generally applicable to LDCs, but it was also the conviction of most neoclassical scholars and the Bretton Woods organizations that the Washington Consensus represents a universal model for policy reform in LDCs and PSCs (Naìm 1999).

In fact, these policy prescriptions appeared to be particularly justified against the background of the economic crisis affecting Latin America in the 1980s. At that time, partly resulting from weak public policies, markets did not function well. GDP had been declining for several years. Budget deficits accounted for 5–10 percent of GDP, and public expenditures were directed toward subsidizing the inefficient state sector rather than used for productive long-term investment. Companies had few incentives to compete in the world market or to meet international quality standards. Initially, governments financed budget deficits by borrowing, especially from abroad, given the relatively low real interest rates. In the course of the 1980s, increasing real interest rates in the United States put limits on continued external borrowing, increased interest payments, and forced many countries to rely on seigniorage resulting in high and volatile inflation. Subsequent experience in the late 1980s and the 1990s has clearly demonstrated that the implementation of most of the policies recommended by the Washington Consensus have been paying off. Meanwhile, several countries, particularly Argentina, Chile, and Mexico, show remarkable records of successful stabilization and economic recovery. However, economic reforms, so far, have not significantly reduced poverty rates in the region, improved income distribution nor have they created the institutional preconditions for higher sustained economic growth. In particular, most Latin American countries still face formidable adjustment needs with respect to enhancing the quality of investments in human resource development, improving the functioning of financial markets, reforming the legal and regulatory framework, and making the public sector more effective and efficient. These challenges necessitate a second wave of reforms that are institutional and structural in nature and for which the Washington Consensus provides only limited guidance.[3]

Certainly, most policy recommendations of the Washington Consensus are essential for markets to work efficiently. They are easy to articulate, straightforward, and focus on economic issues that are of critical importance. A number of empirical studies that analysed the effects of various policy changes on economic performance provide support for the liberalizing program represented by the Washington Consensus.[4] Although their findings differ in detail, there is much overlap among them. Representative findings from that literature show that those LDCs that started out poorest, opened their economies, had relatively low government consumption, avoided high inflation, invested in elementary and secondary education, had low income inequality, and that enjoyed political stability and high quality institutions grew more rapidly than those that did not have these characteristics. In essence, it is not individual policies, but sets of mutually reinforcing policy measures, which are jointly conducive to private investment and economic growth.

And yet, the Washington Consensus raises new questions. Why are the recommended policies not heeded by governments of numerous LDCs and PSCs? If those policies are pursued (more often than not under pressure from the multilateral financial organizations), why do the predicted outcomes not result as quickly as expected?

Experiences from transitional economies in CEE and the former Soviet Union as well as the recent financial and economic crisis in East Asia illustrate that the surge of the neoclassical consensus has been self-limiting. Particularly the systemic change in CEE, which not only encompasses the stabilization and restructuring of the economies but also a fundamental transformation of these countries' political systems and social fabric, reveals substantial shortcomings in the ahistoric neoclassical approach to policy reform. The prescriptions of the Washington Consensus that have been applied to economies in transition proved to be insufficient and misguided in many cases, especially in the successor states of the former USSR. All of these countries (with the exception of the Baltic states) belong to the poorest performers in terms of both economic and political reforms. Failure to get the institutional environment right at the beginning of the transformation process meant that private investors could not rely on stable conditions and that an efficient and socially accepted redirection of resources was hindered. Maybe more important, the failure explicitly to address the problems associated with the states' capacity and capability to initiate and implement a politically feasible and economically effective set of reform measures aggravated the transformational recession in most countries.[5]

Moreover, the stereotypical application of the Washington Consensus policies to alleviate the recent financial and economic crisis in East Asia was misguided from the perspective of both the populations and governments of the affected countries themselves as well as numerous international observers. This is because the problems of the crisis did not result from a lack of fiscal or monetary discipline but were structural in nature. In most cases, governments pursued sound macroeconomic policies, but failed to establish adequate institutional arrangements to supervise and monitor private activities, especially in the financial and banking sectors. Given these structural causes of the economic turmoil, the orthodox conditionality imposed by the IMF on these countries was exaggerated in the area of macroeconomic stabilization and contributed to the severe political unrest, especially in Indonesia.[6] Effective solutions to the current problems will not be found by solely relying on the Washington Consensus. If policy recommendations do not take their political and social consequences into consideration, they may even prove to be counterproductive.[7]

More generally, what made Washington-Consensus type policies so influential and eventually helped the term to become (for right or wrong) a global brand name for neoliberal policies, was the strong pressures from the Bretton Woods organizations to make their financial assistance conditional on adopting and implementing Consensus-inspired economic reforms.[8] However, the effects of these policies did not meet expectations. As Naìm (1999) put it:

Unfortunately, the relative simplicity and presumed reliability of the Washington Consensus was not reflected by the experience with market reforms in this decade. What was implemented was usually an incomplete version of the model and its results were quite different from what politicians promised, the people expected, and the IMF and the World Bank's econometric models had predicted.

Thus after two decades of structural adjustment policies, experiences in most countries have not been encouraging. The outcomes of numerous reforms have not met the original expectations of either the donor community or the recipient countries. In many countries, resistance to Consensus-type policies occurred and made their enforcement politically infeasible. In other countries, governments lacked the credibility, the capacity, and the capability to implement the recommended reform package. Particularly, the combination of political impediments and the enormous administrative complexity of microeconomic reforms significantly slowed down the progress of economic and institutional restructuring in many countries. From a political standpoint, structural reforms are much more demanding than macroeconomic reforms due to their less visible and immediate impact and their relatively high costs which tend to target specific groups of society. Because of this concentration of costs, affected groups have strong incentives to organize themselves to mobilize resistance to reforms. Administratively, structural reforms are usually more complex because they require the participation of a larger number of public agencies as well as societal actors. This involves a greater intensity of coordination and informational demands. Moreover, the implementation of such reforms generally necessitates a larger number of administrative steps, which are, in addition, relatively widely dispersed (Naìm 1999).

As a consequence of these problems, numerous new lending programs did not materialize and domestic economic and social conditions continued to deteriorate. Furthermore, given the threat of increasing political instability in many LDCs, the tolerance of governments for the recipes of adjustment was declining, and lending organizations were faced by increasing political resistance from governments when they sought to impose further reform programs based on more rigorous conditionality (Frischtak 1994). Eventually, however, problems in the implementation of policy reform, existing coordination failures, economies of scale, and externalities in LDCs engendered a rethinking and redefining of the role of the state in economic development (Grindle 1996; Rodrik 1995). Today, even the World Bank (1997: iii) concedes 'that development requires an effective state, one that plays a catalytic, facilitating role, encouraging and complementing the activities of private businesses and individuals'. The Bank concludes that 'state-dominated development has failed. But so has stateless development

(...). History has repeatedly shown that good government is not a luxury but a vital necessity' (ibid.).

In sum, it must be said that the policy prescriptions of the Washington Consensus have been incomplete and flawed for the following reasons:

1. The focus on inflation (which had been the most serious macroeconomic burden in Latin America) called for macroeconomic policies which may not have been most appropriate for achieving long-term growth. It has also diverted attention from other important sources of macroeconomic instability such as weak financial systems and a poor sequencing of financial liberalization. Moreover, policy makers neglected other critical ingredients in a working market economy and sustainable long-term growth, including competition policy, education policies, policies to promote the transfer of technology and to improve transparency, and last but not least the need for effective corporate governance (the lack of which proved to be the Achilles heel of both the Russian and Czech privatization).[9]

2. Neither problems of income and wealth distribution nor those of poverty reduction are explicitly addressed by the Washington Consensus. This omission not only represents a serious failure to address two key problems of underdevelopment, but also causes severe political-economy problems relating to the acceptance of policy reforms in LDCs and PSCs.[10]

3. The call for state minimalism ignores the need for government intervention which results from the existence of externalities, scale economies, incomplete markets, and imperfect information. Particularly in LDCs and PSCs, where market integration is weak and market imperfections such as the lack of functioning capital markets, technological and marketing spillovers, and coordination failures exist, *market-enhancing* government intervention that complements and facilitates private-sector coordination is critical.[11]

4. The postulate of a minimal state also disregards the problem that state officials are the ones who would have to reduce the size of the state and the scope of its interference thereby putting their own interests, jobs, and values at stake.

5. The Washington Consensus ignores its social and political effects and hence the interdependence of the economy and the polity; that is the fact that economic institutions and activities are embedded in a complex fabric of social and political institutions.

6. The Consensus view essentially disregards the role of both political and economic institutions in development and transformation. In particular, it neglects the institutional problems related to policy formulation, implementation, and enforcement. Economic reform is not just a matter of

technical experts getting the prices right. The institutional structures underlying economic policy making play a critical role in the direction of policy reform and the implementation of public policies.[12] Political factors often prevent authorities from realizing reform programs in LDCs and PSCs which, for economic reasons, appear to have sound prospects for accelerating growth and improving living standards. This implies that successful policy reform and economic transformation require a transition of government towards a nexus of institutions supporting a market economy.

7. The Consensus not only ignores the impact of *formal* institutional arrangements but also the influence of *informal* institutions, such as social capital and trust, on the efficacy and feasibility of policy reform and hence on economic performance.[13]

For these reasons, critics argue that the Washington Consensus is largely insufficient as a conceptual basis for policy reforms and does not offer a blueprint for sustained development. Although the above criticisms focus on distinct aspects of the determinants and the efficacy of economic reforms, they are actually linked by a common underlying thread, that is the questions concerning the appropriate role of the state and how to craft an effective politico-institutional foundation for economic development and transition. Basically, these questions concern a country's formal and informal institutions. In order to overcome the deficiencies of the Washington Consensus, institutional analysis needs to be shifted to the center of scholarly attention. Such an analysis must focus on *economic* institutions such as contract enforcement and property rights on the one hand, and a country's *political* institutions on the other, because it is the latter which crucially affect policy formation and bureaucratic implementation as well as the formal and informal interconnectedness between public agencies, private business, and civil society.

The need for institutional reform, while basically acknowledged in theoretical proposals even of neoclassical provenance, was widely ignored in the practice of policy reform. When it was taken into account, policy advisors, economists and policy makers essentially focused on formal legal and economic institutions (for example, law and order, property rights, and central bank independence), though they failed to give these reform measures a high priority on the sequencing agenda. Reforms of political institutions, however, have been left almost completely out of account. While the political and social feasibility and sustainability of policy reforms are widely regarded as crucial factors, this aspect is neither thoroughly discussed nor are recommendations elaborated to improve the politico-institutional foundation of economic development. The Washington Consensus itself does not address either of these two areas of institutional reform.[14]

To be sure, the general policy implications derived from the Consensus had a substantial impact on the policy reforms of numerous countries. However, the way in which these countries sought to implement those implications varied substantially. Furthermore, the original policy prescriptions were soon challenged. Not only have heterodox economists criticized the Consensus from the very beginning (Sender 1999), the policy prescriptions inherent in the Consensus also caused serious and strong controversies among most respected mainstream economists, a fact which seems to reflect confusion rather than consensus (see Box 2.2). These debates became increasingly intensive in the course of the 1990s, especially when experiences with economic crises in countries as diverse as Mexico, Indonesia, South Korea, and Russia revealed that Washington-Consensus type policies were incomplete and inadequate to tackle the 'new' causes of the most recent crisis effectively. Furthermore, new experience showed that lessons derived from earlier market-oriented reform programs missed key elements, the critical importance of which was only demonstrated by the more recent crises. Subsequently, it has become fashionable to postulate the need for so-called *second-generation reforms* in order to assure policy stability and eventual economic success. These particularly include institutional and further structural reforms (at both the national and the international level), which had been ignored or postponed time and again. Hence, not only changes in the international political and economic environment, but also country-specific problems relating to the implementation and enforcement of presumed first-best policies created problems which the Consensus view had not envisioned. These developments forced a search for new ideas and concepts to improve policy reform programs. Thus throughout the 1990s, the core elements of the Washington Consensus have undergone substantial mutations (Naìm 1999).

Towards the end of the 1990s, under the influence of the financial crises in Mexico (1994/95), East Asia, Russia, and Brazil (1997/98) as well as the reform experiences in Latin America, CEE, and the CIS, a new policy agenda has emerged which may eventually lead to a *Post-Washington Consensus*. Whereas this comprises the core components from the earlier agenda, certain new accents and concerns have been emphasized. By revisiting his earlier policy desiderata and incorporating several of the key points raised by his critics, Williamson's (1997) new compilation also stresses issues such as financial sector reform, environmental protection, basic education, and strengthening economic and legal institutions. Among others, even the IMF and the World Bank began recently explicitly to address the

Box 2.2: Washington Consensus or Washington confusion?

'Since the beginning, advocates of the Washington Consensus have been greatly divided about the pace and sequence of the reforms. Profound differences quickly emerged about the need or desirability of what came to be known as the application of a "shock therapy" (...) approach to policy reforms. This approach implied the implementation of as many reforms as quickly as possible. Others argued for a slower, more sequenced pace. This is not a debate just between experts in Washington and others elsewhere. It also rages among insiders. This is illustrated by Strobe Talbott's now famous remark during a 1993 trip to Moscow when he told an anxious Russian media that "what Russia needs is less shock and more therapy". The statement, warmly welcomed by many, was, however, clearly at odds with the line espoused by his colleagues at the US Treasury and by the IMF and World Bank with the active backing of the US government. That debate of course continues today and is far from resolved, with both sides declaring victory using the same facts to back their cases.

A few years later, Joseph Stiglitz, the Chief Economist of the World Bank and former Chairman of President Clinton's Counsel of Economic Advisors, publicly denounced the IMF's handling of the financial crises in Asia and Russia. This led Anders Aslund, a Russian expert at the Carnegie Endowment in Washington to tell The Economist that "without knowing anything [Stiglitz] mouths any stupidity that comes to his head". Ricardo Hausmann, the Chief Economist of the Interamerican Development Bank [IDB] enthusiastically recommends that countries shed their currencies in favor of the US dollar, a policy that would shield them from the ills brought about by international financial volatility. (...) Enrique Iglesias, the President of the IDB, emphasizes that Hausmann's opinions are his own and that the Bank does not endorse them. The Asian crisis prompted MIT's Paul Krugman to call for the governments beset by the crisis to impose controls on capital flows, a solution that, at the time, was immediately rejected by then-Secretary of the US Treasury Robert Rubin,

the IMF's Michel Camdessus, his deputy Stanley Fisher, and Rubin's then-deputy Lawrence Summers, among many others.

Nobel Laureate James Tobin calls for a tax on currency transactions to "put sand in the wheels of international finance" and tame volatility while Nobel laureate Milton Friedman thinks that the problem is perhaps too much sand in the wheels of global finance and calls for, among other measures, the abolition of the IMF. Not so fast, say financier George Soros, Yale's Dean Jeffrey Garten as well as a blue ribbon commission sponsored by the New York-based Council on Foreign Relations. The world is in dire need of a new financial architecture, they claim. Some of them even urge the establishment of new multilateral institutions like an international debt insurance agency, a global central bank or an international bankruptcy court. Others, however, like Barry Eichengreen and Robert Rubin, insist that while the international financial system does require some maintenance and modernization what is really needed is not a general overhaul or new institutions, but better "plumbing", meaning the detailed reexamination and redesign of existing institutions and practices. James Wolfensohn, the President of the World Bank and Stiglitz, his Chief Economist, extol a new approach, the "comprehensive development framework", that the Bank officially adopted in 1999 to guide its lending and advice to its client countries. This leads Columbia University's Jagdish Bhagwati to puzzle (...) about what could explain the mistaken assumptions and outright fallacies on which Wolfensohn and Stiglitz's framework is surely based. He generously concluded that perhaps it was just the result of "plain ignorance".

(...) A point worth reiterating is that these are not the debates between say, French deconstructionist sociologists and American mathematical economists. These are disagreements among some of the most respected and influential individuals in the field and ones that share favorable ideological pre-dispositions towards markets, private capital and free trade and investment (...).' (Naim 1999) challenges of second-generation reforms. At various conferences organized by the Bretton Woods organizations, institutional reforms ranked high on the agenda, including issues relating to corporate governance, market regulation, economic decentralization, social security and tax reform, public sector management, as well as corruption and political governance.[15] Michel Camdessus, then Managing Director of the IMF, implicitly conceded at an IMF-sponsored conference on *Second Generation Reforms* in 1999 that the IMF may have got the sequencing of policy and institutional reforms wrong in earlier years. In his opening remarks to the conference, he stated that:

> Second generation reforms may be seen as the set of measures needed to enable a country to attain, in a sustained way, high-quality growth. (...) First and second generation reforms are not necessarily sequential; indeed the institution-building typically associated with the second generation often can and should occur in parallel with the first generation. (...) I think few would now dispute that sound social, political, and economic institutions are a necessary, if not sufficient, condition for the sustained implementation of sound macroeconomic policies. (Camdessus 1999)

A growing agreement has been emerging that the early Washington Consensus needs to be revised and complemented in order to deal with actual challenges as well as new circumstances. A major criticism of the Washington Consensus is that it has been incomplete and misleading, because it over-emphasizes the appealing reform triad of stabilization, liberalization, and privatization at the expense of the other above-mentioned critical components of and preconditions for economic reforms, which are not only necessary for an effective operation of markets but also of utmost importance for their development. Institutional economists, in particular, have also criticized orthodox stabilization-cum-adjustment programs for neglecting country-specific characteristics, that is that the feasibility and effectiveness of reform policies are path dependent and expectation dependent and hence highly context specific.[16]

Meanwhile, even the Bretton Woods organizations have come to recognize that broadening both the goals of development and transition as well as the set of policy instruments and reforms is indispensable to ensuring the sustainability and quality of growth processes.[17] Today there is a broad agreement that so-called second generation reforms that address the questions of sectoral and enterprise restructuring, institutional change, and improving the legal, regulatory, and administrative functions of governments represent one side of a coin; the other being sound and prudent macroeconomic policies and other ingredients of the original Washington Consensus. Neither side can work properly without the other.

It is to be noted, however, that agreement on the need for second generation reforms by no means implies a consensus concerning their design and key components. This particularly holds (1) for the question of whether or not the state should play an active role in economic development; and (2) for how to transform the state apparatus in LDCs and especially PSCs and to reconstruct (and craft new) political institutions. These questions are of paramount importance because they relate to the politico-institutional foundation of economic policy making. Even if the political objectives and instruments are well-defined, they cannot be achieved and used as conceived, if they lack a secure institutional framework that can guide and ensure policy implementation and enforcement.

The internal organization of state apparatuses is made up of a complicated nexus of institutions that provide incentives (and disincentives) for political decision makers and bureaucrats to carry out public policies. In neoclassical models, however, the state is exogenous to the economic reform process. It is considered a black box which (usually unsuccessfully) seeks to solve problems arising in market processes. This perspective is largely inappropriate for dealing with the *paradox of the adjusting state* which aggravates the problems of policy reform in LDCs and particularly in PSCs. This paradox concerns the ambivalent role of governments during the transition from a state-led model of economic development toward an open, market-oriented economy. While the state (that is the central government, sub-national authorities, the legislature, and the bureaucracy) is required to withdraw from policy interventions and to perform a passive role, economic transition and development usually require nimble and robust political authorities to be in place, ones capable of implementing and enforcing the new market-oriented policy directives. Performing this role is even more complicated if one assigns further market-enhancing tasks to the executive branch because of market imperfections. Making the state more effective so that it can meet new challenges and perform new roles in facilitating private-sector coordination is of utmost importance for feasible and successful policy reform strategies. This central issue, however, was not explicitly included in either the Washington Consensus or neoclassical approaches to policy reform.[18]

Recent theoretical work of institutional economists has explicitly started to open the black box of the state and to focus on political behavior and the role of institutions. By using the tools of the NIE as well as the insights of political scientists and sociologists, persisting deficiencies in the neoclassical model of policy reform can be overcome. The view that the state remains a central variable in economic development, structural change, and the process of policy reform inevitably raises the question of state capability and capacity. Grindle (1996) argues that political leaderships and structures, while often part of the problem, are necessarily also part of the solution for creating a more effective and responsive state. Recognition of the importance of state capabilities and capacities resulting from effective and durable politico-institutional structures and informal institutions is the central element of the newly emerging third wave of theorizing about the role of the state in economic development. The utopian vision of the benevolent state as the ultimate promoter of economic development, proposed by the first wave, has proved to be unrealistic, but so have the optimistic expectations regarding free markets and minimalist states, which characterized the second wave. Grindle (1999: 20) succinctly summarized the key challenge for future research:

> While there is an evolving literature on the political economy of institutional creation and change in terms of those that are important for economic management – central banks, tax agencies, ministries of finance – there remains much work to be done in terms of the reform of the state more generally, including decentralization, civil service reform, and capacity building. Political economists need to consider where the initiative for institutional change comes from, how new institutional models are generated, the way in which the dynamics of institutional creation may differ from those of institutional evolution, and how political and economic actors adapt to such changes.

The following chapters of this study take Grindle's research agenda as a motivation and starting point. They seek to incorporate institutions into the ongoing discussion about economically effective and politically feasible approaches to policy reforms in LDCs and PSCs and explain why analyses of both formal and informal institutions need to be placed at the center of theoretical reasoning and practical policy making. While Part I of this study mainly focuses on the process of institutional change and the role of the state therein, Part II seeks to elaborate a coherent conceptual approach that helps to assess the quality of politico-institutional foundations of economic development and transition in country studies. The subsequent application of this concept to specific cases of policy reforms in various countries illustrates the usefulness of this institutional approach and helps to explain why policy reforms failed in some cases, but succeeded in others. This, in turn, allows lessons to be derived which may eventually become a Post-Washington Consensus.

NOTES

1   See Roemer and Radelet (1991). The following considerations are based on Ahrens (2000).
2.   For discussions of key problems in sequencing and timing policy reform see, for example, Corbo and Fischer (1995), Edwards (1984 and 1989), Fischer (1993), Martinelli and Tommasi (1997), and Sturzenegger and Tommasi (1998) as well as the references therein.
3.   See Stiglitz (1998a), Burki and Perry (1998), and Pou (2000).
4.   See, for example, Aziz and Wescott (1997), Barro (1991), Fischer (1993), Radelet *et al.* (1997), and Sachs and Warner (1995).
5.   See, for example, Amsden *et al.* (1994), Schmieding (1994), and Kolodko (1999). In this context, it is to be noted that – in contrast to the member states of the Commonwealth of Independent States (CIS) – economic liberalization yielded substantial payoffs in Central Europe including the Baltics. This, however, may be mainly attributed to their endeavor to accede to the European Union and hence the requirement to implement the *acquis communautaire*; see Piazolo (1998) and particularly section 6.3.2 in Chapter 6 of this study.
6.   Concerning the causes of the crisis, the role of the IMF, and country-specific analyses (including Indonesia) see, for example, Dornbusch (1998), Feldstein (1998), Goldstein (1998), Radelet (1998), and Radelet and Sachs (1998b).
7.   See Sections 6.2.3 and 6.3.1 in Chapter 6 of this study for further elaboration.
8.   Note in this context that policy reforms that were pursued in the 1980s were remarkably different from those promoted in previous decades. A major reason for this was the fact that a large number of these reforms had been called forth in response to financial crisis and hence significantly enhanced the influence of the IMF, multilateral development banks, and foreign commercial banks. To a higher degree than before, many LDCs were now forced to give these organizations direct access to national policy making. Consequently, international organizations frequently determined the agenda of policy reform which eventually had fundamental effects on the role of governments in numerous countries; see Grindle and Thomas (1991).
9.   See Berglöf and von Thadden (1999) with respect to the crucial importance of corporate governance in the course of development and transition, McKinnon (1992) regarding the order of financial liberalization and Stiglitz (1998a) as well as the references therein for a more thorough discussion of why the prescriptions of the Washington Consensus for stabilization and liberalization – its two core areas – are incomplete and misguided.
10.   Note, for example, that even if market-oriented reforms succeed in terms of raising and equalizing incomes, some losses will be likely to occur and negatively affect powerful vested interests groups. These groups, however, will have both the motive as well as the means to block structural adjustment. This will be particularly the case in a clientelistic regime, the main support of which comes from favored actors of the government who benefit substantially from the regulations and controls which are the principal targets of structural adjustment (Roemer and Radelet 1991).
11.   See Aoki *et al.* (1997a), Krugman (1993), Rodrik (1995), and Stiglitz (1997).
12.   See Weingast (1993 and 1995), North (1995a), and Bates (1999).
13.   See, for example, North (1990a and 1995a), Raiser (1997), Fukuyama (1999), and Lal (1999).
14.   A notable exception is the role of private property rights and an appropriate bankruptcy law, which has been acknowledged even by the advocates of the Washington Consensus; see, for example, Williamson (1990). Of course, the political and social dimensions of policy reforms have been explicitly addressed in the burgeoning literature on the political economy of policy reform. But on the one hand, a consensus on which factors play the most critical roles for the efficacy and implementation of reforms has not been achieved yet. On the other hand, the findings of this strand of the literature had only limited influence on what became the driving force of policy reforms that were guided by the Bretton Woods organizations, namely the Washington Consensus; regarding different aspects of the political economy of policy reforms in LDCs and PSCs, see, for example, Bates and

Krueger (1993), Haggard and Kaufman (1992a and 1995), Nelson (1989 and 1990), Przeworski (1991), Roland (1994), and Williamson (1994). Useful surveys include Haggard and Webb (1993) and Rodrik (1996).

15. In order to gain an impression of the shift in emphasis of the discussion among academics and policy makers on key challenges of economic development and transition, visit the conference websites on the Internet at (1) http://www.worldbank.org/research/abcde/ for the Annual Bank Conferences on Development Economics; and (2) http://www.imf.org/external/pubs/ft/seminar/1999/reforms/index.htm#agenda for an IMF-sponsored conference on second generation reforms.

16. See, for example, North (1990a), Pejovich (1994), and Richter (1999).

17. See Stiglitz (1998a, 1998b, 1998c), Camdessus (1999), and Wolfensohn (1999).

18. See, for example, Aoki *et al.* (1997b) and Streeten (1996).

3. From New Political Economy to New Institutional Economics

Enduring puzzles involving the determinants of economic development and effective policy reform can be solved only if the role and emergence of institutions is thoroughly analysed. When institutions and economic policy are seen as focal points of the development problem, attention needs to focus on the behavior of politicians and political parties, bureaucrats, interest groups, and private actors. The behavior and the decisions of policy makers are influenced by the constituency and various interest groups, and public policies and their outcomes affect the opinion and well-being of citizens as well as the emergence and power of interest groups. For this reason, students of economic development need to study the institutional and procedural relationships between the economy and the polity. Analysing the developmental impact of institutions promises greatly to enhance our understanding of economic policy making and eventually of economic growth processes. Therefore the following will investigate the relevance of applying the NPE and the NIE to the economics of development.[1] In a second step (Chapter 4), the ways in which institutions and institutional change affect the performance of economies in LDCs and PSCs are explored within an analytical demand-and-supply framework relying on the economics of transaction costs and the theory of collective action. More specifically, it will be argued that a critical role is to be attributed to the state concerning the initiation and facilitation of institutional change.

Still governments in numerous LDCs and PSCs appear unable to implement those policies that economists recommend as being more effective and more efficient than persisting strategies for generating growth and fostering development. Governments continue to ignore policy lessons from development experience and pursue policies that are not compatible with the normative prescriptions derived from development economics. Inflationary budgets, inward-oriented policies, as well as policies that create urban bias and factor market distortions and foster deliberate industrialization are still popular among numerous policy makers. However, '(w)hy should reasonable men adopt public policies that have harmful consequences for the societies they govern?' (Bates 1981: 3).

The *New Political Economy (NPE)*, which began to be applied to political phenomena in LDCs in the mid-1970s, offers a theoretical approach in responding to Bates's provoking question. The NPE analyses collective political decision-making processes within given constitutional rules and economic constraints and seeks to explore the determinants of policy reform which result from the rational behavior of policy makers. In the 1980s, the NPE constituted a pivotal component of the neoliberal paradigm. It seemed to be a perfect tool to complement neoclassical analyses of major features of LDC experiences. These include, for example, the over-sized growth of governments relative to private sector activities, the emergence of rent-seeking and corruption, the existence of protectionism, and the related phenomenon of import-substitution policies.

More recently however, the NPE has been succeeded in both academia and research undertaken by development agencies (notably the World Bank) by the *New Institutional Economics (NIE)*, a relatively new branch in economics associated with the work of Coase, North, and Williamson. While the NPE has usefully contributed to the economic analysis of political structures and processes, which are at the heart of economic policy making and policy reform, it does not provide an ample understanding of public action and shows substantial deficiencies in understanding real-world politics in democratic and non-democratic settings alike. The newly emerging discipline of institutional economics, especially in the strand embodied by Douglass North's work, promises to become a more general and more realistic approach to studying the leading questions underlying the complicated task of policy reform. In what follows, the explanatory power of both the NPE and the NIE for analysing policy reforms in LDCs and PSCs will be scrutinized, the concluding argument being that particularly the NIE, combined with useful approaches of the NPE, offers a suitable theoretical framework to analyse policy reform programs and to develop politically feasible and economically effective development strategies.

3.1 THE NEW POLITICAL ECONOMY

The term *New Political Economy* refers to the studies done under various labels, prominent among which have been *economic theory of politics, rent-seeking,* and *public choice.* The most influential pioneers have been Arrow, Downs, Olson, Buchanan and Tullock, as well as Niskanen. With their works on preference aggregation, party competition, interest groups, constitutional economics, and bureaucracy, respectively, these scholars paved the way for the now widely accepted integration of public choice into the social sciences and particularly into economics.[2] The probably most-quoted definition of Public Choice theory[3] was formulated by Mueller (1989: 1–2):

> Public choice can be defined as the economic study of non-market decision making, or simply the application of economics to political science. The subject matter of public choice is the same as that of political science: the theory of the state, voting rules, voter behavior, party politics, the bureaucracy, and so on. The methodology of public choice is that of economics, however. The basic behavioral postulate of public choice, as for economics, is that man is an egoistic, rational, utility maximizer.

The NPE can be generally characterized as an attempt to provide a rigorous and axiomatic general theory of the state, which interprets politics as a market for individual exchanges. Since the NPE (or Public Choice) not only explores political structures and the behavior of politicians but also the behavior of economic pressure groups and economic policy making, it can be explicitly applied to questions of policy reform and economic development.

3.1.1 Features of the New Political Economy

Essentially, the NPE is a neoclassical economic theory of politics based on the assumption of rationality and on methodological individualism. It applies the economic model of exchange to social and especially political relations. Public Choice theorists suggest that marginal analysis and equilibrium analysis can be applied to the study of political markets and objective functions. The concept of utility maximization is central to the NPE and applied to politicians, bureaucrats, and economic agents alike. Individuals seek to maximize their gains from economic and political exchange. They are inclined to use political bodies such as the government, the legislature, and the bureaucracy to protect and to increase these gains. Political behavior is usually explained as mainly (or solely) motivated by individual (material) self-interest. Given the assumption that individuals have stable preferences, changes in behavior are attributed to changing constraints faced by individual actors. Based on these assumptions, the NPE analyses the behavior of individuals involved in political decision-making and the interactions between the economy and the polity. The individualistic approach is often also applied to groups of individuals such as the government, the bureaucracy, and interest groups by presuming homogeneity within the respective groups. The theory does not assume the government to be composed of Platonic guardians or the state to act benevolently in pursuing the public interest. The government and its members are assumed to maximize their utility in terms of their hold on power, income, and prestige subject to administrative, legal, economic, and political constraints.

The impact of institutions on individual behavior is analysed in a comparative way. Public Choice theorists reject Pareto-optimality as a reference point, because it leads to the nirvana fallacy. Instead, they concentrate on comparisons of actual institutional arrangements that could be observed in contemporary or historical settings (Demsetz 1969; Frey 1988).

Recognizing that in reality deriving a social welfare function from the aggregation of individual preferences is generally impossible, adherents to Public Choice theory argue that individuals are better equipped to take advantage of the information of positive institutional analysis and to pursue actions that are consistent with their own preferences. Under the institutional conditions of a functioning democracy, in which preferences can be expressed through voting behavior, the politico-economic interaction implies outcomes that reflect individual preferences as well as possible under given institutional arrangements. This approach to the study of political decision making appears to be superior to the orthodox procedure of economists, which simply assumes the state to pursue first-best policies, because they are rational from the economic perspective. Such assumptions are neither consistent with individualistic behavior nor do they have significant effects in actual politico-economic decision-making processes.

The normative advice resulting from the positive analysis is that the scope of the state's economic regulation and policy making should be reduced as much as possible due to prevailing severe shortcomings of collective institutions *vis-à-vis* the price system. Potential market failures cannot be satisfactorily overcome by governments, because the institutions of the state produce administrative and political failures which are frequently worse than market failures (Frey 1988).

In the beginning, the NPE focused on political structures and processes in developed countries, particularly those having liberal democratic political institutions. In these instances, scholars have applied the tools and techniques of neoclassical economics to formulate an economic theory of log-rolling, legislation, reciprocal patronage, bureaucracy, lobbying, and voting. Prominent has been the use of rent-seeking models to explain domestic economic regulation and foreign trade interventions.[4]

In the mid-1970s, Public Choice theorists began to study political phenomena in LDCs. Early applications addressed mainly rent-seeking problems, for example resulting from tariffs or quantitative trade restrictions.[5] These studies, however, lacked political content, because they neglected political institutions and viewed trade restrictions as simply exogenously imposed. While much is known about the characteristics of LDC states, surprisingly little theoretical work has been undertaken by the NPE to understand the functioning of those polities better; the most notable exception being Bates's (1981) pioneering study on African economies. Scholars began only recently to apply the NPE more extensively to the process of policy making in LDCs by endogenizing political variables and analysing the political determinants of economic policies. The contemporary analysis of policy making in LDCs seeks explicitly to overcome the apolitical and ahistorical character of traditional neoclassical analysis by providing a theory of political behavior in which government is not considered as an exogenous variable. Hence the state is disaggregated and operationalized. The NPE stresses that the behavior of policy makers is shaped by political rather than economic rationality and examines the effects of political motivations and behavior on economic policy making (Meier 1991b).

3.1.2 Rational Politics, Irrational Economics

Central to understanding many works of the NPE is the notion that individuals often cannot accomplish their self-interest through solitary action. Therefore, it appears rational for them to create or to join groups of individuals whose preferences correspond with their own. Thus the pursuit of individual interests can be transformed into group action that enhances the possibility to realize individual goals. Usually such interest groups are better equipped than individuals to make claims on the government in order to achieve their goals. Olson (1965) argues that due to free-rider problems groups tend to be small and narrowly-focused on accomplishing specific goals, the gains of which will only accrue to group members. In politics small groups representing narrowly-defined vested interests emerge, which press the government to deliver goods and services that benefit the specific interests of their members. From the perspective of the NPE, politics can be characterized by competing interest groups seeking to achieve special benefits which can be distributed by the government apparatus. Individual voting behavior is then guided by the motivation to elect those politicians who promise to deliver the desired benefits and to punish those who do not or who failed to do so when they were in office. In this view, public policies reflect the persisting competition among interest groups that try to influence and to control the distribution of public resources on behalf of their members. Interest groups bring specific issues to public attention, add them to the political agenda, and influence decisions through lobbying activities. The reaction of politicians reflects then the distribution of power in society. This strand of the NPE hypothesizes that the composition and power of, and the interrelations between, special interest groups provide the key to understanding public policy formation.[6]

The NPE perceives the existence and competition of interest groups to represent a severe threat to the ability of the government to pursue economically rational policies and to serve the public interest. The logic of collective action tends to bring about a multitude of small and narrowly-focused interest groups which are able to gain access to the political arena and force government to deliver the desired benefits (Olson 1965). Since elected politicians try to respond adequately to a large number of vested interests, the result is the increasing size of government and incoherence of public policies. Consequently market interactions are greatly distorted by government policies that seek to protect a host of special interests through excessive regulation and intervention. To solve this problem, neoclassical political economists advocate a minimal state. In this sense, less politics implies better economics. For if the government is restricted to some core activities such as providing public goods, protecting individual rights, and enforcing private contracts, there are fewer opportunities to please vested interests and hence fewer incentives exist for pressure groups to make unproductive claims on the government (Buchanan 1980). Since in reality, however, the efficient operation of markets is undermined by excessive political interventions, politics and markets are frequently in conflict. The result is public policies reflecting rational choices of policy makers but representing economically irrational actions.

Besides this society-centered approach to understanding the politics of economic policy making, some neoclassical political economists have also focused on exploring the decision-making behavior of political elites from a state-centered perspective. This approach states that policy makers do not merely passively react to vested interests, but are active in pursing their self-interest. Therefore, they will allocate public resources to those who support them and use available political or economic leverage to punish those who oppose their hold on power. As Grindle (1991) argues, political elites actively seek to build coalitions helping them to stay in office by buying political support. Political actions will then reflect less normative preferences or ideological convictions, but rather incorporate any measures which help incumbents to achieve their short-term objective of maintaining power. The policies that emerge under these conditions are incoherent and impede economic growth and development, because they are based on short-term tactical considerations and lack government commitment to their content.[7]

Bureaucrats form another group of public officials whose politically rational behavior may translate into economically irrational actions. Civil servants not merely pursue their own material welfare, but at times they also seek to enhance their power or prestige. Adherents to the NPE argue that bureaucrats, therefore, seek to increase their regulatory power and maximize the financial resources controlled by them and allocate them according to their own preferences, for example by benefiting their ethnic group or home village. The allocation of licenses or decisions regarding the implementation of public infrastructure, education or health projects may be guided by corruption and clientelism rather than by the motivation to serve the public interest (Grindle 1991). Niskanen (1971), the leading Public Choice theorist of bureaucratic behavior, argues that the concerns of managers of public bureaux comprise their pay, reputation, perquisites, power, the bureau's output, and the ease of making changes and of managing their bureaux. According to Niskanen, these factors are positively correlated with the size of the respective bureau's budget. Hence, budget maximization has been considered an adequate proxy describing bureaucratic behavior. This implies that government apparatuses are bigger and burdened with higher costs than necessary. Appropriate measures to impose greater discipline on bureaucrats and to generate an optimal supply of public services include decentralizing the provision of government services, increased exposure of bureaucratic activities to competitive (private) suppliers, reconstruction of bureaucrats' incentives, and strengthening legislative control over appropriation bills.

Another explanation of economically irrational outcomes resulting from rational political behavior is based on the notion of the predatory state. In this context, the state (or the government) itself is conceived as a rationally acting entity that maximizes the economic welfare of a small but powerful political elite at the expense of society as a whole. These states are usually characterized by excessive taxation, overvalued exchange rates, and large but inefficient bureaucracies. Governments of these states rely on rational strategies to enhance their exploitative power by pursuing economically irrational strategies of development. Zaire under Mobutu was the archetype of the predatory state.

The NPE provides a number of compelling arguments that explain the formation and implementation of economically irrational policies. Empirically, the LDCs provide numerous examples supporting the view that public officials and private interest groups exploit the authoritative power of the state and undermine market transactions in order to benefit themselves. There are numerous cases in the developing world of agrarian societies that have initiated development strategies benefiting urban classes and emerging industrialists at the expense of agriculture. Largely inefficient import-substitution policies reflect unproductive strategies of economic development favoring specific economic and political interest groups in many LDCs. Many governments undertake populist policies with some short-term benefits but large long-term social costs. Also, political authorities tend to invest overly in projects rather than provide an overall policy framework that is suitable to transfer the economy onto a higher trajectory of development. The NPE explains these cases by the existence of vested interest groups successfully lobbying for the redirection of public resources to their own benefit or by incentives that drive public officials to misallocate public resources in order to buy political support (Grindle 1991).

3.1.3 Critique of the NPE: Positive Economics, Negative Politics?

In his book *An Economic Theory of Democracy*, Downs (1957) argues that the government should be treated as an integral part of the economy, not as an exogenous force. Private interest motivates politicians to perform the social functions inherent to politics. Yet public policies, by and large, result as unintended by-products of political behavior which is driven by politicians' private motives to maximize their utility in terms of income, power, and prestige. In turn, citizens as voters view elections as a means to select the government that promises to deliver the greatest benefits to them. However, both propositions are flawed to some extent. First of all, most citizens do not have sufficient information to decide which politicians or political parties represent their interests most effectively. Moreover, since a single vote has a negligible weight in general elections, it is not rational for individuals to spend time and other resources to find out. Hence, existing lobby groups are in the position to exert relatively strong influence on public policies.[8] Secondly, political power is not an end in itself, but a means to pursue specific ends. As Grindle (1991) observes, political elites in LDCs are generally not contentless regarding their normative preferences which guide policy making. They usually base their policy choices on explicit notions of what choices constitute 'good policies'. Despite their concern for staying in office, they do not always compromise on policy choices in order to maximize their capacity to retain power. Politicians and political parties often rely on particular support groups or coalition partners for ideological or historical reasons. They may also face political opponents, the support of whom they would never seek, even in their pursuit to keep their hold on power. Acknowledging this implies that the maximization of power should be discarded as a *central* incentive driving political behavior. Furthermore, political decisions vary greatly in their direct relevance to maintaining power. Public investment in infrastructure projects, decentralizing the ministry of education, or restructuring the financial system, for example, are policies of a different dimension than lifting subsidies on basic foodstuffs or a rapid and bold elimination of a protectionist trade regime. Whilst the latter decisions may eventually have the potential to threaten a political regime's survival, the former usually do not.

Five years after his pioneering work Downs (1962) actually acknowledged this kind of mixed motivation guiding political behavior when he attenuated his strong assumptions and stated that politicians, like citizens, have certain visions of what constitutes a good society. Judgement on quality of political leadership is often based on notions of the public or national interest, which may cause citizens to accept policy choices even if they do not correspond with their self-interest. Downs (1962: 23–5) argues that informal institutions such as values and codes of behavior 'are part of the basic culture that is passed on from generation to generation and constantly reinforced through schools, family life, churches, and other institutions engaged in acculturation and social control'. And he concludes that '(a)s social scientists we should analyse the world realistically so that, as ethical men, we can design social mechanisms that utilize men's actual motives to produce social conditions as close as possible to our ideal of "the good society". Failure to be realistic about human nature would lead us to design social mechanisms that do not achieve their desired ends. Conversely, abandoning ideals leads to cynical nihilism' (ibid.: 33). But, as Orchard and Stretton (1997) soberly recognize, the damage had already been done, for it is Downs' original model, without his later amendments, which had driven the Public-Choice paradigm and which leads Tollison (1987) to conclude that those goods provided by governments which are beneficial for the society as a whole are mere by-products of the rent-seeking society. They are an unintended outcome of the competitive struggle for wealth transfers.

The application of the Public Choice tool box to log-rolling, the behavior of interest groups and bureaucrats as well as rent-seeking yields illuminating insights into processes of policy making, but generally suffers from several shortcomings and oversimplifications.[9] For example, studies on log-rolling disregard the possibility that there are legislators who vote for their principled beliefs and are not inclined to trade their votes. On many occasions, bills to be voted on do not directly concern the particular interests of legislators. In these cases, they may vote according to their perception of what serves the public interest or for their conception of 'good government'. Alternatively, they may trade their votes to gain support in other cases which do touch their individual interest. In Public Choice theory, the latter kind of behavior has become the norm and has been illustrated by appropriately selected case studies.

With respect to interest groups, it is argued that big firms, business associations and other pressure groups that are well organized, have substantial resources, and can employ permanent lobbyists, press the government for special favors at the expense of consumers, taxpayers, and society as a whole. Since the costs imposed on individuals are usually marginal and adversely affected individuals are often not well organized, resistance is ineffective and diffuse. Public Choice analyses are based on those cases. However, scholars deny in their theoretical approaches, and neglect in empirical investigations, a great variety of behavior that does not fit into this theoretical paradigm. For example, interest-group activities may also succeed not because they aim to yield concentrated benefits for a few individuals or companies, but because politicians and electors think that the actions lobbied for accord with the public interest or benefit the economy as a whole. Moreover, Public Choice analysts do not consider that some policies and regulations which benefit interest groups, are imposed by governments because authorities are concerned about balance-of-payments problems, low investment levels, or unemployment. Orchard and Stretton (1997), for example, argue that governments in Australia and the United States have often initiated and introduced tariffs, but that these tariffs have also been reduced or even abolished against the interests of those industries which benefited from them, either due to changes in industrial structure or due to a change in theoretical beliefs or in the paradigm underlying economic policy making.

In his seminal work on *The Logic of Collective Action*, Olson (1965) argues that interest groups have crucial competitive advantages in the political market, that groups are effective if they offer concentrated rather than dispersed benefits, that relatively small groups can be more effective than large ones, and that collective group action needs to be compulsory in order to be effective. His theory predicts that the competition among interest groups distorts political outcomes favoring those policies which are promoted by effective pressure groups and provide concentrated benefits at the expense of taxpayers. It is not to be ignored that this happens in developed and emerging democracies as well as in non-democratic settings. However, as a presumably dominant characteristic of a political regime, this prediction of political behavior fails to explain actual political developments in many countries such as consumer protection, environmental regulation, increasing income transfers to politically poorly organized and economically weak groups of society, as well as the expansion of welfare and public health services absorbing increasing shares of governments' budgets. Furthermore, there are numerous examples of collective action based on non-compulsory cooperation, for example if individuals voluntarily cooperate for purposes as diverse as recreation, welfare services, or the protection of neighborhoods. Finally, with respect to bureaucratic behavior, Self (1993) found that Niskanen's reasoning does not provide a general theory. The salaries of bureau managers are often not linked to their budgets. In many cases, government agencies are not monopolistic but often perform functions overlapping with, and duplicating, functions of other bureaux.

In sum, the preceding arguments hold that the NPE 'is most useful for explaining stasis rather than change and "bad" policy choices rather than "good" ones. That is (..) that the perspective is reductionist in a way that impedes efforts to conceptualize or explain what is most sought after by many of its adherents – change and improvement in the nature of development policy in a society' (Grindle 1991: 45). A more appropriate model of policy making should be one that does not assume politics to be either inherently negative or inherently positive regarding the design and pursuit of public policies. Such a model should 'accept politics, not as a spanner in the economics works, but as the central means through which societies seek to resolve conflict over issues of distribution and values. In such a perspective, politically rational behavior would not be viewed as a constraint on the achievement of collectively beneficial public policy' (ibid.). The New Institutional Economics promises to help elaborate such an analytical approach.

3.2 THE NEW INSTITUTIONAL ECONOMICS

In recent years, the occupation with institutions has become the central subject of a new strand of economics, the *New Institutional Economics (NIE)*.[10] Based on the classical works of Coase (1937 and 1960), a huge literature on the economic institutions of capitalism has emerged that seeks to endogenize institutions and investigates more systematically the significance of institutions for economic behavior. The NIE experienced a breakthrough in the economics profession in the 1960s and 1970s. In this context, important pacemakers included Alchian (1961), Calabresi (1961), Buchanan and Tullock (1962), Olson (1965), Davis and North (1971), Williamson (1971, 1975, 1976), and Stiglitz (1974). More recently, this research has been extended to the economic analysis of political institutions.[11] Due to the multidimensional and rapid growth of studies in the field of the NIE, a synthesis of the entire field is beyond the scope of this study. The present purpose, therefore, is the more modest one of relating central insights and hypotheses of the NIE to questions of policy reform and economic performance in LDCs and PSCs.[12]

The emerging literature on institutions has considerably improved our understanding of the roles and functioning of *economic* institutions in *developed* countries. What is not well understood, however, is why institutions in LDCs differ from those in developed countries, how existing institutions evolved over time and why inefficient institutions often persist, how institutions explain differences in policy making, and how they can be politically changed so that the institutional environment can become more conducive to policy reform and economic development.

Standard neoclassical approaches to problems of (under)development failed to make instructive contributions in addressing these challenging questions, because institutions were either taken as given or ignored. Neoclassical analyses usually assume transactions to be costless, information freely available, and governments to be benevolent. This orthodox approach is useful because it allows the determinants and implications of economic efficiency to be analysed under idealized conditions, it yields policy prescriptions which are efficient from a theoretical point of view and it may serve as a benchmark for evaluating actual policies. Neoclassical theorizing, however, has its limits. Its main weakness lies in its neutrality to institutions and its tendency to neglect institutional conditions and the existence of transaction costs. Therefore, neoclassical economics can only be applied to the problems related to the allocation of resources in a very abstract sense.[13] North's (1994a: 359) critique emphasizes exactly this point when he writes that

> Neoclassical theory is simply an inappropriate tool to analyze and prescribe policies that will induce development. It is concerned with the operation of markets, not with how markets develop. How can one prescribe policies when one doesn't understand how economies develop? The very methods employed by neoclassical economists have dictated the subject matter and militated against such a development. That theory in the pristine form that gave it mathematical precision and elegance modeled a frictionless and static world. When applied to economic history and development it focused on technological development and more recently human-capital investment but ignored the incentive structure embodied in institutions that determined the extent of societal investment in those factors. In the analysis of economic performance through time it contained two erroneous assumptions: (i) that institutions do not matter and (ii) that time does not matter.

The NIE as an emerging sub-discipline builds on, modifies, and extends neoclassical theory. It incorporates a considerable variety of conceptual approaches which have developed quite separately. Still the NIE does not represent a fully fledged theory but rather a research program which shows numerous interconnections with other disciplines such as law, philosophy, anthropology, sociology, and political science. Within the economics discipline, affinities exist with evolutionary economics, organization theory, and constitutional economics.

The great variety of approaches subsumed under the term NIE has been united by the conviction that institutions matter for economic performance and that institutions are basically susceptible to economic analysis. Most research in the NIE has been concerned with understanding the effects of institutions on economic behavior, economic performance, and problems of distribution (choice within rules). More recently, scholars also turned their attention to the origins of institutions and the determinants of institutional change over time (choice of rules). The relevance of such research to development economists and practitioners should be obvious. Although it is still modest, the application of the NIE to problems of economic development and policy reform has been growing in recent years.[14]

3.2.1 Definition and Classification of Institutions

In common parlance as well as in academic debates the term *institution* has
been used in a great variety of ways. Basically, two meanings of the term can
be distinguished; (1) institution as a label for organized social groups, that is
organizations such as legislatures, political parties, regulatory agencies, trade
unions, firms, or universities; and (2) as a label for normative rules (Vanberg
1983). According to this distinction, the NIE has been characterized by two
different analytical branches, which are in various ways complementary. The
first defines institutions as normative rules and addresses the questions of
how institutions emerge, change, and affect economic growth and
development. The second branch analyzes organizations, especially the firm
as an economic institution. These two definitions are related to different
levels of analysis. In a macroeconomic perspective, normative rules are the
constraints to economic behavior, and organizations are the players. From a
microanalytic perspective, organizations themselves constrain and structure
human interaction. Organizations operate under specific institutions, rules
and regulations, dealing with budgets, personnel, reporting procedures, and
procurement which constrain the behavior of their members. Therefore,
institutions constitute the incentive structures for the behavior of both
individuals and organizations. If one perceives, according to contract
theoretical approaches, an organization as a nexus of contracts and rules (that
is institutions), a consistent and integrated definition of the term institution
can be agreed upon. This study follows the conception, now widely accepted
among development economists, that institutions are the rules of the game in
an economy and a society,

> the humanly devised constraints that structure human interaction. They are made
> up of formal constraints (e.g., rules, laws, constitutions), informal constraints (e.g.,
> norms of behavior, conventions, self-imposed codes of conduct), and their
> enforcement characteristics. Together they define the incentive structure of
> societies and specifically economies. (North 1994a: 360)

Ostrom (1990: 51) describes institutions in greater detail as

> the sets of working rules that are used to determine who is eligible to make
> decisions in some arena, what actions are allowed or constrained, what aggregation
> rules will be used, what procedures must be followed, what information must or
> must not be provided, and what payoffs will be assigned to individuals dependent
> on their actions (...) All rules contain prescriptions that forbid, permit, or require
> some action or outcome. Working rules are those actually used, monitored, and
> enforced when individuals make choices about the actions they will take. (...)
> Enforcement may be undertaken by others directly involved, agents they hire,
> external enforcers, or any combination of these enforcers. One should not talk

about a 'rule' unless most people whose strategies are affected by it know of its existence and expect others to monitor behavior and to sanction nonconformance.

Hence, the most basic characteristic of institutions is that they include enforceable norms, rules, and behaviors that serve collective purposes and structure and constrain social interaction. They are known to the members of the relevant community or society and applicable in repeated and future situations. Furthermore, institutions should provide predictable, credible, coherent, and evenly enforced rules. Although institutions must provide some degree of stability and predictability, institutional change and adaptation are also necessary. Adaptability helps to ensure that changes in social preferences, technology, political and socio-economic structures, and external factors can be accommodated by incentive structures.

Depending on the level of analysis, the institutional environment needs to be distinguished from institutional arrangements, which together form the overall institutional matrix of a society: 'The institutional environment is the set of fundamental political, social and legal ground rules that establishes the basis for production, exchange and distribution. (...) An institutional arrangement is an arrangement between economic units that governs the way in which these units can cooperate and/or compete' (Davis and North 1971: 6–7).

This systematic distinction underlines that institutions always represent normative rules regardless of the level of analysis. Furthermore, in order to assure the efficacy of rules and a beneficial exchange among actors, involved parties need to be basically capable of enforcing compliance with the agreed upon rules. Therefore, institutions invariably consist of two components; a rule and its enforcement characteristics. This leads us, following Kiwit and Voigt (1995), to a more systematic classification of institutions (Table 3.1). External institutions are those formal rules which are enforced by the coercive monopoly of the state. In contrast, internal institutions are subject to private control and can be classified according to different enforcement characteristics. First, rules could rely on self-enforcement. In this case, violating the rule would make the violator worse off. In game theoretic terminology, this is a pure coordination game implying that compliance is the dominant strategy of all players. Secondly, a rule may be enforced by the imperative self-commitment of the actor. Due to intrinsic motivation, individuals could internalize ethical rules, for example, and comply with them even if that behavior runs counter to their narrowly defined self-interests. Thirdly, enforcement could work through informal societal control, that is explicit sanctions imposed by other actors. Informal enforcement could be achieved by informing others about the non-compliance, thereby damaging the violator's reputation. Finally, internal institutions can rely on enforcement by private organizations (for example, by private courts of arbitration or simply by private power).

Table 3.1: Classification of institutions

kind of rule	kind of enforcement	type of institution	
convention	self-enforcing	type-1-internal	informal institutions
ethical rule	via self-commitment of the actor	type-2-internal	
customs	via informal societal control	type-3-internal	
formal private rules	organized private enforcement	type-4-internal	formal institutions
constitution, laws, regulations	organized enforcement by the state	external	

Source: Voigt and Kiwit (1995); modified

While the control of internal rules relies on horizontal relationships between the actors involved, external institutions are based on a hierarchical enforcement mechanism. But the efficacy of the latter as well as that of formal private rules is always partially backed, complemented or sometimes contradicted by informal institutions such as traditions, routines, codes of conduct, or conventions. This influence of informal institutions may, in some circumstances, reinforce formal rules, but in others it implies hysteresis effects and blocks institutional change, because informal institutions show substantial inertia and change only incrementally (North 1990a).

Since an institutional arrangement is embedded in the institutional environment, its efficacy also depends on the performance of other institutional arrangements. From a theoretical perspective, the interplay of institutions may be characterized by four different relations: They can be neutral to each other, supplement or substitute each other, and they can contradict each other, for example, if compliance with internal institutions requires the violation of an external institution or vice versa. The latter aspect is of particular importance if in a society powerful private groups exist which are able to undermine the state's authority by establishing and enforcing in an organized manner private rules that contradict the constitution or state laws. Moreover, institutional efficiency strongly depends on how well an institution copes with the potential opportunism of involved agents. Substantial differences in institutional efficiency may result from subtle differences in auxiliary institutions. Lin and Nugent (1995) provide an example: the potential opportunistic behavior of managers in business corporations can be mitigated by the existence of competitive stock markets and managerial labor markets, but also by informal institutions such as morality, team spirit, and loyalty. The effectiveness of political institutions also depends on the efficacy of other institutional arrangements. Consider, for example, the effects of adopting constitutions similar to that of the United States in many LDCs in Latin America. While the US constitution has been widely credited with supporting economic development, different enforcement mechanisms, norms of behavior, and ideologies in other countries rendered similar constitutional structures less effective (North 1990a).

3.2.2 The Assumptions, Axioms, and Terminology of the NIE

The NIE in its various branches originally represented an extension of neoclassical economics. It retains the scarcity postulate (which implies competition) and hence the choice theoretic approach of microeconomics. It relies on price theory as a pivotal tool of institutional analysis and views relative price changes as a driving force in institutional change. It modifies neoclassical theory in the sense that it relaxes some of its strong assumptions with respect to the motivations of, and the information available to, individual decision-makers. In particular, more recent works of the NIE abandon instrumental rationality. It is argued that the real world is characterized by incomplete information and limited mental capacity to process information which induces human beings to create institutions that structure the terms of exchange. Moreover, it widens the scope of economics to include the evolution of institutions and political phenomena which are seen as the sources of diverse economic performance over time and across space. Some works of the NIE extend orthodox economic theory by explicitly taking ideologies into consideration. The main assumptions, axioms, and hypotheses of the NIE can be summarized as follows:[15]

1. *Individual-actor approach.* Society, state, political parties, firms, and other organizations are not interpreted as collectivities that behave as if they were individuals. Rather a theory of social phenomena needs to explore the attitudes, motivations, and behavioral patterns of individual actors. The NIE essentially relies on rational-choice theory that retains the tenet of methodological individualism, the claim that social institutions and institutional change must be explained in terms of individual actions and interactions. Furthermore, recent research avoids the assumption that individuals always act in their narrow economic self-interest, make choices in a largely unconstrained environment, have complete information, and have accurate cognitive models.[16]

2. *Individual rationality.* It is hypothesized that utility maximization applies to all individuals including managers, workers, politicians, bureaucrats, and so on; hence it is not organizations (such as firms or political parties) which pursue optimization processes but individuals who seek to maximize utility subject to constraints that result from the institutional arrangements inherent in the organization within which the individuals act. Early contributions to the NIE, in particular, rely on the assumption of complete individual rationality. They assume that all individuals have stable and consistent preferences and seek to maximize utility rationally. This implies that an individual is capable of anticipating all possible future scenarios, weighing all feasible actions against each other, and making instantaneously an optimal decision at no cost (Kreps 1990). More recent research on transaction costs, property rights, and economic history, however, relies on an alternative assumption in order better to account for real-world conditions. Thus preferences are viewed as incomplete and unstable over time.[17] Moreover, the introduction of transaction costs into economic models implies that agents are not any longer completely informed because collecting information is not costless. Also, it is beyond the cognitive limits of individuals to anticipate future developments perfectly and to process available information perfectly. Simon (1961: xxiv) argues that individuals act in a way that is 'intendedly rational but only limitedly so'. Hence, bounded rationality and rational ignorance (that is individual behavior according to which it is rational not to acquire certain types of information given the uncertainties and costs of information search) have become prominent assumptions in the NIE, which increase the importance of incomplete subjective perceptions for making choices (Furubotn and Richter 1997).

3. *Transaction costs.* Institutions are means to exploit the gains from exchange, external economies, and specialization. These gains are realized by an exchange of goods, services, and rights that is based on explicit or implicit contractual relations that entail costs of transacting. It is the consideration of these transaction costs that primarily distinguishes the NIE from neoclassical economics.[18] However, the definition of transaction costs varies among different authors. Williamson (1985: 20–21) distinguishes between *ex ante* and *ex post* costs of contracting, the former including 'the costs of drafting, negotiating, and safeguarding an agreement' and the latter relating to 'maladaption costs, (...), haggling costs [of correcting misalignments, J.A.] (...), setup and running costs [related to the organizational construction (not necessarily the courts) that are supposed to solve potential disputes, and; J.A.], (...) the bonding costs of effecting secure commitments.' By comparison, North (1990a: 27) favors a concept of transaction costs that focuses on information costs.[19]

Transaction costs contain 'the costs of measuring the valuable attributes of what is being exchanged and the costs of protecting rights and policing and enforcing agreements'. More generally, transaction costs comprise the costs of creating, monitoring, enforcing, and restructuring institutions.

The existence of transaction costs has profound implications for resource allocation and economic and political organization, makes the assignment of property rights and the question of economic organization paramount, and implies that the structure of political institutions is to be considered as a key to understanding economic growth and development.

4. *Opportunistic behavior.* New Institutionalists usually take into account that human behavior could be characterized by lacking trustworthiness. Individuals may be inclined not to reveal their true preferences or to provide false information and may seek their self-interest with guile. Williamson (1985: 47) defines opportunism as 'the incomplete or distorted disclosure of information, especially (...) calculated efforts to mislead, distort, disguise, obfuscate, or otherwise confuse'. Opportunism may have harmful economic consequences and makes individual action less predictable. *Ex ante* it is extremely costly to distinguish opportunistic from non-opportunistic actors. Given opportunistic behavior *and* bounded rationality, contractual hazards come into existence to which different modes of contracting will be differentially responsive. Hence, a crucial role of institutions is to suppress opportunistic behavior.

5. *Enforcement mechanisms.* The structure of norms and rules in a society is determined and ensured by a system of monitoring and enforcement devices (a governance structure in the terminology of Williamson (1985)). In general, an economic, political, or social order can be enforced by internal or external mechanisms. Self-enforcing institutions show a particular enforcement mechanism. Central to this mechanism is that all parties to a contract have an incentive to abide by the rules. In this case, honesty yields a higher payoff than dishonest behavior. The only explicit enforcement mechanism is the credible threat to terminate the contract. Self-enforcing institutions play, for example, a crucial role in principal–agent relations and in undertaking policy reform.

6. *Relational contracts.* Contrary to the classical contract that relies on complete information and perfect rationality, the relational contract takes bounded rationality and the uncertainty of the future into account, and relies on the fact that all complex contracts are inevitably incomplete. It describes shared objectives and general principles governing the relationship of contracting parties and shows adequate procedures which guide future contractual arrangements.[20] Note that beyond certain boundaries, such contracts do not represent contracts in the narrow legal sense, but rather general relations between human agents. Relational

contracts play a critical role in principal–agent frameworks. Principals and agents are neither symmetrically informed nor do they have a perfect knowledge of the future. Therefore, they agree on relational contracts that allow them continuously to renegotiate the terms of exchange. Since external enforcement mechanisms are usually not applicable or too costly, and due to transaction-specific investments, *ex-ante* safeguards are required to protect against *ex-post* opportunism.

7. *Ideology.* Human beings' subjective perceptions of the world influence the explicit choices concerning formal rules and the emergence of informal constraints. Therefore ideology, defined as 'the subjective perceptions (models, theories) all people possess to explain the world around them' (North 1990a: 23), shapes institutional change and eventually economic performance. The perceptions are dependent on the way the human mind interprets available information. The models that individuals construct to interpret and explain their environment result from their cultural heritage, everyday problems, and non-local learning. This implies that actors from different societal backgrounds may perceive the same evidence in different ways and hence make different choices. As a result, multiple equilibria can result. Together, institutions and ideology provide a framework for economic and political activity and help agents to cope with conditions of uncertainty and complex situations. If social learning is path dependent, then economic, social, and political development will be uneven and gradual. This may help to explain the poor performance of some economies over long periods.[21]

8. *Path dependency.* Path dependence is another way of saying that history matters.[22] The underlying idea is that historical conditions and small changes in the past can have long-lasting effects. Hence, historical conditions shape present decisions and the future courses of development. Major causes of path dependency include (a) specific investments in physical and human capital, which have been made in the market process contingent on then-existing institutional arrangements; since institutional change would devalue prior investments due to their specificity, economic agents may have an interest in preserving existing institutions; (b) network effects, that is positive externalities accruing to individuals from an increasing number of people who comply with particular institutions; (c) the cognitive embodiment of institutions – a concept inspired by Hayek's (1945) notion of the co-evolution of rules and North's (1992) concept of ideology; in short, cognitive embodiment refers to the path dependence of individual perceptions, i.e. that experiences shape individuals' internal models of the world, which in turn determine their present and future behavior; and (d) the distribution of power in an economy and a society, because powerful individuals and groups seek to secure monopoly rents

and monopoly-related privileges, which may be threatened by changes in institutions and particularly in property rights.[23]

Path dependency has critical implications for policy in that the institutional legacies of the past determine the set of *feasible* options for institutional innovation as well as the actions for both private sector activities and public policies which are available in the present. This means that simply imposing institutional arrangements which proved efficient elsewhere on another economy or polity, or adopting standardized policy recommendations, may be doomed to fail or prove inefficient if those institutions or policies are in conflict with long-standing institutions which evolved in that society over time. This, however, does not imply that any attempt to intervene creatively in development processes would be mistaken or unsuccessful. The evolutionary perspective on path dependence is definitely compatible with a policy approach that seeks to canalize competitive processes through the choice of appropriate competition rules in order to give the competitive process general and desirable functional attributes, but to leave its concrete outcome open.

The preceding presentation of the behavioral assumptions and axioms on which the NIE has been founded as well as concepts of solidarity, loyalty, social transactions, and social capital, which have been introduced into the NIE,[24] make clear that the NIE is not a pure extension of neoclassical economics, but an interdisciplinary research approach that seeks to explain institutional change and the impact of social institutions on economic performance and development.

3.2.3 The Functions of Institutions

Since human beings live in groups and have the propensity to exchange goods and services with each other, behavioral rules governing the way in which actors compete and cooperate are indispensable. Usually the results of an individual's actions do not merely depend on his own efforts, but also on actions of other agents as well. In order to avoid a Hobbesian-type anarchy, external as well as internal institutions are required to structure the behavioral relations among human beings in a community or a society. However, institutions need not necessarily turn out to be efficient from a societal point of view. By contrast, as North (1990a, 1995a) persuasively argues, there is vast evidence that efficient institutions – that is those that foster economic growth – have been rather the exception than the rule throughout history. Sometimes institutions facilitate exchange, promote the development of human capital, encourage technological change, and reduce the costs of transacting; but at other times they support monopolies, thwart the formation of capital, and increase transaction costs. Generally, institutions function as societal constraints which guide and coordinate social interaction. They provide the incentive structure for individual behavior that determines individual choices and dictates the skills and knowledge which are expected to have the highest payoff. They reduce complexity by constraining the set of feasible actions, reduce uncertainty, and stabilize expectations. However, if institutions constrain individual choices too much, the opportunities and incentives to acquire and distribute information and knowledge decentrally will be reduced. This, in turn, badly affects the desirable flexibility of individual action.

Basically, two functions of institutions can be distinguished: an economizing and a redistributive function.[25] The former allows individuals to economize on existing transaction costs and hence to increase their utility within given constraints, or allows them to improve their personal welfare without badly affecting others. From Williamson's (1996a) perspective the basic argument is as follows: since transactions differ with respect to their attributes and modes of contracting, and regarding their competence and costs (with respect to the adaptation to disturbances as well as the mitigation of hazards), economizing on transaction costs can be achieved by aligning transactions with appropriate modes of contracting. This does not mean that institutions generally benefit society at large. In fact, this motive is frequently overcompensated by the redistributive motive, that is the effort to improve one party's welfare at the expense of other parties. The economizing function may be achieved by several distinct means, for example, by relying on market or non-market institutions in order to exploit potential specialization and external economies or economies of scale. Since appropriate institutions may differ in their effectiveness in performing the economizing function, depending on specific circumstances (and may yield different distributive effects), a potential exists for institutional competition. Other ways to improve welfare include the development of institutional mechanisms for risk reduction and the collection of more or better information in order to prevent actors from making mistakes.[26]

Property rights are prominent among institutions economizing on transaction costs. They are formal or informal institutions which determine a party's rights over those assets which it possesses, including their use, control, and the right to transfer.[27] While clearly-defined (private) property rights can substantially contribute to the improvement of the allocation of resources, they also underscore the importance of the redistributive function of institutions, because these rights are usually not neutral concerning the distribution of the net gains of economic exchange and specialization. In reality, the predominant function of numerous institutions relies on the redistributive motive. This is because the relative economic and political powers to impose constraints on others are unequally distributed and institutional competition is often poorly developed. If the redistributive

---

Box 3.1: Institutions, transaction costs, and economic development

'(T)he costs of transacting associated with the exchange process are a fundamental source of the success or failure of economies. (...) There have always been gains from trade (...), but there have also always been obstacles to achieving the gains from trade. These obstacles are not just transportation costs (...); they also are the costs of human organization and the problems of human cooperation and coordination.

These problems of cooperation and coordination can be illustrated by comparing two polar extremes in the exchange process. In one, simple personal exchange, individuals engage in repeated dealings with each other or otherwise have a great deal of knowledge about the other parties in the exchange process. The costs of transacting in such a society are very low because of the dense social network of interaction. Cheating, shirking, opportunism, all characteristics of modern industrial organization, are limited or indeed absent, because they simply do not pay. Norms of behavior are seldom written down and formal contracting typically does not exist. Indeed, there is little need for formal, specific rules. While measured transaction costs in such societies are low (...), production costs are very high, because specialization and division of labor are limited by the extent of the market defined by personal exchange.

At the other extreme, a world of specialization and division of labor, interdependency characterizes the entire structure, and therefore the exchange process extends over time and space. Impersonal exchange characterizes the total exchange process, with people having no individual knowledge of the other partner in exchange. In this form of exchange, the costs of transacting therefore may be high, because of all the problems of measuring what one is getting in exchange and of ensuring that the contracts will be carried out by the other party. In consequence, the gains to be achieved from cheating, shirking, opportunism, etc., rise dramatically. In successful Western societies, these costly aspects of transacting are minimized by elaborate institutional structures devised to constrain the participants and so make the exchange worthwhile. As a result, we have formal contracts, bonding of participants, guarantees, trade names, elaborate monitoring systems, and effective enforcement mechanisms (...). The resources devoted to transacting are large (although small per transaction), but in consequence the productivity associated with the gains from trade are even greater and are responsible for the high rates of growth that have characterized Western societies. However, it should be pointed out right away that the institutions that have made possible relatively low costs of transacting in turn depend upon even more fundamental political economic institutions, ones that undergird the entire system.

The major implication of the institutional structure that makes possible specialization and division of labor and therefore low costs of transacting per unit of exchange is that individuals are able to engage in complex relationships with other individuals about whom they have no personal knowledge. The institutional structure reduces the uncertainties associated with contract fulfillment as a consequence of enforcing reliable forms of exchange. This is possible only as a result of the development of a third party to exchanges, namely government, which specifies property rights and enforces contracts.'

(North 1988: 16–17)

function dominates, overall efficiency of institutional arrangements can hardly be realized. In that case, strengthening the economizing function critically depends on the existence of auxiliary institutions that help to insulate a country's development management from the influence of vested interests.

The relative importance of different institutional arrangements, the underlying costs of transacting, and the functions they perform change considerably in the course of development and particularly in times of major policy reforms (see Box 3.1). Economic and social backwardness of many countries, then, may be explained by persisting institutional inertia and rigidity and failing institutional adaptation to newly emerging technological, social, economic, and political challenges of development (Olson 1996).

After all, institutions can be interpreted as a means that may help to achieve beneficial outcomes of collective action. Since, however, individuals seek to pursue their self-interest, individually rational behavior need not result in group rationality. Hence conflicts of interests could arise, especially if functions of institutions contradict each other or are poorly performed. Efforts at collective action may thus imply problems of shirking, cheating, free-riding and moral hazard, which increase the costs of establishing efficient institutions. In order to alleviate these problems, institutions are required that perform enforcement and monitoring functions and help to increase the efficiency of the economic system. Appropriate institutions may include contracts, private property rights, and a legal system on the one hand and ethical rules, trust, and ideology on the other.

3.2.4 The Intentional Design of Institutions and the Political Steering of Social Processes

A pivotal objective of the NIE is to explain the origin of and the change in institutional arrangements (choice of rules). From an individualistic perspective, there are basically two apparently contradicting views: first of all, following the insights of Scottish moral philosophy (especially the works of David Hume, Adam Ferguson, and Adam Smith) on the one hand and the Austrian School (Carl Menger and Friedrich August von Hayek) on the other, a social order is not the result of conscious design but the spontaneous and unintended outcome of human action. In this context, institutions are interpreted as the unintended outcome of an evolutionary process. A critical aspect of this approach concerns the notion that Adam Smith's *principle of the invisible hand* can be applied to explain institutional change. Evolutionists seek to provide a theoretical rationale and empirical evidence that particular social institutions, that have proved to be socially appropriate and beneficial, represent the unintended outcome of actions of (purely) self-interested individuals. In other words, like market prices which emerge and fulfill their allocative function without the need for any particular agreement, socially beneficial institutions may emerge from the interconnection of self-interested individual endeavors without any systematic coordination. Without doubt, the evolutionary approach presents fundamental insights into the nature and emergence of a social order. But it cannot be usefully applied to explain all institutional arrangements. While normative institutions perceived as 'complexes of normative rules and principles which, either through law or other mechanisms of social control, serve to regulate social action and relationships' (Parsons 1975: 97) are basically susceptible to analysis in an evolutionary framework,[28] with respect to corporate institutions – or the formal institutions which establish organizations – the invisible hand explanation is far less plausible (Vanberg 1983).

This latter aspect is a central point stressed by a second economic approach which is based on contract theory and property rights theory. This approach explains institutional development as a result of (individual) rational cost–benefit calculations. Its implication is that the social and economic order is the outcome of conscious design and contractual agreements. This holds, for example, for the alternative choice of hierarchical versus market transactions, which is shaped by the endeavor to minimize transaction costs (Williamson 1985). This pattern of explanation also holds for changes in property rights which are shaped by the interest of economic agents to internalize externalities (Demsetz 1967). Given these competing views, some remarks are in order about the basic possibility of consciously designing institutions for specific purposes, before addressing the problem of institutional change in greater detail.

Which institutions are basically subject to intentional human design? Due to the bounded rationality of the human mind, individuals can neither know nor compare the consequences of all theoretically possible actions nor can they anticipate all the future changes and design all the optimal institutional arrangements at the same time (Lin 1989a; Kiwit and Voigt 1995). But recall the approach, favored by some scholars, of classifying institutions in normative rules on the one hand and corporate organizations on the other. The establishment of a business firm or a political party is doubtless the conscious outcome of individual action. But it is not conceivable without the existence of further institutions such as contract law and civil law or informal institutions such as trust or specific business ethics. Therefore, organizations may be interpreted as *derived* institutions, which emerge because individuals can take advantage of institutionally legitimized possibilities to act. Thus, Dietl (1993) suggests introducing another classification that distinguishes between fundamental and secondary (derived) institutions. While the former are outcomes of an unintentional evolution, the latter are subject to conscious human design. According to this categorization, all corporate organizations belong to the subset of secondary institutions. Moreover, normative rules can be either fundamental or secondary institutions. Fundamental norms and rules are the outcomes of long-term evolutionary processes, and individuals usually comply with them unconsciously, because they have been internalized in the wake of human socialization processes. Intentionally changing these fundamental institutions exceeds human capabilities. They embody more knowledge than any individual or agency could ever achieve (Hayek 1945 and 1965). Fundamental institutions consist of both formal and informal institutions. While informal rules cannot be intentionally transformed, fundamental formal institutions can basically be changed overnight. However, based on the preceding considerations, one may conclude that an intentional intervention into the fabric of fundamental formal institutions may be socially more harmful than useful.

Fundamental norms and rules are located at the top of the hierarchy of institutions. They provide each individual with basic action and decision rights and duties. Insofar as fundamental institutions grant individuals the right to constrain the choice set of others, secondary institutions may emerge. In turn, secondary institutions themselves can represent the basis for further derived institutions. In this way, a hierarchically-structured fabric of institutions evolves (Figure 3.1). At the lowest hierarchical level, the feasibility to craft institutions intentionally is strongly constrained by superordinate institutions. There are relatively few alternatives of institutional design, all of them with relatively easily calculable consequences. The latitude for institutional design expands if one moves up the hierarchy. But at the same time, the consequences of institutional change become more complex, because the induced effects on all the subordinated levels need to be taken into account. The problems associated with institutional design increase on the way to the top of the hierarchy. On the highest level, if not before, the boundaries of human rationality will be exceeded. On the top level, there are no superordinate or meta-institutions which may constrain the room for institutional design, and the consequences of institutional change are not calculable at all (Dietl 1993).

Basically, the institutional environment of a society represents a coherent whole. This coherence is relatively stable over time, because the pace of potential institutional change decreases if one moves from the bottom of the hierarchy to its top. Fundamental (informal) institutions are subject to an incremental evolutionary process. Due to their relative stability, the existing room for developing new or transforming old secondary institutions remains relatively constant over a longer period of time. This not only represents the precondition of rationally crafting derived institutions, but it also ensures institutional flexibility. In contrast to the evolution of fundamental

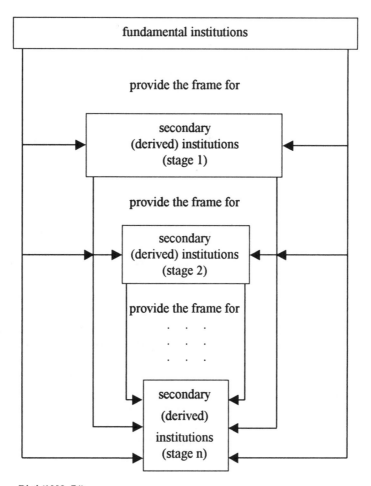

Source: Dietl (1993: 74)

Figure 3.1: A hierarchy of institutions

institutions, the design and transformation of secondary institutions can be carried out by rational human design. In many circumstances, individual actors or groups may even be forced to craft new institutions or to choose a specific institution from a set of alternative feasible institutional arrangements (Dietl 1993); for example a private entrepreneur must decide between an employment contract and a contract of sale if he needs the services of a handyman; or individuals who plan to found a political party must decide what kind of institutional structure the new organization should be based upon. The opportunity to craft institutions rationally, however, does not imply that the developed new rules are efficient either from an individual or a societal perspective. Since the future is open, random events cannot be ruled out, and the actual consequences of institutional transformation cannot be exactly predicted. Like every economic decision, the human design of secondary institutions is subject to uncertainty.

Interpreting the overall institutional matrix of a society, that is, the institutional environment and all institutional arrangements, as a hierarchy implies that the evolutionary approach to institutional change and the economic approach that is based on a rational cost–benefit calculus are complementary rather than contradictory views. The evolutionary approach questions the foundation of contract theory, that is rational constructivism, and hence the feasibility of systematically creating institutions. But it does not completely displace the contract-theoretical rationale. For the evolutionary view is basically compatible with those political interventions into the development process which seek to channel competitive processes by providing appropriate rules of competition. These rules do not attempt to guide the development process towards a concrete outcome, but lend general and desirable characteristics to the competitive process in order to improve its operation. Such an approach relies on the maxim that the pivotal function of public policy is to enhance and support the economic and social order of society ('order policy'). Therefore, it emphasizes the maintenance of a transparent and consistent set of policy rules *vis-à-vis* interventions in development processes. The adherents of order policy would acknowledge that the process of institutional change is inevitably open and undetermined. But they will endeavor to create structural conditions that encourage a performance-based competition among institutions which in turn enhances the adaptive efficiency of society.[29] Such an order-political perspective on the problem of institutional change shifts the analytical focus on the role of political processes, and hence the role of the state.

The importance of explicit institution building has been stressed by political economists as an unalterable prerequisite of successful policy reform, particularly for the transformation processes in PSCs. In this regard, external institutions represent devices that are used by governments for steering the economy and the society as a whole. Furthermore, the state plays a crucial role regarding the supply of formal institutions, because the demand for institutional change, which originates in the private sector, is often associated with severe problems of collective action.[30] This essentially implies three problems resulting from the bounded rationality of policy makers, asymmetric information, as well as the preferences of policy makers and the balance of power in a polity. First, government intervention into the fabric of external institutions may be an unalterable prerequisite of policy reform; for example if a new constitution needs to be established in the course of the transition from socialism to capitalism or if reforms of the legal system must be undertaken to support the adjustment of an economy to a changed political, social or international environment. However, changing external institutions such as the constitution or parts of the legal system implies the danger that fundamental formal institutions, which are embodied in the existing laws and regulations, are unconsciously changed.[31] Governments often show an excessive propensity for political constructivism. But the ultimate consequences of institutional intervention may become so complex that they cannot be fully anticipated. Also, due to the relatively high stability of informal institutions, the possibility of controlling social processes through formal institutions is limited. If policy makers neglect this side condition, they run the risk that informal institutions and formal rules contradict each other thereby reducing the growth potential of an economy (North 1990a; Mummert 1999b). Second, in initiating and facilitating institutional change, policy makers need to recognize the strategic uncertainty of rule-making. This is because other actors such as private households and businesses as well as organizations of the civil society whose welfare and behavior are affected by institutional change will generate feedback effects on policy choices and new institutional arrangements. Since policy making cannot be regarded as a game of perfect information with only two moves, a government changing economic or political rules needs to be capable of anticipating the reactions of other parties and the induced effects on the credibility of public policies. Last but not least, the role of the state in institution building has an ambivalent character. On the one hand, political authorities may reduce economic transaction costs by enforcing the rule of law and hence foster society's welfare. On the other hand, the state may be abused for purposes of redistribution.

These problems underscore that institution building may turn out to be a double-edged sword. The ability to change old and to craft and adopt new institutions is a necessary precondition of successful development management. However, the risk of inducing unanticipated institutional disequilibria or economic distortions is always inherent in imposed institutional change. Policy makers need to be aware of both the risks and the benefits of rule-making if they seek actively to steer economic and social processes. Furthermore, these problems remind us of the significance to be attached to the structural conditions which guide political competition and decision-making. Even on this level, order policy has to play a critical role in enhancing the incentive compatibility of public policies and economic performance.

NOTES

1. This chapter is restricted to discussing the relevance of the NIE and NPE for analysing the political economy of policy reform and the role of institutions in economic development. Regarding comprehensive surveys of these branches of economics see, for example, Dietl (1993), Eggertsson (1990), Frey and Kirchgässner (1994), Furubotn and Richter (1997), Hodgson (1998), Klein (1998), and North (1990a).
2. Readers interested in comprehensive reviews or anthologies of the NPE may read Mueller (1989) or, regarding a critical review, Self (1993). Shorter surveys have been provided by Orchard and Stretton (1997), Frey (1988), and Inman (1987).
3. In what follows the terms *New Political Economy* and *Public Choice* are used interchangeably.
4. See, for example, the early contributions by Downs (1957), Riker (1962), Buchanan and Tullock (1962), Niskanen (1971), and Stigler (1971).
5. See, for example, Krueger (1974) and Bhagwati (1982).
6. See Downs (1957) and Olson (1965, 1982); for a more detailed analysis of this point see Grindle (1991).
7. Note that, as Grindle (1991) points out, this kind of buying political support not only occurs in democratic societies, in which politicians seek to gain support in terms of votes, but also in non-democratic settings. In these cases, the transfer of public resources to powerful groups such as the military, powerful landowners or industrialists, and ethnic or regional groups is used to buy their political support.
8. See Orchard and Stretton (1997). North (1993) and Denzau and North (1994) go even one step further and argue that citizens often do not even know what kind of political actions serve their interests best or do not know in the first place what their individual interests are.
9. The following critique largely draws on Orchard and Stretton (1997).
10. The term *New Institutional Economics* was actually coined by Williamson (1975).
11. See, for example, Aranson (1998), Hall and Taylor (1996), Smith (1992), Moe (1990), North (1990b), and Weingast and Marshall (1988).
12. Relatively complete surveys of the field have been provided by Eggertsson (1990), Furubotn and Richter (1997), and Kasper and Streit (1998). Shorter surveys, which emphasize various strands of the NIE or discuss particular applications, include Klein (1998), Hodgson (1998), Lin and Nugent (1995), Nabli and Nugent (1989a), and North (1994a).
13. The deficits of neoclassical economics had already been identified by older generations of economists such as the adherents of the German *Historische Schule* (particularly Roscher and Schmoller) and the *Old Institutional Economists* like Commons, Veblen, and Mitchell. These scholars rejected the Anglo-Saxon classical theory, but were also suspicious concerning theoretical reasoning based on marginalism as well as profit and utility maximization in general. In contrast to these approaches, the adherents of the NIE rely on the tool kit of neoclassical economics and other analytical methods in order to explain the functioning and emergence of institutional arrangements (Furubotn and Richter 1997). Like the old institutionalists, proponents of the NIE criticize neoclassical economics for neglecting institutions and making unreasonable assumptions about human behavior. But there is little further resemblance between these schools. As Langlois (1986: 5) puts it: 'The problem with many of the early Institutionalists is that they wanted an economics with institutions but without theory; the problem with many neoclassicists is that they want economic theory without institutions; what NIE tries to do is to provide an economics with both theory *and* institutions.' Regarding a more detailed analysis of the distinctions, and the potential for integration, of the NIE and the Old Institutionalism see, for example, Groenewegen *et al.* (1995) and Rutherford (1995). The German roots of the Old (American) Institutionalism are discussed in Richter (1996).
14. See, for example, Bardhan (1989), Nabli and Nugent (1989a), Ostrom, Schroeder, and Wynne (1993), Weingast (1993 and 1995), Levy and Spiller (1994), North (1994a),

Williamson (1995 and 1996a), Harriss, Hunter, and Lewis (1995). For an overview see Lin and Nugent (1995).

15. See North (1995a). For more detailed presentations of the main components of the NIE and the underlying terminology see, for example, North (1990a), Eggertsson (1990), and Furubotn and Richter (1997).

16. See, for example, North (1992 and 1995a) and Ensminger (1992). In this context, North (1990c: 183) asserts that '(h)uman motivation involves more than simple wealth maximization. People do trade wealth or income for other values, and institutions frequently lower the price people pay for their convictions, making them important in choices.'

17. See, for example, Sugden (1986) for an economic theory in which preferences are endogenous.

18. The term *transaction costs* was introduced into economics in Coase's (1937) article on 'The Nature of the Firm', in which he indicated that using the price system is not costless.

19. Note, however, that, although information and transaction costs are related to and overlap each other, they are not identical. While transaction costs solely result from transactions, that is interrelations of individuals or organizations, information costs may also arise for isolated individuals; see Eggertsson (1990).

20. The relational contract was in detail described by Macneil (1974) and introduced into economic theory by Williamson (1976) and Goldberg (1976).

21. See North (1990a, 1992) and Denzau and North (1994).

22. The notion of path dependence has gained wide popularity in the economics profession following the work of David (1985) and Arthur (1988 and 1989) who analysed the development of technologies that show positive network externalities. More recently, the concept has been applied to analysing the determinants of institutional change and the persistence of institutional inertia; see, for example, North (1990a).

23. See, for example, North (1990a), Leipold (1996), and Kiwit and Voigt (1995). The latter argue that network effects play a dominant role for the path dependence of type-1-internal institutions, while cognitive embodiment is crucial regarding type-2 and type-3-internal institutions, and specific investments cause path dependency of formal institutions; see Table 3.1.

24. See, for example, Homans (1958), Hirschman (1969), Lindenberg (1988), Coleman (1990), and Simon (1991).

25. This section particularly draws on Lin (1989a) and Lin and Nugent (1995).

26. Note that there is nothing nonoptimal or irrational about imperfect or incomplete information, because collecting information is not costless. Institutional solutions to overcome the problems related to incomplete or imperfect information, however, may considerably differ depending on the nature of the institutional deficiency. They may be particularly difficult in the case of asymmetric information, when one actor is able to cheat another party through opportunistic behavior; see Lin and Nugent (1995).

27. Note that the key word with respect to private property rights is *control*. Formal ownership is without much value, unless the entrepreneur has sufficient control over the return on his assets. Experiences with Township-Village Enterprises (TVEs) in modern China demonstrate that, even without clearly defined formal property rights, effective control rights may spur business activity. In contrast, shareholders in today's Russia do have formal property rights, but frequently lack devices for effective control over their assets; see Qian and Weingast (1997a) and Che and Qian (1998) for the experiences with TVEs in China.

28. Of course, some normative institutions are in fact subject to conscious design (for example, legislation). Yet in principle, their emergence can be explained as the result of spontaneous dialectic adaptations of separate, self-interested individuals; that is their emergence is conceivable without relying on systematic coordination.

29. According to North (1990a: 81), adaptive efficiency 'provides the incentives to encourage the development of decentralized decision-making processes that will allow societies to

maximize the efforts required to explore alternative ways of solving problems'. The concept of adaptive efficiency is more thoroughly discussed in Chapter 4, section 4.3.

30. This aspect will be explicitly discussed in Chapter 4, section 4.2.

31. Note that numerous fundamental informal institutions have been formalized and embodied in constitutions and laws. Hence, originally unintended institutions assumed the character of conscious intent by legal formalization (Dietl 1993: 72, footnote 63). More specifically, fundamental norms and rules are the outcomes of long-term evolutionary processes, and individuals usually comply with them unconsciously, because they have been internalized in the wake of human socialization processes. Intentionally changing these fundamental institutions exceeds human capabilities. They embody more knowledge than any individual or agency could ever achieve. Numerous fundamental *informal* institutions have been formalized and embodied in constitutions and laws. Hence, originally unintended institutions assumed the character of conscious intent by legal formalization. While informal rules cannot be intentionally transformed, fundamental formal institutions can be basically changed overnight. However, due to their complex nature, an intentional intervention in the fabric of fundamental formal institutions may be socially more harmful than useful.

4. Institutional change and economic performance

In analysing institutions, adherents to the NIE operate at three different levels. As Eggertsson (1990: xiii) puts it:

> (T)here are several levels of analysis in Neoinstitutional Economics, depending on which variables are treated as endogenous. At the first level, the structure of property rights and forms of organization are explicitly modeled but are treated as exogenous, and the emphasis is on their impact on economic outcomes. At the second level, the organization of exchange is endogenized, but the fundamental structure of property rights remains exogenous. Exchange within firms, across formal markets, and in non-market situations is organized by means of contracts that constrain economic agents. (...) At the third level, attempts are made to endogenize both social and political rules and the structure of political institutions by introducing the concept of transaction costs.

Most work in the NIE focuses on the first and second levels. With regard to economic development and policy reform in LDCs, however, the application of the NIE to the problems of economic performance and growth and hence the issues relating to the third level of analysis may be of more relevance, because the attention is shifted to the determinants of institutional change and the effects of different institutions on transaction costs. There is broad evidence that the differential performance of economies and polities over time is sustainably shaped by the process of institutional change. An increasing number of economists persuasively argue that the costs of transacting that derive directly from a society's formal and informal institutions are the key to understanding the performance of economies.[1] Moreover it is recognized that free-rider problems (themselves caused by transaction costs) often hinder the materialization of institutional change. Hence, if institutions affect economic performance, then a theory of economic development needs to comprise a theory explaining institutional change or at least some analytical framework that provides for the integration of institutional analysis into the field of political economy.

The scope and direction of institutional change are by no means random. It can be subject to rigorous economic analysis. In this regard, transaction costs economics and the theory of collective action, in particular, have proved to be powerful tools in analysing institutional innovation and development.[2] Although they developed quite separately, these approaches represent two broad salient strands of the NIE which are highly interdependent and complementary. For analytical purposes, however, it is useful to distinguish these approaches and to investigate the determinants of institutional change in a stylized demand-and-supply framework (Feeny 1993; Lin and Nugent 1995). In this context, transaction cost economics has been useful in examining the determinants of the comparative demand for institutional change, whereas the theory of collective action has proved particularly useful in analysing the factors that shape the supply of alternative institutions.

From a political economy perspective, there are essentially three questions to be addressed relating to institutional change:

- What causes institutional change?
- Why is institutional change critical to policy reform?
- What is the role of the state regarding institutional change?

Before elaborating on these questions, it should be mentioned that, while the differences within the NIE noted so far concern different research interests and the specific context to be analysed, one may also discern certain theoretical disagreements within the NIE.[3] In this respect, the differences between the theoretical approach of Douglass North and his followers (the *Northian* approach) on the one hand and that of Oliver Williamson and his students (the *Williamsonian* approach) on the other are of particular interest for our purposes, that is for questions addressing the interdependence of institutions, policy reform, and economic performance. Not surprisingly therefore, the NIE offers not one universal but several related perspectives on the issues of economic reform and development, which may complement each other.

4.1 THE NAÏVE MODEL: INDUCED INSTITUTIONAL CHANGE

The demand for institutional innovation is typically driven by individuals or members of particular groups who expect a change in rules to yield net benefits for distributional and/or efficiency reasons. Basically, the demand for institutional change and its initiation can originate in both the private and the public sector. Lin (1989a) interprets the former type of innovation as *induced* institutional change resulting from a voluntary change introduced and executed by private individuals or groups which respond to profitable opportunities caused by institutional disequilibria. The latter type represents an *imposed* institutional innovation that refers to a change that is initiated and executed by government fiat. An induced institutional innovation is always a response to profitable opportunities which do not exist or cannot be exploited under the original institutional matrix. In contrast, institutional innovation imposed by the state may (but does not necessarily) occur purely for redistributive purposes in order to provide benefits to specific groups of constituents at the expense of others.

Let us begin with the theory of induced institutional change or what has been coined—in a similar context – the *naïve theory of property rights*.[4] The classic reference here is Demsetz's (1967) classical article, where he asserts 'that the emergence of new property rights takes place in response to the desires of the interacting persons for adjustment to new benefit–cost possibilities'. More specifically, he points out that

(p)roperty rights develop to internalize externalities when the gains of internalization become larger than the cost of internalization. Increased internalization, in the main, results from changes in economic values, changes which stem from the development of new technology and the opening of new markets, changes to which old property rights are poorly attuned. (...) (G)iven a community's tastes (...), the emergence of new private or state-owned property rights will be in response to changes in technology and relative prices.[5]

In this approach institutional innovation appears to be the result of a simple cost–benefit calculation. If the costs of substituting a new for an old institutional arrangement are lower than the expected gross benefits of a new institution, institutional innovation will occur. Indeed, a considerable amount of the literature on property rights has been based on this model.[6] More recently, this model has been extended to include not only property rights but all kinds of economic institutions.

Economic agents will strive for institutional innovation if a new institution appears to be more efficient than an existing one, that is if the new arrangement performs the same or similar functions as the old one but provides more services with given transaction and production costs or if the new institution provides the same services at lower costs. In an institutional equilibrium, no individual has an incentive to use resources in order to change existing institutional arrangements given the behavioral strategies of other individuals. If, however, an institutional disequilibrium occurs, profitable opportunities will arise which, in turn, may induce the innovation of new institutional arrangements that are appropriate to take advantage of these latent gains. Transaction cost economics suggests that privately induced institutional change will actually occur if the marginal transaction costs of change are lower than the expected marginal benefits of the potential new institution. Note in this context that due to the interdependencies of institutions one particular institutional arrangement in disequilibrium implies that the overall institutional matrix is in disequilibrium. Then, given bounded rationality and the existence of positive transaction costs, an economy or society will not instantaneously move from the old to a new equilibrium structure. This is one crucial reason why institutional change is incremental.[7]

Lin and Nugent (1995) classified the factors that may cause an institutional disequilibrium and hence drive the demand for institutional change. They distinguish (1) changes in the demand for institutional services; (2) exogenous changes in the costs of transacting; and (3) changes in the choice set of available and feasible institutions.

1. *Changes in the demand for institutional services.* A demand for new institutional services may result from changes in relative scarcities and prices, technological change, and – due to the interrelated functions of different institutions – from changes in other institutional arrangements. Long-term changes in the relative prices of factors of production will in particular induce a higher demand for the creation or strengthening of property rights in those factors which will have become relatively scarcer. Similarly, changes in the relative prices of products will raise the value of property rights in those factors which are critical inputs to their production.[8] Furthermore, a new institutional service may be needed to deal with scale economies and externalities resulting from changes in production technologies or to modify related income streams to the owners of the factors of production. Finally, changes in certain institutional arrangements can trigger a change in demand for the services of other institutions. Lin (1989b), for example, reports that the factor markets in rural China, which had been suppressed under the system of collective farming, reemerged after the introduction of the household system. From the perspective of policy reform, a most important institutional change that can trigger other institutional innovations concerns major reforms of a country's political or economic order. For example, the transition to democracy and a market economy in Central and Eastern Europe has tremendous effects on informal institutions prevalent in the old system and requires substantial institution building internally to make all societal suborders consistent with each other, and externally to integrate these countries in international orders and structures.

2. *Exogenous changes in the costs of transacting.* Changes in law, ideology, technology or other institutions may cause changes in transaction costs which in turn will trigger a new demand for institutional change. One example where progress in technology may reduce transaction costs is the most recent presidential election process in South Africa where the use of modern information technology substantially reduced transaction costs for

voters. Satellite techniques greatly facilitated the political participation in elections in rural areas and promises to foster further institutional change by inducing mechanisms which give more voice to citizens. Another contemporary example is the introduction of the Internet to which even people in LDCs now have increased access. The Internet will reduce transaction costs related to the international exchange of goods, services, and information and hence will induce widespread institutional change relating to international business transactions (Bhatnagar 1999). Changes in the legal systems in LDCs and PSCs may also reduce transaction costs, for example, if those changes are aimed at simplifying tax legislation. This may induce business people who have operated in the informal sector of the economy to register their businesses officially and to look for new opportunities. A modern market-oriented legal system may also help to create a new type of incentive structure underlying the economy, that is incentives causing people to invest more in long-term productive business operations. As North (1995a: 9) puts it:

> If the highest rate of return in an economy comes from piracy we can expect that the organizations will invest in skills and knowledge that will make them better pirates. Similarly if there are high returns to productive activities we will expect organizations to devote resources to investing in skill and knowledge that will increase productivity.

Moreover, informal institutions such as values, attitudes, and tastes change in the course of development so that institutional arrangements that were once acceptable, like slavery in the United States, may eventually become socially unacceptable. Similarly, ideologies may change over time, the number of ideologies that are in conflict with each other may increase in a society and hence the degree of social cohesion may change. Contingent on the actual changes, changes in people's subjective perceptions of the world explicitly determine choices of formal rules as well as evolving informal institutions (North 1992). This can either impede or support the introduction and execution of institutional innovations that are induced by relative price changes (Nabli and Nugent 1989b).

3. *Changes in the choice set of available and feasible institutions.* The number of feasible institutions for particular institutional services depends *inter alia* on the available knowledge in social science. Advances in the social sciences will improve people's understanding of how their society functions, increase their capabilities of managing existing institutions, and eventually increase the overall knowledge in society of alternative institutions. For example, changes in relevant social science knowledge may affect the behavior of market participants, policy makers and other individuals and the resulting consequences of the impact of group interests

on the regulation of goods and factor markets. Similarly, studies of undesirable outcomes of governmental regulations and programs aimed at income redistribution in LDCs are supposed to have fostered the trend toward deregulation, privatization, and the abandoning of welfare programs.[9]

In the long run, knowledge accumulation and social learning are the main factors that propel the demand for institutional change (North 1990a). Experience helps actors to evaluate the efficacy of existing institutions, identify problems that require new institutional solutions, and develop more effective institutional arrangements. The importance of social learning indicates the critical role of education in fostering institutional adaptation over the long run.

In addition, intensified contacts with other societies may cause a substantial fall in information costs and make people aware of alternative models that exist and that promise to offer more efficient solutions to economic problems. Adopting institutional arrangements from abroad may reduce – but not eliminate – the need to invest in social science research. After all, local knowledge must be available in order to make new institutions consistent with local conditions, because institutional efficiency is contingent on the availability of suitable complementary institutions, which makes a direct institutional transfer particularly difficult (Lin 1989a).

Last but not least, governments can change the feasible set of institutional choices through policy making. If a government introduces new binding constraints on economic activity, this may render an originally inefficient institution a preferred one in the limited choice set. Conversely, by eliminating existing constraints, a government can enlarge the institutional choice set and hence trigger widespread institutional innovation. The shift from the collective farming system to the household system in China provides a good example in this respect.

Adherents to the naïve model argue that a demand for new institutional arrangements will *actually trigger* institutional change and that this change will bring about *efficient* institutional arrangements, because they are the outcome of potential or actual competition among alternative institutions and institutional change is assumed to be voluntary, requiring unanimity among the individuals whose behavior is governed by the institution (Lin 1989a: 19). However, there is broad evidence that efficient institutions are rather the exception than the rule. As North once put it: 'If institutional change results in increasing efficiency, it is usually an accident.'[10] The interesting issue then is to determine which filters apply to the emergence of new formal and informal institutions.

More recently, scholars of economic development have rigorously identified the weaknesses of the naïve model. Although it is quite useful in determining the forces that shape the demand for institutional change and at times drive its initiation, the naïve model remains incomplete because it fails to deal with free-rider problems inherent in group decisions, neglects the impact of political processes, and omits the necessities for, and problems of, institution building as a pivotal component of policy reform.[11] Moreover, North (1989: 665) argues that the naïve model

> leaves out the incremental process by which institutions change (...). What is missing is a more complex study of the way by which the polity evolves and how that translates into the kinds of property rights that will be specified and enforced. Not only may the evolving political institutions spawn property rights that do not induce economic growth but also the consequent organizations may have no incentive to create more productive economic rules. At issue is the incremental character of institutional change as well as the problem of devising institutions that can provide credible commitment so that more efficient bargains can be struck.

More specifically, the model of induced institutional change is flawed and incomplete for essentially three reasons:

1. Throughout history, dysfunctional institutions have tended to survive for long periods of time and new social norms have had great difficulties in emerging. In numerous cases, this can be explained by either collective-action problems, path dependency, imperfect information or high transaction costs-cum-individually-specific perceptions about the degree of institutional disequilibrium. According to the first explanation, free-rider problems may impede institutional change because many institutions show the characteristics of a public good, namely non-excludability and non-rivalry.[12] The public goods aspect offers incentives to free-rides because individuals may find it rational not to participate in contributing voluntarily to the provision of that good or to reveal false preferences regarding the value that is attributed to that good.[13] Free-riding, in turn, will induce a less than optimal provision of the public good. More specifically, the costs of non-compliance with an existing institution, and hence the introduction of a new arrangement, may be too high without cooperation. Thus in a prisoner's dilemma situation it can be individually rational to comply with socially suboptimal institutional arrangements such as castes, which in turn remain in existence (Akerlof 1976). Furthermore, the modification of certain rules requires at times that hierarchically superordinate institutions (for example, rules guiding the change in rules) are also adjusted. This may involve further economic or

political agents in the negotiation and decision-making processes which may impede institutional innovation.

In the second explanation, substantial sunk costs caused by past institutional investments can make the adoption of potentially superior institutions unprofitable (Arthur 1988; Kiwit and Voigt 1995). In addition, individual institutional arrangements are embedded in the overall institutional matrix, which frequently shapes the efficacy of the respective institution to a considerable extent. This may imply a lock-in effect that often makes partial institutional changes more difficult. As a result, institutions that are theoretically conducive to economic development may not be viable because they are not compatible with other components of the existing matrix.

The third explanation holds that uncertainty in the distribution of costs and benefits from change may induce a bias in favor of the status quo (Fernandez and Rodrik 1991). Hence, even if everyone in a society is aware that a particular institution is dysfunctional, this is not a sufficient condition for institutional innovation. Persisting inertia may hinder actual change. According to the fourth explanation, the high transaction costs of crafting and implementing a new institution that promises profitable opportunities in the long run may prevent individuals from undertaking the necessary investment. Institutional change may then be even complicated by the fact that those individuals who will be affected by a potential change, may have different perceptions of the nature of the institutional disequilibrium, its source and degree. Hence different actors may favor different modes of action to achieve a new equilibrium and they may also disagree about how to partition the expected gains from institutional innovation (Lin and Nugent 1995).

2. When new institutions are actually adopted, this change can be and, in fact, has frequently been inefficient. Society as a whole will not necessarily gain from the privately induced adoption of a new institutional arrangement which captures the latent gains arising from institutional disequilibrium. First, even if a group of individuals voluntarily agrees on a new institutional arrangement, the net benefits of which are expected to be positive for each individual, this arrangement will not necessarily enhance the welfare of society.[14] Secondly, change in institutions is also subject to externality problems, because an institutional arrangement is not usually patentable. Thus, an institutional innovation can be imitated by other actors at lower costs. Hence, the overall returns of the new institution to society will exceed the potential returns to the institutional innovator. This implies that investments in formal institutional innovation will be smaller than desirable from a societal point of view (Lin 1989a). Third, the

interpretation of institutional change being efficient neglects the distribution of power within an economy. If, for example, a single actor or a group of individuals is powerful enough to impose institutional change on another party, it can do so even if it makes the other party worse off. Frequently, formal institutions are not created to enhance social efficiency, but to serve the private interests of those who have a sufficiently strong bargaining power to craft new arrangements. This does not affect efficiency in the absence of transaction costs, but if transaction costs are positive it does. Such an institutional change, of course, is not voluntarily initiated and enforced, but it may occur without the involvement of the state. It is obvious that private ordering alone is hardly sufficient to overcome these kinds of institutional failure.

3. Due to the institutional failures mentioned under (1) and (2), and in particular due to collective-action and externality problems inherent in institutional change, incomplete markets, imperfect competition, and imperfect information, government intervention may be potentially desirable from a societal point of view. Since the polity sets and enforces the rules and constraints of the game, including the formal rules of economic exchange, the state needs to play a critical role in facilitating and fostering institutional change and economic development.[15] Precisely in the course of policy reform in LDCs and PSCs, institution building, that is the creation and reform of external institutions that represent the economic constitution of a country and provide the frame for private ordering, is a *conditio sine qua non* for overcoming both market and policy failure. Therefore, the issue of how to create polities in LDCs and PSCs which will be appropriate to provide growth- and development-enhancing economic institutions is at the heart of development policy. Unfortunately, the model of induced institutional change is silent on this problem.

In short, a relatively strong demand for institutional innovation by those actors who will be positively affected may, at times, prove to be sufficient to realize change. This may particularly occur in less complex settings, for example, in a situation between an employer and an employee who negotiate about a contract of employment, or in circumstances in which a larger number of relatively homogeneous actors agree on a new institution which is perceived to benefit everyone. If, however, the potential new institutional arrangement is not well known, its effects cannot be sufficiently anticipated, transaction costs are excessive or if numerous individuals or groups and different interests are involved, the supply side of institutional innovation turns out to be more important. Therefore, to get a more realistic understanding of institutional change in LDCs and PSCs, the supply of institutional change, perceived as a metaphor to deal with the political, economic, and social factors which determine the implementation and enforcement of formal institutional innovation, needs to be taken explicitly into account.

4.2 THE SUPPLY OF INSTITUTIONS: COLLECTIVE-ACTION PROBLEMS AND THE ROLE OF GOVERNMENTS

The theory of collective action represents a suitable tool for identifying the conditions under which institutional change may actually take place even if the previously mentioned obstacles to induced institutional innovation exist. The following considerations begin with a brief summary of some critical conditions which help to accomplish effective collective action. It will be claimed that successful collective action usually presupposes the emergence of interest groups that often seek to better achieve their objectives by gaining access to the state apparatus. Subsequently, the role of the state as a mediator, facilitator, and initiator of institutional change is analysed.

The main issue in studies on collective action is to 'explain collective outcomes in terms of individual motivation' (Hardin 1982: 2) or, in other words, 'to explain the likelihood of success or failure of a given set of self-interested individuals in undertaking actions that may benefit them collectively' (Nabli and Nugent 1989a: 1338). Following the pioneering works of Olson (1965, 1982) and Hardin (1982), a number of mechanisms and conditions have been identified that help to overcome the free-rider problem and hence are favorable to institutional change.

A given institutional innovation may benefit some individuals, but bring losses or uncertainties for others. Thus opposition forces may emerge. Whether or not institutional change will occur, depends on the propensity and the ability of the potential gainers and losers to engage in collective action and eventually on the distribution of power among vested interest groups in a society. If the expected losers are more successful in organizing themselves than the winners, change will not occur unless it is imposed by a third party. But even if there is no potentially losing faction, change may not take place due to high transaction costs. Therefore, groups showing a weak propensity for effective collective action or facing excessive costs of transacting may fail to achieve desirable institutional innovation. Olson (1965: 2) argues forcefully that 'unless the number of individuals is quite small, or unless there is coercion or some other special device to make individuals act in their common interest, *rational, self-interested individuals will not act to achieve their common or group interests'* [original italics].

Olson (1965) shows that effective collective action is contingent on the nature of the group that seeks to achieve a particular objective. Besides group size, critical characteristics which determine success or failure of collective action include the age and purpose of the group. Cooperation among group members is further enhanced if the origins of its members are relatively homogeneous, the goals of group members are complementary though sufficiently differentiated, and if there is a relatively close physical and social proximity among members. Moreover, the sensitivity of group members to expected losses resulting from inaction may play a crucial role as does the distribution of power or wealth within the group. A key condition for effective collective action for medium-sized or large groups is the existence of selective incentives (benefits or penalties) for group members.

The prospects for effective collective action may also be determined by interrelations between different groups. A particular group G1, for example, may be more likely to succeed in collective action the more another group G2 succeeds in an action which conflicts with the interests of the members of G1. Even if G1 is not directly affected by actions of the other group, successful action by G2 may have a demonstration effect that prompts G1 to overcome obstacles to cooperative behavior (Lin and Nugent 1995). Moreover, collective action is more likely to succeed if group members do not have an exit option. Hirschman (1969 and 1981), for example, argues that if there is an exit option for group members and if the available alternative to group action is perceived to be more attractive, then effective collective action will be less likely. In addition, communication within the group and the organizational skills of group members can affect the outcomes of collective action. Nelson (1984), for example, hypothesizes that the better the logic that connects a particular action with its expected outcome is communicated to group members the more likely is successful collective action. Likewise, organizational capability, especially of those group members who are in a leadership position, may play a critical role by strengthening group characteristics which may be more or less favorable to collective action or by transforming homogeneous local groups into effective groups that operate at the state or international level (Olson 1965).

Informal institutions may also help to solve the puzzle of group formation and enhance collective action. In particular, interpersonal or civic trust and other psychological factors (Ferree 1992), the presence of social or civic networks and norms in the community or workplace (Snow *et al.* 1980, Putnam 1993), as well as traditional moral obligations to cooperate in joint activities (Ruttan and Hayami 1984) may ease the dilemmas inherent in collective action and enhance social capital, which eventually can contribute to bringing about better citizen satisfaction, legislative innovativeness, and administrative efficiency. According to Putnam's (1993, 1995) findings, networks and norms of civic engagement, by providing appropriate templates, reduce individuals' propensity for opportunistic behavior, support the creation of social trust and generalized reciprocity, and thereby lubricate economic and political transactions, improve information flows and hence reduce transaction costs and further future economic and political collaboration.

In order to enhance their effectiveness, interest groups usually develop permanent organizations that promote successful collective action through a reduction in start-up costs as well as long-run average costs. Organizations thus help to reduce transaction costs of collective action and, if properly managed, adjust group actions and objectives against exogenous shocks. Also the start-up costs that would result from establishing a new interest group can be avoided in this way. Moreover, organizations may be useful platforms for institutional entrepreneurs who can effectively enhance the prospects for collective action in situations in which group characteristics are not favorable or other obstacles to collective action exist (Nabli and Nugent 1989b).

Due to the free-rider problem, the role of a leader or entrepreneur can be crucial in bringing about institutional change. In this context, it seems appropriate to distinguish between *political* and *institutional entrepreneurs*. According to Hardin (1982: 35), 'political entrepreneurs are people who, for their own career reasons, find it in their private interest to work to provide collective benefits to relevant groups'. In contrast, an institutional entrepreneur is a member of a particular interest group or organization 'who is generally trusted (or feared), or who can guess who is bluffing in the bargaining, or who can simply save bargaining time, [and therefore; J.A.] can sometimes work out an arrangement that is better for all concerned than any outcome that could emerge without entrepreneurial leadership or organization'.[16] If imaginative leaders of a particular interest group organization are able to motivate members, to enhance the degree of interpersonal trust within the group or to strengthen members' identification with the objectives of the group and hence create a certain 'corporate identity' or if leaders are able to provide selective incentives or to suggest actions or arrangements which will leave all group members better off, collective action problems can be eased. Of course, institutional entrepreneurs will make these extra efforts only if they expect material or nonmaterial net gains.

The costs of such entrepreneurial activity will be smaller and the prospects for successful collective action larger the more group leaders are capable of collaborating with other interest groups or gaining access to the state apparatus. In fact, organizations and interest groups often seek indirectly to provide their members with club goods or collective goods by mobilizing government agencies to provide political support, impose desired regulations, and to enforce and monitor them (Hardin 1982). Promoting collective action by means of the state will be particularly effective if political entrepreneurs are available who are eager to win votes. Then even large, geographically dispersed and unorganized interest groups (so-called latent groups) may be provided by the government with collective goods or may get laws and regulations passed which are in their interest, even if these groups are not able to lobby forcefully for them.[17]

Due to the potential interest of governments to demonstrate their responsiveness to the needs of (at least parts of) their electorate, promoting collective action indirectly by means of the state can be more effective than relying on private action. Moreover, tacit government authorization can basically help to legitimize collective action (Nugent 1998). Institutional innovation and policy making may often depend on the power balance among vested interest groups in society. But this is not always the case. The state will not necessarily respond passively to the influence of vested interests. In many countries, even in non-democratic settings, political decisions usually represent some kind of compromise resulting from complex bargaining processes. Also, politicians do not automatically calculate the private returns from all their actions (Grindle 1996). Governments can, and in fact do, influence the constraints of individual actors and interest groups. They can hinder institutional innovations desired by private actors, and they can also foster socially beneficial institutional change for which no organized interest group exists.

As the model of induced institutional change indicates, the demand of private actors for institutional innovation does not automatically entail the emergence of new socially beneficial institutional arrangements. Due to high transaction costs and the public good character of many institutions and also due to collective-action failures, it is possible that desirable institutional change does not occur at all. If change takes place, it may benefit a particular group at the expense of other groups contingent on the balance of power in a society. Therefore, privately induced institutional innovation will not lead to a socially optimal supply of institutions.

Basically, problems resulting from externalities, collective-action, coordination, and institutional failures as well as other market imperfections can be remedied by government action. Given its coercive power, a government can also explicitly address the problem of an unbalanced distribution of private power in a society. Moreover, due to the economies of scale associated with the coercive power, the state can be seen as a natural monopoly that is able to provide public goods and services at least cost. But state action is a double-edged sword. As Lewis (1955: 376) argues: 'No country has made economic progress without positive stimulus from intelligent governments. (...) On the other hand, there are so many examples of the mischief done to economic life by governments that it is easy to fill one's pages with warnings against government participation in economic life.' Similarly North (1981: 20) notes that 'The existence of a state is essential for economic growth; the state, however, is the source of man-made economic decline.' Since the polity has the power to define, implement, and enforce the formal institutions that guide economic exchange, the importance of government policy for economic and social development cannot be overemphasized. But what constitutes an intelligent government? Under what conditions has a government the incentives and ability to design and institute suitable institutional arrangements, which private institutional ordering fails to provide? These fundamental questions will be discussed in greater detail below in Chapter 5. For the moment, we content ourselves with addressing two related, though more basic questions, namely what is the state's role in initiating, facilitating, or complementing institutional change, and what factors principally determine success and failure of government policies?

Initiating, facilitating, and complementing institutional change

Collective-action and institutional failures often result from the inability of private actors to organize themselves, to coordinate investment and production decisions, and to enforce private contracts. Moreover, even if collective action succeeds, the outcome may be socially inefficient due to an unequal distribution of power in the private sector. In these cases, private ordering alone will not yield socially desired results, and it is the state's role to help to overcome these types of institutional failure and to *facilitate* the supply, that is the implementation and enforcement, and at times also the creation of socially beneficial institutions.

First of all, according to Olson (1965), the smallness of groups and their access to selective incentives represent two sufficient conditions for achieving successful collective action. However, groups are not organizations. Many groups whose members share common interests show little propensity for collective action or simply do not have the resources to organize themselves. The unemployed, for example, clearly have a common interest, but there are no LDCs or PSCs where the unemployed are effectively organized for collective action. Neither do most of the poor belong to organizations that further their common interest. Hence, it is the state's role to provide institutional arrangements such as unemployment insurance and poverty alleviation schemes.

Secondly, private-sector institutions basically have considerable comparative advantages *vis-à-vis* state agencies with respect to providing suitable incentives and processing information that is only locally available.

But private institutions cannot solve all market imperfections especially in economies at a low stage of development. For example, coordination failures may be caused by scale economies if factors of production, technologies, and intermediate goods, which are necessary for modern-sector production, are imperfectly tradable in international markets. In this case, individual investments in the modern sector will be profitable only if complementary investments (especially regarding the production of specialized inputs) are undertaken simultaneously. The interdependence of investment and production decisions causes severe coordination problems, because market prices are not adequate signals for the profitability of those activities which involve a large-scale resource reallocation. Rodrik (1995) identified this type of coordination failure in Taiwan and South Korea in the 1960s and 1970s and showed that strategic interventions in the form of government-led coordination of private investment and considerable subsidization played a critical role in enhancing self-sustaining growth.[18]

While coordination problems may basically justify government action, they do not necessarily justify replacing market-based coordination with government-led coordination. Due to information problems, governments may be at a disadvantage *vis-à-vis* private institutions in resolving coordination failures. Instead, institutional arrangements beyond the market may evolve in the non-public sector, including industry and trade associations, farmers' organizations, and financial intermediaries, which may be in a better position to address these problems. Then, governments' primary role is to support the development of these organizations and constructively to interact with them (Aoki *et al.* 1997b). Evenson and Westphal (1995) argue that, in some instances, industry associations acting in the interest of their members have actually been able effectively to diffuse best-practice technology. And they conclude that, more often than not, governments neglect the importance of supporting those private institutions in the provision of what are essentially club goods.

Thirdly, the enforcement of formal, private contracts is another area in which the state must play a critical role. In a world of impersonal exchange, in which economic transactions take place between multiple, specialized, utility maximizing agents who have only limited knowledge about each other and are not involved in repeated business transactions, opportunistic behavior, cheating, and shirking often have a substantial payoff and may trigger non-fulfillment of contracts. Under such circumstances, it often does not pay the involved parties to live up to their agreements. Even if private agents seek to assure compliance by the exchange of hostages, building up reputations, or relying on kinship ties, private contracts may not necessarily be self-enforcing. Based on his studies in economic history and the development of LDCs, North (1990a: 54) concludes that 'the inability of societies to develop effective, low-cost enforcement of contracts is the most important source of both historical stagnation and contemporary underdevelopment in the Third World'. Thus, in a world characterized by impersonal exchange, imperfect information, and hence positive transaction costs, third-party enforcement must accompany complex contracting and the guaranty of property rights. Principally, third-party enforcement can be designed in the form of voluntary *private* institutions. But given the specialized, complex interdependencies of economic transactions, private institutional arrangements assuring cooperative outcomes would not only require a built-in threat of coercion to enforce contracts, but also entail transaction costs which are prohibitive. Enter the state: due to economies of scale with respect to enforcing and policing agreements and its coercive power, the state may act effectively as a third party and enforce contracts at low costs. This, however, leads us, as North (1995a) persuasively argues, to a key dilemma of economic and social development. If the state is the central player in assuring third-party enforcement of formal institutions, how can it be ensured that the enforcers of the state apparatus behave impartially? Given that these enforcers are rational individuals with their own utility functions, their own interests, will guide their decisions. Effective third-party enforcement presupposes not only the ability to detect contract violations and to impose penalties, but also credible commitments on the part of political decision makers, which assure that political actors will enforce contracts impartially.

In sum, it is argued that a market-oriented legal system is required to foster impersonal exchange and hence efficiency. However, game theoretical analyses as well as anecdotal evidence show that legal contract enforcement may be conducive to facilitating anonymous exchange – but not necessarily so. Another, though also imperfect, mechanism for fostering exchange is the informal enforcement of contracts through reputation and personal trust. Greif (1997) shows that there is no single combination of (formal and informal) institutions which ensures optimal contract enforcement. This is because the efficacy and efficiency of alternative institutional matrices depend on existing economic, social, cultural, and political conditions. Hence, institutional reforms need to take into account the interdependencies of the economic, political, and socio-cultural orders of society. But nevertheless, impersonal exchange in a market economy requires the existence of the state as a third party to enforce contracts and to monitor property rights across time and space, because enforcement is typically imperfect and costly if it is privately organized. Informal institutions such as norms and ideologies certainly matter, but the more complex economies and societies become, the higher are the returns on opportunistic behavior. Therefore, a third party with coercive power is essential, and the state has an important role to play in this. But in most LDCs and PSCs, judicial systems are ineffective due to a failure of external institutions. This not only means that legal systems lack transparency and consistency, that existing laws may contradict each other, that laws and regulations are all too often changed arbitrarily, and that important institutions such as a contract law do not exist, but also that there is uncertainty about the behavior of enforcing agents and uniformity with respect to imposing penalties on the violators of contracts. Eventually, self-interested government agents may be inclined to use the coercive power of the state at the expense of the private sector. Adequate constitutional and electoral rules may help to restrain the abuse of political power and overcome opportunistic behavior of public agents. But after all they remain imperfect devices to ensure credible government commitment.[19]

Fourthly, due to an unequal distribution of private power, successful collective action may have deleterious effects on the economy as a whole. On the one hand, powerful organized interest groups may be able to create new institutional arrangements that benefit themselves but harm their business partners or other private agents. In this case, institutional change is solely realized by private action, but it rests by no means on voluntary actions of all parties affected. On the other hand, strong private pressure groups may be capable of capturing the state. It has been convincingly argued elsewhere (Mueller 1983; Olson 1982) that effectively organized narrow interest groups face considerable anti-social incentives and tend to engage in welfare-diminishing distributional struggles. If the state becomes a hostage to pressure groups that favor institutional arrangements that are detrimental to overall societal welfare, efficient institutional change will prove much more difficult to achieve. Note that the interaction of politicians and organized interest groups implies specific investments, the potential loss of which forces the adversely affected pressure groups to oppose institutional change. In particular Olson (1982) emphasizes this fact in his theory of institutional sclerosis and interprets this as a critical cause for the decline of formerly prospering nations.

In contrast to the advanced industrial societies of the West, policy making in many LDCs tends to be less visible, more closed, and essentially centered in the executive branch of government (Grindle and Thomas 1989). Frequently, high-level bureaucrats and government members, not legislators, dominate political agendas. Hence, they are the targets of rent-seekers. Moreover, while large segments of society cannot organize themselves for political activity or some organized groups (that are dependent clients of government agencies or political leaders) lack the capacity to influence the policy agenda, other parties such as ethnic or family groups may be able to influence politics significantly even if they lack public organization. In some cases, it is even difficult to identify the political influence of extra-governmental groups because lobbying takes place informally behind the scenes or because the political power of vested interests is implicit rather than explicit, for example, if policy makers are highly aware of the concerns of foreign investors or the military, even if their interests are not articulated publicly (Grindle 1991).

Solutions to overcome the problem of excessive private power will have to be sought step by step and often only quite indirectly. Besides the need to shield the state from the influence of vested interests through the establishment of specific political institutions, public policies play a critical role. Those LDCs that promote more encompassing, that is inclusive, interest groups and seek to reject the influence of exclusive organizations which are narrowly focused will be better prepared to limit potential harmful effects caused by collective action. However, encompassing interest groups are less likely to exist in LDCs or PSCs, because their emergence is usually the outcome of a time-consuming and effort-intensive process and presupposes a relatively stable and mature political and social environment that does not exist in most LDCs and PSCs, especially in non-democratic settings (Olson 1982). Yet even in these countries, governments or political entrepreneurs may have an interest in encouraging encompassing interest groups, particularly if political success is influenced by popular demonstrations or is contingent on the outcome of popular elections. Furthermore, competition policy may become a powerful tool for governments of less advanced countries to break off powerful private interest groups or, at least, to delimit their functions and economic impact. In this context, removing barriers to market entry by eliminating legal and regulatory impediments to the emergence of potential private competitors, introducing bankruptcy laws and regulations on firms' liability, establishing an independent judiciary, and creating anti-monopoly agencies are measures of utmost importance. Forcing those individuals and groups who are in control of a society's external institutional matrix (cabinet members, legislators, bureaucrats, and judges) to adhere to the principle of competition, which is embodied in the constitution, will help reduce rent-seeking and enhance the equity of opportunity. The protection of rules underlying economic and possibly political competition is a core function of public policy.

Finally, in the course of economic development, existing institutions such as laws, norms, and property rights may gradually become inefficient. Even if some inefficient arrangements may be replaced through private initiatives, some will persist due to diverging social and private costs and benefits and free-rider problems (Lin and Nugent 1995). Therefore, governments can play a critical role in institutional adjustment and innovation.

As Polanyi (1995/1944) argued forcefully, markets cannot unfold their socially beneficial effects if they are not embedded in a fabric of non-market institutions. His argument is that markets can only be sustainable if they are adequately embedded in political and social relations that perform three critical functions comprising the regulation, stabilization, and legitimization of market outcomes. Rodrik (1998) emphasizes precisely this point when he writes that

> every politician knows, the clamor for controls and restrictions overcomes markets when markets produce outcomes that are not endowed with popular legitimacy. Markets are not self-regulating, self-stabilizing, and self-legitimating. That is why every functioning society has regulatory bodies that set the rules of competition, monetary and fiscal institutions that perform stabilizing functions, and social insurance schemes, transfer policies, and other social arrangements that bring market outcomes into conformity with a society's preferences regarding the distribution of risks and rewards.

Besides rules ensuring a competitive environment for economic and political exchange, a number of non-market institutions can be identified which are essential for markets to perform adequately. All of these institutions are public goods, the provision of which is beyond the interest or capacity of private agents. Above all, this concerns a country's political and economic constitution. More specifically, such institutions essentially include the rules guiding macroeconomic stabilization and structural adjustment policies, all measures constituting the legal, regulatory, educational, financial, social, physical, technological, and environmental infrastructure of a market economy, and eventually institutions that facilitate conflict management (Stiglitz 1997; Rodrik 1999). Regarding the choice of formal institutions having a public-good character, a change in relative prices or in similar selection criteria that change transaction costs of alternative institutions according to the naïve model of institutional change, cannot usefully serve as a direct explanatory variable of institution building. These external institutions can only be changed by political decision making. The motivation for institutional reform may then be contingent on political commitment and the type of political order. While in democratic settings, institutional change will be largely determined by political competition, in non-democratic societies political authorities may have significantly more leverage over institutional reform. Nevertheless transaction-cost considerations can still be applied to explain a change in external institutions. To do so, it is useful to distinguish between economic and political transaction costs, the latter comprising the costs of formulating political demands and objectives, the costs of political decision making,[20] and the costs of enforcing political decisions (including the costs incurred by the public administration). Since the polity creates, changes, and enforces external institutions, and helps to enforce formal private rules (type-4 internal institutions) by, for example, protecting property rights and enforcing contracts, political factors (and especially political transaction costs) are a critical determinant of institutional change. This implies that, contingent on the balance of power in a society, socially desirable external institutions will only be encouraged or created if the expected marginal returns which accrue to the political actors exceed the marginal transaction costs of mobilizing resources needed for the innovative activity, that is if the efforts needed for institution building are at least offset by increasing political support, greater prestige, or a sufficient change in other variables that may increase policy makers' utility. If, however, a potential new institution is perceived adversely to affect a powerful interest group, institutional change may not occur, even if it is associated with a high rate of social return. In contrast, socially inefficient innovations may be implemented if the expected net benefits to the political entrepreneurs are positive, and even if the gains to society as a whole are negative (Ruttan and Hayami 1984).

The danger of government failure

Most economists agree that a *laissez-faire* economy neither ensures economic efficiency nor guarantees protection from poverty. Markets fail when actors engage in anti-competitive behavior, when transaction costs prevent the internalization of externalities, and when incomplete information causes moral hazard or adverse selection. Market failures do provide a powerful rationale for government action. Although economic theories of imperfect competition, mechanism design, agency problems, and others have offered a great variety of instruments to address these failures, in practice, interventions have frequently been counterproductive. Governments are not infallible. In the contemporary world, there are numerous sources of policy failure, and their significance varies across time and space. Policy reforms, which are conducive to economic growth in a particular country at a certain point in time, may be ineffective or even harmful for development in the same country at other times. Government interventions which work in one country may prove counterproductive in another.[21] The ingredients of institutional reforms, which are necessary to move a particular country to a higher trajectory of economic growth, as well as the efficacy of new institutional arrangements, depend on a country's stage of development, its degree of integration into international structures, its existing institutional matrix, and the capability and capacity of its government to implement and enforce them. Thus, adequate institutional reform packages are highly context-specific, and so are the sources of potential government failure.

However, several broad politico-institutional explanations for reform failures have been identified in the literature on institutional reforms, which help to understand better the danger of government failure and provide some clues about how to overcome them. The most important factors that may cause government failure include a high degree of discretionary authority of key policy makers, ideological rigidity on the part of the government, principal–agent problems inherent in a country's civil service, interest group conflicts, as well as existing limitations in the available stock of social science knowledge.[22]

Unlike policy makers in a rule-based society, political leaders of states that are based on rule by (moral) authority vested in persons have a substantial degree of absolute personal power and hence discretionary authority over public policy making. If in these cases political rulers do not have an encompassing interest, but seek to maximize their own private wealth, prestige, power, and possibly strive for their particular position in history, they may be tempted to follow myopic personal goals at the expense of the country's overall welfare. Those politicians may do so by violating citizens' rights, ignoring private property rights, overly taxing businesses and private households, confiscating private wealth or investing in politically prestigious projects at the expense of social reforms or anti-poverty programs. Moreover, as North and Weingast (1989) argue, political rulers often act detrimentally to societal interests if their power is seriously challenged by rival competitors and hence their political survival is at stake. In extreme cases, political rulers with excessive discretionary power who strive for maximum surplus extraction may be able to erect a political regime that shows virtually all the characteristics of a predatory state like Mobutu in Zaire or Marcos in the Philippines.[23]

Of course, the discretionary authority of rulers can be, and at times has been, used to foster economic and social development. This may be the case if there is a strong positive linkage between the political leaders' personal wealth and national income growth as in countries like Saudi Arabia. This may also occur if a powerful ruler has an encompassing interest in the well-being of his nation as, for example, in South Korea under Park Chung Hee.[24] After all, the political and economic outcomes of policies conducted under substantial discretionary authority of individual policy makers depend not exclusively but significantly on the personality of the individuals in power.[25]

Earlier, we defined ideology from the perspective of an individual as the subjective perceptions people use to come to terms with their complex environment. But as is well-known, ideology can also be used by political leaders as an economizing device to shape the persuasions, perceptions, and actions of citizens. As a matter of distinction, this kind of influencing of people in the interest of political authorities may be called *organized political ideology*. Political ideologies provide integrated explanations of the present and the past and may help to reduce the transaction costs to policy makers of mobilizing collective action needed for institutional reforms. For example, strong nationalist sentiments in South Korea in the 1960s, reflected in the slogan 'Modernizing the Fatherland' and crucially reinforced by the then existing communist threat from North Korea, helped to mobilize resources needed for industrialization. As Root (1996: 19) puts it:

> Although [President] Park never used the term *capitalism*, he insisted on regaining control of the nation's destiny through modernization. This meant that some groups would lose privileges, while others would gain. By making opposition to reform seem unpatriotic, the theme 'Modernization of the Fatherland' prevented the polarization of society into winners and losers. Modernization became everyone's responsibility.

By using this ideological device Park was able to solidify his power, gain legitimacy, and to carry through radical institutional reforms which significantly contributed to the country's economic takeoff. If political ideologies are appropriate to make citizens believe in the government's legitimacy as well as the rectitude of the existing formal institutions, constituents' compliance with existing laws, regulations, and policies will be enhanced and the transaction costs of state rule reduced. Thus, ideology can be basically used as a critical tool by political authorities to facilitate the supply of institutional innovation.

But ideological rigidity on the part of the government can also retard or block efficient institutional change. Particularly in authoritarian regimes, the political leadership uses political ideologies to inculcate citizens with its own view of the world in order to gain legitimacy and to accomplish its personal goals more successfully. This may, or may not, be consistent with progress in economic development. But in the course of time, institutional disequilibria will occur in the economy due to changes in economic, social, technological, or international conditions or due to newly available sources of information.[26] These disequilibria create or increase the tension between the existing ideology on the one hand and citizens' subjective ideologies as well as the need for policy reforms on the other hand. As long as political rulers stick to their old ideology and the policies derived from it, because they cannot give up their political convictions or fear losing power or legitimacy otherwise, institutional reforms will be, at best, half-hearted (as in the former Soviet Union under Gorbachev), postponed, or not undertaken at all. In extreme cases (like in the former GDR, Romania under Ceaucescu, or Spain under Franco), institutional reforms are only feasible after radical government changes, if the new rulers articulate a new ideology that is consistent with changes in reality.

Another factor that may impede efficient institutional change is bureaucratic discretion. An effective public administration is a *conditio sine qua non* for the implementation and enforcement of policy reform. But bureaucracies are typically plagued with principal–agent problems. Frequently, the personal interests of civil servants are not consistent with the interests of the government, political decision makers are usually not able to monitor bureaucratic behavior effectively, and bureaucrats often have substantial discretionary scope for action. Bureaucratic discretion, in turn, provides incentives to civil servants to collude with extra-governmental interest groups and makes them responsive to rent-seeking and corruption. In addition, discretionary power gives civil servants considerable leverage over policy making. Thus bureaucrats may be inclined to sabotage public policies, because they fear to lose rents, power, and eventually their jobs. This problem has been acute, for example, in PSCs, especially in those cases in which the objective of policy reform is to abolish particular ministries or departments therein (Boycko *et al.* 1996). Moreover, as Winiecki (1990) reports, pre-transformation reforms aimed at decentralizing economic decision-making in the state sector largely failed, because middle-level party functionaries and bureaucrats sabotaged reform efforts for fear of losing privileges, power, and rents.

Moreover, due to redistributive effects, institutional reforms will usually produce losers, who have to bear losses in terms of income, personal wealth, or political power. As discussed above, this may give rise to considerable opposition to new institutional arrangements, especially if the adversely affected groups are well organized and if credible compensation schemes are not in place. Opposition will then be more effective the more the government must rely on the political support of these groups. For example, Feeny (1989) argues that agricultural development in Thailand was impeded because powerful interest groups effectively opposed government investment in irrigation systems, which would have promised them few gains. Similarly, in South Korea the government faces serious problems in limiting the economic power of the *chaebols*. These huge business conglomerates must be considered as major roadblocks to a sustained economic recovery after the Asian crisis and threaten to drive numerous small and medium-sized enterprises from the market. Although the government seeks to enforce measures aimed at restructuring the *chaebols* and enhancing competition through opening up the economy, a radical reform may fail due to political factors. Since the *chaebols* are politically influential and economically significant, the government is unable to dictate their economic restructuring or enforce any major bankruptcy procedures. This would involve a sharp increase in the unemployment rate and a new banking crisis due to the accumulated debts of these conglomerates.[27]

Last but not least, limitations in the available stock of social science knowledge may prove to be an impediment to efficient institutional change. Even if governments actually intend and are politically able to institute efficient institutional reforms, they may fail if they lack adequate information and knowledge either of the ingredients of such reform or of the way to implement them. For example, the adoption of central planning techniques by many LDC governments in the 1950s can be interpreted as having been significantly influenced by the social knowledge and ideas that were dominating the development debate at that time (Krueger 1995). Today policy makers may also fail to create socially desirable new institutions because the policy models used to describe and analyse the economic system are usually imperfect. Often the models are incomplete or even misleading due to imperfect information. Moreover, the need for institution building and its efficacy may depend on the economic or academic background of policy makers; for example, models may yield different policy implications contingent on whether analysts rely on a Keynesian or a neoclassical model of the macroeconomy. Therefore, Eggertsson (1997 and 1998a) concludes that incomplete modeling affects political and economic behavior and influences the creation of institutions as well as the effects which these institutions have on behavior.

Lin and Nugent (1995) argue that social science knowledge is particularly deficient regarding the conduct of institutional reforms in developing countries. This is attributed to failures in applying findings of social science theories to the specific structural characteristics of LDC states. Since these characteristics differ from those in advanced economies, in which most progress in social science has been created, simply transferring institutions that are efficient elsewhere to LDCs may turn out to be counterproductive, whereas institutions that are considered to be inefficient in advanced countries' settings, may prove to be efficient under the specific structural conditions of LDCs. For example, the perception that agrarian institutions such as sharecropping are inefficient was derived from research that (implicitly) assumed the political, economic, and legal institutions of developed countries. More recent research, however, found that given incomplete markets and costly information, sharecropping may be efficient under LDC conditions (Stiglitz 1974 and 1989). Furthermore, the experiences with transformation policies in Russia, for example, indicate that simply applying orthodox stabilization-cum-adjustment policies has not brought about the expected results. This can be essentially explained by the distinct political and cultural conditions and specific economic structures in Russia.

However, with advances in social science knowledge and especially the professional institutionalization of social science and related research, it has, and will continue to, become significantly easier for political decision-makers to (at least) partially substitute acquired new analytical skills and knowledge in social sciences for the relative costly process of learning by trial and error. Ruttan and Hayami (1984) demonstrate, for example, that progress in research has helped better to understand the economic behavior of rural households in LDCs, which, in turn, has increased the efficiency of price policies for products and factors and has improved the design of institutions and the formulation of policies that aim to improve peasants' technological capacities and capabilities. They also observe that enhancements in general education and a better diffusion of education help to improve the public's understanding of social and private costs associated with institutional reforms. This means that the costs to policy makers of crafting new institutions that benefit society as a whole will be reduced and the costs of introducing institutions that are socially undesirable will be raised.

Finally, even if efficient institutional solutions can be identified by policy makers, the problem of proper implementation remains. As yet, there are no generally accepted theoretical approaches that may guide governments through the complicated terrain of implementing policy reforms. Particularly, in the course of systemic transformation in Central and Eastern Europe and socialist states like China, the questions of timing, sequencing, and pacing political, economic, and administrative reforms have come to the forefront of economic and other social science research. Best-practice recipes of how to proceed, however, can hardly be expected. What is still missing is the proper linkage of general theoretical findings and country-specific conditions and needs.

4.3 POLITICAL ECONOMY, INSTITUTIONS, AND ADAPTIVE EFFICIENCY

The preceding sections emphasized that institutional change is a crucial prerequisite to effective policy reform and that institution building on the part of the state is a key component thereof. Sometimes institutional change through private ordering will yield socially undesirable outcomes. At other times, an existing demand for institutional innovation will not materialize at all. The state may provide solutions to overcome institutional inertia and inefficiencies as well as collective action failures. However, the state in LDCs is more often than not beleaguered by inefficient institutional structures itself and hence may represent an impediment to economic development. In this and the next subsection, we provide a synthesis of the foregoing arguments and distill major puzzling questions which have not yet been adequately addressed in the literature on the political economy of policy reform. This will lay the analytical basis for explicitly examining the politico-institutional dimension of economic reform and development policies in Chapter 5.

Particularly, North's theory of institutional change, which seeks to integrate the model of induced institutional change, the pillars of collective action theory and especially the role of informal institutions, has greatly enhanced our understanding of historical and contemporary institutional change in advanced societies and LDCs. Since it explicitly models the interdependencies between the economic, political, and socio-cultural suborders of society, the *Northian* approach goes beyond the realms of traditional institutional analyses. Therefore, it is particularly useful for students who are interested in the critical determinants of economic performance through time and the still puzzling questions concerning the political foundations of economic reforms. The following discussion is aimed at synthesizing the essential pillars of North's model of institutional change in general and the importance of political institutions therein in particular (see Figure 4.1).[28]

North explains the development of, and change in, institutional arrangements through a complex interdependent process among organizations and between them and formal and informal institutions. He explicitly rejects the postulate that only the most efficient institutions will survive over time. On the contrary, institutions may, and in fact do, yield transaction cost-increasing effects and often lead to economic stagnation and even decline.

According to North and his followers, the institutional and organizational structure of a society is the key variable to understanding economic growth and development. While the whole of a society's institutions, that is its institutional matrix consisting of a complex set of formal rules and informal constraints, including their enforcement characteristics, define (together with the traditional constraints of economic theory) the opportunity set available to individual choices, it is individual entrepreneurs (political and economic) and organizations that are the agents of institutional change. The interest groups and organizations of a society evolve as a consequence of the opportunities and hence incentives that are provided by the institutional matrix. Organizations are purposeful entities composed of individuals who act collectively in pursuit of shared objectives. 'The immediate objective of organization may be profit maximizing (for firms) or improving reelection prospects (for political parties); but the ultimate objective is survival because all organizations live in a world of scarcity and hence competition' (North 1995a: 6). North (1995a and b) states five propositions which explain institutional change:

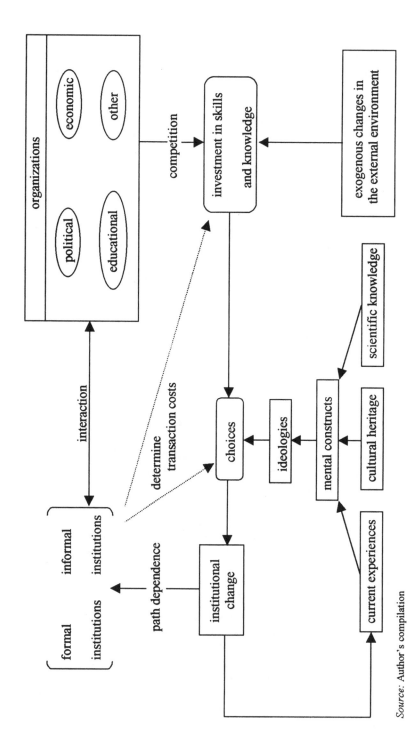

Source: Author's compilation

Figure 4.1: A stylized Northian model of institutional change

1. The existence of scarcity and competition is the starting point to explain institutional change (see Figure 4.1). This setting implies a continuous interaction among organizations and between them and institutions.

2. This endogenous competition as well as exogenous changes such as changes in relative prices or technologies force organizations constantly to acquire new knowledge and skills that are necessary to survive and to achieve immediate objectives. The investment in skills as well as knowledge, in turn, shapes the evolving perceptions of individuals and organizations about present opportunities and choices which will incrementally, though steadily, modify or replace existing institutions by new ones.

3. Since the existing institutional matrix determines the costs of transacting and provides the overall incentive structure, it not only constrains actual choices, but consequently determines the kind of learning that actors perceive to have the highest payoff. This implies that (induced) institutional change will not necessarily be efficient in the sense that more productive, growth-enhancing arrangements will evolve. Since every institutional matrix provides mixed incentives favoring both redistributive and productive activities, the performance of an economy will depend on the relative weights attached to each category. If actors perceive that redistributive activities have the highest returns, organizations are expected to invest in rent-seeking and similar activities. If, however, the maximum payoffs are perceived to result from productive activity, organizations will seek to acquire knowledge and skills that help to increase productivity.[29]

4. The perceptions of individuals and organizational actors, which eventually shape their choices, are essentially influenced by what North (1995a: 7 and 9) calls 'the mental constructs of the players', that is 'the way the mind interprets the information it receives'. These constructs, which are filtered by individuals' cognitive systems, result from genetic evolution, cultural heritage, progress in scientific knowledge, and current experiences such as local learning (Denzau and North 1994; North 1994b). This implies that – given the same facts – the choices of different individuals may be based on different interpretations of the evidence and different perceptions about how the world around them is and how the world ought to be. Hence different subjective ideologies may lead to different actions. Although ideologies economize on transaction costs and facilitate information processing, a sufficient correction of individual perceptions which would imply convergence towards a single equilibrium can hardly be expected. Due to bounded rationality, individuals will lack a complete information feedback regarding the consequences of their choices. Thus,

because of different actions of individuals having the same preferences, multiple equilibria can ensue (North 1992).

5. Institutional change is incremental and subject to path dependence in ideas, ideologies, and institutions. Hence economies cannot reverse their development direction overnight. This is due to the network externalities, economies of scope, and complementarities that are inherent in the institutional matrix. Organizations that exist in a particular society, their internal structure and relations as well as their complex contractual and other relations with other organizational entities in the economy and the polity have been built on the given institutional matrix. Therefore, organizations tend to have an interest in maintaining (most of the elements of) that matrix. Furthermore, the outcomes of current learning processes, which have induced the present institutions, constrain future choices. As organizations evolve over time to capture potential returns more effectively, they will gradually seek to alter the existing institutional constraints; either indirectly through the interaction of organizational behavior and its impact on changing informal rules; or by seeking to alter formal institutions directly. 'In either case', as North (1989: 667) argues vividly

> the change is an incremental process; the result of thousands of individual decisions by organizations and their entrepreneurs which cumulatively are altering the institutional framework over time. Thus short-run profitable opportunities cumulatively create the long-run path of change. The long-run consequences are often unintended for two reasons. First, the entrepreneurs are seldom interested in the larger (and external to them) consequences but the direction of their investment influences the extent to which there is investment in adding to or disseminating the stock of knowledge, encouraging or discouraging factor mobility, etc. Second, there frequently is a significant difference between intended outcomes and actual outcomes. Outcomes frequently diverge from intentions because of the limited capabilities of individuals and the complexity of the problems to be solved.

Major, that is more radical, institutional change may only occur if organizations pursuing different interests come into being and if the emerging inter-organizational conflicts cannot be overcome within the given institutional framework.[30]

The characteristics of institutional change just described do not reveal whether or not this change will be efficient. If we are concerned with the dynamic implications of the interaction among organizations and the interdependencies between organizations and institutions for economic performance, we need to go beyond the static concept of allocative efficiency that presupposes a given institutional framework. Therefore, North introduces the concept of *adaptive efficiency*.[31] This concept rests on the assumption that a sufficiently flexible institutional framework, that will provide low transaction costs, facilitate credible commitment, suitably adjust to a changing demographic, technological, and political environment and smoothly absorb exogenous shocks, is a pivotal *conditio sine qua non* for the emergence of efficient product and factor markets and sustained economic performance. More specifically, a dynamic economic evolution, that results from systematic and continuing investments in learning and the application of the new skills and knowledge to economic and political exchanges, needs to entail specific institutional characteristics if the society is to be shifted onto a higher trajectory of development. These properties, similar to technology development, concern a society's willingness and ability to acquire skills and knowledge in productivity-enhancing activities, to foster innovation, to undertake creative activities, and to take risks. They also concern societal characteristics of overcoming current bottlenecks and problems, for example relating to policy reforms, as they arise and yet to provide secure political and economic rights. While North (1990a) concedes that social science research is far from having elaborated all criteria that ensure adaptive efficiency, he persuasively argues that the institutional matrix is the key that determines the degree to which innovations, trials, and experiments will be encouraged in a given society.[32] For it is the incentives resulting from the overall institutional structure that guide learning processes and the emergence of tacit knowledge. The underlying process of acquiring knowledge then will direct individual actors and organizations gradually to create new institutional arrangements.

Similarly, Eggertsson (1998b) argues that due to bounded rationality as well as incomplete private and public policy models, institutional change is often continuous and incremental. Both the private and the public sector seek to understand and estimate the interdependencies as well as the relevant properties of the societal subsystems. Private agents, for example, seek to identify new margins of business operations; either to find ways of making their productive activities more profitable; or to soften the constraints to their businesses. Government agencies attempt to constrain private actors more effectively by improving their understanding with respect to the relations between policy instruments and targets. All actors gradually revise and update their economic models and accordingly reinterpret the need for, and implications of, institutional rules, constraints, and enforcement mechanisms. Then through the interactions of private and public actors, institutional arrangements change over time. As Eggertsson (1998b: 27) concludes: 'The direction of change can be toward collectively rational outcomes or toward collectively irrational outcomes, and the direction may not be fully understood until relatively late in the game.'

It follows from the preceding arguments that an institutional matrix will be adaptively efficient, yield collectively rational outcomes, and be suitable to resolve conflicts and problems over time, if it

- provides individual actors and organizations with incentives to pursue various trial-and-error searches for conducting activities and hence permits a large number of choices to be made under uncertainty;
- ensures competition, protects well-specified property rights, and enforces bankruptcy laws;
- encourages the emergence of decentralized decision-making mechanisms; and
- ensures feedback effects with respect to identifying relatively inefficient prior actions.

Opportunities for trials and experiments as well as decentralization will enhance the creation of tacit knowledge and encourage the exploration of a great variety of alternatives in order to solve problems of scarcity. This, however, presupposes the existence of entrepreneurship (for the initiation of trials) and competition (for the elimination of errors). Feedback mechanisms also help actors to learn from failures and to correct organizational errors and policy makers to enhance policy adaptability (Pelikan 1987). Note in this context that it is also indispensable for an adaptively efficient institutional matrix to include rules that eliminate not only unsuccessful economic organizations but also failed political entities.

While individual economic and political entrepreneurs and organizations are the agents of institutional change, their bargaining strength and the distributional effects of institutional arrangements are of utmost importance regarding the question of whether or not an economy or society will realize an adaptively efficient path of development. In reality unproductive paths can, and actually often do, persist. North (1990a: 99) describes the problem as follows:

> The increasing returns characteristic of an initial set of institutions that provide disincentives to productive activity will create organizations and interest groups with a stake in the existing constraints. They will shape the polity in their interests. Such institutions provide incentives that may encourage military domination of the polity and economy, religious fanaticism, or plain, simple redistributive organizations, but they provide few rewards from increases in the stock and dissemination of economically useful knowledge. The subjective mental constructs of the participants will evolve an ideology that not only rationalizes the society's structure but accounts for its poor performance. As a result the economy will evolve policies that reinforce the existing incentives and organizations.

Since the institutional matrices of all economies and polities actually provide organizations with varying incentives to pursue unproductive as well as productive activities, historical performance records of societies usually reflect mixed results. Moreover, the same fundamental changes, for example institutional innovations (imposed from outside actors like international organizations) or changes in relative prices, will affect economies differently. While in each economy marginal adjustments will occur, the ensuing changes will reflect the interests and the bargaining power of different actors which have come into existence under different country-specific institutional frameworks. Because of the different institutional matrices, the bargaining power of parties affected by these fundamental changes will also differ. In addition, marginal adaptations to changes will reflect the different ideologies that actors developed in countries with different histories. In sum, this implies that actors in different countries will make different choices even if they are confronted with the same (exogenous) changes.

The preceding argument highlights why efficient institutional change is an extremely complex process. The creation of adaptively efficient economic and political markets cannot be solely achieved by formal institution building. In a given country, formal institutions must complement informal constraints and effective mechanisms of enforcement in order to bring about an internally consistent and coherent overall institutional framework (North 1992). Informal institutions such as conventions, codes of behavior, and self-imposed standards of conduct, however, change slowly. Furthermore, at least to some degree enforcement of new institutions will have to rely on the power of those interest groups and organizations that may have a vital interest in maintaining the old rules of the game. Finally, institutional change may be a substantial source of conflict, because in its course old dominant organizations will be replaced by new ones. If in a particular economy the existence of unproductive opportunities dominates economic and political exchange, how can the emerging, possibly inefficient, development path be reversed? How can economies and polities enhance their capacities and capabilities to form and maintain a well-performing mixture of both types of incentives? Due to the complexity of overall institutional change, simply transferring the formal institutional framework of successful economies to reforming ones will not automatically yield desirable results. As the rush to establish market-oriented economies in LDCs and PSCs indicates, outcomes vary considerably: from Poland and China, which have been success cases so far, to Russia and other successor states of the former Soviet Union, which have shown only limited progress so far – to the countries of sub-Saharan Africa, which remain hopeless cases.

It is largely undisputed that the polity plays a crucial role in establishing and maintaining an adaptively efficient economic order. A competitive polity that provides for the measurement and enforcement of contracts and property rights at low costs, facilitates credible political commitment, ensures the contestability of ideas and access to information, allows government actions to be evaluated, and sets incentives that reward long-term, productive investment and business transactions, is an unalterable prerequisite for reversing an unproductive path of development. In this context, the concept of adaptive efficiency has greatly improved our understanding of economic performance over time. But it still lacks analytical and conceptual rigor. So far, it is a useful but fuzzy approach to understanding (efficient) institutional change. As North himself recognizes (1990a, 1990b), we still know too little of how to create efficient product and factor markets in LDCs and PSCs, and we know even less of what is needed to create a polity that incorporates the institutional and organizational preconditions to implement and enforce necessary economic reforms. Political markets are inherently imperfect due to incomplete models which policy makers use in their attempts to order the economy and other societal suborders; due to complex institutional problems in realizing credible commitments between principals and agents (for example, between voters and legislators and between cabinets members and bureaucrats); due to high information costs; and due to low payoffs to individual constituents with respect to acquiring information.

In summary, economic growth is contingent on the existence of *stable but adjustable* political and economic institutions which provide low transaction costs in impersonal economic and political markets. However, institutional arrangements can neither be taken for granted nor do they come automatically into existence from neoclassical policies aimed at privatization and getting the prices right. By emphasizing that most economic rules are, and need to be, made in the polity, North stresses that institutional change is largely dependent on the power structure or balance among vested interest groups in a society. Although he does not neglect the impact of changes in relative prices and preferences, institutions essentially reflect the relative bargaining strength of political parties, individual policy makers, trade unions, business associations, and other vested interests in the political market. Major changes in formal institutions will only occur if these changes are in the interest of those parties that have sufficient bargaining strength. Therefore, a critical component of policy reform is to encourage the emergence of organizations that support economic and political institutions that are conducive to sustained development. Moreover, since informal rules help to enforce formal institutions and legitimize a new set of formal rules, it is necessary to change both the formal and informal institutions in order to induce a coherent and consistent institutional matrix. But changing informal institutions is time-consuming, so that successful policy reform can usually only be achieved through a lengthy process.[33]

Moreover, the preceding arguments show that the state needs to play a critical role in sustainable and socially beneficial institutional change. After all, the state provides a framework of order within which the economy is built. By undertaking policy reform, the state changes existing and creates new institutional arrangements, even if policy reform merely includes those measures advanced by the Washington Consensus. Furthermore, due to imperfect information, incomplete markets, imperfect competition, and transaction costs, the state can potentially become an important catalyst for economic development. However, this neither implies that governments will inevitably initiate the desired change nor that policy reform is bound to succeed. Governments have not only often failed when they pursued policies that were poor, but also when they did too much or too little for the right policies (Lin and Nugent 1995). Developmental states, therefore, require a politico-institutional foundation that provides policy makers with the incentives and the ability to design and institute institutional arrangements conducive for growth and development, something that a privately induced innovation process fails to provide. Not the minimal state, but the *capable state* is needed in order to make market-oriented policy reform a stable and viable policy choice.

But since political markets are imperfect, institutional arrangements are always a mixture of those that lower transaction costs and those that raise them. Much more research is required to refine the concept of adaptive efficiency. But most likely its nature will remain an abstract and indistinct one because after all adaptive efficiency strongly depends on the context-specificity of economic, social, and political problems. Nevertheless, the notion of adaptive efficiency must be the guide to both policy making and analysing the politico-institutional foundations of economic reforms if we are to strive to find ways to enhance the incentive-compatibility of public policies and economic performance which eventually helps to overcome economic stagnation and decline.

4.4   THE NEED FOR A POLITICO-INSTITUTIONAL FOUNDATION OF POLICY REFORM

The analysis of institutions has profoundly improved our understanding of how economies develop through time. Economic and social development is no longer seen as an inevitable, though gradual, transition from local autarky toward specialization and the division of labor. Instead, the process of development is regarded as being largely determined by the evolution of institutional arrangements which determine the terms of exchange between different agents. Economic growth occurs if institutions provide relatively low transaction costs in impersonal markets, reduce potential hazards of production and trade (such as shirking and opportunism), facilitate capital accumulation and capital mobility, allow pricing and sharing of risks, and encourage cooperation. Consequently, differences in economic performance between LDCs and industrialized countries on the one hand and among LDCs on the other do not ultimately result from countries' natural or technological endowments. Eventually they result from the established economic and political order and the policies pursued by governments. The efficacy of both factors is crucially determined by underlying rules and constraints and particularly by the interplay of economic and political institutions. These are essentially old problems which have already been recognized by the students of classical political economy and political philosophy such as Locke, Montesquieu, and Hobbes.[34] However, few of their insights have been incorporated into modern economics or have influenced economic advisors to LDC and PSC governments. Recently, works of the NIE have been extended to the economic analysis of political institutions which may be defined as those formal rules and informal constraints (including their enforcement characteristics) that directly affect political decision-making processes in the course of economic development. Political institutions, for example, include rules that specify a polity's hierarchical structure, its elementary decision rules, as well as the explicit mechanisms of agenda control. Therefore, these institutions can be considered as devices for the allocation of political power and positions and hence affect political leaders' capability of pursuing their preferences and achieving their goals.[35]

The importance of applying analytical techniques from the NIE to politics and hence addressing the problems concerning the role of political institutions for economic development and policy reform is clearly revealed by the problems of economic transformation and democratic transition in LDCs and particularly in CEE. Usually, advisors focusing on economic transition urgently request governments to get the prices right. Although this is a critical issue of economic reforms, this advice is not sufficient to ensure a successful transformation. Many governments face political and social constraints which hinder them in implementing coherent market-oriented reforms. If, for example, private interest groups have a strong influence on policy making, economic policies may show a significant bias favoring special interests, and do not benefit society as a whole. Even if governments initiate policy reform with a suitable policy mix based on an adequately specified set of economic institutions, economic development may be impeded by political risks resulting from uncertainties about government behavior in the future. As the experiences with failed policy reforms in LDCs indicate, proper advice regarding the formation of policy reform needs to account for the relationship between the economy and the polity. Emerging markets require not merely well-functioning economic institutions such as private property rights, a rational price system, and a well-defined law of contract. They also require a secure political foundation that allows the formation and implementation of economically and socially necessary reforms.

However, institutions can neither be taken for granted nor is institutional change guided by an invisible hand onto some beneficent path. Eventually, the emergence of efficient economic institutions crucially depends on the existence of efficient political markets, because the polity specifies, implements, and enforces the formal rules of economic exchange. But political markets are usually neither perfectly competitive nor efficient. The ability of the state to promote institutional change that benefits the economy as a whole crucially depends on the institutional structure of the polity. This is because different politico-institutional arrangements imply different political transaction costs and hence different incentives for policy makers. Political transaction costs affect the interaction between various branches of government and between political authorities, business elites, and other groups of society. Ultimately they determine political choices. Consequently, economic outcomes are not only responses to market conditions, but also the products of these institutionalized relations (Dixit 1996; Evans 1995).

Hence if initiating and facilitating institutional change by the state is a pivotal component of policy reform and an indispensable condition for its success, we need to recognize that this is only one side of the coin. The flip side is the need to make the state effective in implementing and enforcing institutional and other policies. This requires a thorough analysis of, and a differentiated conceptual approach to, the state apparatus in LDCs and PSCs that avoids an oversimplified treatment of the state as a monolithic entity. Max Weber (1972/1921) defined the state as a compulsory association that successfully claims the monopoly of the legitimate use of physical force within a specific community. Contemporary scholars usually view the state in the *Weberian* tradition, but attempt to usefully amend this definition by reducing the complexity of analysing what states do and what roles they perform. Azarya (1988: 10), for example, argues that the state is 'distinguished from the myriad of other organizations [in society; J.A.] in seeking predominance over them and in aiming to institute binding rules regarding the other organizations' activities, or at least to authorize (...) the other organizations to make such rules for themselves'. But the capability of state actors in achieving objectives such as internal and external security, and effective revenue collection, or in asserting control and autonomy is strongly influenced by the degree of social mobilization, economic conditions, and by the state's internal cohesion and legitimacy. Note also, as discussed earlier, that the pursuit of public interests may conflict with the private interests of individual policy makers and that contention along the boundaries of the state often result from, or are closely linked to, disputes between different levels and branches of government, public agencies as well as diverse interests of bureaucrats.

In its definition of the state, this study essentially follows those outlined in Evans *et al.* (1985), Grindle (1996), and Haber *et al.* (1999). Thus the state is seen as a nexus of institutions for social control, authoritative policy formation and implementation, in which policy makers and social actors interact with each other and influence the path of economic, social, and political development, which in turn shapes the behavior of individuals and groups. In general, state institutions help to mediate conflicting social demands and produce specific policies and rules that govern social interactions within and beyond the political realm. One central purpose of state institutions is to reduce uncertainty about political change. This, first of all, concerns government changes. Institutional arrangements defining mechanisms for government selection significantly shape expectations about who may assume power and what kind of institutional reforms may be expected. Secondly, political change may be associated with fundamental changes in the structural foundation of a polity. This refers to changes in both the general rules that guide political interaction and the rules that govern the evolution of the polity over time. Institutions governing this type of political change, especially a country's constitution, are essential because they shape the strategies which interest groups and individuals pursue to advance their political objectives in the future.

Since the state itself can be perceived as a complex nexus of institutions, which provide the incentive structure for policy makers and determine the process of policy formulation, implementation, and enforcement, institution building as a key component of policy reform has two dimensions: (1) creating the formal *economic* institutions which guide private sector development and coordination; and (2) crafting *political* institutions which are conducive to the proper and sound implementation and enforcement of economic institutions and policies. Therefore, after having discussed the role of governments regarding institutional change in the preceding sections, the following considerations focus on the second dimension, that is the importance of establishing a secure politico-institutional foundation of policy reform.

However, the task relating to this second dimension is subject to what Weingast (1993 and 1995) calls 'the fundamental political dilemma of an economic system'; namely that a strong government, which is required to protect and enforce property rights, is also able to violate these and other citizens' rights and to confiscate private wealth, thereby creating disincentives for private actors to carry out long-term investment and to provide information. This, in turn, blocks thriving markets, and eventually halts development. As North (1990a: 59) puts it bluntly, 'if the state has coercive force, then those who run the state will use that force in their own interest at the expense of the rest of society'. This is why a secure politico-institutional foundation limiting the state's ability to transgress the rights of private actors is indispensable for the emergence of a functioning market economy and for its preservation. As Weingast (1993) observes, the absence of a political foundation of policy reform can lead to an equilibrium trap that is characterized by reform failure despite the choice of 'adequate' economic policies. Such a trap may result from government failure to guarantee publicly that it actually will implement the announced reforms and stick to them beyond the short term. McKinnon (1991) argues that an equilibrium trap may be particularly likely if governments face (unexpected) financial difficulties and if the pressure for quick solutions is relatively high. Then governments will be more likely inclined to intervene in economic processes in order to increase net revenues. Since private investors may anticipate government intervention, uncertainty with respect to economic policies will generate political risk and thus impede long-term economic performance.

More generally, politicians, who reflect multiple interest groups, cannot succeed acting alone, but need to strike bargains about rules and rights with other policy makers, business elites, and social groups with different interests. For example, in order to facilitate private-sector coordination and to foster economic growth, politicians and bureaucrats have to rely on the private sector, which is expected to provide reliable information and to increase private investment. Since future payoffs of alternative political choices, however, are uncertain *ex ante*, policies can be effectively implemented today only if agreements are made that guide future decisions. In order to reduce the costs of political bargaining, legislative exchange, and policy implementation, institutional arrangements must be put in place which facilitate the exchange over both time and space. They need to constitute *ex ante* agreements concerning the cooperation among different policy makers and between them and private business as well as important groups of society.[36] But studies on institutions and transaction costs stress the fact that, while organizations and individuals have numerous incentives to strike bargains, compliance to agreements *ex post* is often a critical problem (North and Weingast 1989). Of course, this kind of problem can be principally overcome by building up a good reputation and repeated play on the part of the agents involved in bargaining. Yet it is well known that there are many circumstances in which these mechanisms alone are insufficient to prevent non-compliance.

The preceding arguments indicate that economic institutions and policies that can be readily revised by policy makers have significantly different implications for economic performance than the same rules and policies when they are not subject to revision or when a revision is associated with high transaction costs. Therefore, for sustained economic development to occur, political institutions must be established that effectively bind political authorities to adhere to prior agreements and to use their powers in the public interest. This problem essentially comes down to the question of how *credible commitments* on the part of policy makers can be realized in order to help to overcome time inconsistent behavior and hence the potentially harmful effects of political discretion, opportunism, and arbitrariness. The argument to be elaborated here is that political institutions may provide the means which are suitable to make commitments credible.

As Shepsle (1991: 247; italics original) defines it, 'a *commitment* is a promise, pledge, vow, covenant, guarantee, or bond to perform in a specified fashion. A commitment is *credible* in either of two senses – the motivational and the imperative, respectively.' A commitment is said to be motivationally credible if it is self-enforcing in the sense that the respective party still wants to honor its commitment at the point in time when it is to be performed. More important in the realm of policy making, however, is commitment in the imperative sense. This means that the respective party 'is unable to act otherwise [at the time of performance; J.A.], whether he or she wants to or not; in this sense a commitment is credible, not because it is compatible with contemporaneous preferences but rather because performance is coerced or discretion to do otherwise is disabled' (ibid.). Since policy makers usually possess varying degrees of discretionary authority and are often not believed to be motivationally credible, they cannot credibly deny that they will behave opportunistically *ex post* even if such a denial would be truthful. They are credible only if they are willing and able to tie their own hands. Hence the necessity for policy makers credibly to commit themselves to policy reforms in the imperative sense underlines the importance of political institutions.

Disabling political discretion requires institutionalizing an asymmetry, that is, making it relatively easy to initiate new policies or to make agreements and making non-compliance relatively difficult. This can be achieved by the division of political labor. For example, the standing committee system of the United States Congress shows considerable advantages over a legislature which is subject to unstructured majority rule. In the former the committees have property rights over their respective jurisdiction and substantial agenda powers. They can exclusively set reform proposals or veto any changes concerning their jurisdictions. In the latter, reform policies are always threatened by potential reneging, because a legislative majority cannot bind its successor legislature and a (coalition) government cannot commit a subsequent government. In the United States, the former system is effective in assuring credible commitments because of another institutional peculiarity; members of Congress are assigned to those committees in the jurisdiction in which they show a vested interest. This implies that the composition of, and majorities in, committees remain largely unaffected even in the case of a substantial turnover in the legislature.[37]

In addition to the legislative committee system, several other institutional arrangements can enhance the credibility of reform policies. These include *inter alia* constitutional provisions and imperatives that, for example, prohibit the expropriation of private property; an independent judiciary; independent regulatory agencies; as well as the empowerment of multiple veto groups that may force unanimity between different political bodies such as the executive and the legislative branch of government. Similarly, institutional procedures may reinforce political structures and enhance the credibility and durability of decisions and policies. For example, procedural arrangements such as mandatory delays, which prescribe several deliberations before a status quo can be changed, raise the transaction costs of policy making and help to disable political discretion.[38]

So far the question of how to make political commitments credible has been discussed with particular respect to the durability and sustainability of public policies. But there is more to it as Lupia and McCubbins (1998a and 1998b) observe. Starting from the premise that a credible government commitment is not necessarily based on reputation, ideologies, partisanships, individual backgrounds, or repeated play, they find that political credibility results from three conditions, the satisfaction of which is significantly facilitated by specific institutional foundations. These determinants include the sincerity (or truthful revelation) condition, the capability condition, and the sustainability condition. All three components are necessary conditions for credible political commitments. First, recall that actions speak louder than words. Even if a government is able to implement reform policies, a lack of sincerity or truthfulness of political decision makers who support reforms by words, but not by deeds, is sufficient to ensure reform failure. Secondly, even if policy makers truthfully reveal what they actually mean, reforms will be doomed to fail and promises will be regarded as non-credible, if the government lacks the capability of technical implementation and of forming appropriate legislative and enforcement coalitions. Third, even if pivotal political actors are sincere and capable, policy reforms will fail if they cannot be sustained over time in the course of government changes or exogenous shocks. This implies that the three conditions are individually necessary and collectively sufficient to make political commitments believable.

Specific institutional arrangements, within which a pivotal political actor makes promises to the citizenry or a policy statement in negotiations with international organizations, can serve as substitutes for his personal attributes with respect to sincerity. An appropriate institutional context needs to increase opportunity and transaction costs for breaking, revising, or reneging on promises (for example, through bonding or signaling mechanisms).[39] Furthermore, in order to satisfy the capability condition, specific institutions are required to ensure technical capability of implementing reforms (for example, a competent and meritocratic public administration and bureaucratic procedures and administrative law setting the terms of delegation) and to ensure the effectiveness of a legislative and enforcement coalition (for example, appropriate agenda control mechanisms and institutional arrangements for the creation of ministerial positions and committees). Finally, in order to ensure the sustainability of reforms, institutions need to be in place which can protect policy reform beyond the enacting government's or political leader's stint of power (for example, veto gates in the governmental process and deliberation councils).

There is a broad consensus in the NIE literature that a credible government commitment is a necessary condition for successful policy reform. In addition, it is widely agreed that suitably designed institutional features (which complement reputation-building and associated punishment strategies) can impose effective restrictions on the *ex-post* behavior of policy makers and are primary devices to enhance the ability of governments to stick to their bargains and to deliver their promises to citizens.[40] Political institutions, in particular a country's constitution, play a critical role because they primarily determine the incentives of political actors and hence political outcomes in the form of economic rules and regulations and policies.

Two qualifiers to the credibility-enhancing effects of political institutions, however, are to be taken into consideration. First of all, whether a society is driven by the rule-of-law depends not only on its political institutions. Since constitutions, laws, and regulations can be politically ignored, altered, or removed, mechanisms must be put in place which allow for the policing of deviations by governments. Weingast's (1993 and 1995) analyses suggest that the effectiveness and maintenance of political institutions defining the legitimate boundaries of the state crucially depend on a consensus among citizens about the limits of government. This consensus, in turn, depends on the interaction of informal (opinions and attitudes of citizens) and formal institutions. In order to create a societal consensus during the development or transformation process, promoting the emergence of a civil society is of utmost importance. Formal institutions may become a focal point to help coordinate and align citizens' informal attitudes, so that (new) formal institutions of policy making and representation can be sustained. Thereafter, the constituency is better prepared to control government behavior and to react in concert against the government if it is perceived to transgress its legitimate boundaries.

Secondly, enhanced credibility through asymmetric institutionalization may come with a cost in that it implies a loss of policy flexibility. If political institutions are in place that effectively bind policy makers' hands today and in the future, it will become increasingly difficult to revise the course of policy reform, if external circumstances or the preferences of the constituencies change over time. Cox and McCubbins (1997) persuasively argue that too many veto points, which are controlled by political actors with diverse interests, may imply state indecisiveness and political stalemate.

These caveats imply that single institutional features alone, which help overcome credibility and incentive-compatibility problems, will be insufficient to ensure successful policy reform. Only a coherent and consistent set of political, economic, and social institutions including both formal rules and informal constraints will lay the structural and procedural basis that is appropriate to secure thriving markets, to ensure policy adaptability, and to implement policy reforms effectively. This finding indicates the need for an overall *governance structure* as a politico-institutional foundation of economic and social development. Hence, in important respects the logic behind political organization shows significant parallels to that underlying economic organization. Regarding the latter, Williamson (1985: 48–9) recognizes that

> Transactions that are subject to *ex post* opportunism will benefit if appropriate safeguards can be devised *ex ante*. Rather than reply to opportunism in kind, therefore, the wise (…) [bargaining party; J.A.] is one who seeks both to give and to receive 'credible commitments.' Incentives may be realigned, and/or superior governance structures within which to organize transactions may be devised.

When institutions and economic policy are seen as the focal points of the development problem, attention needs to focus on questions such as (1) what are the integral components of a politico-institutional foundation of policy reform; and (2) which conditions will be conducive to the emergence of an effective governance structure. The ramifications of the preceding arguments are developed more completely in subsequent chapters.

NOTES

1. For example, when exchange is costly, people may be unable (be it for lack of financial resources or political power) to realize the exchanges which offer them the highest payoffs. See North and Thomas (1973), Nabli and Nugent (1989a), North (1990a), Williamson (1985), and Bardhan (1989) for a critical discussion.

2. The terms *institutional innovation* and *institutional change* are used interchangeably in this study.

3. With respect to the different strands of literature in what is called the NIE see, for example, Lin and Nugent (1995), Clague (1997), Hodgson (1998), and Klein (1998).

4. See Eggertsson (1990) and North (1989). The early attempts at an explanation of institutional change are referred to as the naïve model, because they do not explicitly model political and social institutions.

5. Demsetz (1967: 350).

6. See, for example, Eggertsson (1990) and Pejovich (1997a) for references and examples.

7. Lin (1989a: 18) has put this issue very well: 'The rationality of the human mind, however, is bounded. It is beyond the capacity of the human mind to perceive all the necessary changes and to design all the optimal arrangements at the same time. The process of setting up a new institutional arrangement is also costly in terms of time, effort, and resources. Furthermore, individuals with different experiences and roles in the structure will have different perceptions of the degree and source of disequilibrium. They will also seek different ways of partitioning the gains from the change. For a new set of behavioral rules to be accepted and adopted, negotiation and agreement among individuals is required. Therefore, when disequilibrium occurs, the process of institutional change will most likely start from one arrangement and spread only gradually to other arrangements.'

8. For examples see, for example, Demsetz (1967), North and Thomas (1973, 1977), Ruttan and Hayami (1984), Barzel (1989), and Feeny (1989, 1993).

9. See Lin and Nugent (1995) and also Krueger (1988) for the relevance of knowledge concerning the regulation of the American sugar market.

10. Quoted in Ensminger (1992: 22).

11. Note, however, that the naïve model has been successfully applied to circumstances in which formal political institutions and processes play a minor role and that it has proved to be useful in making broad generalizations regarding property rights changes in prehistoric times; see North and Thomas (1977) and North (1981).

12. As Lin and Nugent (1995) observe, however, not all institutional arrangements are like public goods. In principle, an institutional innovation may be patentable. In that case, the introduction of a new institution resembles the production of a private good, and it can be undertaken without the need for collective action.

13. Moreover, dynamic aspects may play a significant role in causing collective action failures and institutional inertia. Individual decisions to contribute or not to collective action may be interdependent. Thus, concepts such as bandwagon effects (Leibenstein 1950) or critical mass (Granovetter 1978) may play a key role.

14. In this context, it is worth emphasizing that induced institutional change will not bring about more efficient institutions regardless of whether one draws on the naïve model or evolutionary theories of economic development. After all, it depends on the rules of the game, that is the structural conditions guiding institutional competition, or what kinds of institutions will be selected in the course of development (Vanberg 1996).

15. This implies, however, another crucial problem, because the incentives faced by governments and policy makers are not necessarily compatible with the collective interest. Governments have the means to modify the nature and the role of transaction costs and can either reduce their significance or magnify them thereby creating further sources of opportunistic behavior. This problem will be explicitly discussed in Chapter 5.

16. Olson (1965: 176). This distinction is usually not explicitly made in the literature on collective action problems. In some cases, the terms *political* and *institutional entrepreneur* are used as synonyms (Lin 1989a). In other cases, the term *political entrepreneur* describes a politician who seeks to provide collective goods to particular groups (Hardin 1982) or alternatively a leader of an interest group who is capable of overcoming diverse interests of group members and of suggesting institutional innovations which (seem to) leave each group member better off (Olson 1965).

17. See Olson (1965). Of course rational political entrepreneurs will supply collective goods and institutional innovations only as long as the expected marginal returns from the

innovation which accrue to the entrepreneurs exceed the marginal costs of mobilizing the resources that are necessary to provide these goods and institutions. Since the private return that accrues to the political entrepreneurs may be different from the social return, the institutional innovation will not necessarily be provided at a socially optimum level.

18. Similar types of coordination failures also occurred, for example, in the textiles and footwear industries in other East Asian countries. See Stiglitz (1996) and Rodrik (1995) for a more detailed analysis of this argument.

19. In this context, see the skeptical statement in Riker (1976). Regarding the weaknesses of legal systems in Eastern Europe and especially in Russia, see Voigt and Kiwit (1995).

20. The costs of political decision making include the opportunity costs that may result from a potential loss of political support from those social groups which may be badly affected by particular policy actions.

21. See, for example, Evenson and Westphal (1995) who compare similar protectionist policies to restrict technological imports pursued by India and South Korea.

22. The following arguments essentially draw on Lin (1989a) and Lin and Nugent (1995).

23. The notion of the predatory state is discussed in Evans (1995). Regarding the predatory regime in Zaire, see Callaghy (1984), with respect to the Philippines under Marcos see Overholt (1986) and Root (1996).

24. Park's role in Korea's economic development is discussed in Root (1996).

25. Besides the ruler's personality, of course, the existence of potential rival competitors for power (at home and abroad), the (potential) actions of the international community and the like may play important roles as well.

26. An example of a potential new source of information which may gradually undermine a rigid political ideology that is imposed on the people by authoritarian rulers is the Internet. The Chinese government, for example, seeks to restrict people's access to the Internet for fear that information and knowledge transferred from abroad may erode its power.

27. Regarding this problem see 'South Korea. Making a Comeback', *Economist*, 20 February, 1999 and 'Cutting down the chaebol', *Economist*, 14 November, 1998.

28. Besides informal institutions, formal political institutions are central to North's theory of institutional change. In fact, political institutions have received much attention in NIE for a long time. In particular, the rational-choice approach to politics, as outlined in Public Choice (for example, Buchanan and Tullock 1962 and Mueller 1989) as well as in positive political theory (for example, McKelvey 1976; Riker 1981; and Enelow and Hinich 1984), suggests that political institutions can be explained in terms of purposeful human choice. This framework has been applied to elections, legislatures, executives, courts, bureaucracies, and constitutions. Spatial models of voting, for example, illustrate how different voting procedures affect outcomes. The rational-choice perspective has also been used to analyse the effects of political institutions on public policy, including welfare policy, budget, regulation, and technology policy as well as overall macroeconomic policy (Weingast 1996). In his numerous works, North (e.g., 1981, 1990a, 1992, and 1994a) initially builds on the rational-choice model, but increasingly identifies its conceptual weaknesses and extends the model by including the notion of bounded rationality, the concept of ideology, and especially the impact of informal institutions on the creation of formal rules.

29. See North (1990b). Note, in this context, that a society's investment in formal education as well as basic and applied research may possibly be an even more essential determinant of the future development direction of its economy. This kind of investment will basically reflect the perceptions of political decision makers.

30. At times, however, it is not domestic organizations which trigger institutional change but individuals or foreign organizations. There have been situations in which economic reforms have been introduced by powerful political leaders (such as Gorbachev or Salinas) or imposed from the outside (for example, by Bretton Woods organizations' conditionality) and these could in turn slowly induce political changes. From the perspective of collective action, reforms would take place through the following sequence: exogenous policy reform changes the residual rents to assets and induces an intersectoral reallocation of resources

and migration. The resulting changes in income distribution alter the distribution of political power and hence the demands for government policy as well as new institutional arrangements.

31. See North (1990a, 1992, and 1995a) and Pelikan (1985 and 1987) for further elaboration. Pelikan, in particular, proposes an organizationally dynamic approach to comparative economics. Rather than relying on the dichotomy of markets *vs.* hierarchies, he recognizes that real economies are and must be made of both hierarchies and markets. Instead of comparing the functioning of given hierarchies and markets, his approach focuses on the question of how forms of coordination form and re-form. This aspect had already been stressed by Schumpeter (1976/1942: 84) who stated that 'the problem that is usually being visualised is how capitalism administers existing structures, whereas the relevant problem is how it creates and destroys them'.

32. North (1990a: 81–2) argues that '(w)e are far from understanding how to achieve adaptively efficient economies because allocative efficiency and adaptive efficiency may not always be consistent. Allocatively efficient rules would make today's firms and decisions secure – but frequently at the expense of the creative destruction process that Schumpeter had in mind. Moreover, the very nature of the political process encourages the growth of constraints that favor today's influential bargaining groups.'

33. Note that informal institutions are clearly not a policy variable. They can, at best, be changed indirectly, for example, through investments in a country's educational system or progress in social science research.

34. See Weingast (1993) and Bernholz (1993) for an instructive elaboration.

35. See North (1989) as well as the works of Dixit (1996), Kiewiet and McCubbins (1991), Krehbiel (1991), McNollgast (1989), Moe (1990), North (1990b), and Weingast (1984).

36. For a related argument see North (1990a).

37. See Weingast and Marshall (1988), Moe (1990), and Shepsle (1991).

38. Of course, a qualifier must be noted here: some political procedures show opposite effects; sunset legislation, for example, explicitly aims to reconsider and potentially revise existing policies, may impede the ability of policy makers to act according to medium and long-term plans and may undermine political commitments (Shepsle 1991).

39. Effective signaling, however, may be a costly effort and imply a policy-overshooting in order to make reforms credible; see Rodrik (1989). In order to check the accuracy of political statements and promises, scholars should analyse the structural and procedural factors that influence policy making. In this context they may, for example, investigate which actors can impose costs or penalties on the policy maker if he deviates from his promises, what types of costs can actually be imposed, and what are the links between the policy maker and his political supporters. Moreover, opportunity and bargaining costs of a political statement depend on the form of a statement (decree, regulation, coalition agreement, or resolution). Hence, knowing the form of a statement helps verify its accuracy. Verification will also be more likely if independent media, non-governmental organizations, and competing political parties are in place; see the comprehensive study of Lupia and McCubbins (1998b) for a thorough analysis of the institutional subtleties which are necessary and sufficient conditions to identify the sincerity of political statements.

40. See, for example, Weingast and Marshall (1988), North and Weingast (1989), Moe (1990), North (1990a), Borner *et al.* (1995), Weingast (1995), World Bank (1995a), Levy and Spiller (1996), and Lupia and McCubbins (1998a). With respect to the role of institutions for achieving credible commitment in the realm of macroeconomic policies see, for example, Persson and Tabellini (1990).

PART II

Governance: theory and practice

5. Governance and economic performance: conceptual considerations

An economy's ultimate success in narrowing the gap between its actual and potential rate of development critically depends on the political leadership's commitment and ability to implement and enforce appropriate policies. Poor economic management represents, according to Meier (1995: 65), the primary constraint to moving toward a higher trajectory of development. However, as yet, the practice of policy reform, that is the process of replacing inefficient policies with effective ones and the creation of effective management capacities, is not sufficiently understood. Since policy makers base their decisions on political rather than on economic incentives and dominant groups in society as well as public officials are all too often inclined to extract rents from established policies, there is a lack of incentive-compatibility between government policies and economic performance in many countries. What appears to be feasible politics does not necessarily turn out to be good economics. For that reason, students of economic development have been pessimistic regarding the chances of policy reform (Grindle and Thomas 1991). Addressing this problem requires specific study of the institutions related to development management. Taking the institutional structure of the political sphere into consideration implies a differentiated understanding of the political economy of policy reform.

Political scientists and development economists have repeatedly found that an intriguing combination of state strengths and state weaknesses characterize numerous countries in the developing world. On the one hand, most LDC states have been excessively powerful in regulating the economy and directly interfering in economic activity and social behavior. On the other hand, they have been chronically unable to enforce tax laws, resist pressure from interest groups, and implement coherent market-oriented reforms.[1] And yet, some LDC governments have been capable of committing themselves to an active, and sometimes even effective, promotion of national objectives, which did not favor any particular group in society and often contradicted the interests of powerful pressure groups. The emergence of these *developmental states* has been acknowledged in the literature.[2] But, as yet, their institutional, political, and social determinants have not been fully understood.

The disappointing experience with adjustment policies has begun to draw the attention of economic policy makers and international donor organizations to puzzling questions about the logic of government behavior and the institutional foundation of a developmental state. In order to conduct effective adjustment programs, LDC and PSC governments need to assume roles for which they have typically lacked the capacity and capability. The challenge of reforming the state is complicated by decreasingly available financial means which prevents governments from using public resources to minimize political opposition and conflict (Frischtak 1994). The paradox of the adjusting state precisely reflects its lack of institutional, administrative, technical, and political capacities. Regardless of whether a government decides to follow the policy recommendations of the Washington Consensus or whether it opts for a more activist role to overcome coordination failures and other market imperfections, a complex politico-institutional structure needs to be put in place in order to make government more effective in accomplishing whatever tasks it undertakes. Such institutionalization, however, cannot be taken for granted.

This chapter specifically addresses these problems from a conceptual perspective. A concept of governance is developed that can guide comparative politico-economic analysis and serve as an analytical foundation for elaborating country-specific strategies and policies that can be used to overcome politico-institutional impediments to policy reform and economic development. In the next chapter, this concept is empirically tested and subsequently applied to analyse governance structures in East Asia and Central and Eastern Europe (including Russia).

Effective policy reform not only requires credible commitments that political promises are actually delivered to citizens, but it crucially depends on the administrative capacity of state institutions, the relationships between a country's policy making entities and wider segments of society, and the technical and political capability of policy makers to shape and implement the policies which the political leadership seeks to pursue. In this regard, the *governance structure* underlying the process of policy making is of utmost importance. Subsequently, the concept of governance and its importance for successful policy reform are discussed. Following a definition of the term *governance* and an introduction to the concept of governance, the fundamental principles that constitute effective governance are introduced. In a next step, the analysis focuses on institutional problems that are related to creating a strong but limited government and to policy implementation and enforcement. Finally, the role of informal institutions for crafting effective governance structures is taken into account.

5.1 GOVERNANCE: WHAT'S IN A WORD?

The notion of governance is far from being new in the context of political development. On the contrary, it essentially refers to two of the most basic questions posed by political scientists since the foundation of their discipline: 'Who governs?' and 'How well?'[3] While the former question focuses on problems of distribution as well as redistribution, the latter points to problems of 'good government' which are related to institutional effectiveness and performance. However, the second question was largely disregarded by empirical political scientists due to the inevitable involvement of normative judgments. An exception to this general neglect of institutional performance has been the empirical research on political development in the 1960s and early 1970s.[4] In the mid-1980s, occupation with these questions reappeared in political sociology, when a new generation of researchers (re)directed scholarly attention to the issue of state capacity including its determinants.[5] As Skocpol (1985: 16), a leading proponent of the sociological approach, puts it, 'the capacity of states to implement strategies and policies deserve close analysis in their own right'. The proposed explanations for differences in states' capacities and capabilities include the level of economic development, bureaucratic structures, social structural conditions, elite strategies, class coalitions, political culture, historical heritages, and the international context of LDCs. The newly revived interest in the state, its relations to society, and its role in economic and social development has been due to various recent events and considerations. But six developments may have been of particular importance in motivating recent research: these include the widespread failure of economic adjustment programs as well as the misuse of public funds and corruption in many LDCs, the collapse of centrally planned economies, the fiscal crisis of welfare states, the collapse of nation states and the occurrence of humanitarian emergencies, the role of the state in the high-performing East Asian economies and more recently its role in the Asian crisis. Reinforced by these problems and developments, the questions pursued by political sociologists have been increasingly taken into account by empirical researchers in political science, public choice, and development economics as well as by international organizations.[6]

It was the World Bank (1989), which gave governance a prominent role on the economic development agenda, when it attributed the crisis of Sub-Saharan Africa to governance problems. The Bank specifically identified phenomena such as widespread corruption, the excessive personalization of political power, the neglect of human rights, and the persistence of non-accountable and non-elected governments as being key impediments to sustained development. Since the beginning of the 1990s, an increasing flow of scholarly publications and political pronouncements from major Western governments, NGOs as well as bilateral and multilateral development agencies followed; all of them dealing with issues relating to governance problems in LDCs and PSCs. Of course, as in political science, the discussion of appropriate political and institutional side conditions to sustained economic growth has a long history in economics, too, and is at least as old as the discipline of development economics and official development cooperation. It could even be found in so-called technocratic approaches such as Rostow's take-off scenarios.[7] What is new and notable about the new interest in the role of the state and political and social institutions in economic development is that the need for improved state action and institution building in the economic *and* political realm is postulated by an increasing number of scholars and policy makers. What is more, recent debates seek to elaborate a coherent and consistent approach to bring the issues of state capability and capacity to the fore of problems related to policy reform. The ongoing discourse in both academia and politics increasingly seeks to overcome the minimal-state doctrine prevalent in the 1980s and to integrate non-economic impediments to development under the label of governance.

Yet, whenever terms of political or economic philosophy are used in everyday language, caution is advisable. If these terms occur with increasing frequency in political soap-box oratory, increased alertness is required. The courted term may quickly lose its content-oriented substance and become meaningless. This is what happened to the concept of *governance* over the last decade. Until the beginning of the 1990s, the term governance was rarely used by development economists and policy makers. Since then, however, there has been a heightened awareness that the quality of a country's governance structure is a key determinant of its ability to pursue sustainable economic and social development. But as yet, a clear and operational definition of the term, agreed upon by a majority of scholars and policy makers, has not been formulated. At present, there is a confusing variety of definitions which greatly differ with respect to issues, problems, or objectives that are taken into account (see Box 5.1). Often, the term is used as a catchphrase in political discussions, and users of the term either do not offer any definition or seek to incorporate too many aspects so that the underlying concept turns out to be useless.[8] Some definitions prove to be completely redundant, for example, if governance is perceived as *good government*.[9] Some scholars highlight several substantive characteristics of a governance concept but either do not explicitly refer to governance or do not offer a proper definition.[10] Finally, some scholars interpret governance as an end in itself, while others see it as an analytical frame or as a means to promote sustainable development (Kjær 1996). The discussion on what constitutes

---

Box 5.1: Definitions of governance

- Governance capacity is defined 'as the ability to coordinate the aggregation of diverging interests and thus promote policy that can be credibly taken to represent the public interest'. (Frischtak 1994: vii)
- Governance is 'an interactive process by which state and social actors reciprocally probe for a consensus on the rules of the political game'. (Bratton and van de Walle 1992: 30)
- Governance means 'identifying economic and social objectives, and (...), charting a course designed to move society in that direction'. (Boeninger)[11]
- 'Governance (...) is the conscious management of regime structures with a view to enhancing the legitimacy of the public realm'. (Hydén 1992: 7)
- Governance is the 'capacity to establish and sustain workable relations between individuals and institutional actors in order to promote collective goals'. (Chazan 1992)
- Governance signifies 'the capacity to define and implement policies'. (Kjær 1996: 6, italics omitted)
- 'Governance is the science of government behavior and performance'. (Dethier 1999a: 5)

'good' governance still goes on in studies on development economics, the New Institutional Economics, political development, public economics, and in studies in public administration.[12]

Non-economists as well as development cooperation and aid agencies of Western governments tend to prefer a broad and often a politically non-neutral approach to governance that not only comprises the creation of market-oriented economic institutions but, at least equally important, the pursuit of democratization, the enhancement of human rights, political stability, and the enhancement of political legitimacy as an end in itself.[13] Economists, by contrast, frequently employ a too narrow and technocratic concept that focuses on public sector management, accounting and auditing standards, reform of the economic bureaucracy, problems of fiscal federalism, and the like.[14] Notwithstanding that these factors are critical to effective economic policy making, this approach overlooks other variables which have a significant impact on how economic policies are agreed upon, how they are implemented and enforced, and to what extent private agents comply with the established rules of the game. It ignores that development-enhancing governance is not easily available off-the-rack, but presupposes particular kinds of politics in order to institute and sustain it.[15]

In the realm of policy reform, some recent studies on the obstacles to structural adjustment address several critical elements for a suitable conceptualization of the term, but do not explicitly refer to the notion of governance.[16] Other approaches seek to conceptualize the term by addressing aspects which are critical from the perspective of economic reform, but the underlying definitions remain vague and hardly operational for practical matters. This is, for example, the flavor of the definition used by the World Bank (1992: 1) which defines governance according to Webster's Dictionary[17] as

> the manner in which power is exercised in the management of a country's economic and social resources for development. Good governance (...) is synonymous with sound development management.

Other conceptual approaches to governance view democratic government as an unalterable prerequisite for successful adjustment. In that sense, 'good' governance corresponds to democracy and keeps government small, ensuring that economics dominates over politics. Due to the historical experiences of industrialized countries and the assumption that democracy may provide a remedy against a big and potentially corrupt government, democratic institutions and processes are regarded as effective devices to secure thriving markets. However, the concept of democracy seems to be too broad for a proper operationalization. Furthermore, the derived thesis that democracy will automatically foster economic growth and development is empirically not well supported.[18] Hence, one may agree with Frischtak (1994: 12–13), who states that '(t)o build attributes to specific political regimes into the very concept of governance – quite apart from the fact that these attributes and norms may be worth promoting in their own right – detracts from the analytical utility and credibility of the concept'.

In order to address practical problems of policy making and policy reforms in LDCs and PSCs, a proper terminology and concept of governance is required that not only goes beyond the broad dimensions of democracy and autocracy but that avoids any prejudgments of the character or locus of real policy making (as the concepts of *government* or *leadership* do).[19] The definition ought to incorporate all key agents and institutions pivotal to reform and development and represent a suitable foundation for elaborating context-specific development strategies. A definition that avoids the vagueness of the terminology referred to above and is more practicable may be derived from conceptual considerations that address key issues of policy reform.[20] One conceptual underpinning to governance identifies the institutional capacities of state apparatuses as the crucial constraint to successful policy reform. This approach outflanks the debate on big versus small government and, instead, focuses on specific characteristics of the government machinery such as autonomy, rationality, efficiency, and technocratic capability which make public administrations less dependent on the disruptions of politics. Indeed, institution building has been increasingly recognized by the development community as a key ingredient of policy reform. This conception highlights some of the key constraints faced by adjusting states. But it will unfold its inherent potential to improve our understanding of the political economy of policy reform only if it can (1) succeed in identifying the conditions which will allow states to develop the required institutional capacity; and (2) adequately incorporate state–society relations in its analytical framework.

Another concept worth noting adds the dimension of informal institutions (culture, habits, traditions), which shape individual behavior and subjective perceptions, to the governance framework. This concept has been particularly influenced by experiences from sub-Saharan Africa, where artificially imposed political institutions as well as externally imposed standard development strategies were often interpreted as the root cause for the long-lasting crisis of governance and resulting adjustment failures.[21] Since economic and political transactions are embedded in networks of informal institutions (Granovetter 1985) including trust and personalistic relationships, the policy prescriptions inherent in this approach suggest that both development strategies and reform policies ought to be compatible with cultural characteristics and that effective governance needs to take the belief systems persisting in society into consideration (North 1992 and 1995a). With respect to sub-Saharan African countries, this conception would advocate the transition from strongly hierarchical, state-centered polities toward organizational arrangements which encourage self-governance of local communities and strengthen non-governmental organizations. This line of reasoning adds an important aspect to the discussion on governance, which has usually been neglected by the economics profession. It also implies that, because development is path dependent, there is no universal model of effective governance to be successfully applied to all LDCs and PSCs.[22]

This conception may be of particular importance for the systemic transformation of PSCs. For as several scholars have argued, the transition towards capitalism may be impeded by informal institutions which evolved in PSCs before and during socialist rule.[23] These include, for example, widespread pro-collectivist attitudes, nationalism, communalism, and habituation to political hierarchy. The philosophical heritage has neither been conducive to individualism nor to performance-contingent rewards nor to a constitutional state. '(P)eople see the gains from exchange as a redistribution of wealth within the community rather than as rewards for creating new value' (Pejovich 1994: 520). Also, many East Europeans did not perceive capitalism as a system based on self-responsibility, self-determination, and competition, but rather as a system automatically providing a great variety of goods and large incomes, the realization of which would neither require reducing 'socialist' welfare benefits nor changing the traditional work ethos. Therefore, 'the transition process was a crude awakening that capitalism is not merely about being rich' (ibid.: 522). These factors made the transformation process path dependent and induced hysteresis effects, so that capitalist behavioral norms as postulated by neoclassical reasoning could not emerge in the short run. This also means that creating capitalist institutions by fiat following textbook models will not yield the intended effects and involve acceptance problems, as the resurgence of pro-collectivist political parties indicates. Instead, it is argued that policy makers should seek citizens' compliance to transformation policies by allowing them to experiment with alternative institutions and to adopt those arrangements that succeed in the market test. A market for institutions (for example, regarding the choice of contractual agreements and the design of property-rights structures)[24] in association with the transfer of productive assets to non-elites would provide the underprivileged with upward mobility, contribute to overcoming hysteresis effects, and encourage a consensus for the support of economic reforms.

A third concept, which is closely related to problems of policy reform, views governance as an approach that comprises the establishment of abstract, universal rules, their enforcement mechanisms, as well as stable and transparent mechanisms of conflict resolution. This conception refrains from making any normative judgment concerning specific political regimes and rather follows Weber's (1972/1921) notion of the modern state. Weber proposed that the operation of markets requires a high degree of calculability based on legal rationality, the rational administration of justice, and a relatively insulated bureaucracy (characterized by a functional definition of duties and full-time devotion to administrative tasks), the work of which is not only based on instrumental rationality, but essentially on the development and enforcement of universal legal norms. In a similar way to Weber, who conceived that his ideal-type of state is most conducive to the functioning of modern capitalist societies, this conception also suggests that its notion of governance is the key to creating an environment conducive to policy making and business activities.

Last but not least, a fourth concept is important and should be taken into account. This is the notion of governance as introduced into the NIE by Williamson (1985, 1991, and 1995). This concept has been essentially applied to the modern theory of the firm. For our purposes, this approach is of great relevance for two reasons. First of all, the research conducted by Williamson and his followers on governance structures has made *governance* a technical term in the NIE with a distinct meaning and connotation. In order to avoid any misunderstandings, it is necessary to indicate the differences between this micro-analytic approach to governance and the concept to be developed in this study. Secondly, despite the differences in analytical perspectives and subject-matters, Williamson's approach may be a useful cornerstone to develop a governance concept that is suitable to analyse problems related to the political economy of policy reform and that may eventually contribute to the development of an adequate politico-institutional foundation of economic development.

Governance in Williamson's terminology refers to the organizational relations among economic actors.[25] Governance structures are defined as modes of contracting or as organizational constructions such as the firm.[26] Williamson (1996a: 4–5, emphasis in original) argues that '(n)ot only does transaction cost economics concur that the transaction is the basic unit of analysis, but governance is the means by which <u>order</u> is accomplished in a relation where potential <u>conflict</u> threatens to undo or upset opportunities to realize <u>mutual</u> gains. (...) Order is thus established by looking ahead, perceiving potential hazards, and factoring these hazards back into the design of governance, thereby to mitigate the hazards.'

Scholars of transaction cost economics argue that almost all transactions need to be guided by a governance structure in order to protect the parties involved in these transactions from the hazards that are associated with bilateral or multilateral exchanges. The appropriate institutions of governance depend on the attributes of the actual transactions. This micro-analytic approach to governance is characterized by the assumption that – due to bounded rationality – complex contracts are inevitably incomplete. Since, in reality, the future is full of genuine surprises, the availability of contracting options to transacting parties is limited. This, in turn, induces transaction costs associated with economic organization.[27] While uncertainty is relatively unimportant with respect to simple transactions (for example, the procurement of a component off-the-shelf), more complex transacting (for example, purchasing and installing specialized equipment) requires more sophisticated modes of contracting. Such contracts, however, will be incomplete and will only provide solutions for some conceivable contingencies. Examples are relational contracts (that is, agreements which define shared objectives as well as general principles which ought to govern the relations between the contracting parties) and implicit contracts (that is, unstated agreements which all parties are assumed to understand).

But transactions not only differ with respect to the uncertainty about future events and the actions of other parties that are involved, but also regarding the complexity of the terms of exchange, the frequency of specific transactions, and asset specificity. While all these characteristics matter for the establishment of appropriate governance institutions, the latter aspect is perceived to be of particular relevance for the mode of economic organization. Asset specificity is defined by Williamson (1985: 55) as 'durable investments that are undertaken in support of particular transactions, the opportunity cost of which investments is much lower in best alternative uses or by alternative users should the original transaction be prematurely terminated'. Asset specificity hence refers to various investments that are specific to particular relationships including, for example, investment in specialized human and physical capital as well as intangibles such as R&D, tacit knowledge, and capabilities. The phenomenon of asset specificity may imply severe problems. For after completion of the contract, the parties involved are to a certain degree locked in. Formal law offers only limited protection because many contracts are incomplete and court ordering may be beset with insurmountable problems. Hence, the party that makes smaller specific investments has an incentive to behave opportunistically (hold-up problem). This is often anticipated by the other party which seeks to protect itself against *ex-post* opportunism through private ordering. Court ordering therefore often needs to be complemented by private safeguards. The degree to which this is required for a specific transaction determines the choice of the governance structure by which this transaction is to be monitored and enforced.

Williamson (1995) argues that adaptation of economic agents and entities is the key problem concerning economic organization, and he concludes that a 'high-performance system will align transactions with governance structures in relation to their adaptive needs' (ibid.: 176). Contingent on the complexity of the transactions, adequate governance structures that further adaptation can be found along a wide spectrum. The spot market where anonymous exchange takes place represents the first pole that is sufficient for simple terms of transactions, because market prices provide incentives that are powerful enough to exploit profit opportunities and to make economic agents quickly adapt their individual plans to changing constraints and opportunities. However, when asset specificity plays a crucial role or when the number of market participants is relatively small, bilaterally coordinating investment decisions could be useful and joint ownership of these specific assets could be efficient. Hence, the fully integrated firm lies at the second pole of the spectrum, that is, a situation in which all transacting parties operate under unified ownership as well as control. Such hierarchies provide better protection against opportunistic behavior and entail relatively efficient institutional arrangements for coordinated decision making. But in contrast to decentralized governance structures, hierarchies may provide weaker incentives to managers with respect to profit maximization and may incur relatively high bureaucratic costs. Between hierarchy and markets, a number of hybrid modes of contracting exist including complex, long-term bilateral or multilateral contracts as well as arrangements of partial ownership. Hence moving along the spectrum from spot markets to a hierarchical form of organization implies a trade-off between adaptive properties and high-powered incentives typical for markets and the coordinating properties and safeguards provided by firms.

In sum, Williamson's approach to governance rests on three concepts comprising credible commitment, bureaucratization, and remediableness: first of all, complex transactions will take place only if opportunistic behavior on the part of the transacting parties can be avoided as much as possible. Therefore, it is necessary to identify, explicate, and mitigate possible contractual hazards, many of which lie in the details of organization and transactions. Hence, farsighted economic agents 'will recognize that better terms can be had by devising *ex ante* safeguards that communicate confidence [i.e., credible commitments; J.A.] by deterring *ex post* opportunism' (Williamson 1996a: 9; original italics). Credible commitments may involve reciprocal acts such as the exchange of hostages to safeguard a particular relationship. Hostages can basically yield *ex ante* as well as *ex post* effects; the former relying on screening and the latter on bonding mechanisms. In particular, the *ex post* effects can help to make agreements self-enforcing.[28]

Secondly, since all forms of economic organization are subject to opportunism, it is necessary to see firms and (public) bureaux as governance structures beset by agency problems rather than as technical entities that are characterized by stewardship behavior. The advantages of hierarchical forms of organizations *vis-à-vis* the market lie in their ability to foster coordination by internalizing externalities or coordinated adaptation to shocks. But organizational integration is not always an advantage. Asymmetries of information within firms and bureaux and between those who manage the organizations and those who are in charge of control tend to degrade incentive structures. This problem is aggravated by the propensity of transacting parties to seek their own advantage. Furthermore, a bureaucratic organization such as a large firm or a public agency is subject to changes over time, when members of the organization acquire more knowledge, and strategizing and coalitions emerge among the different parts of the organization. Because of the trade-off between coordination benefits and efficient incentives, it depends on the context whether hierarchies, markets, or hybrid forms of organization represent an effective governance structure.

Finally, the concept of remediableness refers to 'a comparative institutional criterion, according to which the appropriate test of "failures" of all kinds – markets, hierarchies, and bureaux alike – is this: an extant mode of organization for which no *feasible* superior alternative can be described and implemented with net gains is presumed to be efficient' (Williamson 1996a: 17–18; emphasis added). This criterion highlights the need not to compare actual forms of organization with any hypothetical ideal, but to analyse the cost-effectiveness and relative efficiency of alternative feasible institutional arrangements in practice. Institutions that seem to be inefficient by reference to an ideal though hypothetical model may actually be an effective mechanism to cope with poorly defined or costly-to-enforce property rights.

Williamson's approach to governance is essentially a constructive approach to institution building that is usually applied to organizational problems of developed market economies. It takes ideologies as well as the political and the property rights framework (and essentially the entire institutional environment) as a given. Moreover, it states that institutional arrangements are explicitly designed to reduce the costs of transacting, and it examines single organizations as relatively efficient solutions to the problems of structuring economic activity.[29] As we have argued in Part I of this study, these assumptions and conclusions do not hold in many circumstances that can be found in LDC and PSC settings. Nevertheless, Williamson's approach offers some useful inputs to the development of a policy-oriented (societal) notion of governance. His emphasis on opportunistic behavior, the significance of relational and implicit contracts, the utmost importance attributed to credible commitments, his view of governance as a means to establish order – all are factors that play a critical role in the process of policy reform as well.

Governance from a micro-analytic perspective has been an integral part of the NIE for a long time. By contrast, the interest in (societal) governance structures from a policy-oriented perspective, which has been becoming increasingly important in discussions about policy reform in LDCs and PSCs, has resulted from practical policy-oriented problems in underdevelopment as well as from political and other social science studies. Although policy-oriented governance has been clearly related to problems of institution building, the NIE has not yet played a significant role in elaborating a conceptual basis for this type of governance; either in the literature or in practical matters.[30] The different conceptual approaches discussed above promise to enhance our understanding of this (societal) type of governance, to overcome the existing deficits in NIE research, and to yield an appropriate comprehension of the term. For the purposes of this study, therefore, the following definition is proposed:

> Governance is the capacity of a country's institutional matrix (in which individual actors, firms, social groups, civic organizations and policy makers interact with

each other) to implement and enforce public policies and to improve private-sector coordination.

By this definition, governance *per se* is neither good nor bad. But for a particular country, the governance structure, that is the underlying institutional matrix (comprising formal and informal political, economic, and social institutions), is critical because different types of governance frameworks can have different development outcomes. For example, in its concrete form, a governance structure may promote the efficacy of policy reform or prove to be harmful for economic and social development. In some cases, governance structures may further the public interest over the narrow interests of powerful stakeholders. In other cases, it may give preference to economic over political or social development. In some countries, governance structures may favor short-term growth at the expense of sustainable long-term development, whereas other countries may have established frameworks which produce the opposite effects. Certain forms of governance may isolate a country's citizens from external influences, whereas other forms may overly favor external political or business interests.

In general, a governance structure affects the incentives of politicians, bureaucrats, and private economic agents alike and determines the terms of exchange among citizens and between them and government officials. This implies that the capacity of an existing governance structure is not only crucial for the proper use of public resources and donor transfers to LDCs and PSCs but plays a key role with regard to (1) the formation, implementation, and enforcement of economic and social policies as well as development projects; and (2) private sector development and coordination. Based on the above definition, the subsequent considerations emphasize and discuss only those governance issues which constitute the political foundation of policy reform *and* are basically subject to political design. On the one hand, this implies that the following analysis primarily focuses on political institutions. The importance of economic institutions such as property rights, private contracting, anti-trust regulations, and corporate governance has received broad attention in the literature and is not discussed at length in this study.[31] Moreover, the role of informal institutions is only implicitly analysed in as far as informal constraints can or should be taken into account when crafting political institutions. On the other hand, this implies that governance is not restricted to what Dethier (1999a) calls *public governance* (that is, the quality of government, its internal organization, and the laws and decisions made by public officials). The term also encompasses the institutional relations between different levels of government as well as between the government and society.

The analytical approach to governance not only focuses on issues such as prices, discretionary power, and voting rules as determinants of individual behavior and political and economic outcomes, but draws attention to the role of information, incentives, as well as control rights over scarce resources. Government (like market) failure is frequently rooted in informational, transactional, and political constraints. Informational constraints that limit efficiency include adverse selection and moral hazard. Transactional constraints evolve chiefly due to the incompleteness of contracts. Inherent in governance structures are agency relationships which are frequently more complex in the political sphere than in the economic realm. Multiple principal–agent problems which are inherent in policy reform can take different forms: (1) the government acts as an agent of the constituents; (2) government agencies and bureaux act as the agents of the political leadership. Moreover, even legislatures, courts, private interest groups, and media possibly try simultaneously to influence the decisions of agencies, which often have to perform different (conflicting) tasks; and (3) bureaucrats also act as principals for private firms whose behavior is to be influenced. Thus, multi-principal/multi-task agencies embedded in a multiple-level principal–agent framework exist in reality, which further aggravates the problems of the classical principal–agent game (Dixit 1996). Under these circumstances, the formulation and implementation of public policies are subject to various restrictions (imperfect and asymmetric information, difficulties in monitoring bureaucratic input and output as well as private agents, opportunistic behavior, multiplicity of interests, bounded rationality, and time inconsistency), all of which cause political transaction costs.

Instead of imposing additional formal constraints on administrative units, as is often observed in government bureaucracies (Wilson 1989), effective governance requires more sophisticated institutional arrangements with powerful incentive schemes and screening, signaling, and monitoring mechanisms, which imply a fusion of interests of politicians, bureaucrats, business people, and non-elites. In this context, it is to be noted that institutional arrangements which may contribute to mitigate these principal–agent problems are typically characterized by a trade-off between risk sharing and efficiency so that the outcome is usually a second best. The foregoing also indicates that political and legal institutions not only determine the mandates of public agencies and officials (relating to the scope of the activities assigned to them), the feasible instruments of policy making as well as the procedural processes that have to be observed. They also determine the degree to which vested interests can influence public policies and the degree of incentive-compatibility of economic performance and policy making (Dethier 1999a). The quality of a country's governance structure matters in the presence of these constraints. Hence, effective development management not only requires that the 'right' policies and policy instruments be selected, but also that suitable institutional incentive schemes that ensure credible government commitment be created.

A governance structure is *effective* if it ensures that policies and projects conducted by governments are properly implemented and enforced, that private businesses can thrive within a given legal and regulatory framework which is not subject to arbitrary political interference, and eventually that the adaptive efficiency (in the Northian sense) of both the polity and the economy is enhanced. From this perspective, effective governance is independent of the basic character of a political system (the regime type). Thus, in itself our governance framework is drawn up as a politically neutral concept, and for the purposes of this study it ought to be. Numerous empirical studies suggest that there is no evidence that either democratic or non-democratic states are better suited to initiate and consolidate policy reforms effectively and to promote sustained economic development.[32] Furthermore, even democracies differ considerably from one another along various dimensions, including their structural characteristics (for example, parliamentary vs. presidential systems), the degree of political stability, the openness of their policy making processes, the degrees of political participation, and their developmental outcomes. As we will argue below, some of the most successful economic performers over the last three or four decades have been (at least in their early stages of economic take-off) non-democracies. Notwithstanding that democratization may be a desirable objective in itself and that sustained economic and social progress may further democratic development over time, the governance concept proposed here rests on the premise that a democratic order is neither necessary nor sufficient for successful policy reform.

The notion of effective governance is not only important for sustained development of LDCs. It is not only an analytical tool to understand better the obstacles to effective economic reforms, to find ways of overcoming market and government failures, and to explore the political opportunities to make institutional change more efficient. Particularly in many economies in transition, more is at stake if policy reforms fail, including the collapse of social and public organizations and institutions in the course of the systemic transformation, as well as the danger of political, economic, and social instabilities and a substantial loss of public legitimacy.

The study of governance as defined here is performance-oriented. It examines how well a polity is capable of establishing institutional arrangements and mobilizing and managing physical, human, and social capital so as to strengthen the preconditions for sustained catch-up processes. When the ways are to be explored in which politics and especially political institutions may strengthen the public realm and its role in economic and social progress, the notion of governance takes on distinctive importance. The general proposition here is that the more that development management is reflected by the qualities that are associated with effective governance the more it induces political legitimacy and the more private agents will comply with the given rules and regulations and accept policy changes.[33]

5.2 THE DIMENSIONS OF EFFECTIVE GOVERNANCE

The multi-faceted concept of governance is of critical relevance for the formulation and implementation of overall development strategies and policies, for the change of economic, political, and social institutions, and for the quality enhancement of sectoral projects. *Effective* governance is a normative concept with distinct principles or norms which must be realized in order to achieve a particular set of objectives. For the purposes of this study, these objectives comprise the improvement of the adaptive efficiency of a national economy and polity, the enhancement of the incentive compatibility of policy making and economic performance, and hence the effective enforcement of policy reforms and, ultimately, sustained economic development. While acknowledging the relative (and invariably subjective) nature of any assessment of governance, it is useful to attempt to define as explicitly as possible the norms and principles that could be used for such an assessment in the context of economic policy reform.[34]

While market performance is usually induced through choice and exit options available to economic agents, government performance requires other channels which help to discipline political authorities through the exercise of voice (Hirschman 1969). The capacity of institutions and the capabilities of policy makers to implement and enforce reform programs reflect five fundamental principles that guide the strategic interactions among public officials and between them and private agents. These key principles constitute effective governance structures. They include accountability, credibility, participation, predictability, and transparency, all of which are required for the sound management of public resources, an enabling environment for the private sector and a productive partnership between the public and private sectors that does not degrade into closed circles of influence and privilege. Governance provides the overall perspective from which these principles are derived.[35] Credibility or credible commitment (in the sense used by Lupia and McCubbins (1998a and 1998b)) represents the all-embracing principle constituting effective governance.[36] As numerous theoretical and empirical studies as well as case studies indicate, without commitments that are credible on the part of the policy makers neither effective policy reform nor sustained development can be expected.[37] At best half-hearted reforms or single development projects are likely to be conducted in their absence. Ensuring political commitment is not a simple controlling-the-controller problem (Borner *et al.* 1995). As discussed in Section 4.4 of Chapter 4, the Lupia/McCubbins approach to credible political commitment rests on three conditions, namely sincerity, capability, and sustainability. Various institutional arrangements exist that could help to fulfill these conditions better. Since, however, these governance-enhancing institutions may differ from country to country, we propose to define the dimensions of effective governance according to four core principles which together promise to enhance the credibility of a government's commitments and eventually the quality of an overall governance structure.

Accountability is not only a morale, but an important instrument to survive politically.[38] Often, democratic rules, and especially elections, are conceived as the crucial standard that constitutes accountability. But experiences in LDCs, particularly in an East Asian context, indicate that political accountability and accountability for public-policy performance are not necessarily the same. Accountability for the outcomes of policies cannot be guaranteed by political elections (Root 1996). Broadly defined political accountability may become less effective the more roles governments assume and the more actions are undertaken by the state. Then mechanisms that strengthen micro-level accountability become more important with respect to both government activities at the regional and local levels as well as to functional or sector-specific actions.

Basically, accountability means making politicians and bureaucrats responsible for their actions and overall government policies and avoiding the capture of the state by narrow interests. Mechanisms that constitute accountability involve not only the de-politicization of the public administration but also networks of institutional arrangements linking the different branches of government, various government ministries, public agencies and bureaux, public organizations and external audit agencies as well as public organizations and non-governmental organizations, intermediaries, and the private sector. Lack of accountability may reduce the credibility of political authorities as economic partners. This could eventually trigger private investors to reduce productive, long-term investment and thus imply sovereign risk. But public accountability, in particular, is difficult to ensure. This is because in most cases evaluation needs to focus on inputs (usually on public expenditures) due to the difficulties related to measuring public outputs or the effects of government action. Additionally, in numerous countries independent, external watchdog or monitoring agencies are absent. Instead, governments rely on internal, hierarchical control mechanisms which are often ineffective due to collusion between different individuals or public bureaux.

What kind of accountability mechanisms work varies widely among countries and is subject to context-specificity. Factors such as the existing political institutions, bureaucratic capacities, the degree to which private agents have access to information and the means to use exit and voice options, history as well as cultural characteristics, all play an important role. To be effective, accountability presupposes the definition of expected performance criteria relating to the compliance with certain rules or the achievement of particular performance levels. With respect to policy reform, accountability refers to the design of development-enhancing reform programs, making these congruent with their implementation and enforcement and eventually ensuring an efficient use, stewardship, and allocation of resources. This requires, on the one hand, competent policy making, that is adequate government capacities and capabilities to take and implement decisions at the right time and to manage public service delivery, and, on the other hand, the establishment of agencies of restraint (such as anti-corruption offices and ombudsmen) and monitoring devices both for overall economic policies as well as public procurement and investment. Hence, criteria and oversight mechanisms need to be introduced both at the national and sub-national levels which assess public officials' performance and ensure the observance of standards and norms. Economic accountability, especially with regard to public finances, needs to rely on devices such as accounting and auditing systems that are suitable to evaluate the performance of public agencies. Moreover, not only are governments to be held accountable for their actions, but private economic actors as well. This need underlines the importance of legal and regulatory institutions and competition policy.

Participation is often an objective of development in itself because it is expected to enhance citizens' independence, autonomy, and self-reliance. But participation also plays a critical role in strengthening governance structures. More specifically, it reinforces accountability because it provides the means by which citizens may exercise influence and control over decisions and actions of their governors.[39] It thus stresses the voice option of citizens to hold public officials responsible if they transgress their rights or fail to observe their duties. This requires institutionalized channels through which individuals can actively participate in enforcing rules, for example, procedurally simple access to independent judicial agencies and swift use of legal institutions in order to remedy the outcomes of discriminatory actions or policy incompetence on the part of the political authorities (Borner *et al.* 1995). An obvious, though imperfect, instrument for exerting political pressure from below is elections in democratic states. But opposition forces can even influence policies in authoritarian regimes as, for example, in South Korea where opposition to the regime triggered a change in social policies.

Participation also provides channels to make policies more responsive to the needs of the beneficiaries. The outcomes of public policies often depend on the cooperation and support of societal groups which are affected by them. This may require more or less citizen representation, which could range from consultative committees to community councils to a popularly elected legislature or forms of direct democracy. Similarly, participatory mechanisms can reinforce accountability at the micro level and make development projects more effective by allowing beneficiaries to become actively involved in project design and implementation.

Participation usually goes hand in hand with some sort of decentralization, especially when there is a unity of interest of the local elite and the poor or other broad segments of the local community. But to be effective, it sometimes requires the support of the central government.[40] This particularly holds, for example, with respect to issues such as land reform or the provision of agricultural credit. In situations in which the allocation or distribution of scarce resources and goods is at stake, the local elite may be inclined to undermine reform efforts. Central legislation may also be needed to provide access to education, credit, and health care; that is services that are often prerequisites for enabling the poor to participate. Without central support, powerful elites at the local level may capture participatory decentralized organizations. Moreover, finance of these organizations frequently depends on central government involvement.

But note that participation is no panacea that will work in all areas at all times. Effective participation necessitates transparent institutional arrangements that will actually be enforced. Moreover, there are areas in which participatory mechanisms have to be modified or complemented, for example, regarding development issues that require technical know-how and decisions such as exchange rate policies, the design and implementation of irrigation projects, or the introduction of a credit system, all of which need technical expertise. Then the question is rather how to hold these experts accountable to the public and to ensure their cultural and social sensitivity. A simple call for participation is insufficient. This general postulate needs to be supplemented by institutional arrangements and administrative structures which ensure proper formulation and implementation of policies and which determine what decisions are to be taken by whom at what point in time.

Predictability relates to the clearly-defined laws and policies that regulate the economy and society as a whole, to the clear and explicit communication of the laws and other rules to the business sector and private actors (including citizens' rights and duties) as well as to their consistent and impartial application and enforcement. Generally, it is absent in societies that are based on rules by authority that is vested in individual persons. Effective predictability is contingent on the existence of a rule-based system that binds public officials and private actors alike. This is an essential precondition for stabilized expectations of domestic and foreign entrepreneurs and their investment decisions. It also helps to provide assurance against arbitrary political interference in private transactions. Adequate organizations and institutions are the key to enhance predictability. These comprise, for example, independent central banks, anti-trust agencies, an independent judiciary as well as institutional arrangements protecting government ministries and agencies against political opportunism and insulating the economic bureaucracy from the influence of special interests. Moreover, in order to create the preconditions for enhancing the adaptive efficiency of both the political and economic order, publicly-known amendment procedures must be in place which allow the rules to be changed if they fail to serve their purposes.

Transparency emphasizes the need for timely, relevant, and reliable information about market conditions, technological developments, information-intensive businesses such as those operating in capital markets, government policies and future actions and so on to be made available to economic actors if a competitive market-based economy is to flourish. Governments 'may enjoy two important advantages with regard to the production and diffusion of information: credibility and economies of scale' (Klitgaard 1991: 81), and, in fact, they usually play a central role even in LDCs and PSCs not only in providing information, but also in setting requirements for private organizations to disclose their information. Publicly providing information and facilitating the exchange of information between the public and the private sector can help to reduce transaction costs and be superior to pure market search. Moreover, the transparent provision of information on policy making and implementation (in association with clear and straightforward decision-making procedures) helps to reduce opportunities for corrupt behavior, improves the analysis and articulation of public policy choices, and enhances their acceptance.

These four principles are clearly interrelated and reinforce each other. Institutional arrangements that further these principles are expected to provide those incentives that are conducive to effective policy making and developmental outcomes. More fundamentally, the adherence to these principles enhances the prospects for the emergence of an adaptively efficient institutional matrix, the foundations of which were discussed in Section 4.3 of Chapter 4. Obviously, the full realization of these principles, especially accountability, participation, and transparency, can hardly be expected to occur in totalitarian or other non-democratic regimes. At first glance, the adherence to these principles seems to contradict our politically-neutral concept of governance. Notice, however, that in the developmental states of East Asia, most of which successfully managed to catch up with more advanced economies under rather authoritarian regimes, key elements of effective governance were not absent. Therefore, it is useful to deepen the analysis of governance structures in order better to understand their contributions towards making policy reforms more effective. Following Wohlmuth (1998), we propose to distinguish between governance issues at the macro, the meso, and the micro level of a societal order. Effective macro-level governance may come close to the notion of a liberal democracy by referring to the full realization of the five core principles of governance including *inter alia* the adherence to the rule of law, separation of powers, overall administrative accountability, and freedom of association and expression. Meso- and micro-level governance issues refer to circumstances at sub-national and sectoral levels and specific functions or parts of governments such as particular government agencies and ministries and their relations with the private sector. In these subordinated realms, actual conditions may reflect the overall principles to varying degrees. Hence, we follow Wohlmuth (1998: 9) in presuming that '(w)hatever the quality and extent of macro-governance, the degree of meso- and micro-governance can vary by quality and extent'. Even in countries with unfavorable structures of macro-level governance, functioning institutional structures at the meso and micro level can exist. This implies that effective governance sub-structures can be found in particular sectors, regions, and communities as well as in some parts of the economic bureaucracy which enhance the prospects of reforms and promote development. This fact is important to note as it helps to explain how effective overall governance structures may evolve over time; a problem to be discussed in Section 7.1 of Chapter 7.

5.3 IMPROVING THE QUALITY OF POLICY MAKING THROUGH INSTITUTION BUILDING

Effective governance, like the notion of governance proper, refers not to a single type of system, but to a set of disparate institutional systems. Systems of effective governance represent a subgroup of all governance structures, which is distinguished by its developmental outcomes and its relatively high degree of adaptive efficiency. These systems are characterized by a flexible *market-enhancing governance structure* (MEGS), which shows comparatively high degrees of accountability, participation, predictability, and transparency. The purpose of this section is to elaborate what it takes to institute such a structure. Although the required steps and their institutional components are interdependent and mutually reinforcing, it is useful analytically to distinguish various levels of institution building. These include (1) the need to enhance state capability and hence to create a state that is able to protect property rights, enforce contracts, and implement policy reforms; (2) the need to limit state authority in order to avoid predatory government behavior; (3) the need for capacity building as a precondition for technically, administratively, and politically implementing and enforcing reform policies; and (4) the need to create key economic institutions for enhancing and sustaining markets. In addition, the question of informal institutions must be explicitly addressed. Since there are limits to intentional institution building and due to the potential conflict between existing informal rules and norms on the one hand and politically crafted formal institutions on the other hand, it is to be discussed how, if at all, the impact of informal arrangements can be taken into account in governance-related institution building. These conceptual-theoretical considerations provide the starting point and benchmark for the discussion of empirical investigations on governance (Chapter 6, Section 6.1), particular country cases (Chapter 6, Sections 6.2 and 6.3), and eventually the question of how flexible MEGS can evolve over time (Chapter 7, Section 7.1). An essential benefit of this approach to effective governance is that it provides the basis for a comparative theory of governance, because it allows the economic performance of countries with different governance-related characteristics to be predicted.

5.3.1 State Strength, Administrative Capability, and Credible Commitments

MEGS essentially rest on three subgroups of institutions: formal political norms, rules, and regulations, formal economic institutions, and informal constraints. Regarding the functioning of a market-oriented economy, all of these institutional arrangements including their enforcement characteristics play crucial roles. To understand the political foundation of policy reform, however, we must begin with the set of institutions that govern policy making, that is the *political institutions* of society. In this context, political institutions comprise the formal rules and informal constraints (including their enforcement characteristics) that directly affect political decision-making processes in the course of economic development.[41] The political institutions of a country's governance structure play a dominant role with respect to problems of initiating, implementing, and sustaining economic reform policies, because they determine how different actors are involved in political processes, what kinds of reforms are politically feasible, and how the behavior of individual actors is shaped. After all, the structure of political institutions shapes the interactions of individuals to determine the outcomes of public policies.

Competent statecraft has been, and remains, critical to economic development. But successful government action is unconceivable without state authority, organizational coherence as well as well-structured relations with society. The effectiveness of governance structures in general and political institutions in particular is essentially shaped by the incentive structures they provide resulting from the structural characteristics of states. 'Different kinds of state structures create different capacities for action. Structures define the range of roles that the state is capable of playing. Outcomes depend both on whether the roles fit the context and on how well they are executed' (Evans 1995: 11). Moreover, government activities usually vary across sectors. What kind of role governments can play is contingent on the organizational and technological characteristics of a given sector. The effectiveness and consequences of public policies in turn depend on the institutional capacity of the state and on how well the government is prepared to resist the pressure of vested interests. But government capacities and capabilities are always in short supply given the demands on the state. This led the World Bank in its 1997 *World Development Report* to suggest a two-part strategy. The first step for a government is to match its role to actual capability, that is to reduce its tasks and realize a better focus of policies. The subsequent and time-consuming step is to build additional capabilities, that is to reinvigorate, and in many cases to invigorate, formal institutions and to safeguard sensible policies in order to enhance the state's ability to conduct and foster collective action efficiently. This refers, for example, to the need to make state agencies subject to enhanced competition, to improve the performance of public bureaux, and to make government more responsive to the needs of citizens. Institution building, however, not only means enhancing technical or administrative capacity but also instituting norms and rules that provide government officials with incentives to pursue collective ends while restraining arbitrary action and corruption. But what are the appropriate institutional arrangements that align incentives of political officials and citizen welfare? How do governments commit themselves to efficiently providing public goods and preserving market incentives?

In numerous LDCs and PSCs, the public administration is inefficient and unable to manage policy reforms. Legal systems are often based on imprecise and weak laws and regulations, opening the door for substantial executive or administrative discretion. Policy makers frequently collaborate or act in collusion with precisely those powerful private actors they are actually supposed to control and supervise. Such states are weak or soft in Myrdal's (1968, 1970) sense. They are essentially based on nepotism and personal connection. Under these circumstances, governments are unable to implement policies that contradict the interests of powerful pressure groups or the bureaucracy. They cannot credibly precommit to particular policies and merely react to demands and actions of private actors, pressure groups, and political parties. Typically, interventionist policies cannot be implemented and enforced in a consistent manner. Policies of soft states are dominated by too many market-distorting interventions (resulting from rent-seeking activities of lobbying groups), while market-enhancing interventions (to correct market or coordination failures) are neglected (Bardhan 1995). This implies that economic reform measures, property rights, and contracts are not durable. Moreover, in states that lack the mechanisms to control public officials, policy makers can act independently. For example, one part of the government may announce a policy reform, while other parts block its implementation. In these cases, the lack of effective enforcement devices makes rules meaningless and hinders private business activities unless a powerful political actor, such as an inner circle of the executive or the president's family, intervenes. Recall, for example, the role of the Communist Party's Politburo in the former Soviet Union or the style of policy making in Russia under Yeltsin, in the Philippines under Marcos, or in Indonesia under the rule of Suharto. Weak states, which are not capable of enforcing the basic conditions for enhancing and preserving competitive markets, can hardly sustain or even initiate policy reforms. Instead, cronyism and nepotism play an important role in sustaining the exchange of goods and services. Since under these circumstances collusion between public officials and powerful private interest groups is likely to occur, a soft state may easily become a so-called predatory state (Root and Weingast 1996).

Thus, the first (tentative) part of an answer to the above questions is to create a strong state as postulated by many studies on the role of the state in economic development.[42] These studies share the conviction that state strength is a necessary condition for undertaking growth-enhancing economic reforms. States are regarded as strong if they show at least two characteristics which help to overcome problems of collective action: (1) States must be autonomous and hence insulated from the influence of private pressure groups in order to formulate policies independently. (2) States need to exhibit high degrees of centralization and internal cohesion in order to overcome collective action and principal–agent problems and to implement policies effectively (Doner 1992). A strong state is conceived as a *conditio sine qua non* for enhancing the capability and sustainability of policy making. State strength helps to avoid the capture of the state apparatus by narrowly defined interest groups, enhances political stability as well as the long-term predictability of the political system and hence can contribute to stabilizing the expectations of private entrepreneurs and prolonging the time horizon of policy makers.

Frequently, the postulate of a strong state is associated with the notion of the so-called *capitalist developmental state*. The term is due to Johnson (1982), who originally introduced the idea of the developmental state into modern Japan's history of industrial policy.[43] The theory of the capitalist developmental state was inductively developed based on the experiences of the fast-growing economies of Japan, South Korea, and Taiwan in order to underline the differences between the market economies in the West, notably the United States and Great Britain, and those in North East Asia.[44] In Chang's (1999: 192) words: A state is called developmental if it 'can create and regulate the economic and political relationships that can support sustained industrialization (...) [and if it; J.A.] takes the goals of long-term growth and structural change seriously, "politically" manages the economy to ease the conflicts inevitable during the process of such change (but with a firm eye on the long-term goals), and engages in institutional adaptation and innovation to achieve those goals.' According to Johnson (1987: 140, 142–3),

> (d)evelopmental states are generated and come to the fore because of the desire to break out of the stagnation of dependency and underdevelopment; the truly successful ones understand that they need the market to maintain efficiency, motivate the people over the long term, and serve as a check on institutionalized corruption while they are battling against underdevelopment. (...) A developmental elite creates political stability over the long term, maintains sufficient equality in distribution to prevent class or sectoral exploitation (land reform is critical), sets national goals and standards that are internationally oriented and based on nonideological external referents, creates (or at least recognizes) a bureaucratic elite capable of administering the system, and insulates its bureaucrats from direct political influence so that they can function technocratically. It does *not* monopolize economic management or decision making, guarantee full employment, allow ideology to confuse its thinking, permit the development of political pluralism that might challenge its goals, or waste valuable resources by suppressing noncritical sectors (it discriminates against them with disincentives and then ignores them).

The main characteristics of the developmental states in North East Asia, although realized to varying degrees across countries and within countries over time include: (1) stable political rule ensured by a political-administrative elite that does not accede to political pressures which could impede economic growth; (2) cooperation between the public and the private sector that is guided by a pilot economic planning agency; (3) continuing investment in universal education and policies that aim at a more equitable distribution of opportunities and wealth; and (4) a government whose members understand the need for market-conforming policies and interventions (Johnson 1987, 1999).

A most critical feature of a strong (developmental) state is the necessity to ensure the autonomy of both the economic bureaucracy and the political elite who are in charge of strategy formulation, actual decision making, and implementation. The challenge lies in avoiding the situation where policy makers become captives of their major 'clients', especially of those who represent big private business. In order to avoid public–private cooperation leading to the formation of policy goals that are plainly reducible to private sector interests, institutional arrangements, the access of policy makers to funds, and the sources of their political power play a significant role. State autonomy from vested interests is more likely to evolve the more funds can be developed that are not provided from private business (for example, through direct contributions or loans from abroad as in South Korea or through the operation of SOEs as in Taiwan).[45] Of at least equal importance is the independence of the economic administration proper. Economic policies need to have a long-run focus, be consistent, and rely on complementary policy instruments. This holds for public policies in general and even more for selective industrial policies. Therefore, policy makers who seek to implement a coherent, long-term development strategy must be able (at least partly) to depoliticize economic decision making. This is why most contemporary adherents to the developmental state regard bureaucratic autonomy from social entanglements as a constituent characteristic of developmental states. In these states, depoliticization is facilitated through a separation of reigning and ruling actors. While politicians determine broad policy goals and protect the public administration from vested interests, the bureaucrats are in charge of planning and implementing policies and guiding the economy. Moreover, as Pempel (1999a: 160) notes, 'technocrats and bureaucrats enjoy disproportionately high levels of power and wield a variety of tools to enforce their will. State actors are also relatively free from major populist pressures, most especially from organized labor and organized peasants.'

The organizational design of, and the incentives within, the public sector are crucial to the developmental consequences of government policies.[46] Any kind of coherent policy reform necessitates the establishment of a public administration that is capable of implementing and enforcing overall macroeconomic policies, property rights, and specific policy measures. But how can such a bureaucracy be created? In *Economy and Society*, Max Weber (1972/1921) offered a powerful hypothesis as to what type of internal organization of the state is appropriate to give polities the capacity to enhance markets and promote economic growth. He proposed that the operation of markets requires a high degree of calculability based on legal rationality. This is to be provided by the development of formal law and the rational administration of justice. In his framework, the bureaucracy, characterized by a functional definition of duties, full-time devotion to administrative tasks, and relative independence of societal pressures, is an important tool in the construction of an advanced market economy. For Weber, the state's ability to enhance and complement markets depends on the administration representing a corporately coherent entity in which bureaucrats see the pursuit of corporate goals as the best way to increase their individual welfare. A corporate identity that aligns bureaucrats' objectives with those of the political leadership, requires civil servants to be shielded from societal pressures. Insulating the administration is helped by giving bureaucrats a distinctive status.

Administrative professionalism is a necessary but not a sufficient condition for development-enhancing outcomes of public policies. Other institutional key features of a Weberian-type bureaucracy include replacing political appointments and dismissals by meritocratic standards in promotion and in recruitment based on competitive examinations, providing civil servants with opportunities for long-term career rewards, and setting transparent rules for hiring and firing. This will improve the expertise in the bureaucracy, create commitment, and increase the administration's effectiveness.[47] However, for making meritocratic personnel policies work, governments need to place strong emphasis on education policies in order to create a pool of highly qualified potential civil servants. The establishment of an effective public administration is a complex task. But it is not as time-consuming and difficult as one might expect. Countries as diverse as South Korea and Taiwan or France and Austria, whose bureaucracies were considered to be incompetent, ineffective, and non-meritocratic in the first half of the 20th century and even into the 1950s, managed within some 20 years to establish high-quality public administrations through comprehensive civil service reforms.[48]

The preceding arguments illustrate the importance of state strength and bureaucratic capability. But the ability to formulate reform policies independently and to implement them properly will only yield developmental improvements if the announcements, promises, and actions of policy makers are credible. And at this point there is a significant weakness in the notion of a strong state and the theory of developmental states. If a development-oriented political leadership is in power in such a state, it will have some means at its disposal to signal and document its commitment, for example, through specific investments in the educational and health infrastructure, through opening up the economy (and hence allowing for international competition between governments for mobile resources), or through joining international organizations such as the IMF or the WTO and thereby binding its own hands (at least in some areas of policy making). Such policies, in association with a competent and sufficiently independent bureaucracy, may contribute to the fulfillment of the capability condition, which – as we argued earlier in Chapter 4, Section 4.4 – is necessary for credible political commitments. However, as long as institutional safeguards are absent which effectively bind the executive to its promises and hold it accountable for its actions, the remaining preconditions for credible commitments cannot be fulfilled, in other words the sincerity condition that ensures the truthfulness of political intentions and announcements and the sustainability condition that ensures compliance with rules and promises over time. Development-enhancing outcomes of public policies are particularly unlikely if a political leadership is in power that lacks legitimacy and shows no encompassing interest in development. In this case, the structural characteristics of strong or developmental states can easily be abused by arbitrary government action at the cost of the population at large.

5.3.2 Limiting State Strength

State strength is a necessary but insufficient characteristic of a flexible MEGS. Strong and unlimited states represent a serious threat to economic development. Although the illustration of the developmental state indicates that there may be important lessons for other LDCs and also PSCs, it also reveals that this type of state shows important characteristics which can be neither easily created in other countries nor are they desirable from a political, social, or moral standpoint. This refers to the precondition that a political elite needs to be in power that is credibly committed to fostering long-term economic development. If such an elite is absent, a developmental state may quickly degenerate into a predatory state. Moreover, as Johnson (1987) observes, although development and authoritarianism do not necessarily go hand in hand, successful developmental states have often been based on a soft authoritarian political system, which can, and often does, imply enormously damaging side effects such as the violation of human rights or the political suppression of organized labor.

Strong governments that face no constitutional or other institutional limits are too powerful. Since there are no safeguards that hinder policy makers from altering rights, laws, and regulations at will or from undertaking confiscatory policies, it is almost impossible to make credible commitments to private actors. Even if political authorities are willing and able to take the future consequences of their actions into account and incorporate their anticipations in current policy choices, weak political property rights may pose substantial hazards. For if politicians today cannot adequately tie the hands of their successors, the sustainability of policy reform will be insecure and front-loaded projects may be preferred. Similarly, credibility may be impossible if the short-time horizons of politicians induce them to seize private assets or to reward special constituencies at the expense of long-term investments (Williamson 1995). Finally, political leaders who are more familiar with power considerations than with efficiency reasoning may simply ignore the importance of credible commitments for private investment. In this context, Mikhail Gorbachev's request to foreign companies in 1990 to make investments in the USSR illustrates the point: 'Those [companies] who are with us now have good prospects of participating in our great country ... [whereas those who wait] will remain observers for years to come – *we will see to it'.*[49] This kind of carrot-and-stick politics towards international investors and the open readiness to exercise bureaucratic discretion causes substantial contractual hazard. It not only threatens those companies that have already undertaken investments but also increases the option value of waiting for potential future investors. As Williamson (1995) argues, the lesson to be learned here is that rules that provide relatively few degrees of freedom can have crucial advantages over political discretion that allows for more degrees of freedom.

The failure of policy makers to provide credible commitments causes substantial political risk with the consequence that private investments are reduced and potentially beneficial effects of economic reforms are undermined. If political power is unlimited, transactions involving the government as a contracting party are usually insecure. In order to stimulate market participation, such governments need to rely on protectionist measures like trade protection, monopoly rights, or other privileges to particular economic groups (Root and Weingast 1996). Thus, the four main characteristics of developmental states are insufficient in themselves for instituting a MEGS, because they alone do not ensure that the 'fundamental dilemma of an economic system' (Weingast 1995: 1) can be overcome. The dilemma lies in the fact that a strong government capable of protecting and enforcing legal rights and effectively implementing reforms is also capable of violating these rights and of confiscating citizens' wealth, thereby creating disincentives for private actors to carry out long-term investment and to provide information, which in turn blocks thriving markets, and eventually halts development. This fundamental dilemma revolves around the question of what kinds of political institutions are required for a thriving market economy to become a feasible and stable policy choice. The answer is that political institutions must be designed that help to overcome the short time horizon of many public officials, ensure a predictable and secure political foundation of policy reform and hence establish a *strong but limited government.* As adherents to the NIE emphasize, such institutions need to credibly commit policy makers to enhancing and preserving markets and, as a precondition thereof, to binding limits on discretionary and arbitrary political behavior in the future.[50] As Shepsle (1999: 16) puts it, clearly mindful of the lack of 'enlightened' political leadership in most LDCs:

A (...) problem implicit in the *WDR [World Development Report 1997;* J.A.], and commonly articulated by social planners elsewhere, is to believe that 'enlightenment' is the only asset available to mitigate the perverse incentives associated with the short time horizons of officials. Successful development, noncorrupt performance, and credible commitment, it is true, require (some) politicians to resist short-term temptations (...). And it is also true that their own aspirations often dispose them in the opposite direction. The general solution, however, is *not* 'enlightened leadership,' for if this were generally available there would not be a problem in the first place. The solution is to channel private aspirations in more constructive ways. This is the classic Madisonian problem of institutional design. In crafting a constitution for a new nation, Madison took for granted that men were not angels, but rather were ambitious and self-interested. Through institutional design he sought to 'pit ambition against ambition.' He did not depend up 'enlightenment,' nor upon insulating policymaking from politics, as planners sometimes suggest. Successfully designed institutional arrangements, it appears to me as it did to Madison, may serve as a substitute for enlightenment, and is essential in a world in which the latter is in short supply.

The problem, of course, is what kind of political institutions produce a flexible MEGS that allow society effectively to cope with policy-related problems and other conflicts as they arise, reduce opportunistic government behavior, and yet ensure a relatively high degree of stability of political and economic rights. Here, *self-enforcement* is of critical importance. For a MEGS to evolve and to survive, public officials (and also private actors) must have incentives to abide by the system's rules. Policy makers must find it in their own interest to observe a set of private rights as well as the limits on government behavior. This implies that the political institutions of a MEGS need to be self-enforcing. The central hypothesis of the notion of self-enforcement is that individuals are only honest and comply with existing rules if this behavior is more rewarding (or less costly) than dishonesty or non-compliance.[51] Hence, self-enforcement may require relatively high political transaction costs to be incurred by policy makers if they do not stick to their promises or do not abide by the rules of the game. Depending on the specific situation, these may include the expected costs of losing power in popular elections or decreasing government revenues when, due to political instability or excessive discretionary behavior, private companies postpone investment, increasingly operate in the informal sector, or shift their business activities and move their resources outside the country.

The preceding considerations illustrate that the notion of the strong state being a necessary and sufficient condition for sustained development is misleading and that the theory of the developmental state is incomplete as long as it ignores the need for institutional arrangements that ensure credible political commitments. And, in fact, as we will argue below, the developmental states in North East Asia as well as other high-performing Asian economies (HPAEs) actually managed to reduce unproductive rent-seeking behavior[52] and have been able to commit their administrations to pursuing an encompassing interest and to cooperating productively with the private sector. These and other contemporary and historical examples as well as theoretical reasoning suggest pointers on the political crafting of a self-enforcing MEGS that can mitigate the complex coordination and collective-action problems associated with policy reform and help to establish strong but limited governments.[53]

In general, such a MEGS includes institutions that monitor the behavior of public officials and penalize misbehavior, reduce information asymmetries, stabilize expectations, and provide economic actors with exit and/or voice options. A relatively basic mechanism for reducing governmental discretion and document commitment is openness, that is, granting the possibility of external exit to the private sector by introducing competition between countries. The risk of mobile factors leaving the country increases the costs of abusing political power, because it means a reduction of the government's tax base. Moreover, the external-exit threat becomes even more powerful over the long run. The longer an economy takes part in the international division of labor, the more specialized its production activities become. If the government of such an economy were to transgress the rights of private entrepreneurs, the economic loss would be substantial, because widespread exit would render the allocation of domestic resources less efficient (Borner *et al.* 1995).

Possibly more effective mechanisms to prompt political authorities to abide by rules and regulations and sustainably to promote economic development may be found in the internal organization of the state. This refers to an elaborate system of institutions which allows for and facilitates the punishment of bureaucrats and politicians if they do not observe the rules. It also concerns institutions that incur relatively low political transaction costs in order to facilitate legislative exchange, to monitor bureaucratic behavior better, and to improve public sector management as well as the interaction of the various branches of government, business representatives, and social groups.[54] In other respects, however, institutions are required that impose relatively high political transaction costs on public officials. As indicated above, this is particularly important in order to prompt policy makers to comply with the rules of the game and to enhance the incentive compatibility of public policies and economic performance. In order to impose credible limits on their own authority, policy makers need to tie their own hands by establishing suitably designed political rules, the revision or transgression of which is associated with high costs. Governance mechanisms that can effectively control governments and help to increase the accountability of policy making generally stress participation in one way or another. Control through participatory mechanisms means that both public and private actors are involved in monitoring political behavior, enforcing rules, and sanctioning non-compliance through transparent institutionalized channels. Of course, participation does not ensure that policy makers are 'enlightened' people. Existing loopholes may still be used for the pursuit of personal interests. But institutionalized participation will considerably reduce the number of actual loopholes (Borner *et al.* 1995).

However, formally establishing an elaborate system of institutionalized control is not sufficient, because policy makers may still have incentives to circumvent rules and reestablish a monopoly of political power. Hence, *de jure* institutional reforms will not be automatically translated into *de facto* reform. Whether or not formal political institutions will actually be obeyed and deviant behavior punished depends, on the one hand, on the informal institutions prevalent in a given society and, on the other hand, on the existence of auxiliary institutions that help to prevent collusion of dominant political (and economic) powers. A relatively effective means to raise the transaction costs of establishing power cartels is to institute several independent channels of control over government agencies and individual public officials. Another complementary means is to establish institutions that provide citizens with information about political activities and help to coordinate their actions so that they can react in concert if political officials transgress private rights.[55]

Basically, five different credibility-enhancing institutional arrangements are conceivable that help to prevent policy makers from acting opportunistically and are conducive to the emergence of a MEGS. These comprise institutional checks and balances through horizontal separation of powers, periodic elections, the involvement of broad interest groups in political decision making, the vertical separation of powers through decentralization and, more importantly, federalism, and effective watchdog organizations.[56] This is not to say that a full realization of all these institutions is an unalterable prerequisite to ensuring credible commitment. As we will see below in Chapter 6, Sections 6.2 and 6.3, even gradual and partial, though critical institutional reforms may impose binding limits on policy makers and enhance governance effectiveness. But in general, these institutions are mutually reinforcing. Each additional channel of participation makes it more difficult and costly for public officials to disobey rules and thus strengthens the accountability of policy making.

Besides international competition, it is the organizational and institutional design of, and the incentives within, the polity that are crucial to the developmental consequences of government policies. An adequate institutional environment for policy reform needs to provide mechanisms for the resolution of conflict, enhance political and social stability through transparent rules and processes for solving collective problems, and create public trust on the basis of a common sense of legitimate authority.[57] Governance structures are effective if they provide suitable means to adequately adjust political transaction costs and to mitigate the multiple principal–agent problems that are inherent in policy reform. This implies that a MEGS requires a *strong but limited government*; strong in the sense that it is able credibly to precommit itself to policies that are in the public interest, and to establish an independent bureaucracy capable of implementing and enforcing those policies; limited in the sense that both the government and the public administration are prevented from confiscating private wealth and are held accountable for their activities. By establishing strong but limited governments, institutions can be designed and incentives created that channel the behavior of political decision makers into those activities which are compatible with sustained economic development and prompt private business to carry out long-term investment and provide the authorities with information that is necessary to make feasible policy choices.

5.3.3 Capacity Building, Implementation, and Enforcement

Successful economic reforms not only require a secure political foundation, but also the institutional means to implement and enforce political decisions, public policies, and regulations. Strategies, programs, and decisions aiming at economic change neither change policy nor yield anticipated and intended results automatically. Even if policies are well-designed, considerable implementation problems may occur. In numerous LDCs and PSCs, public services are delivered with poor quality or at high costs. At times they are not delivered at all, at other times, delivery is dogged by fraud, waste, and corruption. Frequently, politicians intervene in day-to-day activities, and bureaucrats often have limited flexibility to respond well to changing policy needs. In many countries, governments have a monopoly in providing certain goods and services, but lack accountability for using inputs, let alone for achieving results. Moreover, sought-after changes may not materialize due to opposition to policy reform either from inside the public sector or from powerful interest groups that may be negatively affected by new policies (Pradhan 1998; Grindle and Thomas 1991). For these reasons, capacity building is another critical pillar for establishing a MEGS. Without it, the implementation and enforcement of public policies is not conceivable. Capacity building is a term which is often used synonymously, or in combination with, governance. But actually it refers to key actions proposed to achieve the core principles of governance in the public sector. Confusing these two terms would imply that capacity building work in the narrow sense may be interpreted as governance in the broad sense. Each attempt at capacity building would thus be considered a governance activity with the danger that policy makers do not take the complexity of a governance structure into account, but tend to tackle governance problems in a piecemeal, ad hoc approach.

Capacity building includes three components: (1) institution building (that is replacing a less efficient by a more efficient set of rules and functions); (2) organizational restructuring (that is the design of organizational forms better suited to the new set of rules and functions); and (3) human resource development (that is in particular training). Hence, capacity building is not to be confused with a pure training exercise. Capacity describes 'the ability to perform appropriate tasks effectively, efficiently and sustainably. In turn, capacity building refers to improvements in the ability of public sector organizations, either singly or in cooperation with other organizations, to perform appropriate tasks' (Grindle and Hilderbrand 1995: 445). Beyond irreducible functions of the public sector such as securing law and order and establishing the basic rules of the game for political and economic interaction, appropriate tasks are context-specific.[58] It is to be noted that training without institution building and organizational restructuring will have no sustainable effect if the existing institutions do not match with the proposed policies. New capacity is needed to help to assure the rule of law and open access to public information. But capacity building also includes the need to ensure that diverse social groups are able to get needed information and participate in the making of public policy.

Essentially, five interdependent dimensions determine public-sector capacity and hence represent starting points for capacity building measures (see Figure 5.1).[59] These comprise:

- the *action environment* (including general political, economic, and social factors) in which political authorities operate. Figure 5.1 displays several factors that may have a critical impact on the capacity of the public sector. Notice that policy interventions that aim to improve the conditions set by the action environment are time consuming and are slow to materialize, because this involves trying to change basic societal structures;
- *general public sector institutions* which include basic institutional arrangements such as the procedures and rules guiding public operations and officials, concurrent policies, government responsibilities for development policies and projects as well as formal and informal arrangements that determine the distribution of power within the public sector. The efficacy of all these factors depends on adequate budgetary support and hence on current or future financial constraints;
- the *task network,* referring to the various organizations that need to be involved for the accomplishment of a particular task. Public-sector performance is linked to the quality of coordination and communication between these network organizations and to the ability of all

organizations to perform their responsibilities effectively. These networks (which may also include non-public organizations) usually consist of primary, secondary, and supporting organizations. While primary organizations (for example, the budget office of a ministry of finance) take the lead in task performance, secondary entities (for example, a statistical office) are often necessary to provide required services and supporting units (such as a training center for computer-based operations) to improve the technical and organizational skills that are indispensable for performing the task;

- *organizations* as the basic entities of a task network. Organizational structures, resources, and processes as well as management techniques determine how objectives are chosen, operations are structured, authority relations are defined, and incentive structures are formed. These factors essentially affect the behavioral patterns of individuals who work in a given organization and hence have substantial effects on an organization's output;

- *human resource development (HRD)*, that is the focus on improving human skills, attracting professional, technical, and managerial talents to careers in the public sector, and how training and promotion schemes affect performance.

These dimensions of capacity building emphasize that in order to provide a secure political foundation of policy reforms, the credibility-enhancing institutional arrangements mentioned above (which are components of the action environment) are to be further complemented by control and incentive mechanisms which help to improve public sector management. These may, for example, comprise:[60]

- the existence of a minimal level of bureaucratic processes and structures including organization charts, reporting relationships, job descriptions, information systems, and supply lines;

- competitive wages and meritocratic procedures for recruitment and promotion of bureaucrats that can attract more talented individuals and increase integrity and professionalism;

- the introduction of hard budget constraints that help to delimit the influence of external actors on government expenditures and measure bureaucrats' ability in macroeconomic management;

- independent personnel agencies which reduce external pressure on appointments and patronage;

- statutory boards partitioning the policy space by assigning single policies to special agencies that help monitor civil servants' performance;

- the break-up of ministries into focused business-oriented entities headed by executive officers working on output-based and fixed-term contracts with substantial managerial autonomy;
- prudent accounting procedures and independent external and internal auditing mechanisms;
- publication of government documents and data (for example, statutes and rules, proceedings of legislative bodies, budgets, and revenues), possibly complemented by freedom of information acts;
- anti-corruption agencies which reduce bureaucrats' propensity to use their specific information for extra-legal activities as well as ombudsmen who can help enhance the accountability of public agencies by offering a forum for translating citizens' complaints into reforms;
- the use of market-like mechanisms such as auctions for the procurement of goods and services as well as for the allocation of public resources, partially contracting out government activity, and performance contracting;
- client surveys which can make the quality of public service delivery more transparent and generate external pressure for improving performance; and
- socially connecting an independent bureaucracy through institutional arrangements that link the public and the private sector in order to encourage the mutual exchange of information between the public administration and the business community, enhance the bureaucracy's flexibility, and support a consensual and transparent process of policy formulation.

Of course, establishing a rule-based, professional public administration is a gradual process, and quick fixes through creating 'enclaves of excellence' is hardly sustainable, although those administrative islands may yield useful demonstration effects. Moreover, not all of these and other mechanisms can be usefully applied in any given country. If the action environment or the human resource base is shallow or if informal norms in the public sector deviate considerably from formal institutions, the new formal institutions and modern management methods will not simply materialize on introduction. Instead, priority has to be given to more basic institutional reforms, training of bureaucrats, merit-based recruitment and promotion, strengthening financial accountability and rule-based compliance, introducing hard budget constraints, making the flow of public resources more predictable, and providing greater clarity of administrative purposes and bureaucratic tasks. In these cases, sophisticated institutional devices must be postponed until the necessary capabilities are in place.[61]

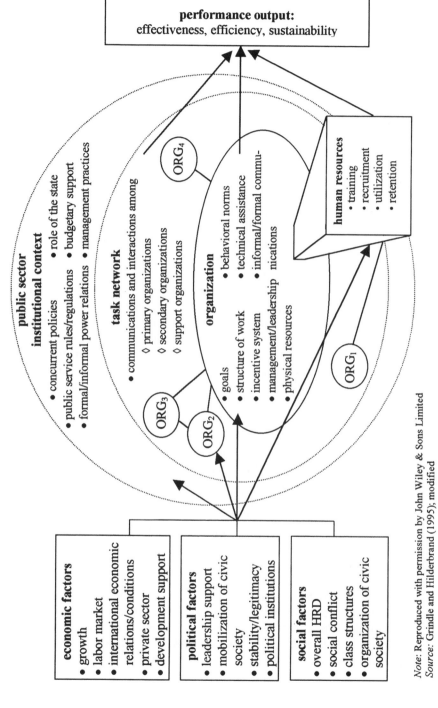

Note: Reproduced with permission by John Wiley & Sons Limited
Source: Grindle and Hilderbrand (1995); modified

Figure 5.1: Dimensions of public-sector capacity

But basically all of these elements of a 'rationalized bureaucracy' (Campos *et al.* 1994: 10) represent effective signaling devices that can be used by governments to document their commitment to impartiality and competence and to create trust in the private sector that authorities will comply with the rules of the game and deliver the promised policies. Notice, however, that the specific demands on administrative capability and capacity may differ considerably over time and across sectors, and they depend on the concrete kind of policy that is pursued by the government. Moreover, when an economy gradually moves toward a higher level of development in the course of time, demands on bureaucratic quality will change. New challenges require new skills and new institutional arrangements. This is, for example, the case if the government's role changes from the direct provision of public goods to out-contracting, setting the terms of procurement, and defining regulatory rules. The availability of new organizational, managerial, and technical skills is also important if centralized institutional arrangements guiding policy making are to be replaced by decentralized or polycentric arrangements (Ostrom, Schroeder, and Wynne 1993). These examples illustrate that effective bureaucratic governance needs to be interpreted as being subject to a dynamic process. Policy makers have to take care that policies match institutions and vice versa. Effective governance requires continual fine tuning and the adjustment of institutions and policy solutions to changing technological, social, economic, and political environments. This also implies that policy makers must not divorce themselves from the implementation of policy reforms once a decision for reform has been taken. Instead, the realization of change presupposes the development of implementation and enforcement strategies that take into account that implementation represents an interactive process that requires ongoing monitoring and decision making in order to react to anticipated and actual reactions to reform initiatives. Such reactions can occur at any point during the implementation process and may influence decision makers and public managers at various political or administrative levels. This means that policy interventions to improve institutional, administrative, technical, and political capacity have to be continuously scrutinized and adjusted in order to ensure pragmatic policy making and policy adaptability that are not only necessary to react quickly to changing needs and developments but also to anticipate and overcome potential resistance to reforms.[62]

Furthermore, in order to support vigorous markets, the government must operate in partnership with the private sector. In particular, the importance of task networks which often need to include NGOs or private intermediate organizations such as employers associations, trade unions, or consumer associations indicates that crafting strong public sector institutions, an elaborate system of checks and balances, and a capable independent public administration do not suffice for successful policy reform. Since the public sector and especially the economic bureaucracy need to rely on information and feedback from the private sector to design and implement public policies properly, institutionalized links must be in place which allow for consultation, cooperation, and coordination. As mentioned earlier, a Weberian-type bureaucracy based on objective rules for bureaucratic activities and appointments represents an unalterable prerequisite for granting independence to the administration by shielding its technocratic elite from pressures of vested interests. But a serious problem with Weber's view of the bureaucracy is that it overemphasizes the insulation of the public administration from the economy.[63] A completely insulated bureaucracy would lack the ability to rely on decentralized private information and implementation. Evans (1992) modifies Weber's approach in this regard and argues that a developmental state requires a bureaucracy showing the corporate coherence of the Weberian ideal type, being relatively independent of societal pressures, though sufficiently embedded in society. This would imply that bureaucrats possess 'accurate intelligence, inventiveness, active agency and sophisticated responseness [sic] to a changing economic reality'.[64] The involvement of the business community in public policy making through institutionalized channels represents an adequate means of establishing a state–business interface by which the mutual exchange of information can be encouraged, risk sharing facilitated, bureaucratic flexibility enhanced, and a consensual process of policy formulation realized. This seemingly contradictory combination of bureaucratic autonomy and social connectedness, which Evans (1995) calls *embedded autonomy*, may represent the institutional basis for effective state involvement because it enhances the accountability for public-policy performance and balances the administration's independence. Furthermore, socially connecting the economic bureaucracy with the business sector and other segments of society entails an active monitoring process of (changing) endogenous needs, which helps policy makers to deal with uncertainty. Note, however, that the importance of embeddedness differs depending on the tasks and functions of government agencies. Cooperation between administrators and representatives of various industries is significant in areas of industrial, technological, and infrastructure policy. It is clearly less important, or may even be counterproductive, in areas such as the tax administration where monitoring devices and other hierarchical forms of control are necessary.

Public–private partnerships can rely on co-production or institutional arrangements which enhance the cooperation between public agencies, business, NGOs, and other public or private organizations. In the aftermath of the Asian crisis, it has become fashionable to reject any political attempts to intensify government–business relationships as an industrial policy to spur private investment. It is argued that close links between government and business lead to cronyism, nepotism, and collusion. In some cases, as in South Korea, the autonomy of the state can be compromised if business conglomerates acquire substantial political influence (Mody 1998). But, like a minimal state that will not be able to meet the diverse challenges of coordination and other market failures, an autonomous public administration will not be capable of effectively overcoming market failures and implementing industrial policies, if it lacks reliable information about markets, technological bottlenecks, and local or sectoral needs that can only be provided by private actors. The critical question is not whether policy making should rely on public–private deliberations, but how these forms of consultation and cooperation should be institutionally designed in order to reduce potential economic and political risks.

5.3.4 Key Economic Institutions

The fourth pillar constituting a MEGS concerns formal economic institutions.[65] Today, it is widely recognized that macroeconomic stabilization, privatization, and price reforms, though necessary components of policy reforms, are insufficient and that adequate economic rules and regulations must be in place to make incentives work and markets perform well, to reduce transaction uncertainties between private actors, and hence to support private sector development and coordination. In the 1990s, three disparate developments helped to reinforce the efforts to put institutions on the reform agenda of policy makers. The first one was the failure of price liberalization and privatization in the Russian Federation and other successor states of the USSR due to a lack of a market-oriented regulatory, legal, and political framework. Another one was the dissatisfaction with economic reforms in Latin American countries and the insight that these policy reforms neglected the importance of safety nets and social insurance. The third one was the Asian crisis in 1997/98 which revealed that financial liberalization without prudent regulation can have disastrous consequences (Rodrik 1999).

Meanwhile, even the Bretton Woods organizations and Western policy advisors have come to recognize that not only broadening the goals of development and transition but also the set of policy instruments and reforms is indispensable to ensure the sustainability and quality of growth processes.[66] The set of reforms that is needed to complement orthodox macroeconomic-cum-adjustment policies, is collectively referred to as *second generation reforms*. This label, however, is misleading, because the reforms of the so-called first and second generation are not necessarily sequential. As adherents to the NIE have argued for a long time, institution and capacity building which are now typically associated with second generation reforms need to occur prior to, or parallel with, the reforms of the first generation. At best, the labels *first* and *second* illustrate a historic view of the systemic transformation or of economic development in general. What had been ignored, neglected, or postponed during the first phase of policy reform, needs to be taken into account in the next generation. Today, there is a broad agreement that so-called second generation reforms that address the questions of sectoral and enterprise restructuring, institutional change, and improving the legal, regulatory, and administrative functions of governments represent one side of a coin; the other being sound and prudent macroeconomic policies and other ingredients of the so-called Washington Consensus. One side cannot work properly without the other.[67]

But which are the key economic institutions that matter for market performance and private sector development? A useful starting point is the set of *constitutive principles* of a market economy elaborated by the German *ordo* liberal school and, in particular, by Walter Eucken (1990/1952). *Ordo* liberals derive their prescriptions for public policy making from the notion of *order* which is a fundamental precondition for making governance structures effective.

> Order means that repetitive events or actions fit into a discernible pattern which allows people to have confidence that the pattern of future actions, on which they may depend, can be predicted reasonably well. If the world is ordered, complexity, and hence the knowledge problem, is reduced and economic agents are better able to specialise. Institutions serve to facilitate the emergence of order.[68]

Adherents to the *ordo* liberal school favor order policy (that is, supporting and enhancing the economic and social order of society) over process intervention. This maxim is essentially based on three axioms including that (1) cognitive abilities of individuals are limited so that an order that allows recognizable patterns to be uncovered, will improve living standards though an enhanced division of labor and give citizens distinctive realms of freedom; (2) individual freedom is an unalterable prerequisite of competition; and (3) order is required to make binding commitments possible and to enforce formal rules in order to overcome problems of asymmetric information and the temptations of opportunistic behavior (Kasper and Streit 1998).

Public policy making that is based on the commitment to conduct order policy consistently will not only ensure that individual freedoms are more secure but that economic coordination is more effective and rent-seeking and discrimination are limited. Arbitrary, ad hoc interventions and conscious discretionary policy making (for example, to smooth cyclical economic swings with respect to aggregate demand), it is argued, will attenuate market signals, create economic disturbances and destabilize private actors' expectations (Eucken 1990/1952). Government interventions into economic processes should only be undertaken if they are market compatible, that is if they 'do not interfere with the price mechanism and with the automatism of the market derived from it' (Röpke 1950: 160).

The primary focus of *ordo* liberals is on competition, because competitive structures display basic controlling and knowledge-generating functions which serve to operate a complex market system efficiently. This implies that all policy measures ought to be market conforming. By the same token, redistribution policies should be rejected unless they aim at ensuring the opportunity of equality for individuals and firms in a way that does not erode competitive signals. Thus, universal institutional arrangements that apply equally to all economic actors are more desirable than discriminatory interventions and specific directives (Kasper and Streit 1998).

The constitutive principles of order policy which promise to enhance and maintain competitive markets include a flexible system of market prices, monetary stability, private property rights,[69] open markets (that is, freedom of both entry as well as exit), the liability of all economic actors for their actions and commitments, freedom of contract, and the steadiness of economic policy making. Since the proper functioning of a competitive order is based on the decentralized *ex post* coordination of individual plans and actions through market transactions, establishing a system of flexible market prices will be the focal point of creating and maintaining a market economy. Only a price system that reflects the scarcities of goods, services, and the factors of production can efficiently fulfill the functions of a competitive system. This is why Eucken postulates a primacy of monetary stability. But basically all constitutive principles are interdependent and this is why they need to be realized simultaneously in order to promote private sector development effectively and to establish a functioning market economy. In addition, these principles need to be complemented by so-called *regulating principles*, because actual market-oriented economies may contain weaknesses and deficits that require correction. Eucken thus emphasizes the need for anti-trust policies in order to prevent the emergence of monopolistic power, the need to correct income distribution (for example, through a progressive income tax) in order to enhance social justice, the need for social safety nets and the protection of employees, and the need for institutions that help internalize external effects.[70]

However important these principles may be for the proper functioning of market economies, the *ordo* liberal school shows two basic weaknesses. On the one hand, it has not provided an answer to the question of how to acquire the institutions necessary to fulfill these principles and how policy makers can credibly commit themselves to conduct order policy instead of relying on interventionist measures which may serve narrow interests. On the other hand, the *ordo* liberals have somewhat neglected the dynamic aspects of a growing developing country the economy of which may be burdened with substantial market and coordination failures. To begin with the second qualifier, it is to be noted that markets not only fail due to anti-competitive behavior but also due to relatively high transaction costs preventing privately induced technological change and due to adverse selection and moral hazard resulting from incomplete information. More modern economic theories including those of imperfect competition and principal–agents relations have recognized these failures and developed regulatory instruments to cope with them. In reality, all successful market economies rely on a set of regulatory organizations and institutions which oversee product and factor markets. With respect to LDCs (and also PSCs), where market failures are more pervasive than in industrialized countries, it is essential to understand that regulation may go beyond issues such as securities regulation, financial supervision, and anti-trust. Rodrik (1995 and 1999), Hellmann et al. (1997), and Lau (1997) among others convincingly argue that especially coordination failures and imperfect capital markets require strategic government interventions in order to trigger socially desirable private investment. By referring to the experiences in East Asia and notably in Taiwan and South Korea in the 1960s and 1970s, they show that governments effectively coordinated private investment decisions, provided targeted subsidization and thus helped to initiate a process of sustained growth. However, while institutional arrangements such as financial restraint, staggered entry procedures regulating market access, and the provision of contingent rents worked well in these countries, similar arrangements failed in others.[71] This fact does not call into question the usefulness of specific policy interventions *per se*, but indicates the need to understand better the institutional, economic, and political factors that determine the effectiveness of government interventions in a given country setting.[72]

Moreover, with respect to industrial policy and more specifically technology policy, students of economic development have come to realize that LDCs do not simply select and costlessly apply technological innovations that have occurred in more advanced industrial countries and that are regarded as appropriate for domestic use. Certainly, relatively backward economies can, as Gershenkron (1962) observed, take advantage of the technological knowledge of advanced countries. But they can only do so if they have acquired sufficient technological capabilities and institutional capacities to identify suitable technologies and to adapt, absorb, and improve the technologies imported from abroad. Since such a competence has numerous externalities, government activism in facilitating and encouraging the process of technological change is critical. Moreover, circumstantial sensitivity and tacitness in applying technologies make it extremely difficult, if not impossible, for LDCs to rely on a best-practice approach or to formulate a blueprint for national technological policies and their implementation. To a large extent, technological progress and economic performance depend on the organizational and institutional environment in which the industrial sector operates. Besides the macroeconomic policy framework, a country's technological infrastructure is of critical importance, that is its education system, private and public research organizations, the network of technological and scientific associations, and its legal institutions such as intellectual property rights as well as contract laws that provide incentives to develop and exchange technologies. The technological infrastructure backs up technological efforts of private firms by providing standards, information, scientific knowledge, and facilities which cannot be established and operated by individual firms.[73] Following this line of reasoning, unconventional though modern approaches identify a strong need for public policies including selective interventions to facilitate, encourage, protect, and induce technological activities in LDCs (Lall 1992 and 1997; Pack and Westphal 1986).

An important lesson from these observations is that socially beneficial economic institutions may vary across countries and even over time within a given country. The last point becomes clear if one looks, for example, at South Korea in the 1990s when close institutional relationships between the *chaebols* and the government, which had a positive overall impact on the economy at earlier stages of development, increasingly became dysfunctional.[74]

Most of the institutional ingredients for a functioning market economy proposed by the German *ordo* liberals have not been rejected by modern economists but essentially taken for granted. As argued earlier, however, these institutions do not evolve automatically. This fact calls attention to the first qualifier mentioned above: how can these institutions be acquired? This question, in fact, needs to be addressed from two perspectives. First of all, it relates to the political institutions of a country's governance structure and how these deal with problems of implementing and enforcing new economic institutions. As argued in the preceding sections, the politico-institutional component of a country's governance structure is a major determinant for the success or failure of policy reform, including institutional reform. The more the political and administrative institutions are suitable to realize the fundamental principles that constitute effective governance, the easier is the acquisition, implementation, and enforcement of market-enhancing economic institutions. Secondly, the above question relates to the problem of strategy choice. What is the most conducive way to establish a distinct set of formal economic institutions? This question, in turn, is similar to the discussion about big-bang approaches versus gradualism in overall policy reform. Basically, two strategies to institution building can be distinguished; the first favoring the adoption of an institutional blueprint from advanced industrial economies, the second emphasizing the need to develop economic institutions locally by using indigenous experiences, experimentation, and local knowledge. While the first strategy suggests advantage be taken of the experiences of successful economies through importing their entire formal institutional framework at one stroke, the second strategy is by nature more gradual and hence time consuming.

At first glance, the big-bang approach to institution building is distinguished by its procedural clarity, conceptual simplicity, and straightforwardness. It represents an attractive alternative to policy designers because it seems to offer a useful 'how-to manual' that can be as easily articulated as the policy prescriptions inherent in the *Washington Consensus*. This approach appears to be particularly feasible if the development objectives of a given country are clear-cut and sufficiently realistic to be achieved within a certain period of time. This was, for example, the case with respect to the former German Democratic Republic (GDR) that, in the course of unification with the Federal Republic of Germany (FRG), 'simply' adopted the whole institutional framework of the latter.[75] Also, the substantial progress in transition in Poland compared to other less successful PSCs may be (at least partly) attributed to the fact that both the Polish post-socialist governments and broad segments of society have had clearly defined objectives of transition, that is, that Poland should become a full member of the European Union (EU) as fast as possible. However, most LDCs and PSCs cannot rely on 'big brothers' such as the FRG or the EU. In addition, development objectives are usually not so clear-cut and well defined. Even if a developing country seeks to emulate the development trajectory of more advanced countries and seeks to copy their institutional frameworks, the question arises as to which country ought to be the role model. The institutional matrices of modern capitalist economies are far from being the same. This becomes obvious if one compares the economic as well as the social and political orders of the United States, the EU, and Japan, or the institutional settings within the EU, for example, those of Sweden and the United Kingdom. All of these countries display a great variety of stabilizing, legitimizing, and regulatory institutions that guide economic exchange. This implies, as Rodrik (1999) correctly emphasizes, that the institutional foundation of a successful market economy cannot be uniquely determined. Hence, the existence of, and the need for, institutional diversity has to be accepted as well as the fact that even the most advanced economies are constantly under pressure to search for new institutional arrangements that are suitable to overcome existing problems more effectively (that is, at lower costs or with higher social benefits) and to meet practical challenges in the future (Unger 1998).

Furthermore, the great variety of successful market economies indicates that the economic institutions of capitalism do not represent a 'general purpose technology' that promises sustainably to increase total factor productivity and to shift the frontier of production possibilities significantly outwards in any given country just by acquiring it off-the-shelf. The caveat against transferring institutions that have proved to be socially beneficial elsewhere to other countries, especially if these are at a different stage of development, was already stressed in Part I of this study. Adherents to a more gradual approach to institution building emphasize that the efficacy of the economic institutions of a market economy is contingent on particular local problems, capacities, preferences, and needs.[76] Similar to technology policy, tacitness and circumstantial sensitivity in implementing and operating economic institutions such as social security programs, social partnerships, rules guiding the representation of minorities, currency boards, or labor market regulations make it difficult to rely on best-practice approaches. Imported institutions may fail to meet the specificity requirements of local needs, and institutional blueprints are usually incomplete because the knowledge that is necessary to use these institutions properly can often not be delivered but has to be acquired through local learning and experimenting.

Although these are convincing points made by the adherents to gradualism, this mode of institution building is not without dangers either. A first caveat reminds us again of the importance of a secure political foundation underlying policy reform, namely that gradualism may come in different forms and shapes. For example, the gradual approach to economic transition in most successor states of the USSR is less a reflection of self-conscious and rule-based experimentation with the desire to build more efficient institutions, but more an outcome of political instability, pork-barrel politics, rent-seeking, and efforts to block market-oriented reforms. In contrast, the gradual approach to institution and capacity building in East Asian countries such as Taiwan, South Korea, and China during their recent history followed a more programmatic approach that sought to enhance local knowledge and meet local needs.[77] A second caveat against gradualism stresses the costs of reinventing the wheel again and again. As Rodrik (1999) argues, gradualism may waste resources and time if policy makers do not take advantage of institutional arbitrage. In some particular (mostly technical or legal) areas, institutional arrangements can be adopted from more advanced countries. This holds, for example, for the institutions underlying the operation of central banks, anti-trust agencies as well as financial regulations or auditing and accounting standards.

Considering the preceding arguments, one may conclude that the successful acquisition of economic institutions that help to establish a MEGS depends, on the one hand, on a secure political foundation of policy reform that ensures credible commitments and the capacity to implement new institutions and, on the other hand, on the strategy of institution building. Important lessons can be learned by LDCs and PSCs from the experiences of more advanced economies. But a simple transplantation of institutions from one country to another is basically associated with severe problems. This makes gradualism the superior way of establishing and maintaining a local economic order, especially if policy makers are not dogmatic and use institutional arbitrage where it is appropriate.

5.3.5 The Importance of Informal Institutions

Before synthesizing the preceding arguments regarding the question of what kind of institutions constitute a flexible MEGS, some thoughts need to be given to the importance of informal constraints and their impact on governance. Since formal *and* informal rules together determine the process of policy formulation as well as its outcomes, both types of institutions are embodied in our concept of governance. From the perspective of policy and institutional design, formal rules usually receive the primary, if not exclusive, attention of reformers. At first glance, this disregard of informal institutions seems to be justified with respect to governance-related policies because it lies in the nature of informal institutions that they can neither be enforced by the state nor are they directly amenable to political design. However, informal constraints can play a significant role in the capacity of a country's institutional matrix to implement and enforce policies and to enhance private sector development. As has been emphasized by North (1981, 1990a, 1992), Kiwit and Voigt (1995), Cooter (1997), and Pejovich (1997b) among others, informal institutions such as social norms, moral values, or (individual) ideologies do not necessarily support or reinforce formal rules and regulations, but actually rather often block institutional reform or render overall economic reforms inefficient. Thus any efforts to reform formal institutions must contend with the persistence of inherited informal constraints which may or may not be socially efficient within a new political, economic, or social environment. The argument goes that especially in LDCs and PSCs traditional informal constraints significantly differ from informal institutions in advanced industrialized countries and therefore may make the formal economic institutions that constitute a functioning market economy less effective. This could not only mean large-scale institutional failure but eventually, due to effects of path dependency, lead to a lock-in situation that keeps a given country on a relatively low trajectory of economic growth and development (North 1995a). This, in turn, raises the question of how formal institutional innovations need to be designed in order to translate *de jure* into *de facto* reforms. How can policy makers ensure that existing and new formal rules actually determine the choice of economic actors?

The literature on institutional reform has been quite silent regarding this question. Either it has ignored the question altogether or it has called for reconciling (new) formal institutions with existing informal ones. That means that the former should be crafted with a keen eye to encouraging convergence between formal institutions and informal constraints so that any contradictions between these two types are reduced (Dia 1996, Raiser 1997, and Voigt and Kiwit 1998). However, such an approach is misleading and incomplete. It is misleading because it is not a feasible option for policy making in LDCs and PSCs to wait with market-oriented policy reform until socially inefficient, informal institutions have eventually vanished. Moreover, if informal institutions that conflict with formal market institutions or impede economic exchange are accommodated through institutional reform, how should these socially inefficient, informal constraints ever disappear? The approach is incomplete because it fails to distinguish between different kinds of formal institutions and to recognize that their efficacy may be differently shaped by informal constraints.

To solve these problems of institutional policy, Mummert (1999b) suggests a more differentiated approach to investigating how informal institutions matter for institutional policies. He distinguishes between two types of formal institutions: (1) market order-oriented institutions which are established to build the structural and institutional framework of a market economy that allows a spontaneous economic order of action to evolve (these institutions essentially include Eucken's constitutive principles); and (2) task-oriented institutions which, in the presence of market failures or particular preferences of constituents, are established to achieve specific tasks or ends by politically intervening in processes of self-coordination. The contents of these institutions differ according to the different policy objectives that they are designed to promote. In Mummert's (1999b: 5–6; emphasis in original) words:

> In order to achieve specific tasks formal institutions have to be very specific in guiding the behavior of the respective actors. They describe the ends the individual actors have to pursue and sometimes even the means they are allowed to use while doing so. Thus, these formal task-oriented institutions constrain the individual actors considerably. By contrast, the formal institutions that allow for market coordination have to constrain the individual actors to a much lesser extent. Such market order-oriented institutions ideally forbid simply to use certain means while the actors do not have to fulfill certain tasks but can act according to their individual preferences.

Conflicts between informal and formal institutions presuppose that the normative contents of these rules contradict each other. Hence, a conflict is more likely with respect to formal task-oriented institutions because they define specific objectives or prescribe particular actions which economic actors have to perform in order to accomplish these objectives.[78] Regarding formal market order-oriented institutions, conflicts are less likely because economic actors are allowed to act as they wish unless they violate or harm the rights of others. Conflicts with informal constraints would be only conceivable if an informal institution prescribes actions which are prohibited by the formal institutions.[79] But even if institutional conflict is unlikely with respect to (re)invigorating market order-oriented institutions, this does not mean that informal institutions have no impact on economic performance. This is because informal rules may affect the quality and the dynamics of the spontaneous market processes which emerge within the framework constituted by market-order institutions.[80] This implies that, from the perspective of institutional policy, one needs to distinguish between the task compatibility of informal institutions on the one hand and their market compatibility on the other hand.

Task compatibility. Whether actual contradictions between formal task-oriented institutions and informal norms actually lead to growth-impeding conflicts eventually depends on the hierarchical relationship between these two types of institutions. As Hayek (1993/1976: 24) argues,

> rules which are logically inconsistent in the sense that they may lead in any given situation to requirements or prohibitions of acts of any one person which are mutually contradictory, may yet be made compatible if they stand in a relation of superiority or inferiority to each other, so that the system of rules itself determines which of the rules is to 'overrule' the other.

Hence, informal institutions which contradict formal ones will undermine institutional reforms only if they are not perceived or accepted by economic actors to be subordinated to the formal task-oriented rules and regulations. Therefore, the legitimacy of formal institutions as it is perceived by individual actors is the crucial factor that eventually decides whether informal constraints will become impediments to institutional reforms (Mummert 1999b). This emphasis on legitimacy brings us back to the importance of political institutions for a flexible MEGS to evolve. The political institutions determine the mechanisms according to which formal economic institutions are established, altered, or eliminated and hence considerably determine their legitimacy. This fact adds a further characteristic to our concept of a MEGS which political institutions need to exhibit. These institutions should not only provide for a secure foundation of policy making that ensures proper implementation of reforms but they must also be generally accepted by the population and based on a social consensus that makes institutional reforms legitimate. The emergence of such a consensus strongly depends on the capacity of a given society to overcome the problems of interpersonal and inter-group cooperation. The more fragmented a society is, the more difficult is consensus building. As Dollar and Svensson (1998), Easterly and Levine (1997), and Adelman and Morris (1967) observe, especially ethnic heterogeneity and fragmentation negatively affects inter-group cooperation, the efficacy of policy reforms, and economic growth.[81]

Market compatibility. Basically one can distinguish between informal institutions that have a positive, a negative, or no impact on market processes. Informal institutions that support market exchange and private sector development do so by reducing transaction costs. Such institutions may include the reputation of a trading company, norms emphasizing honesty in contract fulfillment, commercial codes of conduct, private mechanisms of conflict resolution, or more generally, for example, the rules underlying a protestant ethic. Informal institutions that imply relatively high transaction costs tend to hamper market coordination, for example, if these norms forbid interest being taken for lending money. However, as Mummert (1999b) argues, it is not solely the normative content of informal institutions that determines the degree to which these norms impede or support market coordination but, at least equally important, the number of economic actors to which the normative prescriptions of these institutions apply. Thus, it makes a difference whether market-impeding informal institutions are prevalent throughout a given society or whether their acceptance and obedience is restricted to a certain sub-national jurisdiction, community, ethnic group, particular kinships, or certain business groups. The same essentially holds for market-enhancing norms. Hence, actually existing barriers to entry into and exit from different societal groups play an important role regarding the effects of informal institutions on the dynamics of a market system. The lower the entry barriers are, or the less fragmented a society is, the greater the likelihood that market-enhancing norms will unfold their positive impact on market exchange. With respect to informal constraints which may restrain market exchange, the fragmentation of society also matters. If obstacles to institutional reforms exist in a few distinct subgroups of society, this will impede market transactions within and with these groups. This, in turn, will make competition less intensive and yield adverse consequences for economic growth. If, however, entry and exit barriers to group membership are relatively low, the opportunity costs for individual economic actors resulting from complying with restraining rules will decrease and hence market processes could be strengthened (Herrmann-Pillath 1993 and Mummert 1999b).

For the purposes of this study, the crucial question arising from the preceding arguments concerns the implications for institutional policies. With respect to market order-oriented institutions, no direct conflict with informal institutions is to be expected. Thus, an adaptation of these formal rules to informal constraints is not necessary. On the contrary, a possibly rapid introduction of these formal rules is advisable in order to establish the institutional framework that constitutes a functioning market economy and hence to increase the degree of competition between economic agents. Moreover, these formal rules may help to reinforce potentially existing informal institutions, which show market-enhancing characteristics, and gradually undermine growth-impeding institutions because they raise the opportunity costs of complying with socially inefficient informal norms. Hence, they may act as focal points that help realign citizens' informal attitudes. In contrast, the establishment of formal task-oriented institutions may be directly associated with institutional conflicts especially if they lack legitimacy. This makes it necessary for reformers clearly to articulate the advantages of task-oriented institutions and communicate them to different segments of society. Depending on the task that is to be performed by a particular institution, the involvement in institution building procedures of those actors who may benefit from them and possibly also of those actors who fear to be adversely affected by them helps to foster a social consensus. In other words, inclusionary strategies of institution building which emphasize political consultation and participation would be superior to a hierarchical top-down implementation of formal institutions. Sometimes, however, institution builders are well advised if they do not avoid potential conflict, for example, if new laws are explicitly introduced in order to alter informal institutions by using their moral weight or the coercive power of the state. This may be important in such instances as anti-discrimination or anti-slavery laws or laws that seek to protect consumers or eliminate child labor.

Another way to alleviate potential conflicts between informal and formal institutions is to increase the stock of social capital in order to overcome problems of coordination and cooperation within societies.[82] According to the definition suggested by Fukuyama (1999),

> social capital is an instantiated informal norm that promotes cooperation between two or more individuals. The norms that constitute social capital can range from a norm of reciprocity between two friends, all the way up to complex and elaborately articulated doctrines like Christianity or Confucianism. They must be instantiated in an actual human relationship (...). By this definition, trust, networks, civil society, and the like which have been associated with social capital are all epiphenominal, arising as a result of social capital but not constituting social capital itself. Not just any set of instantiated norms constitutes social capital; they must lead to cooperation in groups and therefore are related to traditional virtues

like honesty, the keeping of commitments, reliable performance of duties, reciprocity, and the like.

Social capital predominantly refers to relationships within groups but often creates externalities. This suggests that it may have positive as well as negative effects on overall economic and political development. As Fukuyama (1999) illustrates:

> An example of a positive externality is Puritanism's injunction, described by Max Weber, to treat all people morally, and not just members of the sib or family. The potential for cooperation thus spreads beyond the immediate group of people sharing Puritan norms. Negative externalities abound, as well. Many groups achieve internal cohesion at the expense of outsiders, who can be treated with suspicion, hostility, or outright hatred. Both the Ku Klux Klan and the Mafia achieve cooperative ends on the basis of shared norms, and therefore have social capital, but they also produce abundant negative externalities for the larger society in which they are embedded.

From an economic perspective, the primary function of social capital is to reduce those transaction costs that arise in association with formal coordination devices such as contracts, administrative rules, and hierarchies. Of course, coordinated action within a group can be basically achieved without social capital. But this would require the existence of a range of formal institutional arrangements that allow for or facilitate negotiating, litigating, and monitoring procedures; all of which cause substantial transaction costs. Moreover, since most complex agreements are based on relational contracts, social capital may help to ensure compliance with and hence enforce these agreements (Panther 1999).

In emerging as well as in advanced economies, informal institutions remain essential coordination mechanisms. With an increasing complexity of services and business transactions, effective formal monitoring devices become increasingly costly to implement and operate. In these instances, internalized professional codes of conduct and standards may help to lower these transaction costs. Note in this context, that, for example, a highly educated engineer in the software industry is frequently more knowledgeable about certain technical issues than her supervisor and can hence better assess her productivity. Similarly, an experienced civil servant responsible for public procurement can make procurement more efficient if he uses his personal judgment rather than sticking strictly to detailed procurement guidelines. Hence, the decentralization of business transactions, production decisions, and policy making is important for taking advantage of local knowledge and accelerating decision making.[83] But the potential efficiency gains can only be realized and the expected reductions in transaction costs (that are associated with rigid hierarchies) will only materialize if opportunistic behavior can be avoided and distrust between workers and managers or subordinated government representatives and their superiors can be overcome. In the absence of effective formal monitoring devices, the social capital that has been accumulated by the respective actors matters for enhancing cooperative behavior and attenuating the principal–agent problems resulting from a relatively autonomous scope for action. This observation that a continuously smooth and efficient operation of markets and hierarchies requires culturally shared norms and interpersonal trust (or what has been called the 'noncontractual elements of contract'[84]) has been stressed by sociologists such as Durkheim (1960/1933), Granovetter (1985), Evans *et al.* (1985), and Rueschemeyer (1986) for a long time.

Besides its economic function, social capital has an important political function. As mentioned earlier, it is the foundation from which trust and the structures of a civil society can emerge. Thus, social capital is an essential precondition to enable segments of society to organize themselves.[85] In particular, a vibrant civil society is seen as a critical factor that helps to balance state power and reduces excessive individualism.[86] Moreover, it facilitates participation in policy making and hence allows for effective administrative decentralization and makes the political system more flexible and responsive to citizens' needs. However, there is also a reverse side of the coin. As Fukuyama (1999) concedes, if a civil society also comprises powerful organizations representing narrowly defined interests, unproductive rent-seeking behavior may mean that the politicization of the public realm will become excessive, leading to substantial distortions of public policies or political deadlock.

Due to its positive economic and political functions, social capital plays a crucial role for both facilitating economic exchange and hence strengthening market processes within a framework of formal market order-oriented institutions and enhancing the accountability of and participation in policy making. Therefore, reformist policy makers as well as ordinary citizens or the organizations in which they are organized may have a strong interest in increasing society's stock of social capital. But since social capital represents an informal institution, it is not directly amenable to human design. But that does not mean that institutional reformers cannot influence the stock of social capital in a given society at all. They can actually do so by using indirect measures. Due to potentially negative effects of social capital on overall economic and political development, these measures should aim at enhancing social capital in a way in which cooperation is not only strengthened within but also between groups so that potential externalities are internalized and shared norms can be used to achieve cooperative ends at a broader societal level. In that sense, increasing social capital aims at attenuating growth-impeding informal institutions and at strengthening those informal norms and rules which are conducive to market-based transactions and which help legitimize formal political and economic institutions. As mentioned earlier, measures to restrain rent-seeking behavior concern the design of political institutions and require relatively insulated policy making bodies.

With respect to increasing the stock of social capital or creating new forms thereof, however, only a few obvious levers exist for governments. Policy makers need to be aware of actually existing forms of social capital. But they can neither reverse potentially negative effects nor simply duplicate positive impacts on the society as a whole. Since the development of social capital is path dependent, political measures can at best gradually seek to influence future developments without being able, however, to anticipate fully the consequences of their political interference. This fact reinforces our caveat against simply transferring formal institutions or organizational structures from one country to another without taking differences in informal institutions into account. The adherents of the theory of the developmental state, for example, argue that several distinct formal institutions are necessary for economic prosperity; including a powerful economic planning agency like MITI in Japan. But whether such an organization can have a positive impact on development not only depends on the technocratic ability to make policy, but on cultural factors and hence on the existing levels of social capital as well. For example, would an organization like MITI have the same effects in the United Kingdom or in Russia? As Fukuyama (1995) emphasizes, different societies may have developed different cultural capacities for effective institution building. In Japan, the levels of corruption and rent-seeking have been relatively low. But that has not been the case in other countries (for example, in Africa or Latin America) which have given strong policy making powers to agencies that are comparable to MITI.

The most promising lever for governments to enhance social capital is the fostering of education. Since educational organizations not only generate human capital but also impart social norms and rules, they represent a primary source of social capital. This not only holds for education at the primary and secondary level but for tertiary and even professional education as well. For example, professional training and advanced education for civil servants as well as creating an *esprit de corps* represent effective safeguards against political corruption. Increasing social capital within the public administration through informal networks can generate a corporate identity and an internal cohesion that cannot be achieved by meritocracy alone.[87] In association with an emphasis on the formal competence of bureaucrats, as well as merit-based recruitment and performance-related promotion, these 'nonbureaucratic elements of bureaucracy' (Evans 1995: 49) can reinforce the formal organizational structures of public administrations.

A more indirect means for the state to support the growth of interpersonal and inter-group trust and hence cooperative behavior is to ensure secure private property rights as well as public safety. In the absence of these public goods, private businesses and ordinary citizens may be exposed to the power of illegal private organizations such as the Mafia-like groups in Russia in the 1990s (Voigt and Kiwit 1995). In a safe and stable environment that facilitates public interaction of individuals, trust is much more likely to arise as an outcome of repeated interactions between individual actors.

Similarly, since societal segmentation, especially in traditional societies, has been a considerable source of institutional conflict, governments may seek to foster cooperation between different social groups by encouraging what Granovetter (1973) calls *weak ties*, that is the existence of individual actors within distinct social networks who are capable of moving between various groups and who therefore facilitate the communication of information and ideas as well as the transfer of human resources and the spread of innovational activities throughout society. Such weak ties automatically emerge in the course of development if the number of overlapping social groups allowing for multiple memberships gradually increases. But governments can indirectly support this development by fostering universal education, economic competition, and the political participation of local or ethnic groups.

Another maxim for the state is to avoid overly strict centralization. If the state assumes too many activities that could be better undertaken by members of the civil society or the private sector, it may easily destroy social capital, because people will lose their ability to cooperate with one another. The examples provided by Fukuyama (1999) with respect to French and Soviet history illustrate this point:

> France had a rich civil society at the end of the Middle Ages, but horizontal trust between individuals weakened as a result of a centralizing state that set Frenchmen (...) [against; J.A.] each other through a system of petty privileges and status distinctions. The same thing occurred in the former Soviet Union after the Bolshevik Revolution, where the Communist Party consciously sought to undermine all forms of horizontal association in favor of vertical ties between Party-State and individual. This has left post-Soviet society bereft of both trust and a durable civil society. There are, of course, good reasons why countries should restrict the size of their state sectors for economic reasons. On top of this, one can add a cultural motive of preserving a sphere for individual action and initiative in building civil associations.

Yet another means of generating social capital is to integrate society into international structures and hence take advantage of globalization. On the one hand, globalization may have negative consequences for LDCs and PSCs, especially if indigenous cultures are broken down or traditions are threatened.

On the other hand, globalization also opens up opportunities to take advantage of new ideas and practices and to establish international networks, not only for business corporations, but also for all kinds of members of civil society. This may help to overcome dysfunctional informal and formal institutions. The problem then is how to channel the various impacts of globalization into the domestic society in a way that contributes to overall social and economic development. This again refers to the rules and regulations that guide the internationalization process and eventually involves the question of how far the political institutions of society meet the core principles of effective governance (particularly accountability and participation).

In sum, informal constraints do matter for economic and social development and the effectiveness of policy reform. However, institutional conflicts will not necessarily result from any given attempt at institutional or policy reform. As far as formal market-order institutions are concerned, clashes with informal rules are relatively unlikely and therefore these formal institutions should be introduced as quickly as possible in order to ensure smooth functioning of the market system. With respect to task-oriented institutions, caution is advised. An essential precondition to avoiding institutional conflict is to ensure legitimacy of both formal economic and political institutions. Furthermore, legitimacy is important in yet another respect: informal institutions not only affect economic development due to their path dependence but also due to their *expectation dependence*, that is 'the influence of expectations of the future on the present' (Richter 1999). In order to incorporate expectation dependence adequately into current policy making, the legitimacy of policy reform and its acceptance need to be ensured. Besides a steady and consistent economic policy and participatory political institutions, the scientific justification of pursued reform strategies and the articulation of concrete policy measures in a readily comprehensible manner can play a critical role in this context. Moreover, governments can seek to overcome potential incompatibilities of formal and informal institutions by increasing the stock of society's social capital through a policy dialogue with the members of civil society and other indirect measures.

Due to the influence of informal institutions and the impossibility of fully anticipating future conflict situations through formal rules, policy reform is always a complex evolutionary process, the outcome of which can be hardly predicted. Governments can and need to become active players in shaping economic and social development, but they also need to be aware of the limits of political interference and economic reforms. Therefore, a MEGS ought to be perceived as a nexus of relational contracts, the efficacy of which depends on the interplay between formal and informal institutions and the gradual change in informal constraints during the course of development. In order to cope with the problems associated with path and expectation dependence, a flexible MEGS needs to be adaptively efficient in North's sense.

5.3.6 The Components of a Market-Enhancing Governance Structure

To conclude the conceptual-theoretical analysis of which factors constitute a flexible MEGS, the following considerations synthesize the main arguments of the preceding sections and identify useful starting-points for governance-related policies as well as the channels through which governance affects economic performance. According to our definition of governance, the main thread guiding governance-related policies concerns the capacity of institutions to implement policy reforms effectively and enhance private sector development. The notion of effective governance does not make any concrete prescriptions for the design of public policies. Such an approach takes into account that no blueprint is available for policy reforms that foster economic growth and development. Different reform strategies may be advisable, depending on the preferences of policy makers or citizens, the balance of political or economic power in a society, the impact of informal constraints on formal institution building, and the extent and kind of market and coordination failures. While in some instances, the policy desiderata inherent in the Washington Consensus may be both economically efficient and politically feasible, governments in other instances may need to rely on more activist measures in order to overcome severe market imperfections or to meet societal demands such as those for a more equal distribution of income and wealth. This implies that governance structures always need to be tailored to the particular country-specific context.

The ultimate objective of governance-related policies is gradually to create an adaptively efficient polity and economy that is suited to overcoming problems of underdevelopment and transition, and to deal properly with emerging new policy challenges as they arise. This implies that the concept underlying a MEGS has to be understood as a dynamic approach, the concrete form of which needs to vary across countries according to their specific characteristics, and within countries over time according their stage of development.[88] The structural foundations of a MEGS must be relatively durable to allow for stabilizing expectations of both public officials and private economic actors. But they must also be sufficiently flexible in order to allow for institutional innovations, for adjusting institutions if new forms of conflict resolution are needed, and for feedback mechanisms that facilitate policy revisions in cases of failures. This implies that a MEGS is effective if it ensures the proper implementation, enforcement, and sustainability of policy reforms. It is (sufficiently) flexible if it ensures a relatively high degree of policy adaptability to a changing political, economic, international, and technological environment.

Basically five realms guiding political and economic exchange can be distinguished which together make up the institutional set of any given society and determine its quality of governance. This, first of all, concerns the public sector. The relevant institutions include the core public sector institutions that govern the functioning of a country's political bodies (its executive branch of government at the central and sub-national levels, the legislature including political committees, the judiciary, and its public administration, including regulatory agencies) as well as the institutions that determine the policy making process. Regarding the latter, the degree of decentralization and its concrete form in a given country are expected to play a crucial role for the quality of governance. The second realm is the state–society interface, that is the institutions linking the policies of the public sector with the needs and activities of the private sector and civil society. In this context, institutions as diverse as deliberation councils, public–private partnerships in production activities, and the direct involvement of citizens and NGOs in the design and implementation of development projects at the local level may play a critical role. The third area that is crucial for the quality of governance involves the formal economic institutions that determine the terms of exchange in the market place. Some of these institutions may be internal, that is, crafted and enforced through private ordering by domestic firms, economic intermediary organizations (for example, business associations and trade unions), and transnational corporations. Others will be necessarily external, that is, imposed and enforced by the state. Fourthly, the international structures in which a given country is embedded play an essential role, because they determine to what extent the country takes part in, and is constrained through, the international division of labor. On the one hand, this concerns the international competition that domestic enterprises face and the impact of foreign investors on the domestic economy and their influence on domestic policy making. On the other hand, this relates to contractual relations with foreign governments as well as the regulations and constraints that are associated with a country's membership in international organizations such as the IMF, WTO, or the ILO. In particular through potential conditionalities attached to their lending operations, organizations like the IMF or the World Bank not only influence the processes guiding the international flow of goods, services, and capital, but also the design of external economic institutions and reforms of the public sector. The fifth realm of governance is a society's informal institutions, including its social capital, which can have a relatively strong impact on the quality and the results of policy making but which cannot be (directly) altered through political design.

Hence, these realms represent the basic starting points for governance-enhancing policies.[89] But their concrete form in any given country depends on a variety of channels of influence which are summarized in a stylized manner in Figure 5.2.[90] This implies that domestic political actors, although they basically have the means and the power to shape all realms of governance except for the set of informal institutions prevalent in society, are not the only key agents for establishing, reforming, and sustaining the institutional matrix. Although the emergence of effective governance always presupposes political commitment and leadership at the national level or at least at local/regional levels of policy making, strong intermediary associations and dynamic entrepreneurs can reinforce public policies and possibly also compensate (at least temporarily) for policy failures or help gradually to remove rigid governance mechanisms that impede innovative activities. Important roles can and ought to be assumed by business associations, civic organizations, private firms, local governments, and international organizations. But, of course, the opposite may also occur, namely that governance-enhancing policies are undermined by domestic, non-political or foreign players.

These considerations lead to a twofold conclusion: first, even in the absence of binding political commitment at either the central or sub-national levels of government, domestic non-political and foreign actors may seek to enhance the quality of governance through private ordering, building coalitions with reform-minded parts of the government or other political factions, or by putting political pressure on the government to comply with international rules and to apply international standards in policy making. In general, however, this will only partially improve the quality of governance due to the coercive power of the state. The second conclusion, therefore, is that in order gradually to craft a sustainable MEGS, credible political commitment is a *conditio sine qua non*. This presupposes the existence of reform-minded political forces which are in power or at least have the means to influence institutional change through appropriate coalition and consensus building. If this is the case, then governance-enhancing policies can be undertaken.

The fundamental pillars constituting a MEGS include the creation of a strong but limited government, comprehensive and coherent capacity building measures, as well as the implementation and enforcement of key economic institutions that ensure a proper functioning of market processes and a dynamic development of the private sector. With respect to the practical problems of policy reform, utmost significance must be attached to capacity building measures because they not only aim at human resource development and the restructuring of specific public-sector organizations but also at changing fundamental political institutions (such as election laws) and making the operation of economic institutions more efficient. Practically it is the extent, quality, and coherence of capacity building measures that ultimately determine the credibility of political commitments and the degree to which the core principles of governance (accountability, participation, predictability, and transparency) are realized (see Box 5.2)[91].

Last but not least comes the question of what are the channels through which governance affects economic performance. These essentially concern the political institutions which determine the formulation and implementation of public policies and the economic institutions that determine the terms of market exchange. The quality of governance influences economic growth and development in manifold, though indirect, ways, and the effects are contingent on the actions of a great variety of actors. The impact that enhanced governance can unfold ranges from improving the technical competence to conduct macroeconomic stabilization policies, to ensuring a more efficient provision of public goods at the central and the local level, to enhancing the efficacy of privatization programs, to overcoming potential resistance to reforms, and to promoting the dynamic efficiency of market transactions. Governance can shape economic performance in a bottom-up and in a top-down manner. The former influence, for example, relates to issues such as political decentralization, fiscal federalism, and subsidiarity as well as the impact of local institutions and sub-national policies. The latter concerns the institutional components of policy issues like country-wide deregulation policies, social security programs, and monetary policy. Finally, it is to be noted that enhanced governance may indirectly affect economic growth through both fostering factor accumulation and increasing total factor productivity. For example, labor participation ratios may be increased through adequate education policies or reforming rules for hiring and firing. Investment ratios can be increased through sound macroeconomic policies, credible government commitments to protect private property rights, and a market-oriented financial sector that is subject to prudent regulation. Total factor productivity can be positively affected, for example, by governance-related policies that seek to foster technological and industrial development and facilitate overall structural change.

In sum, the conceptual approach to building effective governance structures, which has been developed in the preceding sections, improves our understanding of the politico-institutional problems associated with economic reforms in LDCs and PSCs and suggests a great variety of starting points for policy and institutional reforms which may help to improve the quality of policy making. The conceptual framework is suitable to identify the key components of a MEGS, the main actors who can shape institutional change, as well as the potential channels through which governance affects economic

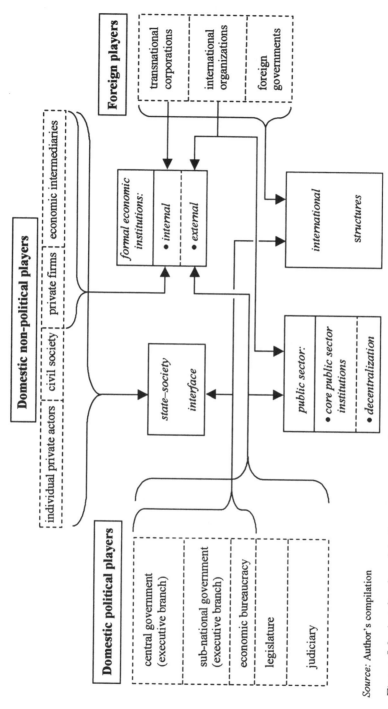

Source: Author's compilation

Figure 5.2: A stylized model of governance: realms and players

performance. But due to the abstract nature of this approach and the fact that effective governance is highly context- and time-specific, concrete case studies need to be analysed in order to understand how governance-related policies work (or do not work) in practice and to distill potential lessons from specific country examples which may guide theoretical research and practical policy making.

Box 5.2: Principles and capacity building measures for constituting MEGS	
Governance	capacity building
Credibility	veto-rights; bonding/signaling mechanisms; agenda control mechanisms; separation of powers;
Accountability	public sector management; public enterprise management and reform; public financial management; civil service reform;
Participation	participation of beneficiaries and affected groups in projects; public–private partnerships, deliberation councils, and industrial districts; decentralization of economic functions and empowerment of local government; cooperation with NGOs;
Predictability	legal and regulatory reform; legal framework for private sector development;
Transparency	disclosure of information; clarity about government rules and regulations; transparency in political decision making and public policy implementation.

Notes

1. In reality, of course, LDC states differ considerably with respect to the dimensions recorded here as weaknesses and strengths. To simplify the argument, this paper follows Frischtak (1994) and uses the Weberian ideal-type of state as a reference model. Thus, the analytical model of the state, used here, does not result from empirical characteristics of any LDC state and may be tested only with regard to its conceptual suitability.

2. See, for example, Evans (1989, 1995), Huff (1995), and Leftwich (1995).

3. See Putnam *et al.* (1988) for a brief review.

4. See, for example, Huntington (1968), Huntington and Dominguez (1975), and Weiner and Huntington (1987).

5. See, for example, Evans *et al.* (1985), Skocpol (1985), and Evans (1992).

6. See, for example, Meier (1991a), Grindle and Thomas (1991), Grindle (1996), World Bank (1996 and 1997), and Bardhan (1997a).

7. For example, Rostow (1958: 155) argued: 'Initial changes in method require that some group in the society have the will and the authority to install and diffuse new production techniques; and a perpetuation of the growth process requires that such a leading group expands in authority and that the society as a whole responds to the impulses set up by the initial changes (...). It is likely to require political, social and institutional changes which will both perpetuate an initial increase in the scale of investment and result in the regular acceptance and absorption of innovations.'

8. This holds, for example, if the term *good governance* is supposed to mean promoting sustainable economic and social development, democratization, participatory development, fostering the enforcement of human rights, and improving environmental standards; see, for example, Leisinger (1995).

9. This definition simply creates a new term without providing any new conceptualization. What makes it particularly problematic is the use of the adjective *good*, which only reflects subjective perceptions.

10. See, for example, Doner (1992) and Thomas (1996).

11. Quoted in Doornbos (1995: 383).

12. Recent studies on governance and related concepts applied in the context of economic development include in the realm of development economics, for example, Auroi (1992), Bardhan (1993, 1997a, and 1997b), Dethier (1999a and b), Evans (1995 and 1998), Elsenhans (1996), Goldsmith (1995), Leftwich (1993 and 1994) and Wohlmuth (1998); in the realm of the NIE, for example, Dixit (1996), North (1995b), Weingast (1995), and Williamson (1996a); as well as in political development the studies by Grindle (1996) and Grindle and Thomas (1991). In public economics, notable publications include World Bank (1995a), Tanzi (1996) and La Porta et al. (1999). With respect to contributions in the field of public administration see, in particular, recent publications in the journals *Public Administration and Development, Governance. An International Journal of Policy and Administrations* as well as in the *IDS Bulletin,* Vol. 23, No. 4 (1992) on 'New Forms of Public Administration'.

13. See, for example, Chalker (1991), Aberbach and Rockman (1992), Santiso (1999) and the contributions in Hydén and Bratton (1992) as well as in the IDS Bulletin on 'Good Government' (*IDS Bulletin*, Vol. 24, No. 1, 1993).

14. See, for example, Dhonte and Kapur (1997), IMF (1997), and Dillinger and Fay (1999).

15. See Leftwich (1993 and 1996) for extensive elaboration of this argument.

16. See, for example, Bardhan (1995), Boycko et al. (1996), Martimort (1996), and Streeten (1993). The following considerations are based on Ahrens (2000).

17. See Webster's *New Universal Unabridged Dictionary*, London: Dorset & Baber, 1979.

18. See, for example, Barro (1994) and de Haan and Siermann (1995).

19. As will be argued below, governance does not presuppose, as the concept of *government* does, that political authority needs to result from the formal legal institutional arrangements

of a state. Neither does it imply, as the concept of *leadership* does, that political control is necessarily assumed by official political elites or the head of state; see Hydén (1992).

20. The following considerations on the conceptual use of the term essentially draw on Frischtak (1994).

21. Frischtak (1994) points out that this conception may also reflect the positive development experiences of countries such as South Korea and Japan, which succeeded in modernizing without giving up their cultural traits.

22. Regarding the cultural dimensions of governance in an African context, see Martin (1992).

23. See, for example, Mummert (1999a), Pejovich (1994), and North (1995a).

24. See Pejovich (1994); preconditions for a market for institutions to work effectively comprise a stable and credible legal system, equal protection of all property rights, and the freedom of exchange and law of contract.

25. The following considerations on micro-analytic governance essentially draw on Williamson (1985, 1995, and 1996a) and Klein (1998).

26. Firms are seen as being similar to markets in the sense that both are realms in which individuals transact. In the micro-analytic branch of the NIE, especially in the agency literature, the firm as an entity is not a major subject of analysis, but rather a practical label for a set of contracting relationships agreements between managers and owners, employees and managers, and the company and its suppliers and customers. Accordingly, the firm is seen as a nexus of contractual agreements, 'a legal fiction which serves as a focus for a complete process in which the conflicting objectives of individuals (...) are brought into equilibrium within a framework of contractual relations' (Jensen and Meckling 1976: 311–12). Thus the focus is on how particular contracts can alleviate these conflicts. The firm's boundary is then an issue of secondary importance; see Klein (1998) for a review of the corresponding literature.

27. Notice that complete contracts specify a particular course of action, terms of exchange, or a decision that are contingent on all conceivable future conditions which may be relevant for a specific transaction. For example, textbook models relying on the notion of competitive general equilibrium, assume all contractual agreements to be complete. Although the future cannot be anticipated with certainty, the probability distributions of all imaginable future states of affairs are assumed to be known. 'In an important sense, the model is "timeless": all relevant future contingencies are considered in the *ex ante* contracting stage, so there are no decisions to be made – no actions to be taken at all, really – as the future plays itself out' (Klein 1998: 14; original italics).

28. See Williamson (1985, chapters 7 and 8) for an elaboration of the hostage model.

29. Concerning the differences between the approaches of North and Williamson, see Eggertsson (1990), North (1990c), and Ensminger (1992).

30. Major exceptions in this regard include North (1990a and 1995a), Weingast (1993 and 1995), and Bardhan (1997a).

31. See Chapter 5, section 3.4. See, for example, Barzel (1989), Berglöf and von Thadden (1999), Williamson (1975, 1985, and 1996b), and World Bank (1997).

32. See, for example, Barro (1994), de Haan and Siermann (1995), and Siermann (1998).

33. Political legitimacy is not considered as the ultimate objective of effective governance but rather as a side condition; regarding a different perspective on this issue see Hydén (1992). Concerning the importance of political legitimacy for overcoming potential conflicts between formal and informal institutions, see Chapter 5, Section 5.3.5.

34. Note in this context that our conceptual approach to effective governance presupposes political stability in a given country. According to Haber *et al.* (1999), 'a political system is stable, or self-preserving, (1) if there is common knowledge about the selection mechanism to replace governments and the rules that manage political action, and (2) the institutional arrangements that specify this political system are self-enforcing. (...) these two conditions imply that there is one and only one political system in place at any given time.' In the absence of political stability, the approach to establishing effective governance structures as it is discussed in this study is hardly feasible, because it presupposes a certain degree of regime durability that cannot be ensured in a politically unstable environment that is

characterized by a relatively high chance of external political shocks, violence, and social disruptions. Yet, political instability does not necessarily imply economic stagnation. As Haber *et al.* (1999) illustrate by using the example of Revolutionary Mexico, a governance structure that integrates political and economic interests through vertical political integration of politically powerful factions and economic elites may turn out as the only feasible, though theoretically second-best, approach that is suitable to foster economic performance sustainably. This study essentially omits the problem of political stability and only considers it in its weak form in Chapter 6, Section 6.3.1 on Russia.

35. The studies by Brautigam (1992), World Bank (1992), and Root (1996) are partly based on the same principles. For different, though related, approaches, see Hydén (1992) and Boeninger (1992).

36. Notice in this context that democratic rules alone are neither a necessary nor a sufficient condition for political credibility, although democratization processes may be conducive to the emergence of political credibility over time. In their empirical investigation, Borner *et al.* (1995) observe that while modern industrialized countries show relatively high degrees of political credibility mainly due to democratic participation, numerous democratic LDCs still lack credibility. On the other hand, they find that several rapidly developing countries that fail the democracy test have found distinct institutional mechanisms which enhance credibility.

37. See, for example, Borner et al. (1995), Levy and Spiller (1996), and Cox and McCubbins (1997).

38. The following arguments are based on World Bank (1992), Hydén (1992), Root (1996), and Streeten (1997). For a discussion of the importance of accountability for economic policy making see Przeworski (1995).

39. Effective accountability is based on two distinct but related processes: a process of appraisal, which is necessary to investigate and monitor the performance of public agencies, and a sanctioning process, which allows authoritative action to be taken in order to reward good performance or penalize bad performance. Adequate channels of participation help reinforce both processes.

40. South Korea's experience with respect to financing primary education provides an instructive example of how the collaboration of parents, the private sector, local organizations, and the central government can jointly produce effective results. Central and local governments contribute to financing schools as do parent–teacher associations, and the latter are involved in decision making. Parents, in turn, finance large parts of the education at the secondary and tertiary level; see Salmen (1990).

41. Hence, political institutions represent a certain subset of all those institutions which affect economic development; see North (1990a).

42. Most of these studies focus on East Asian development; see, for example, Lamb (1987), Migdal (1988), Killick (1989), Wade (1990), and Werlin (1991).

43. Of course, the idea that the state could be developmental was already inherent in the early writings on development policy including the works of Myrdal, Baran, Rosenstein-Rodan, and Kuznets; see Chang (1999).

44. See Johnson (1999). Note, however, that the theory of the developmental state has not been exclusively applied to North East Asia. See, for example, the contributions in Woo-Cumings (1999) for applications to India as well as to Latin American and European countries.

45. In Japan, more subtle mechanisms were in place that ensured relative independence of the state from private business. Although big private business provided substantial funds to the ruling Liberal Democratic Party (LDP), it did not have a dominant impact on or influence over public policies. The reason was that the LDP, although it supported private business, had to rely on the support of the farming population to stay in power; see Johnson (1987).

46. See Campos and Root (1996), Evans (1995), Qian and Weingast (1997a), Stiglitz (1998a), and World Bank (1997).

47. A professional bureaucracy that is characterized by internal promotion instead of political appointments also allows for a lengthening of the time period which public officials are

willing to wait for the realization of the benefits of their policies. This increases the share of public resources devoted to long-term investment projects such as infrastructure and eventually leads to higher economic growth (Evans and Rauch 1995).

48. See Root (1996), Evans (1995), as well as Chang and Cheema (2002).

49. *International Herald Tribune*, June 5, 1990; quoted in Williamson (1995: 187).

50. See North (1995a), Weingast (1993, 1995, and 1997), and Williamson (1995).

51. See Telser (1980). The notion of self-enforcement was introduced into the NIE by Klein, Crawford, and Alchian (1978).

52. Rent-seeking is generally viewed as an unproductive activity. Therefore, the term *unproductive rent-seeking* appears to be a tautology. But as we will argue in Chapter 6, Section 6.2, there are in fact special forms of rent-seeking – the pursuit of so-called *contingent* or *learning rents* – which are productive.

53. See Chapter 6, Section 6.2 with regard to experiences in, and potential lessons from, the HPAEs, Weingast (1995) and North and Weingast (1989) for the historical evolution of a strong but limited state in England; Root (1994) for a historical study on France and England; Montinola *et al.* (1995) for the experiences in contemporary China; and Weiss (1998) for analyses of state capacity and the impact of political institutions on economic performance in East Asia, Sweden, and Germany.

54. See the next section for a conceptual approach to capacity building in the public sector and for examples.

55. See Parikh and Weingast (1997), Borner *et al.* (1995) and especially Mummert (1999a) for problems related to the problem of how to translate *de jure* into *de facto* institutional reform.

56. Regarding further elaboration on these institutions, see, for example, Borner et al. (1995), Dixit (1996), Persson *et al.* (1997), Rodrik (1995), Root (1996), and Weingast (1993).

57. In this respect, see Knack and Keefer (1997a), who find in their cross-country analysis that social capital matters for economic performance. Civic norms and trust are relatively strong in societies with relatively high incomes and equal income distribution, with institutions restraining predatory state action, and with educated, ethnically homogeneous populations. They argue that in countries in which interpersonal trust is relatively low, the provision of formal institutional rules monitoring economic exchange is of particular importance.

58. Regarding the question as to which tasks and transactions are basically to be conducted by a public bureaucracy and for which a private mode of organization is better suited, see Williamson (1999).

59. The following mainly draws on Grindle and Hilderbrand (1995).

60. For a more detailed discussion of the following mechanisms with respect to public sector management in LDCs and PSCs see, for example, Campos *et al.* (1994), Evans (1995), Grindle and Hilderbrand (1995), Evans and Rauch (1995), Campos and Root (1996), Campos and Pradhan (1996), Pradhan (1998), World Bank (1997), and Stiglitz (1998b).

61. In general, constraints with respect to the operation of single organizations or organizational networks as well as human resource development are more tractable and can be more quickly remedied than constraints at the level of the action environment. But the case studies discussed in Grindle and Hilderbrand (1995) indicate that all dimensions of capacity building are strongly interdependent. This implies that narrowly focused efforts at capacity building will not be effective, especially if the most binding constraints are ignored.

62. For a comprehensive discussion of the strategic management of reform implementation see Grindle and Thomas (1991).

63. Another problem with the Weberian perspective is that it underemphasizes what Evans (1995: 71) calls the 'nonbureaucratic elements of bureaucracy'. Informal networks may create a corporate identity and foster the internal coherence of a public administration which cannot be ensured by merit-based procedures alone. However, the nature as well as the effects of such networks are contingent on the selection process that is used to choose civil servants. Such networks have positively affected public sector performance in several industrialized, but also in less developed, countries, notably in East Asia; as Evans (1995:

71–72) observes with respect to the Japanese experience: 'Solidarity groups, like the Japanese batsu, built on an amalgam of meritocratic selection, intensive socialization, and quasi-primordial ties, play a crucial role in the internal cohesion of effective bureaucracies. Their presence provides critical reinforcement for the compliance to organizational norms and sanctions that Weber took for granted. Their absence makes it harder to prevent devolution into individual maximization and the "marketization" of state offices'.

64. Evans (1992: 148). Note, however, that such embeddedness may increase state capacity to facilitate policy reform at the initial stages of development, but later may become an impediment to growth. This might cause serious problems in future policy making and calls for a continuous adjustment of the institutional foundations of economic policy making.

65. Although the role of economic institutions had been relatively neglected by mainstream economists in their works on policy reform in LDCs until the 1980s, it gained considerable prominence during the last decade, *inter alia* due to the growing impact of the NIE in the field of economics. Today, the importance of economic institutions is widely recognized, and numerous theoretical and empirical studies have elaborated the substantial relevance of those institutions for the success of economic reforms and the proper functioning of markets; see, for example, Williamson (1985), Knack and Keefer (1995), Kasper and Streit (1998), and Rodrik (1999). Therefore, this section does not reconstruct the discussion on economic institutions, but restricts itself to the identification of those institutional arrangements which perform key roles in flexible MEGS and suggests ways of acquiring them.

66. See Stiglitz (1998a, 1998b, 1998c), Camdessus (1999), Wolfensohn (1999), Aslund (1999) as well as the contributions to the IMF Conference on Second Generation Reforms, Washington, DC, 8–9 November, 1999. Internet Website: http://www.imf.org/external/pubs/ft/seminar/1999/reforms/index.htm.

67. Note in this context the efforts of the World Bank to introduce the so-called *Comprehensive Development Framework*; for further information on this project see the Internet Website http://www.worldbank.org/cdf/.

68. Kasper and Streit (1998: 151; emphasis omitted).

69. Notice in this regard that to be effective, private property rights must go hand in hand with control rights. Ownership will be meaningless if economic actors cannot actually control the use of their assets and do not have control over their returns. In today's Russia, for example, shareholders have formal property rights but they frequently cannot effectively control enterprises. In contrast, as Qian and Weingast (1997a) observe, the experience of township and village enterprises in China suggests that control rights may be established and can foster entrepreneurial activities even if property rights are not clearly defined. Thus formal legislation is neither a necessary nor a sufficient condition for ensuring effective control. In practice, Rodrik (1999) concludes, the efficacy of control rights is contingent not only on legislation but also on private enforcement as well as informal norms such as customs and tradition.

70. See Eucken (1990/1952). Notice in this connection that our references to *ordo* liberal ideas are restricted to the policy prescriptions concerning the economic order. Actually, the *ordo* liberal approach is much broader in that it not only emphasizes the interrelations of institutional frameworks of various product and factor markets but also the interdependence of all suborders of society comprising the economic, the political, and the social order. This implies that economic, social, legal, and other policies need to be compatible so that the institutions of different suborders mutually support each other; see, for example, Böhm (1950) and Leipold (1994).

71. With respect to the use of the mentioned policy instruments and institutions and the role of governments in East Asia in overcoming coordination failures, see Chapter 6, Section 6.2.

72. To foster this understanding, case studies are required which help explain the success and failure of various types of government intervention. With respect to selective government policies in East Asia, see Chapter 6, Section 6.2.1.

73. See Ergas (1987), Lall (1992), and Evenson and Westphal (1995).

74. With respect to the South Korean case, see the more detailed discussion in Chapter 6, Section 6.2.3.
75. Regarding the economic, institutional, and political transformation of the former GDR, see, for example, Sinn and Sinn (1993), Willgerodt (1994), Brücker (1995), Eisen and Wollmann (1996), and Mummert and Wohlgemuth (1998).
76. See, for example, Qian (1999) as well as Lau, Qian, and Roland (2000) who argue that the institutional peculiarities of the development process in China are solutions to local informational and political problems for the solution of which no blueprint exists.
77. See Chapter 6, Sections 6.2 and 6.3.1 for further elaboration on this point.
78. Thus, the introduction of formal task-oriented institutions may trigger institutional conflicts if these formal institutions prescribe ends or means that conflict with the ends and/or means prescribed by informal institutions. This is, for example, the case if the formal rules require criminal behavior to be reported to the state authorities, whereas informal institutions prescribe that criminals be protected if they belong to one's own ethnic group or family. Another example is merit-based procedures in public administrations to recruit and promote bureaucrats, which may contradict social norms that favor nepotism.
79. Such a conflict would be conceivable if, for example, social norms existed that prescribe non-compliance with contractual agreements or the expropriation of third parties' property. However, as Mummert (1999b) observes, such prescriptions, if they exist at all, can only be found in inter-group relations, but not within groups.
80. Note in this context that the formal rules constituting a market-based economy do not necessarily relate to high and sustained economic growth. Even if the same set of formal institutions is established and equally enforced in two different countries, economic outcomes may differ due to different resource endowments, innovation rates, or preferences. As Mummert (1999b: 8) nicely illustrates, 'within the same framework of formal institutions a society consisting solely of "before Christmas Scrooges" would generate a pattern of behavior that would be very different from a society full of "after Christmas Scrooges".'
81. The transition toward a market economy and a democratic order in the PSCs provides rich illustrative material supporting this point. Particularly in the former USSR and former Yugoslavia, diverse ethnic groups, different nationalities, as well as communal groups jointly supported the dissolution of the socialist system. But after political independence had been realized, the emerging conflicts among these groups especially in the Russian Federation and Serbia hindered a social consensus on policy making and undermined the legitimacy of the new formal institutions.
82. See, for example, Coleman (1988 and 1990), who recently brought the term into wider use, but also Ostrom (1990), Putnam (1993), Fukuyama (1995), and Evans (1997).
83. These examples have been taken from Fukuyama (1999).
84. Evans (1995: 26); this is a paraphrase of the gist of Durkheim's dialog with Spencer in *The Division of Labor in Society*; see Durkheim (1960/1933).
85. Note that if a civil society includes numerous groups and associations that enable and empower citizens to organize themselves, political authorities will have less powerful arguments to justify government intervention in the private sector.
86. See in this context, for example, Putnam (1993) who investigates the effects of social capital on local government performance in Italy. He essentially attributes government inefficiencies and widespread corruption in Southern Italy to the prevalent low levels of social capital.
87. Such informal networks can be internal or external. An example of the former might be networks consisting of civil servants who graduated from the same university, while the latter might include state–society relations, such as deliberation councils; see Johnson (1982), Okimoto (1989), and Evans (1995) for examples drawing on Japanese experiences.
88. Emerging new policy challenges may, for example, result from increasing globalization, external economic shocks, or a changing balance of economic or political power within a given society. Country-specific characteristics that may necessitate different forms of effective governance concern, for example, distinct historical developments and hence

informal institutions, different political systems (democratic or non-democratic regimes, parliamentary or presidential systems), or different comparative advantages of countries. Moreover, the stage of development of any given country matters for the adequacy of its governance structure because the extent of market integration, the degree of market failures, and the degree of openness may vary in the course of development, as may the capacity and the capability of governments and bureaucracies to undertake reform policies.

89. More specific points of departure for governance-enhancing policies are context- and time-specific and will be discussed in the next chapter which deals with practical problems of governance in selected LDCs and PSCs.

90. Note that Figure 5.2 simply seeks to synthesize the potential impact of different players on the distinct realms of governance and to show the complexity of governance-related policies. The arrows indicate major channels of influence which may actually differ across countries according to their political, economic, and social structures. The fifth realm of governance, that of informal institutions, is disregarded in Figure 5.2 because they cannot be directly influenced by political or economic actors.

91. Box 5.2 presents examples of capacity building measures which may help enhance the fulfillment of the fundamental principles underlying a MEGS. While particular measures are related to single principles, this should not imply that there are no overlappings. For example, civil service reform may not only aim at enhancing the accountability of policy making but also its predictability and transparency. This classification has been made according to the presumably major channel of influence. Moreover, credibility is considered to be the overall principle in our governance framework. That means that all capacity building efforts to fulfill the other four principles will indirectly help to accomplish credibility. If particular mechanisms such as the separation of powers are separately mentioned, this should indicate their particular relevance for enhancing credibility.

6. Governance in practice: evidence from less developed countries and economies in transition

The conceptual approach to instituting a flexible MEGS suggests that there is no universal model that can ensure effective governance in the course of economic development and transformation. Instead, policy reform and particularly institution building should be guided by an effort to achieve as high a level as possible of four core principles, namely accountability, participation, predictability, and transparency. The main hypothesis is that whatever institution building improves a country's scores on these principles will enhance the ability of policy makers credibly to (pre)commit themselves to deliver their promises to citizens, to formulate socially beneficial policies, to implement and sustain these policies, and hence to foster economic growth. Drawing on the evidence provided by LDCs and PSCs, this hypothesis is tested empirically here, in our first step, using cross-country regressions and analysing the development of various institutional indicators across countries and over time (Section 6.1).

Moreover, the theoretical arguments provide some pointers as to which broad institutional realms are of particular significance for making governance more effective. These include (1) the institutions that integrate a given country into international structures; (2) the organizational design and the incentives within the public sector; (3) the institutions linking the public and private sector; and (4) the formal economic institutions in a given country. All of these areas are basically amenable to intentional and constructive institution building. Therefore, in a second step (sections 2 and 3), we discuss several case studies in order to identify the distinct and concrete characteristics of governance structures. In this context, we include both 'success cases' and 'failures' in our analysis. While it is generally desirable that institutional reforms aim at improvements in all of these areas, the case studies show that – depending on a country's stage of development, its existing capacities, the potential impact of informal institutions, and the international constraints that it faces – MEGS can be constituted in different ways and with different emphasis given to the distinct institutional realms mentioned above.[1] Thus, as will be argued in the following subsections, the concept of embedded autonomy was, for example, a critical pillar of effective governance in the HPAEs, especially in North East Asia, whereas China's remarkable economic performance has been mainly attributed to its decentralization policies. In contrast, successful economies in transition such as Poland, Hungary, and the Czech Republic benefited greatly from the likely accession to the EU that has been realistically envisaged from the very beginning of the transformation processes. These 'success cases' will be discussed and compared with experiences of countries like Russia and India, in which governance structures have been relatively weak and policy and institutional reforms so far less successful. The objectives of this comparative approach are to distill potential lessons for governance-related policies from successful cases while acknowledging country-specific characteristics, to identify the differences in governance structures in countries that face similar development or transition challenges and hence similar problems of policy reform (such as Poland and Hungary or China and India), and to explore ways in which a flexible MEGS might be brought to evolve over time (Chapter 7, Section 7.1). Finally comes the question of how international organizations may support the development of MEGS in their member countries (Chapter 7, Section 7.2).

For essentially three reasons, particular attention is given in the subsequent sections to the economic performance and the policy-making regimes of PSCs and LDCs in Central and Eastern Europe and East Asia. First of all, the HPAEs, a subgroup of East Asian countries, are among the very few countries that experienced exceptionally high growth rates and sustained them over the last four decades. Therefore, an analysis of these countries' institutions and governance structures promises to yield important lessons for other countries. Secondly, most of the HPAEs were seriously affected by the Asian Crisis in 1997/98. This has often been attributed to a lack of supervisory and regulatory financial institutions, nepotism, and cronyism. But most of these countries managed to resume economic growth relatively quickly. This raises the question of whether the Asian Crisis was indeed a crisis of governance and, if so, how policy makers managed to overcome structural rigidities and institutional impediments. Thirdly, the economies in transition in CEE are explicitly taken into consideration because the systemic transformation is basically a transformation of governance structures which comprises institution building in virtually all suborders of society. This implies that policy reform packages cannot be simply prescribed but that they must be based on a new politico-institutional foundation that will be diametrically opposed to the former socialist one. Neither a theory nor clear-cut pragmatic policy implications exist that can guide such a transition. Yet, the first decade of transition witnessed a few transition economies that outperformed the majority of PSCs. It is therefore worthwhile to analyse the differences in policy making among these countries and to look for potential lessons from other success cases such as the HPAEs.[2]

6.1 INSTITUTIONS MATTER: THE EMPIRICAL EVIDENCE

Until recently, empirical analyses of the institutional determinants of economic performance were rare.[3] Due, however, to new comprehensive data sets which have become available recently, this gap in research could be partially closed. Since the beginning of the 1990s, there is an emerging empirical literature that tackles the demanding task of measuring institutional differences and their impact on economic performance, both over time and across countries. This literature brought about a number of striking results and insights and supported the major findings of earlier theoretical works. Some studies even seek explicitly to incorporate governance aspects into their empirical investigations. By reviewing the major contributions to this strand of empirical research, this section provides some evidence on the impact of political and economic institutions as well as on the institutional changes that go hand in hand with economic performance and especially economic growth.

Recent empirical analyses that investigate the relation between different institutional indicators and economic performance are listed in Table 6.1. The first part of Table 6.1 comprises studies that analyse the relationship between formal institutions and economic performance by essentially using subjective indicators of institutional quality.[4] They provide evidence that improvements in formal institutional arrangements are associated with economic growth thereby supporting our theoretical hypotheses. Moreover, four studies (Knack and Keefer 1997a, La Porta *et al.* 1997b, Panther 1999, and Zak and Knack 1999) explicitly take the importance of informal institutions into account and analyse the impact of trust on economic performance. They find that trust and civic cooperation have positive effects on economic growth.

Basically, the part of the literature that focuses on the presumed effects of formal institutions on economic growth can be separated into two main approaches: the first one builds on the seminal paper by Barro (1991) who included measures of political stability as a proxy for institutional quality in his cross-country analysis of long-term growth. He concluded that the significantly adverse effect of his proxies (number of coups and political assassinations) on growth reflects the uncertainty of property rights. Five important studies which followed in this direction have been provided by Knack and Keefer (1995), Brunetti *et al.* (1997a, b, and c), and Rodrik

Table 6.1: Empirical evidence of the relationship between institutions and economic and social development

Authors	Methodological Approach	Main Findings
	I. Impact of Institutions on Economic Growth	
Knack and Keefer (1995)	Cross-country regressions using two subjective indexes of institutional development. One composite index combines variables such as quality of the bureaucracy, corruption in government, rule of law, expropriation risk, and repudiation of contracts by government. The other combines variables such as bureaucratic delays, nationalization, potential, contract enforceability and infrastructure quality.	Institutions that protect property rights are crucial for economic growth.
		Institutional development increases the rates of convergence between developed and developing countries
Mauro (1995)	Cross-country regressions using subjective indexes of corruption, the amount of red tape, the efficiency of the judicial system, and various categories of political stability.	Corruption is negatively linked with economic growth.
Fischer, Sahay, and Végh (1996)	Pooled cross-section times series regressions using the cumulative liberalization index (computed by de Melo, Denzier, and Gelb (1997)) as an indicator of structural reforms together with initial conditions and macroeconomic policy variables to explain annual growth in PSCs over the period 1992-1994.	Market-oriented institutions have a significant impact on economic growth.
Brunetti, Kisunko, and Weder (1997a, b, and c)	Surveys of business establishments around the world to construct an index of the 'credibility of rules', composed of 'the predictability of rule-making, subjective perceptions of political instability, security of persons and property, predictability of judicial enforcement, and corruption'. Cross-firm and cross-country regressions test the relationship between the credibility index and economic growth.	Credibility promotes investment and economic growth.

Authors	Methodological Approach	Main Findings
I. Impact of Institutions on Economic Growth		
Chong and Calderón (1997a)	Geweke decomposition to test the causality and feedback between institutional measures (such as contract enforceability, nationalization potential, infrastructure quality, bureaucratic delays, and a composite index of the above four) and economic growth.	Improving institutional development promotes economic growth in developing countries.
Knack and Keefer (1997b)	Cross-country regressions using institutional variables such as the rule of law, the pervasiveness of corruption, the risk of expropriation, and contract repudiation.	Institutions are important determinants of 'convergence' – weak institutional systems prevent poor countries from catching up.
Knack and Keefer (1997a)	Cross-country regressions using indicators of trust and civic norms from the World Values Surveys by Inglehart (1994). The indicators can be interpreted as proxies for the quality of informal institutions.	Trust and civic cooperation have significant impacts on economic performance.
La Porta et al. (1997b)	Cross-country regressions using measures of trust from the World Values Surveys.	Trust has important effects on economic performance.
Havrylysyhyn, Izvorski, and van Rooden (1998)	A stylized cross-country regression analysis using panel data for 25 PSCs based on a model with fixed effects and a full lag structure on policy variables.	Including institutional variables representing the political and legal framework adds explanatory power, especially when the impact of the institutional environment is modeled to increase over time.
Ahrens and Meurers (2000)	Cross-country regressions including most PSCs using subjective and objective indicators of institutional quality. The variables are summarized in subgroups and subsequently assigned to the four fundamental governance dimensions developed above in Chapter 5, Section 5.2.	The quality of formal institutions has significantly positive effects on FDI and economic growth in economies in transition.

Authors	Methodological Approach	Main Findings
	I. Impact of Institutions on Economic Growth	
Zak and Knack (1999)	Cross-country regressions using indicators of trust from the World Values Surveys.	Low trust environments reduce investment and the rate of economic growth. Trust is higher in economically, socially, and ethnically more homogeneous societies and in countries where social and legal mechanisms for reducing opportunistic behavior are better developed.
Rodrik (1997)	Cross-country regressions using subjective indicators of institutional quality and an instrumental variable approach.	Institutional differences (together with variables for initial income and education) explain almost perfectly the differences in growth rates of the East Asian countries for the period 1960–1994.
Panther (1999)	Using factor analytic methods, a civicness indicator is extracted for 11 economies in transition that reflects trust in impersonal institutions and the attractiveness of non-democratic regimes to democratic government.	Civicness promotes both liberal-democratic institutional reform and economic performance.
Campos and Nugent (1999)	Cross-country regressions using subjective institutional variables that are assigned to distinct governance domains.	All governance variables show the expected effects on economic growth. But the relative importance of these indicators and the degree of substitutability/complementarity among them vary by region.
Kaufmann, Kraay, and Zoido-Lobatón (1999)	Cross-section regressions (including 150 countries) using an unobserved component model. More than 300 governance indicators are assigned to six distinct governance domains.	There is a strong causal relationship between the quality of governance and development outcomes.

Authors	Methodological Approach	Main Findings
	II. Impact of Institutions on Financial Development	
La Porta et al. (1997a)	Cross-country regressions using measures of legal rules protecting investors and the quality of their enforcement (measures include rule of law, shareholder rights, one-share equals one-vote, and creditor rights). The data on these qualitative, but objective variables (except for rule of law) are presented in La Porta et al. (1998).	Countries with better investor protections have bigger and broader equity and debt markets.
Levine (1997)	Panel regressions using institutional variables (such as creditor rights, enforcement of contracts, and accounting standards) as instrumental variables.	Countries with more developed institutions (legal and regulatory systems) have better-developed financial intermediaries, and consequently grow faster.
Cull (1998)	Cross-country regressions in levels and differences.	Explicit deposit insurance is positively correlated with subsequent increases in financial depth if adopted when government credibility and institutional development are high.
Demirgüc-Kunt and Detragiache (1998)	Panel logit regressions using rule of law, corruption, and contract enforcement as measures for institutional development as determinants of the probability of financial crisis after interest-rate liberalization.	Banking crises are more likely to occur after financial liberalization. However, the effect of financial liberalization on fragility of the banking sector is weaker when the institutions are more developed.

III. Impact of Institutions on Social Development

Authors	Methodological Approach	Main Findings
Chong and Calderón (1997b)	Cross-country regressions using measures of risk of expropriation, risk of contract repudiation, law and order, corruption in government, and quality of bureaucracy for institutional development, and measures proposed by Foster, Greer, and Thorbecke (1984) for poverty.	Improvements in institutional efficiency reduce the degree, severity, and incidence of poverty.
Chong and Calderón (1998)	Cross-country regressions using a composite index of institutional efficiency based on measures of corruption of government, quality of bureaucracy, law-and-order tradition, risk of expropriation, and risk of contract repudiation.	For poor countries, institutional efficiency is positively correlated with income inequality, and for rich countries it is negatively linked with income inequality.
Campos and Nugent (1999)	Cross-country regressions using subjective indicators of institutional quality, which are assigned to distinct governance domains, to explain development performance across regions, countries, and time.	Improvements in institutional quality (such as the rule of law, bureaucratic quality, and government accountability) help to reduce infant mortality and illiteracy.

Sources: Burki and Perry (1998) and author's compilation

(1997). The former employ the data from the International Country Risk Guide (ICRG) and from Business Environmental Risk Intelligence (BERI) and find that institutions that protect property rights have a significant positive impact on growth and investment. Furthermore, they find stronger evidence for conditional convergence if growth is controlled for institutions. Brunetti *et al.* use the results of a worldwide business survey to construct several indicators of institutional uncertainty,[5] which are related to economic growth and investment in LDCs and growth and FDI in PSCs. These three complementary studies confirm the positive impact of high scores on their institutional variables, especially on their credibility index, and on growth and investment which prove to be robust in combination with different additional economic and political variables typically employed in growth analysis (for example, inflation or political rights). Finally, Rodrik (1997) focuses explicitly on high-performance economies in East Asia[6] and shows that an index of subjective institutional indicators is exceptionally well suited for rank-ordering these countries with respect to their growth performance. His rather parsimonious model specification accounts for almost all of the variation in economic growth among these economies, even if the quality of institutions is instrumented by using exogenous determinants.

The other main approach capitalizes on the extensive data collection of institutional variables and the regularly updated publication of institutional indicators. Researchers of this strand seek to trace the year-by-year impact of institutional development in PSCs on economic performance over time, applying mixed time-series/cross-section models while exploiting the typically U-shaped recovery path of transition economies. Prominent representatives of this branch are Fischer, Sahay, and Végh (1996), who utilize a cumulative liberalization index as an indicator of structural reforms together with initial conditions and macroeconomic policy variables to explain annual growth over the period 1992–1994. For their sample of 25 PSCs, they find that market-oriented institutions have a significant impact on economic growth. Havrylysyhyn, Izvorski, and van Rooden (1998) extend this analysis for annual growth rates over the period 1991–1998. They also start from a basic specification by which growth is explained by the contemporaneous inflation rate, the contemporaneous and lagged values of a structural reform index, and two 'clusters' of initial conditions. They find that including institutional variables representing the political and legal framework adds explanatory power to their specification, especially when the impact of the institutional environment is modeled to increase over time. A common feature of both methodologies is to document a general influence of institutions on economic performance without explicitly referring to a concept of governance, thus ignoring different dimensions of governance which are necessary to analyse the foundations of institution building and policy reform in a consistent and coherent manner.

More recent approaches that seek to overcome this deficit are Campos and Nugent (1999), Kaufmann, Kraay, and Zoido-Lobatón (1999), and Ahrens and Meurers (2000). All of these studies explicitly introduce a concept of governance as a basis of their econometric analyses. Kaufmann, Kraay, and Zoido-Lobatón use the concept of governance proposed by the World Bank (1992). This governance framework includes four major components: (i) public sector management, (ii) accountability, (iii) legal framework for development, and (iv) transparency and information. The framework of Campos and Nugent is similar to the governance concept developed in this study: they see five components to be associated with effective governance: (a) accountability, (b) efficiency of the bureaucracy, (c) an appropriate legal framework, (d) transparency, and (e) participation. Finally, Ahrens and Meurers seek to operationalize exactly the governance framework of this study by assigning various institutional indicators to the four core dimensions of governance (accountability, participation, predictability, and transparency).

The first two studies link their dimensions of governance to several development objectives (GDP per capita, illiteracy, and infant mortality). Campos and Nugent focus on the relevance of individual dimensions for distinct regions of the world. They fail, however, to separate the institutional variables they employed according to their framework of governance and carry out their analysis with an arbitrary selection of proxies for the governance dimensions. They analyse complementarity or substitutability between their dimensions by allowing for interactive terms in the regressions of their development indicators. Kaufmann, Kraay, and Zoido-Lobatón determine six domains, which they assume to represent their concept of governance, and construct an indicator for each domain, condensing data by an unobserved component model. By using a rather parsimonious model, they also find evidence that their governance domains contribute to effective development indicators for a sample of 160 countries.

Ahrens and Meurers (2000) seek to link this more comprehensive analysis of governance with the classical exploratory study of growth performance over a longer term. They focus on PSCs, because these emerging market economies are conceived to be particularly sensitive to (changes in) institutional quality. As a second indicator for economic performance and prospects for future growth they selected foreign direct investment (FDI). This is adequate in the context of transition economies because, on the one hand, there appears to be more uncertainty in overall investment figures in these countries[7] and, on the other hand, FDI not only alleviates the transition-specific shortage of savings, but also promotes technology transfer and the restructuring of the economy, both of which are indispensable for accelerating the convergence to developed market economies. They considered per capita figures for both growth and FDI to sustain comparability across countries.[8] As a result, they find that almost all institutional variables they employed are significant, at least at the 10 percent level, in both the regression on growth and the one on FDI.[9] Moreover, by principal component analysis, they extracted a common factor for each triple of institutional variables that has been assigned to the respective four governance dimensions.[10] The factors for *accountability* and *transparency* are at least significant at a 5 percent level on both growth and FDI, and the factors for *participation* and *predictability* at least at a 10 percent level.

In sum, all of these studies which explicitly aim to incorporate a governance framework in their analyses find a significantly positive impact of the quality of formal institutions on economic performance and particularly economic growth, thereby confirming the findings of earlier studies. What is more, however, these analyses illustrate that a conceptual-theoretic framework of effective governance such as that developed in this study can be usefully operationalized and employed in econometric analyses. Despite still-existing weaknesses of empirical studies (to be discussed below), this result is encouraging because it constitutes an explicit link between the theory of governance and the empirical evidence and helps to identify potentially effective channels of influence to be used by policy makers in a consistent and coherent manner.

Sections II and III of Table 6.1 include some studies analysing the potential impact of institutions on structural or social development. In these areas, the number of available studies is still relatively small. The second section of Table 6.1 includes investigations that analyse the relationship between (mostly) objective institutional indicators and financial sector development. Especially, sound legal and regulatory systems are found to have a significant impact on the development of financial intermediaries and markets. Furthermore, Levine (1997) also finds that more developed formal institutions enhance financial deepening and hence indirectly promote economic growth. Another study (Demirgüc-Kunt and Detragiache 1998) confirms the often-made hypothesis that proper institutions are critical for macroeconomic and financial stabilization, because they reduce the probability of banking crises in the aftermath of financial liberalization. Finally, Cull (1998) observes that deposit insurance schemes can contribute to financial deepening, but only if the quality of other formal institutions (like the rule of law) is relatively high. The third section of Table 6.1 includes two studies that analyse the relationship between essentially formal institutions and poverty reduction and income inequality, respectively. By using subjective measures of institutional quality, these studies indicate that improvements in institutional efficiency may reduce poverty in LDCs in spite of an ambiguous relation between formal institutions and income inequality. Another study by Campos and Nugent (1999) finds a positive correlation not only between improvements in subjective indicators of institutional performance and economic growth but also between the former and reductions in infant mortality and illiteracy.

After having reviewed the empirical evidence found for a broad sample of countries, it is useful to assess where Central and Eastern Europe as well as East Asia (the two regions upon which this study explicitly focuses) stand in terms of institutional development *vis-à-vis* other regions and relative to their recent past. Figures 6.1 – 6.8 show the evolution of distinct institutional indicators over time for various regions of the world.[11] The numbers have been calculated as a simple average of each indicator by region. These figures are based on the subjective indicators provided by the International Country Risk Guide (ICRG) for two reasons: first, these indicators are available for numerous LDCs and PSCs and for a relatively long period of time (1982–1995). Secondly, these variables represent institutional measures that reflect important aspects of our governance dimensions. The five indicators include (i) the risk of repudiation of contracts; (ii) the risk of expropriation of private property; (iii) corruption in government; (iv) a rule-of-law index; and (v) the quality of the bureaucracy. Additionally, a composite index of institutional quality for all years has been constructed by calculating the sum of the scores

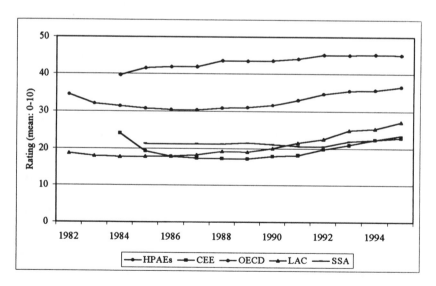

Figure 6.1:   Institutional quality by regions: composite institutional index, 1982–95

that were given to each country for each of the five indicators. Because of their different scales, the institutional indicators were re-scaled to a common scale ranging from zero to 10.[12]

Figure 6.1 shows that – in terms of the composite index – CEE countries are lagging behind all regions except sub-Saharan Africa (SSA). Remarkably, while institutional quality had significantly deteriorated in the 1980s, contributing to the demise of the formerly socialist regimes, it considerably improved in the course of the systemic transformation. As expected, the HPAEs outperformed all other regions except for the OECD countries and even managed partially to close the gap in institutional quality *vis-à-vis* the latter. Moreover, it is evident that all developing regions (except for SSA) have experienced considerable improvements, especially since the late 1980s, indicating that formal institutional quality can in fact occur relatively quickly.

From Figures 6.2–6.6, we can see clearly that the HPAEs have outperformed all other developing regions on all fronts and have significantly approached the standards of OECD countries. CEE as a region is lagging far behind the HPAEs with respect to all indicators and, despite some improvements over time, performs just as well as (or only slightly better than) SSA countries on average. Regarding contract enforceability and the risk of expropriation, the East Asian countries experienced substantial progress on both fronts since the mid-1980s, as did the economies in the Latin American and Caribbean (LAC) region; probably because of the structural reforms that had been implemented across the regions since the 1980s.[13] Furthermore, the HPAEs managed to maintain (or to improve slightly) their comparatively high scores with respect to the rule of law and the quality of their bureaucracies. A serious problem that may have negatively affected the efficacy of governance in East Asia is the increasing degree in government corruption. CEE countries experienced some progress concerning contract enforceability and the protection of property rights. But their law-and-order regimes have remained relatively weak and even more so the quality of their bureaucracies. In association with the persisting high levels of corruption this documents the crucial importance of restructuring the public administration in these countries.

The regional averages, however, mask the institutional diversity that exists within regions. Therefore, Figures 6.7 and 6.8 illustrate the evolution of the composite institutional index within the CEE and the East Asian region, respectively. Figure 6.7 clearly shows the same tripartite division in East Asian countries that can also be identified with respect to growth performance.[14] Hong Kong, Singapore, South Korea, and Taiwan (that is the Newly Industrialized Countries (NICs) as they were labeled long ago) have not only outperformed the rest of East Asia in terms of economic growth but also in terms of institutional development. These countries have been

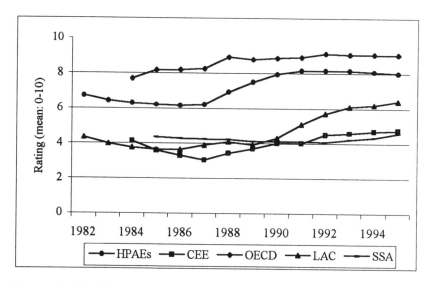

Note: A rise in the index represents a reduction in the risk of contract repudiation.

Figure 6.2: Risk of repudiation of contracts index by regions, 1982–95

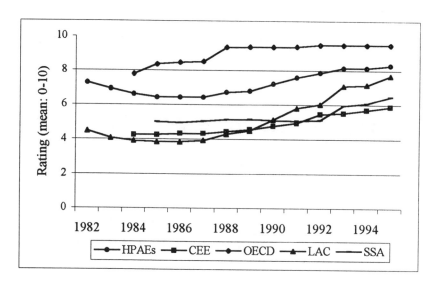

Note: A rise in the index represents a reduction in the risk of expropriation.

Figure 6.3: Risk of expropriation index by regions, 1982–95

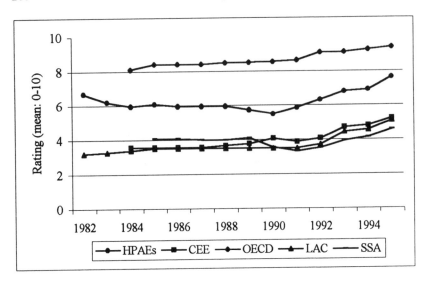

Figure 6.4: Rule-of-law index by regions, 1982–95

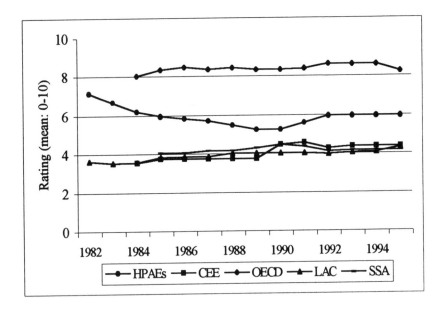

Note: A rise in the index represents a reduction of corruption.

Figure 6.5: Corruption in government index by regions, 1982–95

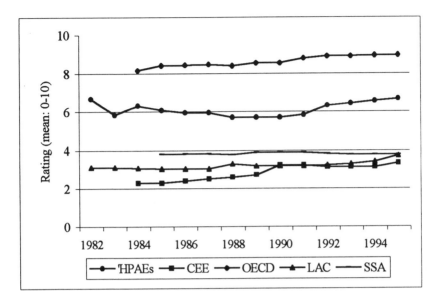

Figure 6.6: Quality of the bureaucracy index by regions, 1982–95

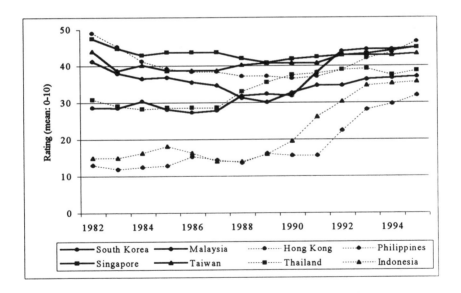

Figure 6.7: Institutional change in East Asia by countries: composite institutional index

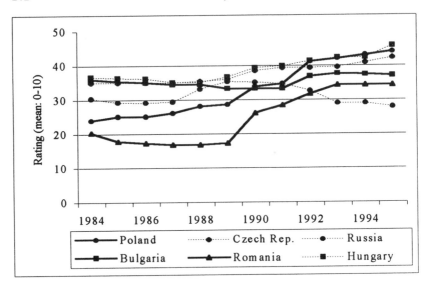

Figure 6.8: Institutional change in CEE by countries: composite institutional index

followed by Thailand, Malaysia, and more recently Indonesia regarding improvements in institutional quality, whereas the Philippines, which are not included in the HPAEs, have lagged behind in spite of substantial progress achieved since the beginning of the 1990s.

As Figure 6.8 shows, a similar tripartite division with respect to institutional performance can be identified in CEE. While the EU accession candidates, the Czech Republic, Hungary, and Poland, are the top performers with scores well above 80 percent of the maximum scores, Bulgaria and Romania are significantly lagging behind, and Russia even more so, being bottom of the sample of countries.[15] Looking at the development of institutional quality over time allows for two additional, instructive insights: first, whereas the former USSR had outperformed Poland in terms of institutional quality in the mid-1980s and even managed further to improve institutional performance in the reform-oriented Gorbachev years, its institutional development as a whole follows an inverted U-shaped pattern. This probably reflects the political crisis and the vacuum of power that adversely affected the efficacy and sustainability of the big-bang transformation program that the Russian government had sought to implement at the beginning of the 1990s.[16] Recalling the enormous decline in production figures and GDP as well as the significant deterioration of social indicators such as life expectancy and income equality which Russia experienced in the 1990s, this development supports the hypothesis that a sound politico-institutional foundation is a *conditio sine qua non* for effective policy reforms.[17] Secondly, in contrast to the Russian Federation, countries such as Romania and most notably Poland, although having faced more unfavorable starting conditions, managed relatively quickly to upgrade their politico-economic structures in institutional terms. Overall, these developments not only correspond to the growth records of these countries over the last decade, but directly reflect the extent and efficacy of structural and institutional reforms conducted by these countries since the beginning of the transition process.[18]

Figures 6.9–6.18 provide some further evidence on where the East Asian and Central and Eastern European countries stand in institutional terms in the mid-1990s. By using the most up-to-date measures of the various indicators on a country-by-country basis, these figures illustrate recent differences within regions. With respect to CEE, significant differences on all fronts can be detected between the EU accession candidates on the one hand, and the rest of the sample on the other. While the former have already achieved levels of institutional quality which are close to the standards of the EU countries, particularly Russia and Yugoslavia are lagging behind. Note, however, as already pointed out above for the region as a whole, that the quality of the bureaucracy is still relatively weak even in countries such as the Czech Republic and Poland. This indicates that these countries still face substantial adjustment pressures for their public sectors in order to meet the requirements of the so-called *aquis communautaire,* the fulfillment of which is an unalterable precondition for EU membership.[19] Furthermore, the relatively low quality of the bureaucracies in association with insufficient contract enforceability and low scores on the rule-of-law index[20] reflect the persistent weakness of political institutions in Russia and Yugoslavia and somewhat less pronouncedly in Albania and Romania as well. These weaknesses suggest that the politico-institutional foundation of policy making represents a serious impediment to effective structural adjustment policies and a dynamic development of the private sector.

Regarding East Asia, Figures 6.14–6.18 include all countries for which data are available, thus comprising not only the HPAEs and the Philippines but also China and Vietnam, two of the most dynamic developing countries still under socialist rule. Especially, the NICs show institutional scores which are close to or even equal the maximum scores. Of particular significance is the very low risk of expropriation of private property and the high enforceability of private contracts throughout the region (except for Vietnam) reflecting an internationally comparatively favorable investment climate. With respect to corruption, the rule-of-law index, and bureaucratic quality, East Asia exhibits a more mixed picture. Corruption in Hong Kong has been relatively low for a long time, reflecting the continuous effectiveness of its

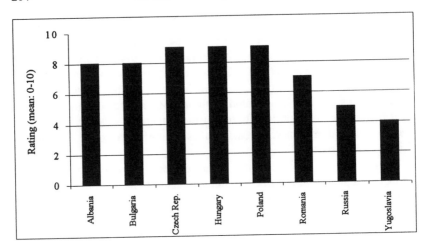

Note: A high score in the index means a low level of risk.

Figure 6.9: Risk of repudiation of contracts index by CEE countries in 1995

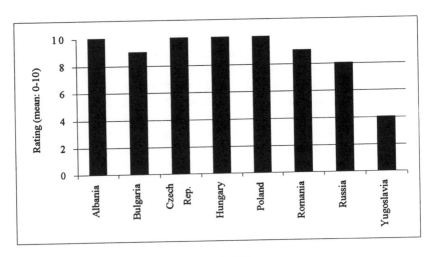

Note: A high score in the index means a low level of risk.

Figure 6.10: Risk of expropriation index by CEE countries in 1995

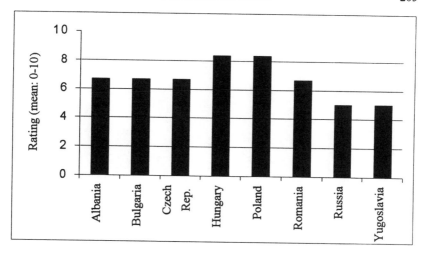

Note: A high score in the index means a low level of corruption.

Figure 6.11: Corruption in government in CEE countries in 1995

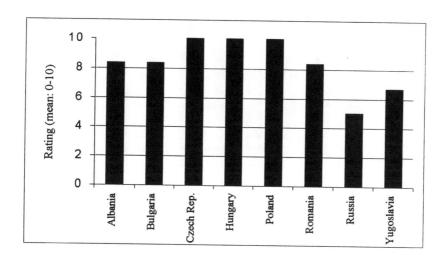

Figure 6.12: Rule-of-law index by CEE countries in 1995

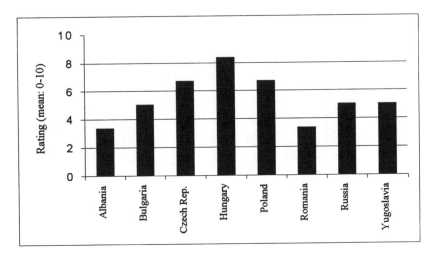

Figure 6.13: Bureaucratic quality index by CEE countries in 1995

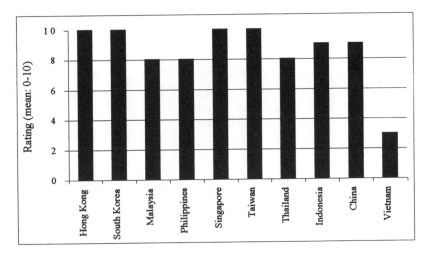

Note: A high score in the index means a low level of risk.

Figure 6.14: Risk of repudiation of contracts index by East Asian countries in 1995

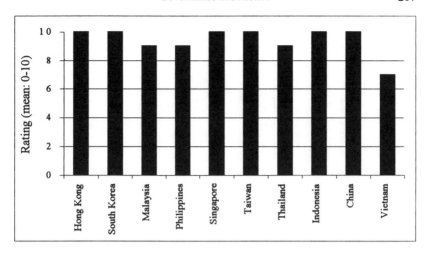

Note: A high score in the index means a low level of risk.

Figure 6.15: Risk of expropriation index by East Asian countries in 1995

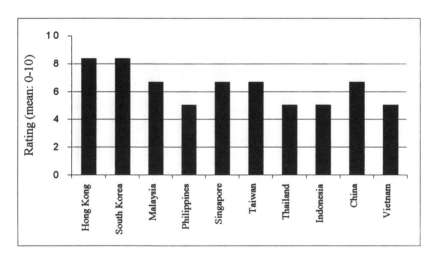

Note: A high score in the index means a low level of corruption.

Figure 6.16: Corruption in government in East Asian countries in 1995

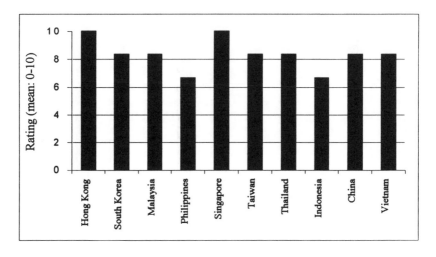

Figure 6.17: Rule-of-law index by East Asian countries in 1995

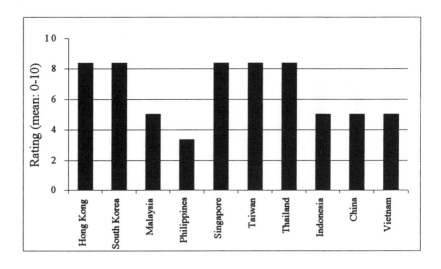

Figure 6.18: Bureaucratic quality index by East Asian countries in 1995

early established anti-corruption agency. More recently, South Korea has become similarly successful in overcoming corruptive practices that were persistent until the mid-1990s. In contrast, corruption is still much more pronounced in Thailand, the Philippines, and Indonesia, a symptom of widespread nepotism and cronyism especially in the latter two countries. This observation corresponds to the relatively low scores of these countries on the rule-of-law index. Finally, regarding bureaucratic quality, the sample seems to be divided in two. Whereas the NICs plus Thailand score very high on this index and hence seem to be well prepared to formulate and implement economic policies in a relatively autonomous manner, the public administrations in the other countries remain relatively weak, thus reflecting insufficient capacities to conduct institutionally and technically more challenging reform measures.

Finally, an explicit focus on transformation economies in CEE and East Asia shows that different paths of transition may imply substantial institutional progress. Figure 6.19 compares the development of institutional quality of the HPAEs on the one hand, and of China and Vietnam on the other; the Philippine case serving as a further reference point. While Vietnam, a poor socialist developing country that started its economic transition only in the mid-1980s, performs similarly to the capitalist Philippine economy, China, by pursuing a gradual transition strategy that had started already in 1978, managed to catch up and more recently even to surpass the HPAEs taken as a group. This shows that even under socialist rule, in a non-democratic setting, and by relying on piecemeal market-oriented reforms, substantial institutional progress can be achieved in a relatively short period of time, one that enhances the country's attractiveness as an investment location and helps to spur economic growth. This insight is confirmed by Figure 6.20 which compares economies in transition in both East Asia and CEE. While Vietnam has achieved some progress over time and now shows an overall institutional performance that is comparable to that of Russia, China has almost caught up with the top performers in CEE, all of which are EU accession candidates. Interestingly, while Poland and the Czech Republic have favored a big-bang style transformation in many areas of policy making, both Hungary and China have explicitly pursued a gradual approach. This again suggests that up front neither transformation strategy can be generally said to be superior and that the design of feasible policy reforms will depend on country-specific characteristics.

As a whole, the evidence presented here documents that in both regions several countries still suffer from a serious institution gap relative to the high performers in the respective group which have continuously approached the standards of the most advanced economies. Whereas the latter are well prepared to undertake further structural reforms and to catch up with the

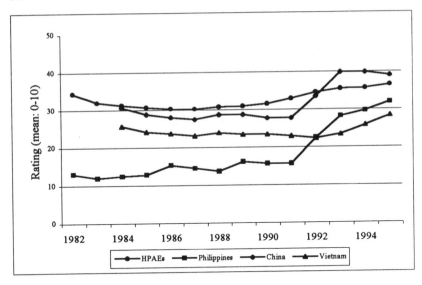

Figure 6.19: Institutional change in East Asia, the HPAEs and economies in transition, composite institutional index

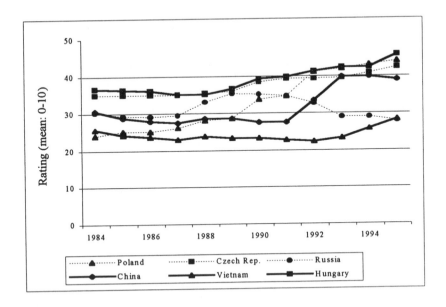

Figure 6.20: Institutional change in transition economies – CEE and Asia compared, composite institutional index

OECD countries further, the former badly need to enhance the quality of their legal and political institutions and thus to create the institutional foundation of policy reforms which may eventually lead to sustained long-term growth. Especially, the relatively low scores on the rule-of-law and the bureaucratic-quality indicators in many countries reinforce the need to undertake innovative reforms of public sector institutions in general and the judicial systems in particular. The empirical results also suggest that indicators of formal institutions can significantly change over relatively short periods of time. This contradicts the pessimistic views advanced by the literature on path dependence and evolutionary economics and implies that formal institutions are not as unchangeable and immutable as these strands of the literature have proposed. Thus, the feasibility space regarding institutional policy choices may be wider than frequently assumed.[21]

The interpretations of Figures 6.1–6.20 combined with the empirical studies listed in Table 6.1 provide clear evidence that formal and informal institutions matter for economic performance and also appear empirically to support the hypotheses derived from our conceptual-theoretic concept of a MEGS. But before we finish this section on the empirical evidence, a word of caution is in order. By looking at the data, we can merely state that our theoretical hypotheses and the implied policy implications cannot be rejected. Due to various methodological problems, it is extremely difficult to identify distinct causalities between institutional and economic or political variables and to measure the (relative) efficiency of different institutional arrangements. Important methodological problems relating to these studies concern the problems of finding adequate data that measure institutional quality in general and the various dimensions of governance in particular, and to correctly specify the econometric model.

Data problems occur for different reasons. For example, measuring government efficiency in providing public goods requires data on inputs (like public expenditures) as well as outputs (like illiteracy rates, infant mortality, and educational achievements). These data *per se*, however, do not directly measure government efficiency, because political authorities usually do not use public resources equally effectively. Moreover, measuring productivity relating to public goods and services is difficult not only due to unobservable attributes such as effort but also due to insufficiently comparable data indicating, for example, the appropriate number of public agents that are required for the efficient provision of collective goods and services such as legislation, regulation, law and order, and defense (Dethier 1999a). Another major problem is that virtually all variables measuring institutional performance or governance are by necessity proxies, because either the 'true' explanatory variables are unobservable or the number of relevant variables is too large to be included in econometric analyses. As mentioned above, these proxies include both objective and subjective indicators. While objective indicators (such as the application of accounting standards or the existence of bankruptcy laws) reflect the formal existence of institutional arrangements and are relatively easy to measure and to compare across countries, this does not hold for their enforcement. In this connection, subjective indicators play a critical role because they are more suitable to assess the quality and the actual implementation and enforcement of formal institutions. However, subjective indicators also show considerable weaknesses which have to be borne in mind when interpreting the data. First, these indicators essentially reflect the perceptions of those individuals questioned in surveys and of professional political and economic analysts. These perceptions will undoubtedly be affected by objective political and social conditions in a given country and do not necessarily reflect institutional quality. Secondly, and related to the foregoing, the overall economic performance of a given country may considerably affect the perceptions especially of foreign analysts which could bias the estimates of the relations between the institutional variables and economic growth (Burki and Perry 1998). Thirdly, the judgment and assessments of a given rating agency may be more or less affected by the judgment and assessments of other rating agencies.

Another methodological challenge is properly to specify an econometric model for testing theoretical hypotheses. As Dethier (1999a: 38) argues, researchers may be '"fooled" by the data', because they deal with proxy variables which could make them think that they measure one thing, when they are actually measuring something else. For example, by using the ICRG indicator 'rule of law', scholars may believe that they estimate the relation between the security of private property rights and economic growth, when they in fact analyse the relation between economic growth and people's acquiescence in formally established institutions.[22] By the same token, researchers may not exactly know whether they measure direct (first-order) effects between two particular variables or rather second- or third-order effects. In this context, it is also noteworthy that the causality between institutional and economic variables is extremely complex. While some effects may be contemporaneous, others may be subject to specific lag structures. Some institutional arrangements, such as India's caste structure, have deep historical roots so that it is hardly possible to collect useful data (Dethier 1999a).

Yet another problem exists with regard to the challenge of directly using our conceptual-theoretic approach to MEGS in empirical studies. As Ahrens and Meurers (2000) argue, while the assignment of distinct institutional variables to the different dimensions of governance is a useful step which leads to a number of significant results, the correlation between these variables is relatively high and there are no variables available that affect only one dimension of governance.[23] Given this correlation, the 'true' relationship between governance indicators and economic growth cannot be identified (Dethier 1999a). This also implies that independent sources of governance can hardly be empirically identified. On the one hand, this may be attributed to the existing interdependencies of various governance dimensions. On the other hand, this result may reflect the inadequacy of the available data sets. Thus, a useful step for future research would be to collect further data through cross-country surveys, the methodological approach of which should be directed at the specific requirements of our conceptual governance framework. Such a data collection effort is, however, beyond the scope of this study.

Moreover, the results of cross-country analyses are highly sensitive to model specification. As Levine and Renelt (1992: 960) conclude, '(n)ational policies appear to be a complex package, and future researchers may wish to focus on macroeconomic policy regimes and interactions among policies as opposed to the independent influence of any particular policy'. While Levine and Renelt only used economic variables, specification problems can be expected to be even more severe if institutional variables are added to the model. This implies that scholars need to be very cautious in concluding that a robust partial correlation which they may find between an institutional indicator and economic performance means that the institutional variable (directly) causes economic growth (Dethier 1999a). Further methodological problems, to mention them only briefly, relate to the omission of relevant variables because they are not observable or because data are not available (this may mean that the regression equation does not coincide with the structure that one is seeking to recover), to the existence of simultaneous equation bias, or to serially correlated residuals as well as lagged dependent variables. Regarding the latter problems, instrumental variable techniques may help attenuate or even overcome the problem.[24]

In sum, it is to be concluded that statistical studies analysing the effects of institutional indicators on economic performance are considerably constrained. Although such studies may help to clarify some conceptual issues and broadly support theoretical findings, they usually fail to identify distinct causal relationships between variables and hence to provide clearly applicable policy implications. Even if institutional indicators are statistically significant and help to predict economic growth and the success of development projects, the interpretation of the coefficients is not as straightforward as desired by researchers. Empirical studies are helpful devices to complement theoretical work, but given the heterogeneity among countries, they are inappropriate to analyse the economic effects of different institutions and to sufficiently understand how context- and time-specificity matter for the efficacy of public policies and institution building. As

Klitgaard (1994) argues, governments can positively and negatively affect economic development in numerous ways. Through public policy making, they can vest rights, change prices for goods, services, and factors of production and also constrain their use, alter information structures, adjudicate and preempt disputes, contracts as well as mechanisms for control and coordination, mobilize resources, and affect or reinforce tastes, preferences, and values. They are also able to violate rights, interfere with private economic decisions, and confiscate private wealth. Most of the effects of these policy measures cannot be satisfactorily captured by cross-country statistical studies. This implies that we must complement econometric studies with the kinds of research which political scientists, sociologists, and institutional economists do provide. Therefore, in order to examine the importance of those effects that cannot be properly measured in cross-country statistical studies, one needs to go beyond statistical comparisons. A promising methodology is to analyse case studies. In particular, case studies suggest that many different features of the political, economic, and cultural environment affect the formation, implementation, and eventually the success of public policies and formal institutions.[25] Therefore, the discussion of selected case studies from East Asia as well as Central and Eastern Europe, including both exceptionally good economic performers as well as 'failures', will be the focus of the subsequent sections.

6.2 THE INSTITUTIONAL FOUNDATION OF DEVELOPMENTAL STATES: EAST ASIA

The rise of East Asian economic power during the last four decades has been dramatic. The six fastest-growing economies in the region (China, Hong Kong, Japan, Singapore, South Korea, and Taiwan) realized about 5 percent per capita growth annually between 1965 and 1995 (measured in international purchasing power parity), and economic growth in three other high performers from South East Asia (Indonesia, Malaysia, and Thailand) accounted for about 3.5 percent per year. In contrast, the other East Asian economies performed poorly, and the economic growth of the rest of the LDCs in the world averaged only 1.5 percent a year.[26] Foreign-trade growth of the nine top performers has been similarly remarkable: from 1965–1990, the newly emerging economies in East Asia increased their share of total world exports from 8 to 18 percent and their respective share of manufactured exports from 9 to 21 percent (Rowen 1998).

The group of fast-growing East Asian economies can be classified roughly according to their economic growth records into four subgroups: while Japan, being already industrialized and a member of the G7 countries, represents a class of its own, the second class includes the so-called NICs, South Korea and Taiwan (formerly Japanese colonies the development strategies of which, especially South Korea's, followed the Japanese model) as well as the city-states Singapore and Hong Kong, which – being important international entrepôts – have been exploiting their locational advantages. All the NICs have relatively few natural resources, are ethnically relatively homogeneous (except for Singapore), and share a number of cultural similarities. These four countries have been growing rapidly for several decades and approached or even joined the ranks of the so-called high-income economies. A third group comprises the ethnically more diverse countries Indonesia, Malaysia, and Thailand which have considerably more natural resources than the NICs. These countries have joined the group of East Asia's high-performing economies more recently, that is within the last 25 years. Finally, China is fourth – representing a distinct world in itself, a huge country in which economic progress has been proceeding rapidly, but very unevenly across provinces. The following analysis explicitly focuses on the second and third subgroups, that is the relatively small high-performing Asian economies (HPAEs). While it also makes partial references to Japan due to its function as a role model especially in North East Asia, it leaves out China, the development performance of which will be explicitly discussed in Section 6.3.1.[27]

A basic, simple though clearly correct, explanation of the sources of the East Asian exceptionalism has been that these countries adopted unusually good economic policies.[28] The HPAEs have been distinguished by their sound macroeconomic management as well as suitable financial, educational, and technological policies. All countries encouraged market processes basically based on private property, were open to foreign trade and foreign direct investment,[29] realized by-and-large positive real interest rates, avoided an overvaluation of their currencies, limited price controls, realized low tax levels and government consumption, did not over-regulate industry, and did not favor industry at the expense of agriculture. Consequently, neoclassical scholars concluded that getting the fundamentals right was the key to economic success (Krueger 1993 and Rowen 1998).

However, in all HPAEs (with the exception of Hong Kong), policy making actually went far beyond what the World Bank (1991) called market-friendly policies.[30] In fact, governments conducted numerous, diverse, but selective interventions. Development strategies included the maintenance of state-owned enterprises and banks, the provision of physical and intellectual infrastructure, the promotion of technology programs, governments directly influencing private investment, the provision of implicit and explicit subsidies to specific industries, import protection, control over trade unions, and financial market regulations (Rowen 1998 and Stiglitz 1996). While neoclassicals argued that government interference was irrelevant or even harmful to resource allocation and economic development, adherents to the developmental-state (or revisionist) view gave considerable credit to state interventions. Revisionists claim that market and coordination failures had been pervasive in East Asia particularly at the early stages of economic development. Thus, government activism and intervention needs to be regarded as a *conditio sine qua non* for remediation. In East Asia, economic success was fostered by the ability of strong states to govern the market and to pursue selectively targeted industrial policies. Adherents to this view forcibly argue that strong governments in East Asia succeeded in achieving these objectives.[31]

Reinforced by the market-enhancing view (Aoki *et al.* 1997a), which emphasizes the role of governments to support and complement rather than supplant private coordination, a new consensus has begun to emerge recently that governments of the HPAEs have been much more active and successful in promoting and supplementing markets than adherents of the neoclassical theory concede. Activist states in East Asia did not only promote economic development, but government policies and economic administrations were essential to market success.[32] However, facing the poor performance of other LDCs with activist states, it was not government interventions *per se* that were conducive to growth. So how is it to be explained that the HPAEs managed to avoid the disasters that resulted from interventionist policies elsewhere? What are the factors that made these countries what has been called developmental states?

It will be argued in the following subsections that traditional policy-oriented attempts at an explanation of the East Asian Miracle miss two decisive factors: the role of institutions and a differentiated analysis of the role of the state in economic development. The main thesis is that – besides the formulation of consistent reform policies – the concept of governance, as it has been applied in distinct settings of political institutions in the HPAEs, has played a crucial role in the success of economic reforms and eventually in the emergence of sustained paths of development. In order to support this thesis, two central sets of questions have to be explicitly raised, which have been either controversially discussed or not yet adequately addressed in the literature:

- Why were interventionist policies adopted; why and how did they work effectively?

- How were country-specific policy mixes agreed upon in the course of political decision-making processes, how were they successfully implemented and eventually enforced?

In order to address these questions, the following subsection provides a brief overview of the activist policies in East Asia. Subsequently, we seek to close the explanatory gap concerning the East Asian exceptionalism by highlighting the importance of an overall shared-growth strategy and analysing the mechanics of policy formulation, implementation, and enforcement. Finally comes the question of whether the recent Asian crisis was a crisis of governance and, if so, whether or not the whole model of East Asian development must be called into question as was called for by some observers.

6.2.1 Getting interventions right

Why were interventionist policies adopted and why did they work effectively? Economic theory identified several necessary conditions for markets to yield efficient results. These comprise the absence of externalities and public goods, perfect competition, a complete set of functioning factor and product markets, and perfect information.[33] To some extent, these conditions are insufficiently satisfied in any economy, which is one reason that even successful industrialized countries are in fact mixed economies, where governments play a significant economic role. Since market failures can be observed on a much broader scale in LDCs, reservations regarding the functioning of market mechanisms are of particular relevance in developing countries. However, government activism may not necessarily imply a more efficient resource allocation, as the decay of the formerly socialist economies and the crises of rent-seeking societies in many parts of the developing world have clearly indicated. The crucial mistake of these countries was the propensity to overcome market failures by replacing markets. Instead, policy makers in East Asia sought to exploit the *complementarities* between market processes and government activities. In that sense, rethinking the state meant less government intervention in areas where markets basically worked or could be made to work and more interventions in those areas in which market failures persisted or markets did not exist (World Bank 1991 and 1993).

At the early stages of East Asian development, market imperfections did not only consist of technological and marketing spillovers and nonexistent or weak (especially capital) markets, but particularly of coordination failures. Notably in South Korea and Taiwan, which shared favorable initial conditions at the beginning of the 1960s with a relatively skilled labor force and low income inequality (see Tables 6.2 and 6.3 in Section 6.2.2), the economy could not take off, although capital accumulation showed a high latent return. Scale economies caused a twofold coordination failure inducing a rate of return to individual private investment that was significantly lower than the potential social return. First, increasing returns to scale associated with a capital shortage or imperfect capital markets may imply that small firms do not get access to capital. Then, government intervention may be an adequate means to lower capital costs and to improve economic efficiency. Secondly, scale economies may cause a coordination failure if factors of production, technologies, and intermediate goods, which are necessary for modern-sector production, are imperfectly tradable in international markets. In this case, individual investments in the modern sector will be profitable only if complementary investments (especially regarding the production of specialized inputs) are undertaken simultaneously. The interdependence of investment and production decisions causes severe coordination problems, because market prices inadequately provide signals regarding the profitability of those activities which imply a large-scale resource reallocation. Rodrik (1995) identified this type of coordination failure in Taiwan and South Korea, but it also occurred, for example, in the textiles and footwear industries in other HPAEs.[34]

Besides ensuring macroeconomic stability, governments in the HPAEs undertook a set of interventionist measures aimed at creating markets and improving the ability of private agents to overcome coordination problems and other market imperfections. Government activism proved to be successful because markets and government intervention were not interpreted as alternative mechanisms of resource allocation. Policy makers did not try to supplant markets by establishing a command-and-control economy, but rather sought to complement markets and established institutions which caused public policies to play a market-enhancing role (Aoki *et al.* 1997b).

Advocates of the market-enhancing view identify complementarities between private coordination within a firm or across firms and the design of the institutional matrix. Therefore, government's role is not to substitute for private-sector coordination, but to create an institutional environment that supports private coordination.[35] A central point of government intervention in East Asia was that it – contrary to common perception – did not imply extensive rent-seeking behavior. The reason is that interventions did not create rents, but policy-induced *rent opportunities* (contingent rents) for Schumpeterian entrepreneurs, which promised larger returns than those resulting from competition without interventions and whose exploitation depended on private agents' own efforts to conduct business and to meet objective and transparent rules enforced by competent and impartial referees. The most widely used type of contingent rents was export contests for preferential access to credit or foreign exchange and export subsidies. This instrument limited rent-seeking because firms were rewarded on the basis of their actual performance. In contrast to unconditional subsidies, contingent rents fostered competition and facilitated the resolution of coordination problems in the private sector.[36]

Besides rewards indexed to performance, various other policy instruments improved the flow of information among private entrepreneurs and between them and the government and induced cooperation and coordination in the institutions of the private sector. These include deliberation councils, staggered-entry strategies, the creation of industrial parks for high-technology industries, and administrative guidance.[37] According to the market-enhancing view, public policies need to show a bias towards private-sector institutions whenever feasible, because these institutions are basically more appropriate for solving coordination problems due to their built-in self-regulating properties like competition and their more suitable responsiveness to local information.[38]

In contrast to numerous other LDCs which rigidly maintained unsuccessful policies, economic policy making in the HPAEs has been characterized by a high degree of *pragmatic flexibility* regarding the use of different policy instruments. Measures that worked well were retained, while those that failed were abandoned. Governments have been capable of responding adequately to a changing economic environment and of learning from mistakes, and have hence acquired a high degree of *policy adaptability* (World Bank 1991 and 1993).

Single interventions did not ensure success. It was the mixture of market-oriented policies and country-specific interventions which proved to be suitable to overcome market failures, to encourage competition, and to create the basis for economic growth. The real East Asian Miracle seems to be political rather than economic. Why did policy makers pursue these policies? How were incentives created within the public sector which guaranteed that bureaucrats and politicians did not rely on opportunistic behavior, but sought to enhance efficiency and to reduce rent-seeking and corruption? And which institutions induced the pragmatic flexibility in tactical policy making and the high degree of policy adaptability?

6.2.2 Political economy of policy reform: governance in the HPAEs

The developmental states in East Asia have been based on a politico-institutional structure that made policy reform combined with shared growth strategies a politically feasible option. The complex coordination problems associated with policy reform were overcome by politically-crafted, self-enforcing governance structures. Besides international competition, it has been the organizational design and the incentives within the public sector and the institutions linking the public and private sector that have been crucial to the developmental consequences of government activism. Authorities in the HPAEs built a complex set of political institutions involving the government, the bureaucracy, business elites, and other social groups in the process of policy formulation, implementation, and enforcement. The cooperation of these actors, reflecting different interests, required policy choices, the costs and benefits of which were largely unknown *ex ante*. In order to intervene effectively in the economy and to foster economic growth, politicians and bureaucrats had to rely on the private sector, which was expected to provide reliable information and to increase private investment. Therefore, authorities established institutions which constituted governments' credible commitment to deliver their promises to business and non-elites.

Although state interventions have been quite different across countries, similarly structured governance frameworks were established, all of which incorporated *one fundamental political and two institutional principles* as a basis of policy making:[39]

- the governments' credible commitment to an overall strategy of shared growth;
- crafting a meritocratic Weberian-type bureaucracy; and
- establishing specific state–business–society interfaces.

The formal institutional arrangements based on these principles provided mechanisms of consensual conflict resolution, enhanced political and social stability through transparent rules about how to solve collective problems, and created public trust on the basis of a common sense of legitimate authority. These governance structures proved to be adequate means to reduce political transaction costs and to mitigate multiple principal–agent problems which are inherent in policy reform. The HPAEs managed to overcome or to attenuate various constraints to effective policy making (such as imperfect and asymmetric information, difficulties in monitoring bureaucratic input and output, opportunistic behavior, multiplicity of interests, bounded rationality, and time inconsistency) comparatively well. In order to achieve this, they established sophisticated institutions with powerful incentive schemes and screening, signaling, and monitoring mechanisms, which encouraged a fusion of interests of politicians, bureaucrats, business, and non-elites. Furthermore, governments induced incentive-compatibility of public policies and economic performance and enhanced both their reputation and legitimacy through a subtle system of checks and balances, delegation of authority, and specific credible commitment devices.

East Asian history shows that state activities have not been exclusively motivated by self-aggrandizement or self-interested politicians merely pursuing their own (material) welfare and capturing individual rents, but that political elites may have an *encompassing* or *national interest* (Bardhan 1995). The HPAEs realized rapid and sustained economic growth *in association with* significantly improving income distribution,[40] thereby disproving Kuznet's hypothesis that in early stages of economic transition income inequality tends to increase (Kuznets 1955). *Shared growth* became the driving force to improve human welfare, substantially resulting in a significant increase in life expectancy, a considerable reduction of absolute poverty, and a rapid improvement of other economic and social indicators, thereby outperforming most LDCs and sometimes even surpassing industrialized economies.[41]

Table 6.2: Human capital indicators in East Asia and comparator countries, actual versus predicted values, c. 1960

	per-capita growth	primary enrollment ratio		secondary enrollment ratio		literacy rate	
	1965–89	actual	predicted	actual	predicted	actual	predicted
HPAEs							
Hong Kong	6.3	0.87	0.83	0.24	0.23	0.70	0.59
Indonesia	4.4	0.67	0.51	0.06	0.07	0.39	0.25
Japan	4.3	1.03	0.92	0.74	0.29	0.98	0.70
Korea	7.0	0.94	0.57	0.27	0.10	0.71	0.31
Malaysia	4.0	0.96	0.68	0.19	0.15	0.53	0.43
Singapore	7.0	1.11	0.78	0.32	0.21	0.50	0.54
Taiwan	6.17*	0.96	0.62	0.28	0.12	0.54	0.36
Thailand	4.2	0.83	0.57	0.12	0.10	0.68	0.31
others							
Dominican Republic	2.5	0.98	0.64	0.07	0.13	0.65	0.39
Philippines	1.6	0.95	0.62	0.26	0.12	0.72	0.36
Paraguay	3.0	0.98	0.65	0.11	0.14	0.75	0.40
Sri Lanka	3.0	0.95	0.65	0.27	0.14	0.75	0.39

Note: * 1960–89
Sources: World Bank (1991), Rodrik (1995 and 1996)

This remarkable record can be partly explained by specific initial conditions the East Asian countries shared prior to their economic take-off. By the early 1960s, the level of education was much higher than expected given their levels of income, and the distribution of wealth and income was relatively equal by international standards (Tables 6.2 and 6.3). The first condition facilitated the creation of a competent civil service and the shift to modern-sector production. The second condition helped to shield economic policy making from vested interests – particularly in the relatively homogeneous societies of North East Asia where no powerful class dominated economic or political life – and implied a lack of redistributional pressures, which facilitated growth-oriented macroeconomic policies.[42]

Table 6.3: Gini indices for HPAEs and comparator countries

	land ownership c. 1960	income 1965–70	income 1971–80	income 1981–90
HPAEs				
Hong Kong	n.a.	0.49	0.42	0.39
Indonesia	n.a.	0.40	0.41	0.30
Korea	0.39	0.34	0.38	0.33
Malaysia	0.47	0.50	0.48	0.42
Taiwan	0.46	0.32	0.36	0.30
Singapore	n.a.	0.50	0.45	0.41
Thailand	0.46	0.44	0.38	0.37
unweighted average	0.45	0.43	0.41	0.36
others				
Argentina	0.87	0.43	0.41	0.43
Brazil	0.85	0.57	0.60	0.60
India	0.52	0.40	0.41	n.a.
Kenya	0.69	n.a.	0.59	n.a.
Mexico	0.69	0.58	0.52	0.53
Philippines	0.53	0.48	0.45	0.39
unweighted average	0.69	0.49	0.50	0.49

Sources: Rodrik (1996), Root (1996).

However, Rodrik's (1995) conclusion that specific initial conditions in the HPAEs have been crucial and limit the relevance of their public policies to other LDCs is not convincing. The existence of favorable initial conditions is no guarantee for sustained economic growth as the experiences of other countries indicate (Table 6.2). Also, some East Asian countries such as Indonesia, Malaysia, and Thailand had less favorable conditions and nevertheless realized high growth rates. Finally, it has to be explained why and how all HPAEs further improved income and wealth distribution in the course of development (Table 6.3). Therefore, favorable initial conditions cannot be regarded as the single most important explanatory factor. Instead, the exceptional East Asian development record, it is argued here, results from specific public policies and a particular institutional environment.

Figure 6.21 portrays the politico-institutional approach to understanding the developmental governance structures in the HPAEs. The figure shows the interaction of different players on the political stage within a specific set of institutions resulting in consensual policy making based on transparent and predictable rules. These allowed different policy choices which helped to exploit the latent growth potential and made shared growth possible.

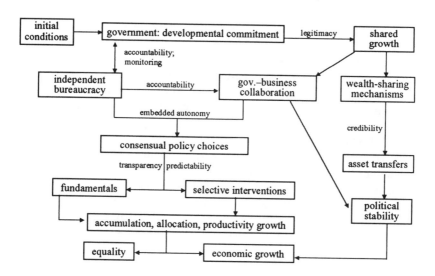

Source: Author's compilation

Figure 6.21: A politico-institutional approach to economic development in East Asia

When they came to power, all governments (except the Japanese) faced serious military and political (communist) threats, either internal or external.[43] Furthermore, particularly governments in Indonesia, South Korea, and Taiwan needed to establish political legitimacy, because these military regimes came to power by force. Gaining legitimacy was not only important to enhance internal political stability but also to receive badly needed financial assistance from the advanced industrialized countries. Therefore, governments created large social bases whose economic interests were directly associated with the political regimes' success. An overall strategy of *shared economic growth* seemed to be appropriate to attain legitimacy.[44] However, policies promoting growth may be difficult to launch or to sustain. Business elites may prefer to maintain the status quo, because reform policies that foster competition induce uncertainties about their future wealth. Also, adjustment and growth policies initially tend to require sacrifices from non-elites involving the danger of political or social unrest. Therefore, initiating as well as sustaining growth policies represents a coordination problem, which can only be overcome if authorities manage credibly to assure both elites and non-elites that they will benefit from growth (World Bank 1993). The adopted shared-growth strategy in East Asia incorporated credible means to convince everybody that governments would deliver their promises. First, it promoted growth by cooperating with the business elites mainly through consultative committees (see below) and prompting them to undertake long-term investments and modernize organizational and management structures; this was the precondition for growth and thus for economic gains to be shared. Secondly, citizens were compensated for short-term costs of economic adjustment through explicit wealth-sharing mechanisms in the form of *real* asset transfers (Campos and Root 1996 and Root 1996). These included among others land reform and rural development in South Korea and Taiwan, public housing programs in Hong Kong and Singapore, promoting labor-intensive manufacturing most notably in South Korea and Taiwan and worker cooperatives in Indonesia and Singapore, improving primary and secondary education in almost all HPAEs[45] and rural infrastructure, notably in Indonesia and Malaysia. Furthermore, almost all HPAEs, most remarkably Japan, Taiwan, and even South Korea, emphatically promoted the creation of small- and medium-sized enterprises through technology and marketing support systems and financial assistance.[46] Thereby, governments strengthened broader-based private sector development and in association with fostering rural development helped to reduce poverty and income inequality.[47] The most explicit wealth sharing mechanism was introduced in Malaysia under the New Economic Policy scheme (1971–1991), which aimed at sharing the fruits of economic growth widely across all societal strata. One specific goal of this scheme prescribed equity targets favoring the ethnic Malays (the Bumiputras) who should hold a 30 percent share of the corporate sector's equity by 1990. Although the target could not be fully achieved, the results were tangible as the equity share of the Bumiputras increased from 2.4 percent in 1970 to 19.2 percent in 1990 (Campos and Root 1996).

Since asset transfers served as credible signaling devices documenting authorities' commitment to sustainable development and assuring constituents that they would benefit from future growth, they also implied a societal consensus to reforms and support for the political regime.[48] Giving *real* assets to non-elites made citizens expect that they would have the opportunity to improve their individual position on the social welfare ladder and to realize long-term gains from economic reforms. The principle of shared growth served as a strategy to credibly signal HPAE leaders' commitment to sustainable economic development, thereby creating win–win coalitions, prompting the population to support growth policies, fostering private investment, and reducing rent-seeking.[49] It made non-elites more self-reliant, gave them an interest in the long-term success of the political regime, and hence strengthened their political support of the government and eventually led to more political stability. Therefore, shared-growth strategies helped to turn good economics into good politics. By providing non-elites with real assets, they reduced the time lag in which economic adjustment policies became popular and made ordinary people more cooperative and willing to bear short-term sacrifices due to expected future returns.

The second pillar of policy reform was public sector reform to enhance the bureaucratic capability that was necessary for shared growth. Political leaders in East Asia established rules that brought bureaucrats' incentives in line with governments' goals. These rules affected the incentives of bureaucrats differently across countries ranging from a narrow circle of technocrats in Indonesia to virtually the whole public administration in Singapore. However, in each case a *Weberian-type bureaucracy* was created resulting in a *corporate identity* which induced bureaucrats to identify with the objectives of the political leadership. This corporate coherence created 'a competent, powerful but accountable group of bureaucrats (...). The creation of this economic bureaucracy stands out as one of the most original and successful of the institutional innovations that distinguish the HPAEs from the patterns characteristic of Latin America and Africa.'[50] The Weberian-type bureaucracy based on objective rules for bureaucratic activities and appointments represented an unalterable prerequisite of granting independence to the administration by shielding its technocratic elite from pressures of vested interests.[51] Thus, the bureaucracies of the HPAEs became relatively autonomous; similar to MITI in Japan 'in the sense of being capable of independently formulating its own goals and able to count on those who work within it to see implementing these goals as important to their individual careers' (Evans 1995: 50). Independence of other branches of government and of interest group pressures was the precondition to address collective-action and coordination problems, helping the private sector to attain solutions which would have been difficult to reach otherwise.[52]

Preventing bureaucrats from short-run opportunistic behavior required a change of their risk-reward calculations. Governments achieved this by promising them long-term benefits and career prospects and committing themselves to sustainable economic growth perceived as a precondition to receiving long-term returns. Political leaders managed credibly to signal that growth was their top priority not only by initiating appropriate policies, but by radically replacing incompetent personnel as well as setting and effectively controlling performance targets for ministers and bureaucrats (see Box 6.1). Political commitment to economic growth thus credibly changed bureaucrats' expectations. Supporting governments' policies promised to be more profitable for them than opportunistic behavior. Moreover, bureaucrats' competency has been enhanced by meritocratic recruitment and promotion in combination with competitive, well-defined career paths allowing for quite a high degree of upward mobility. While civil service organizations in most countries recruit from top educational organizations, the specific rules guiding personnel selection and promotion differ across countries. Whereas formally institutionalized systems (emphasizing entry examinations and professional performance) dominate in Japan and South Korea and similarly in Singapore (stressing academic performance, personal recruitment interviews, and professional performance), entry exams in Thailand and Indonesia are relatively perfunctory.[53] In the latter cases, recruitment depends on the completion of university degrees, preferably from foreign academic organizations.[54] Despite these differences, most systems have considerably helped to reduce favoritism and to select talented individuals. Furthermore, civil servants are provided with salaries, benefits, and allowances much closer to those of the private sector than in other LDCs. In sum, objective and meritocratic rules guiding public sector employment and management in association with competitive remuneration packages have proved to be effective devices in recruiting and promoting qualified civil servants and in reducing political interference in personnel decisions. By the same token, the Philippines and also Indonesia, which have instituted less stringent and less objective rules and do not provide competitive compensation packages, have the weakest economic bureaucracies in the region (Root 1996 and Cheng *et al.* 1998).

The common attention of all HPAEs to crafting state capacity by strengthening the public administration represents a clear confirmation that institutional and policy reform go hand in hand. Capability, competence, and

Box 6.1: Leadership, institutions, and bureaucratic performance in East Asia

In order to restructure the economic bureaucracy and to prepare it for a shared-growth strategy, the authority and power of individual political leaders in association with appropriately designed institutions played a critical role at the early stages of the economic take-off processes. Campos and Root (1996: 140–141) summarize the findings of their field research as follows:[55]

'In Singapore, Lee Kuan Yew removed corrupt officials after publicly shaming them, thus signaling his determination to cut ties to the past (...) The new bureaucracy was small, so responsibilities were unambiguously assigned and Lee could closely supervise performance. Adopting sometimes draconian measures for acquiring evidence and meting out justice, he established a Corruption Control Committee to find and penalize wrongdoers. The message was that leadership expects nothing but the best.

In Indonesia, Soeharto manifested his commitment to growth by following the advice of his technocrats during times of economic crisis. (...) In a further signal of his acceptance of the technocrats – and his determination to provide a sound macroeconomic framework for shared growth – he had a balanced budget requirement inserted into the constitution in 1967. (...) When oil prices collapsed in 1983 he again followed the difficult advice of the technocrats: open the economy, deregulate, and encourage export investment to bring in foreign exchange. He did so, although the liberalization jeopardized the rents of powerful regime supporters.

General Park reorganized Korea's economic bureaucracy around the newly created Economic Planning Board (...). Moreover, when his first five-year plan did not produce results he began his famous New Year visits – visits to each of his ministers to discuss goals and strategies to implement those goals. Park returned the following year to each minister and went through the promises sentence by sentence. Those ministers who achieved less than 80 percent of what they promised were fired. (...) Each department had to define its performance objectives in terms that were clear to all. Ministers learned to communicate the need for precise targets to their subordinates (...).

In Taiwan, the need for a reputable economic bureaucracy to monitor and guide economic development was foremost in the minds of the KMT [Kuomintang; J.A.] leaders. (...) Integrity was instilled in the civil service by examples set early in the regime's history. When Wang Zeng-Yi, Chiang Kai-Shek's brother-in-law, was successfully impeached by the Control Yuan, a clear signal was sent about the regime's commitment to accountability. Even the premier's closest relations were not protected from the standards that applied to all public servants. The use of insider advantages by officials was actively and purposely resisted by the creation of an independent examination board to monitor recruitment into the civil service. The Control Yuan had complete powers of impeachment and investigation over all members of the government.'

independence are essential attributes of an effective public administration. But these characteristics do not suffice to institute a MEGS unless they are complemented by appropriate mechanisms that hold politicians and civil servants accountable for their actions. Therefore, in order to balance bureaucratic independence and accountability, governments established different ways to delegate authority and responsibility, and they successfully guarded themselves against opportunistic behavior by monitoring mechanisms. The introduction of hard budget constraints, notably in Japan, Malaysia, and Indonesia, delimited the influence of external actors on government expenditures and additionally measured civil servants' ability in macroeconomic management. In Japan, independent personnel agencies helped to reduce external pressure on appointments and patronage. In Singapore, numerous statutory boards were used, which partitioned the policy space by assigning single policies to special agencies; this institutional mechanism helped to monitor bureaucrats' performance. In several countries, particularly in Hong Kong and Singapore, decisive anti-corruption measures significantly reduced civil servants' propensity to use their specific information and considerable power for extra-legal activities.[56] Finally, administrative guidance (providing the bureaucracy with broad mandates but restricted enforcement powers) suitably balanced independence and accountability. This holds particularly for Japan and South Korea, and to some extent for Taiwan. Policies were basically implemented by using a carrot and stick strategy, that is by giving substantial incentives to private business and exercising selective, though transparent, coercion. Moreover, private actors have been explicitly involved in the process of policy formulation and implementation in order better to assure voluntary compliance. Thus, multilateral negotiating processes emerged, which indirectly helped to monitor the bureaucracy.[57]

This leads us to the third pillar of policy reform. A solely insulated bureaucracy would not only imply an overly strong state apparatus that may be unresponsive to citizens' needs but would also be unable to rely on decentralized private information and implementation. Therefore, the direct involvement of private business and other actors in public policy making through institutionalized channels represented the most important institution to establish a state–business–society interface by which a consensual process of policy formulation was realized, the bureaucracy's flexibility was enhanced, the mutual exchange of information was encouraged, and the preconditions of sustained and shared growth were created. Thus, the notion of *embedded autonomy* (the seemingly contradictory combination of bureaucratic autonomy and social connectedness) was the institutional basis for effective state involvement.

Conventional wisdom often explains economic success in East Asia by the persistence of authoritarian regimes whose political leaders pursued policies largely unconstrained by institutions (Haggard and Moon 1990). However, the outward appearance of a state does not say very much about its actual structure of rule. Obviously the political authorities in East Asia did not follow their counterparts in other developing countries who often based their power on the support of specific, loyal business groups which were granted monopoly status and given additional assets at the expense of other (non-loyal) groups for their political support (World Bank 1992). In those countries, authorities did not establish a system of political checks and balances, and the large extent of the rulers' (arbitrary) political discretion and uncertainty about their future actions induced companies not to provide information to authorities and to reduce long-term investment, hence, impeding industrialization and economic growth.

A closer look at the political institutions in the HPAEs reveals that their leaderships have actually been confronted with institutions delimiting their power, and they even constrained themselves by delegating decision-making power and explicitly involving economic elites and other social groups in the process of policy formulation and implementation (Root 1996 and Doner 1992). In Japan, South Korea, Singapore, Malaysia, and Thailand, the coordination of public policies and private business activities was predominantly realized through consultative committees, that is mainly *sectoral deliberation councils*, which represented a forum to discuss policy issues and market trends. Their main task as a quasi-legislative body was to collaborate on the formulation and implementation of sector-specific or overall public policies, rules, and regulations. In addition, they helped critically to scrutinize industrial policy programs and to monitor bureaucratic activities. Council members included government officials, academics, representatives from the business community, and sometimes also delegates from trade unions or consumer associations, depending on the council's area of responsibility. In addition, *functional* deliberation councils played important roles. In Singapore, for example, a National Wages Council (NWC) was established as a tripartite body comprising the government as well as labor and employer representatives (including multinationals). In its annual deliberations, the NWC elaborates on general employment-related problems and specifically on wage policies, seeking to tie wage increases to productivity gains. The efficacy of these deliberations has been ensured by two working rules, the unanimity rule of decision making and the non-attribution rule which prescribes that comments and statements will not be publicly attributed to the individual who made them. These rules facilitate a free and open discussion of critical issues and foster consensual policy making (Campos and Root 1996). Due to their multilateral nature and their repetitive activities, these councils served as a crucial institutional device to promote cooperation and consultation and to limit the power of the state. This way, governments demonstrated their commitment not to confiscate private assets, directly or indirectly, and they enhanced both their credibility and authority by the devolution of power.

Deliberation councils also helped to improve the overall information basis and the quality of decision-making. Particularly in LDCs, in which markets lack institutional foundations or other market failures persist, imperfect or asymmetric information may cause the malfunctioning of markets. Then, the pursuit of private interests may not lead to efficient outcomes.[58] Facing the coordination failures in East Asia, authorities needed to undertake interventionist measures which required the provision of private-sector information. On the other hand, in order to stabilize expectations and to improve companies' planning activities, the business community was interested in knowing the government's attitude towards specific projects and which policy changes were to be expected (Haggard 1998). For these reasons, both publicly providing information and facilitating the exchange of information through encouraging the development of functional intermediaries (like manufacturers' associations) and close government–business collaboration reduces transaction costs and can be superior to pure market search.[59] By using private-sector information, the bureaucracy elaborated action plans that were communicated back to the representatives of the private sector. Public–private deliberations thus constituted an integrated and highly flexible decision-making process that was able to digest and take advantage of market and technical information which was uncovered during the implementation of earlier decisions. Continuous monitoring of policy implementation helped to revise old and to set new policy priorities or to change sequential implementation steps (Pack and Westphal 1986). Opportunistic behavior was essentially avoided by the repetitive character of negotiations as well as the fact that the rules governing industries were agreed upon by the councils. This, in turn, enhanced government credibility, ensured council members that the rules were not arbitrarily altered, and prompted private actors to concentrate on market competition instead of lobbying.[60]

Eventually, deliberation councils turned out to be effective institutional devices to reduce transaction costs, rent-seeking, and information asymmetries in the economic policy dialogue and to legitimize public policies. They improved economic efficiency through an effective exchange of information, committed the government through binding and transparent rules that governed policy making, and helped both the government and the private agents to adjust flexibly to a changing political and economic environment. Since violating or changing the rules that underlie these councils was costly for all participants, they became stable devices for long-term policy making.[61] Most importantly, since these councils suitably served to hold the executive accountable for its policies,[62] to create transparency about government decisions, rules, regulations, and policy implementation, and to enhance the predictability of public policies, they provided effective institutional safeguards to bind authorities to their promises. Hence they significantly helped to limit strong governments; an important fact that had been neglected by the theory of the developmental state discussed earlier.[63]

The foregoing arguments concerning governance structures in the HPAEs can be essentially recapitulated in seven policy conclusions: (1) the ability to craft and adopt specifically-tailored institutional structures is as important to effective governance as the formulation of policies; (2) effective governance structures and hence developmental outcomes depend on the legitimacy of the political leadership, the roles that policy makers pursue, and the general character of state structure; (3) political legitimacy is an indispensable side-condition to both an emerging societal consensus in favor of shared-growth strategies and an autonomous bureaucracy embedded in a dense network of external relations,[64] (4) internal cohesiveness-cum-social connectedness entails comprehensive consultation, cooperation, and coordination mechanisms which enhance compliance with government policies and create a self-enforcing governance structure to limit state strength; (5) participation, an independent, but accountable administration, and social consensus create a strong but limited government that guarantees political stability and increases governance capacity; (6) a Western-style democracy is *not* a universal model of development. Effective governance is independent of the form of government (the regime type); (7) while the initiation of economic reforms may be facilitated by the discretionary authority of elites and political institutions that insulate policy making from distributive claims of interest groups, their consolidation requires stabilized expectations regarding a new set of incentive structures and the confidence that these cannot be altered at the individual discretion of policy makers. Governments need to construct broad coalitions of political support and impersonal institutional channels for communication with affected economic and political interests, which make consolidation a stable policy choice.

In sum, the experiences of the HPAEs convincingly indicate that governance structures are basically subject to political design as far as formal institutions are concerned. By establishing institutions that ensure predictability, accountability, and transparency of policy making, as well as participation of business elites and other social groups, the HPAEs brought about a societal consensus to growth-oriented policies and enhanced the incentive-compatibility of government policies and economic performance. This helped especially the high performers in Northeast Asia to initiate and manage the transition from network states based on rule by moral authority vested in persons, to rule-based societies with strong-but-limited governments.

6.2.3 Myth or miracle: governance and economic performance after the Asian crisis

In 1997–1998, a widely unexpected tidal wave of financial and economic troubles swept across East Asia. Currencies plummeted, stock markets plunged, numerous commercial banks failed, GDP stagnated and even shrank, unemployment figures soared, and living standards declined. What had been known as the East Asian Miracle became the Asian Crisis and not only threatened development successes of the past four decades but also questioned the role-model character of these countries' development strategies. It would be beyond the scope of this study to portray the chronology of the crisis fully, to analyse its causes thoroughly, and to discuss the various policy responses of the affected countries.[65] Rather, this section seeks to explore to what extent the Asian Crisis was a crisis of governance as was maintained by some observers.

In contrast to previous currency and financial crises, the East Asian one did not result from major abortive developments of macroeconomic variables. On the contrary, the overall macroeconomic landscape prior to the crisis looked sound in virtually all HPAEs. Economic growth rates had been sustainably high, budget deficits low (some countries even realized budget surpluses), inflation was low to moderate, and the savings rates were among the highest in the world (see Table 6.4).

Table 6.4: Sound and solid: economic fundamentals in pre-crisis East Asia

(in percent)

	GDP growth		inflation rate		fiscal balance/GDP		savings/GDP	
	1990–95	1996	1990–95	1996	1990–95	1996	1990–95	1996
Indonesia	8.0	7.8	8.7	7.9	0.2	0.2	31.0	27.3
Malaysia	8.9	8.6	3.7	3.5	-0.4	0.7	36.6	42.6
Philippines	2.3	5.8	10.6	9.1	-1.1	0.3	16.6	18.5
Singapore	8.6	6.9	2.7	1.4	9.4	6.8	47.0	51.2
South Korea	7.8	7.1	6.6	5.0	0.2	0.5	35.6	33.7
Taiwan	6.4	5.7	3.8	3.1	-5.0	-6.6	26.9	25.1
Thailand	9.0	5.5	5.0	5.9	3.2	2.4	34.4	33.7

Source: ADB (1999a)

Nevertheless, several warning indicators had reached critical limits which (in hindsight) could have been interpreted as indicating future financial and economic problems, if not the scale of the crisis (see Tables 6.5–6.7).[66] First of all, national currencies had been pegged to the US dollar. But rapid economic growth and enormous net capital inflows (the effects of which on the domestic money supply could not be fully sterilized) meant domestic inflation rates that were higher than inflation in the US. Hence, national currencies (especially in South East Asia) appreciated in real terms. The international competitiveness of the HPAEs was additionally affected by the depreciation of the Chinese yuan and especially the Japanese yen; Japan being the most important trading partner of the East Asian countries. Secondly, the real appreciation helped to slow down export growth and increase import values. Current account deficits thus increased substantially in most countries. Thirdly, the current account deficits were essentially financed through private net capital inflows from abroad. Inflows mushroomed, especially after the Mexican Tequila crisis in 1994–95. While FDI played an important role, especially in Malaysia, the bulk of inflows consisted of portfolio investments and other, mainly short-term private flows (including bank loans). Consequently, the stock of foreign debt increased much more rapidly than currency reserves implying alarming debt-reserve levels particularly in Indonesia, Singapore, South Korea, and Thailand. Fourthly, domestic credit expansion was extraordinarily high in most countries; even given the high rates of economic growth.[67] This fact leads observers to suppose that loans were not exclusively provided to financially well-checked investment projects. And actually, it shows that financial intermediaries especially in Indonesia, South Korea, and Thailand rapidly accumulated short-term foreign debts by mid-1997 and, at the same time, provided long-term credit for risky projects. This alarming fact eventually resulted in a large number of bad loans, accounting for roughly 20 percent in Thailand and 17 and 16 percent in Indonesia and South Korea, respectively, by the end of 1997.[68] Fifthly, indicators of corporate financing gave cause for concern as well: even if debt-to-equity ratios have been traditionally high in East Asian countries due to the relative importance of the banking sector regarding corporate financing,[69] these ratios reached alarming numbers in South Korea and Thailand, where they exceeded 350 and 230 percent, respectively, in 1996. What is more, in most countries the ratio of short-term to total debt exceeded 50 and in Malaysia and Thailand even 60 percent.

Finally, if increasing inflows of capital come upon a relatively limited number of profitable long-term investment projects, the demand for assets such as real estate and stocks will increase. Since the supply of these assets is relatively non-elastic in the short run, large price increases will occur (possibly reinforced by subsequent speculation) which will imply an asset

Table 6.5: Pre-crisis warning indicators (1)

	current account/GDP			short-term debt	currency reserves*	debt–reserve ratio
	1990–95	1996	1997	(billions US$)	(billions US$)	
Indonesia	-2.5	-3.4	-1.4	34.66	20.34	1.7
Malaysia	-5.8	-5.0	-5.3	16.27	26.59	0.61
Philippines	-3.7	-4.7	-5.3	8.29	9.78	0.85
Singapore	0.6	15.4	15.4	196.6	80.66	2.44
South Korea	-1.2	-4.7	-1.8	70.18	34.07	2.06
Taiwan	4.2	4.0	2.7	21.97	90.02	0.24
Thailand	-3.9	-7.9	-2.0	45.57	31.36	1.45

Note: * Second quarter of 1997

Source: ADB (1999a)

Table 6.6: Pre-crisis warning indicators (2)

	broad money (M2) (percent of GDP)			private sector credit[1] (percent of GDP)			corporate financing (1)	(2)
	1980	1990	1995	1980	1990	1995	1996	1996
Indonesia	17	40	48	10	47	53	1.88	0.54
Malaysia	52	66	91	38	71	85	1.18	0.64
Philippines	24	34	50	31	19	38	1.29	0.48
Singapore	64	91	84	71	82	91	1.05	0.58
South Korea	33	38	44	42	57	61	3.55	0.57
Taiwan	66	148	194	55	100	149	0.80	0.59
Thailand	38	70	79	30	65	98	2.36	0.63

Notes:
[1] Private sector credit includes lending by the monetary authorities and deposit money banks; it excludes lending by other banking institutions, for which data are not available for most of the countries listed.
(1) Debt-to-equity ratio
(2) Short-term debt to total debt ratio

Sources: ADB (1999a) and IMF (1998b)

Table 6.7: Pre-crisis warning indicators (3)

	Net private capital flows[1] (percent of GDP; annual averages)							
	1975–82	83–91	92–96	1994	1995	1996	1997	Change 96–97
Indonesia								
Net private capital flows	1.1	2.6	4.8	0.3	3.5	6.1	0.0	-6.1
Net direct investment	0.5	0.6	1.8					
Net portfolio investment	0.1	0.1	0.7					
Other net investment	0.5	1.9	2.3					
Short-term liabilities	-0.8	1.4	2.4					
Malaysia								
Net private capital flows	5.1	4.1	10.5	1.2	6.2	8.4	-3.0	-11.4
Net direct investment	3.7	3.6	6.5					
Net portfolio investment	—	—	—					
Other net investment	1.4	0.5	4.0					
Short-term liabilities	0.8	0.5	3.5					
Philippines								
Net private capital flows	5.5	-0.8	4.8	7.9	8.4	12.7	0.4	-12.3
Net direct investment	0.5	1.0	1.7					
Net portfolio investment	0.1	0.1	0.1					
Other net investment	5.0	-1.9	3.0					
Short-term liabilities	2.9	-2.0	2.3					
South Korea								
Net private capital flows	5.7	-0.4	3.2	1.2	0.2	4.9	-6.0	-10.9
Net direct investment	0.1	0.1	-0.3					
Net portfolio investment	0.1	0.3	2.4					
Other net investment	5.5	-0.8	1.1					
Short-term liabilities	3.6	0.6	2.7					
Taiwan								
Net private capital flows	1.9	-2.2	-2.5	n.a.	n.a.	n.a.	n.a.	n.a.
Net direct investment	0.3	-0.9	-0.6					
Net portfolio investment	0.1	-0.3	0.2					
Other net investment	1.5	-1.0	-2.0					
Short-term liabilities	-0.6	2.0	1.4					
Thailand								
Net private capital flows	4.0	5.7	8.8	14.3	17.3	14.5	-2.0	-16.5
Net direct investment	0.4	1.3	1.0					
Net portfolio investment	—	0.8	2.2					
Other net investment	3.5	3.6	5.7					
Short-term liabilities	1.7	2.8	4.7					

Notes:

[1] Because of data limitations, other net investment may include some official flows.
The sign '—' indicates that the figure is zero or negligible.

Sources: IMF (1998b) and World Bank (1998)

inflation. If the asset bubble bursts, numerous investors will suffer from substantial losses. If these losses lead to an increase in bad loans, the solvency of financial intermediaries may be adversely affected. The problem is aggravated if it is foreign banks who are the creditors of domestic debtors. Then, a domestically-grown crisis can easily spill over to currency markets putting the exchange rate under severe pressure. This is what seemed to have happened, particularly in Thailand, where the Asian Crisis originated, and to some extent also in Indonesia, the Philippines, and South Korea.

These warning indicators had not been properly registered in the global financial markets and had been virtually ignored by all actors including the IMF. Yet these indicators reflect some deeper causes of the crisis. On the one hand, the causes include internal factors such as policy mistakes of governments in East Asia (for example, the maintenance of fixed exchange rates for too long and a premature financial liberalization), distorted incentives and market structures (especially regarding the financial and capital markets), nontransparent accounting and auditing practices of companies and banks, and implicit government guarantees to companies and banks regarding foreign borrowing. On the other hand, causes of the crisis relate to external factors. This line of reasoning refers to foreign banks and investors that failed to assess investment risks properly and, given the seemingly endless duration of the Asian Miracle, were captivated by 'irrational exuberance'.[70] Other external factors that played a critical role include the actions of international organizations such as the IMF and foreign governments, especially the US Treasury and the Japanese authorities. These actors played a crucial role in two regards. First, the IMF and the US Treasury contributed to the emergence of the crisis by pressuring the East Asian economies to liberalize prematurely their financial sectors, although a number of internal institutional and structural preconditions thereof had not been put in place. Moreover, the Fund's earlier role in bailing out crisis-ridden economies elsewhere may have caused moral hazard behavior on the part of international investors who accordingly perceived the risk of potential losses in the event of a crisis to be relatively low. Secondly, it is argued that both the IMF and foreign governments deepened the crisis, once it had started, by insufficiently contributing to bail-out funds. In addition, the Fund has been blamed for attaching overly excessive austerity programs and structural reforms to its bail-out conditionality. In doing so, it not only ignored the sound economic fundamentals in the crisis-affected countries but also political and social factors in a country like Indonesia that rendered the Fund's policies counterproductive.[71]

By now, the major determinants of the crisis have been quite well understood, although a consensus about the relative weight of the different causes has not yet emerged. Today, most scholars agree that the crisis was caused by both internal and external factors and by the actions (as well as omitted actions) of a great variety of actors (see Table 6.8).

Table 6.8: Perceived causes of the East Asian crisis: actors and actions

Actors	Actions
governments of crisis-affected countries	corruption, collusion, nepotism, crony capitalism; insufficient democracy; distorted markets, fixed exchange rate regimes; implicit government guarantees to companies and banks regarding foreign borrowing; premature capital-account liberalization; lack of regional cooperation;
foreign banks	sloppy credit-risk analysis; excessive confidence in currency pegs; moral hazard behavior, panic;
domestic banks	ditto;
investors, foreign and domestic	ditto;
domestic companies	ditto; occult accounting practices; family control;
the IMF	pressure for premature financial liberalization; moral hazard; bail-out conditionality of excessive austerity and excessive emphasis on structural reforms;
the US Treasury	pressure for premature financial liberalization; insufficient contribution to bail-out funds;
the Japanese Government	insufficient demand stimulus at home; insufficient contribution to bail-out funds abroad;
'the Japanese Economy'	two-thirds of the Asian economy, in seventh year of stagnation and getting worse;
'Globalization'	free floating responsibility.

Source: Adapted from Wade (1999)

The great diversity of actual and perceived causes of the crisis as well as the different extent to which the above warning indicators reached critical levels in various countries document that there is no mono-causal explanation. Moreover, this fact suggests that the causes and troubles have varied substantially across countries so that different explanations are required. Finally, it partially reflects the attempt of different actors to shift the blame; as Wade (1999: 135) puts it succinctly: 'The main external actors (the IMF and the US Treasury) blame national actors, governments blame outsiders, and national populations blame everyone but themselves.' Accordingly, Wade (1998: 1535) broadly distinguishes two contending strands of thinking which seek to explain the crisis: (1) the 'death throes of Asian state capitalism' and (2) 'panic triggering debt deflation in a basically sound but under-regulated system'. The first explanation has been favored by international investors such as George Soros and Washington-based policy makers and organizations (including Alan Greenspan, the chairman of the US Federal Reserve, the IMF, and the US Treasury, but with the notable exception of the World Bank). This view questions the overall validity of the Asian style of economic policy making and development. It suggests, or even explicitly requests, that the Western (in other words: Anglo-American) form of free market capitalism is superior to any alternative and hence to be universally applied.[72] *The Economist* (in its 7–13 March, 1998 issue) supported this interpretation by identifying six (alleged) myths of East Asian success. Chief among these was the perception that the governments in East Asia were small and that there was 'good' governance. The article argues that, while the share of public expenditures and revenues in GDP was relatively small, most governments conducted inefficient industrial policies that distorted market incentives and triggered the emergence of large underground economies.[73] The article further points out that governments only looked good as long as the economies boomed. Now, given the economic turmoil, institutional weaknesses are uncovered. These essentially include unreliable legal and regulatory systems, insufficient regulation and supervision of banks, and a lack of transparency in the corporate sector. According to this first explanation, most, if not all, of the blame is to be put on the governments in East Asia which made the Asian problems homegrown. Domestic policy mistakes, government interventions, and close relations between the state and private business are conceived to have led to crony capitalism and corruption.

There is certainly some truth in these arguments, and in fact there have been a number of serious obstacles to maintaining high growth rates and technologically upgrading the economies particularly in South East Asia. One criticism emphatically proposed by Krugman (1994) and Young (1995) among others was that East Asian growth mainly resulted from factor accumulation and hardly from productivity increases.[74] This implies that, due to diminishing returns, there are some natural limits to continued fast growth unless some significant progress in fostering sustained total factor productivity growth can be accomplished. Moreover, especially in Malaysia and Thailand, severe skill shortages have occurred that have already caused private companies to move production elsewhere. Furthermore, throughout the region, all kinds of infrastructure have been chronically congested. But one should keep in mind that these latter two problems are problems of economic success. Finally, one must concede that cozy relations between political authorities and the *chaebols* in South Korea and the *konglomerats* in Indonesia have fueled collusion and corruption and that government favors and political connections also played a central role in allocating funds in Malaysia. But such obstacles have been much less significant in other East Asian countries.[75] In sum, these problems do indeed indicate severe institutional weaknesses and call for a number of structural reforms in order to continue the previous pace of economic development. But they can be hardly referred to if one seeks to explore the causes of the recent crisis, which was essentially a currency and financial crisis. However, another obstacle did play a critical role. This was the lax regulation of the financial sectors, the lack of prudent banking supervision as well as insufficient auditing and opaque accounting practices in virtually all countries.

This latter criticism has also been acknowledged by the second explanation that, however, interprets external factors as having been crucial variables causing the crisis. This alternative view holds that it was financial panic on the part of international investors in association with under-regulated financial markets which was responsible for the severity of the crisis. Jeffrey Sachs, for example, argued:

> Asia is reeling not from a crisis of fundamentals but a self-fulfilling withdrawal of short-term loans, one that is fueled by each investor's recognition that all other investors are withdrawing their claims. Since short-term debts exceed foreign exchange reserves, it is 'rational' for each investor to join in the panic.[76]

And Joseph Stiglitz, then chief economist at the World Bank, implicitly criticized the IMF and explained that

> (r)ecent developments (...) underscore the challenges presented by a world of mobile capital – even for countries with strong economic fundamentals. The rapid growth and large influx of foreign investment created economic strain. In addition, heavy foreign investment combined with weak financial regulation [allowed; J.A.] lenders in many southeast Asian countries to rapidly expand credit, often to risky borrowers, making the financial system more vulnerable. (...) Inadequate oversight, not over-regulation, caused these problems. Consequently, our emphasis should not be on deregulation, but on finding the right regulatory regime to reestablish stability and confidence.[77]

Hence, while the adherents of this view clearly concede policy mistakes and institutional weaknesses within the crisis-affected regions, they also point to the persistent institutional shortcomings of the international financial architecture and the policies of foreign actors.

With the benefit of hindsight, it seems to become increasingly evident that none of these extreme viewpoints provide a full explanation. In particular, the strength of the economic recovery in all East Asian countries in 1999 and most recent growth forecasts for 2000 cast serious doubts on the extreme claim of fundamental structural imbalances and misleading development strategies (see Figure 6.22).[78] If the economic and political problems were as systemic as presumed by the first viewpoint, one would have expected an incomplete, gradual, and regionally uneven recovery. Instead, there is growing awareness of the fact that both internal and external factors caused the crisis, the importance of which varied across countries. Moreover, there is quite broad agreement that the domestic financial system played a critical role in causing the crisis.[79] As mentioned above, there is evidence of severe distortions in the banking and financial sectors of several East Asian countries. But these problems have existed for a long time. Furthermore, there are numerous other countries with weak financial systems, which have not suffered from crises. Hence, for a crisis on the scale of East Asia's to occur, there must be a link between the weak financial and banking sector and one or more triggering events. These latter factors comprise the overly rapid financial liberalization, including capital account convertibility, the induced huge inflows of short-term private capital which accelerated in the 1990s, and moral hazard behavior on the part of international investors and domestic financial intermediaries.

First of all, the rapid shift towards financial liberalization and capital account convertibility caused enormous strains for the rather unsophisticated financial systems which had traditionally focused on simply intermediating funds between domestic investors and savers. There were newly emerging opportunities to borrow in international capital markets at low interest rates and investing at home at much higher rates (combined with pegged exchange rates). Domestic financial intermediaries underestimated the risks that were involved in such transactions. Thus, unhedged and mismatched currency positions of domestic banks and companies appear to have been major factors behind the crisis. Secondly, these problems were aggravated by implicit government guarantees to bail out enterprises and banks in the case of failed investments. This induced moral hazard behavior which eventually led to overinvestment, reinforced excessive external borrowing, and implied a lack of concern for excessive risks associated with certain projects, particularly in the real estate sector. Thirdly, moral hazard behavior could also be observed on the part of foreign banks which believed that they could reckon on the IMF to bail out debtors in the event of a crisis. Fourthly, governments were unprepared to respond adequately to pressures on domestic currencies. They held inadequate levels of currency reserves and were reluctant to raise rates of interest due to concerns about the adverse consequences of their

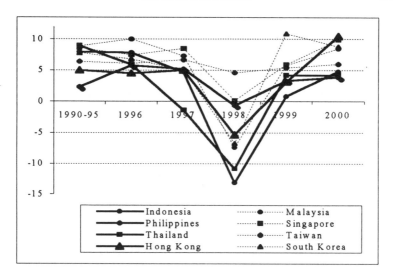

Source: ADB (1999a and 2001)

Figure 6.22: V for victory: real GDP growth before and after the crisis (percent per annum)

overextended financial systems. Finally, although the East Asian countries did not need to attract more funds (the savings rates accounted for 30 percent or more in most countries), the IMF played a key role in pushing East Asian countries too rapidly toward capital account opening without ensuring a proper sequencing of reforms and without insisting *a priori* on establishing the institutional preconditions thereof.[80]

In sum, the recent currency and financial crisis in East Asia should be viewed as an interruption of economic growth and not as the end of an era of specific development strategies. As Furman and Stiglitz (1998) point out, the miracle was real. The effects of the recent crisis do not come close to undoing the economic accomplishments of the HPAEs since the mid-1960s. Primarily, the crisis is to be traced to the failure of institutional change to keep pace with rapid economic growth. This particularly concerns the modernization and expansion of the financial systems. But in countries such as South Korea and Indonesia, this also holds for reforming and adjusting government–business relations. Close ties between political authorities and large business conglomerates proved to be effective at the early stages of economic development. But since the *chaebols* became politically too powerful over time in South Korea and since Indonesia did not manage the transition from personal to impersonal rule during the Suharto era, the government–business interfaces degenerated into closed circles of political decision making, which after all aggravated the recent economic troubles in these countries. This set of factors surely reflects problems of governance, but they do not constitute a crisis of the overall governance structures that had underpinned sustained economic development in the HPAEs. Rather, they again indicate that effective governance must be interpreted as a dynamic process that requires continuous fine tuning and adapting institutional arrangements to a changing political, economic, social, and technological environment. The rapid recovery of all crisis-affected countries (see Figure 6.22) shows that their overall governance frameworks are robust and sufficiently flexible to react quickly to external shocks. But this fact should not tempt East Asian governments to postpone necessary structural adjustments. These not only concern the modernization of their financial and corporate sectors, but also the need to adapt effectively to new challenges through institution building. Above all, these challenges relate to the problems of an aging population, increasing urbanization, further integration into the world economy, and growing demands for political participation. Consequently, these countries will face increased strains on public budgets, pressures for further reforms of the legal and regulatory systems, and the need to enhance the flexibility and responsiveness of political institutions.

6.3 GOVERNANCE AND SYSTEMIC TRANSFORMATION

The HPAEs can look back on almost four decades of sustained economic growth and development that has taken place *within* a market-oriented economic order. In hindsight, it shows that getting the prices right was neither a necessary nor a sufficient condition to ensure this remarkable economic performance. Getting the policies right seems to be a more correct explanation. But eventually, as the previous section set forth, getting the institutions right is the most accurate and fundamental rationale of the development performance of these countries. It was distinct and country-specific sets of institutions that as a whole produced flexible MEGS which facilitated policy formation and adaptability, made its implementation effective, and allowed these countries to share the benefits of economic growth widely.

More recently, the number of high-performing countries in the East Asian region increased: the club of top performer has been joined by two socialist economies, China and Vietnam, which started their market-oriented reforms in 1978 and 1986, respectively. China has benefited from over two decades of rapid growth, averaging 9.3 percent between 1978 and 1997, and Vietnam has experienced average GDP growth of 7.4 percent between 1986 and 1997. Both countries have weathered the recent regional crisis fairly well with continuing positive growth rates albeit at a somewhat lower level than in previous years.[81] These two countries have been the first socialist economies to take up the challenge of creating a market-based economic order. They were soon followed by other socialist countries in Asia such as Laos and Mongolia, the latter joining the by then global shift from centrally planned to market-oriented economies that culminated in the dramatic political and economic transformation in Central and Eastern Europe (CEE) and the former USSR. While the Asian economies in transition essentially strive to institute new hybrid systems, so-called socialist market economies, the CEE countries including Russia seek simultaneously to establish Western-style market economies and democratic orders. Hence, what distinguishes these economies (or better: societies) in transition from other LDCs or emerging markets is that their policy reforms are not embedded in a relatively stable institutional order that is incrementally changing in the course of economic development. Rather, comprehensive policy reforms and large-scale institutional change have to go hand in hand. While this challenge has already been clearly visible in the Asian transition economies, it is even more pronounced in the twofold transformations in CEE. This fact calls attention to the importance of economic and political governance during transition. Experiences show that neither a so-called shock therapy nor gradualism will automatically succeed and lead to sustained economic development. Recent empirical studies (for example, World Bank 1996, Wolf 1999, and EBRD 1999) document that it is not the speed of transition that matters but the quality of economic and political institutions which play a critical role for successful stabilization and structural adjustment.

As yet, however, neither a general theory of systemic transformation is available nor do generally accepted governance guidelines exist that can guide policy makers through the complicated terrain of policy and institutional reform. This section therefore seeks to deepen our understanding of the role played by governance in a successful systemic transformation and of which factors determine its quality in different countries. This is done by means of example, focusing on two distinct groups of countries that comprise both success cases and failures. The first group includes three large countries: China, India, and Russia. While these countries greatly differ with respect to their political, social, and economic orders and the pursued transition strategies, they nevertheless share a history of pervasive state intervention and socialist management and very similar governance-related problems (especially regarding the governability of a large country, decentralization, and poverty reduction). The second group consists of Central European transition economies (the Czech and Slovak Republics, Hungary, and Poland), that show similar legacies from their socialist past and seek access to the European Union (EU). It will be particularly argued that while some lessons can be learnt from the successful HPAEs, their highly centralized governance structures are in general not transferable to other countries.

6.3.1 Large countries: China, India, and Russia

The conceptual approach to effective governance, discussed earlier, suggests that a universal model constituting a MEGS cannot be identified. Institutional mechanisms that produce development-enhancing governance structures are contingent on a wide variety of country-specific factors. These include the initial conditions of policy reforms, the degree to which a country is integrated in international structures, the actual design of its polity and economy, the balance of political power in society, existing ethnic or religious clefts, the preferences of policy makers and citizens, and the size of the country. Hence, actual governance structures vary substantially across both space and time. While it shows that the notion of embedded autonomy in a highly centralized version worked well in a subgroup of small East Asian economies, especially at early stages of their development, this is hardly to be expected to hold for countries that are much larger and more heterogeneous than the HPAEs.

Nevertheless, the four core principles of effective governance (accountability, participation, predictability, and transparency) suggested by our conceptual approach are hypothesized to be useful orientation lines for governance-related policies. Hence, from the viewpoint of the political economy of policy reform, the crucial question is how the quality of a given country's institutions can be sustainably enhanced along these governance dimensions. With respect to large, heterogeneous, and conflict-ridden countries, it has been argued for a long time that decentralization and particularly (fiscal) federalism may serve as an appropriate politico-institutional foundation for economic reforms.[82] But actually, federal states have differed widely in their political and economic performance. Some federal countries such as the United States belong to the richest, technologically most advanced, and least corrupt countries in the world. Others, like Mexico and India, have remained very poor and have experienced disappointing growth records. Russia, another country with a *de jure* federal structure, has been mired in negative growth and plagued by widespread corruption, while China, though very poor, has one of the fastest growing economies in the world.

The performance of these countries, of course, varies in part due to a number of variables other than federalism that affect a country's development success. Nevertheless, we follow Parikh and Weingast (1997) and argue that performance differences can actually be traced back to systematically varying characteristics of federal systems. Although all federal systems are distinguished by a hierarchy of central and sub-national governments, different institutional characteristics of the federal architecture significantly account for differences in federal performance. Hence, if federalism is conceived to help constitute a MEGS, we should explore the kind of institutions which can bring about a distinct federal system that strengthens and reinforces the four core principles of governance. Such a system should help maintain and enhance markets and implement policy reforms in an effective manner.

In order to fulfill this task, we introduce a comparative theory of market-preserving federalism developed by Weingast (1995) and others. Subsequently, this theory will be applied to three large transition economies: China, India, and Russia. The focus on China is obvious because the remarkable success of its economic reforms has been mainly and convincingly attributed to its decentralization policies. Hence, the Chinese experience may yield some valuable lessons for other large countries.

India is included in our sample for several reasons: first, it is sometimes called the next Asian Tiger because of its vast development potential which the Indian government has recently begun to unleash by introducing bold economic reforms (Root 1998b); secondly, India is an economy in transition as well, because those comprehensive policy reforms that commenced only in 1991 represent an obvious break with its socialist past and seek to replace the old state-led development strategy by a market-oriented one; and thirdly, although India is a *de jure* federal state, *de facto* it is so only to a very limited extent. The in fact centralized nature of the Indian state represents a serious impediment to the implementation of comprehensive structural reforms. Moreover, increasing trends of regionalism and the alienation and marginalization of large segments of society have shown that excessive concentration and centralization of political powers in governmental structures and the major political parties have undermined democratic processes (Mukarji and Arora 1992; Verma 1994). Therefore, the success of current reforms ultimately depends on political reforms and in particular on political decentralization.

Finally, Russia is taken explicitly into consideration, not only because of its political and economic importance in global terms, but also because, after one decade of transition, it has remained a hopeless case. While it had begun the systemic transformation with a seemingly shock therapy-like program under the Gaidar government in 1992, all subsequent reform efforts were of a piecemeal character. Until the end of the 1990s, virtually none of the many economic reform attempts materialized as expected (except for some temporarily limited successes in macroeconomic stabilization). Production figures and living standards continued to decline, social indicators (such as life expectancy) deteriorated substantially, unemployment soared, and poverty increased significantly. Above all, political factors proved to be the most severe obstacles to the systemic transformation and economic progress. Initially, it was the vacuum of political powers in which the transition process was trapped. Subsequently, the government's reform policies were blocked by a parliament dominated by anti-reformist communist and nationalist forces. And more recently, the collusion between corrupt government officials and the new oligarchs has posed a serious threat to market-oriented reforms. Moreover, the highly centralized manner of ruling through presidential decrees and at times through sheer military force has proved to be counterproductive and yielded, in the case of Chechnya, disastrous results. In sum, lack of effective governance seems to be the single most important cause for the continuing Russian transformation crisis. Consequent political reforms, and especially the creation of a *de facto* federal structure, are argued to be necessary steps towards creating a politico-institutional foundation making market-oriented economic reforms a stable and viable policy choice.

Market-preserving federalism[83]
The traditional economic arguments in favor of federalism are essentially threefold: (1) according to Hayek (1945), central governments cannot accumulate sufficient information to tailor economic policies to specific regional and local circumstances. Lower level governments possess much better information about individual projects as well as citizens' preferences, and therefore they are better prepared to conduct policies that have a regional or local impact; (2) following the seminal work of Tiebout (1956), economists have emphasized the benefits of competition between sub-national jurisdictions. Competition not only implies a more efficient policy mix across jurisdictions, one that accounts for the different preferences of citizens, but also forces policy makers to anticipate the political and economic consequences that will result from their decisions;[84] and (3) a major principle that has been proposed by the works on fiscal federalism is that a given public good should be provided by the lowest level government that is able to produce that good.[85] Moreover, political scientists emphasize a number of non-economic benefits resulting from federalism. Many scholars argue, for example, that federal structures help to avoid or reduce political conflicts especially in geographically polarized and ethnically or religiously divided societies, because they alleviate inter-group fights for political power which are likely to occur in centralized systems. In other large, but more homogeneous societies, federalism may contribute to overcome problems related to vast geographic distances, to facilitate public administration, and to account for differences in regional or local historical experiences (Horowitz 1985 and Bednar *et al.* 1996).

While stressing the potential benefits that federalism may provide, most theoretical approaches ignore a more fundamental issue, that is the question of how the institutions constituting federal structures are maintained. For example, assigning political authority to different levels of government is not merely a technical problem for solving problems of economic efficiency, it is also a fundamental political issue, namely how to allocate political power to different political units at different jurisdictional levels. In fact, if not *de jure*, numerous contemporary federal orders diverge in terms of the assignment of political powers over public expenditures and revenues from economists' prescriptions. Frequently, policy makers manage successfully to circumvent or undermine the rules of federalism and thereby call the potential benefits of the whole system into question (Parikh and Weingast 1997). The modern literature on federalism attributes this systemic failure to insufficient and ineffective institutional safeguards, which do not provide political officials with the incentives to comply with the rules of the game.[86] In order to overcome this obstacle, 'the rules and constraints of federalism must be self-enforcing: Political officials must find it in their interests to abide by a series of rules and to respect a series of citizen rights' (ibid.: 1595). This requires, for example, institutional safeguards which, on the one hand, hinder central governments' interference in the domains of sub-national jurisdictions and, on the other hand, discourage lower-level governments from encroaching on the common domestic market.

The elementary functions of federalism comprise a subdivison of power through vertical separation and the integration of heterogeneous societies. Its main purpose is the mediation of contrasting social, economic, and political objectives. Basically, two extreme versions of federalism can be distinguished: a centripetal variant (in the form of a unitary state) and a centrifugal one (in the form of an alliance or a confederation); the former aiming for complete integration and equalization of living conditions, and the latter favoring autonomy, self-reliance, and the diversity of living conditions. In reality, federal systems are located somewhere between these extremes of a bipolar continuum. But their location is not ultimately fixed, because tensions between unity and diversity, integration and autonomy as well as the political culture and institutions of a country might alter the original orientation. This basic classification emphasizes that political institutions play a major role in the functioning and effects of a federal system. However, it does not address the 'fundamental political dilemma of an economic system' (Weingast 1995: 1), namely that a strong government capable of protecting and enforcing legal rights is also able to violate these rights and to confiscate citizens' wealth, thereby creating disincentives for private actors to carry out long-term investment and to provide information, blocking thriving markets, and eventually halting development. Federalism can only survive and unfold its market-enhancing role if political decision makers have incentives to abide by its underlying rules. Therefore, self-enforcing political institutions are required as a governance structure which limits political discretion concerning the economy and credibly commits the government to honor rules and rights and to preserve markets.

Based on the postulate that a limited, self-enforcing government is required to take advantage of federalism's benefits which are proposed by economists, Parikh and Weingast (1997: 1597) and others developed an axiomatic approach to studying actual federal structures. This concept provides the analytical foundation for a 'comparative theory of federalism', which allows scholars to predict the political and economic performance of federalisms that exhibit different institutional characteristics. Moreover, this approach recognizes that federalism *per se* does not promote economic development. Rather, it is a distinct type of federalism – market-preserving federalism – that is conducive to economic performance. Market-preserving federalism (MPF) constitutes one type of centrifugal federalism and represents an appropriate governance structure because it establishes a balance of power which promotes the accountability of political decision makers, enhances the participation of lower-level political entities, and makes political commitments credible. The principle institutional foundations of MPF include:[87]

C1.   a two- (or more) level government hierarchy with a clear assignment of competencies ensuring autonomy to each government (central and subordinated) within its realm of authority;

C2.   institutionalized autonomy of all governments, which cannot be altered at the discretion of either the central government or sub-national governments;

C3.   sub-national governments with primary authority over the economy of their respective jurisdiction;

C4.   a central government that ensures a common market and prevents the erection of barriers against the mobility of goods and factors of production across sub-national jurisdictions;

C5.   all governments are subject to hard budget constraints.

Fulfilling these conditions will bring about an ideal kind of self-enforcing federalism. C1 is the basic characteristic defining federalism as a decentralized system. However, not all decentralized systems constitute a centrifugal type of federalism. Therefore, C2 relates to the critical problem of enforcing MPF. It constitutionally delimits the discretionary power of the central government and prevents the reversal of the devolution of power. This condition serves as a device for credible commitment and helps to make MPF self-enforcing. The remaining criteria address the relationship between authority and economic issues and lend the system its market-preserving character. While C3 puts limits on the discretionary power of the central government to conduct economic policies and compromise the system of MPF and establishes competition among sub-national jurisdictions, C4 ensures that this competition is beneficial for the country as a whole. Constraining the discretionary authority of all governments, C3 and C4 ensure that (thriving) markets are not destroyed by political discretion. These two conditions also limit the central government's authority to providing national public goods and policing misbehavior by lower-level governments. C5 addresses both transfers of fiscal revenues between different levels of government and borrowing through channels of the financial system. Hard budget constraints ensure fiscal prudence at all levels of government, preventing higher-level governments from bailing out subordinated ones and linking regional and local revenues to economic outcomes, thus providing incentives for regional and local politicians to care about the consequences of their policy choices.[88] Though more difficult to enforce for the central government, this condition is also necessary to prevent monetary discretion becoming a means of stretching sub-national governments' authority. However, the more expenditure obligations are shifted to lower-level governments, the greater is the separation of fiscal policies and monetary policy in the economy and the easier it is to realize the independence of the central bank.[89]

MPF brings about several economic effects which are beneficial for the country as a whole.[90] First, neither the national nor any lower government has a regulatory authority that governs the economy in its entirety. Secondly, it creates competition among all jurisdictions. Regional or local restrictions have comparative disadvantages for enterprises, prompting them to move to other jurisdictions. This will have negative effects on regional and local tax revenues and eventually on economic activity. Thus, subordinated governments have to compete for factors of production by offering appropriate sets of public policies and local public goods. Thirdly, hard budget constraints imply that sub-national governments face the risk of going bankrupt. This is an incentive for prudent fiscal management in order to maintain the respective governments' ability to provide necessary public goods. Fourthly, inherent to MPF is a demonstration function. Economically successful jurisdictions serve as a model for less successful ones. This results in important feedback effects which offer an opportunity for readjusting politicians' expectations, revising inappropriate policy choices, and imitating strategies of other jurisdictions. Fifthly, MPF establishes the political foundation of markets. Private actors are provided with long-term security protecting them from political predation. The opportunities for government intervention due to specific political objectives, which threaten to distort markets, are substantially reduced. Finally, through the devolution of political and economic authority, MPF sustainably constrains the authority of the central government over the economy, thereby limiting the power of a strong government. This makes MPF self-enforcing and lends the system an important degree of durability, which allows the continuation of economic reforms beyond the commitment of politicians who started them. Since, however, the government apparatus is basically a site of conflict, institutions need to be put in place that ensure the compliance of all governments with the conditions constituting MPF. Institutionalized conflict resolution requires a constitution in which the division of authority between the different levels of government is embodied and competencies are clearly assigned to the central and sub-national governments, with the least possible reliance on concurrent responsibilities. Moreover, an independent judiciary needs to oversee adherence to the agreed rules, and lower governments should have the right to appeal to the courts in case the central government tries to encroach on sub-national affairs.[91]

After inception of an MPF-like system, a considerable diversity of experiments and policy choices undertaken by lower-level governments can be expected to appear. This is most likely because individuals in different jurisdictions (especially in large countries) will have significantly different interests, capabilities, and expectations and because political authorities as well as civic organizations may act according to different ideologies and theories. In turn, as the outcomes of new experiments and policies become known across jurisdictions, political officials as well as citizens are likely to update their perceptions and expectations regarding the consequences of different policy choices. Thus, inherent in the demonstration function of MPF is a set of feedback effects which a unitary system cannot provide. This characteristic is crucial for enhancing the adaptive efficiency of the overall institutional matrix of a given country and hence for instituting a *flexible* MEGS. Nevertheless, the expected processes of learning and imitation are not expected to induce a uniform appearance of all jurisdictions for several reasons: (1) since different branches of industry necessitate the existence of different kinds of (local) public goods, they may be located in different geographical areas; (2) resource endowments and market access may differ among jurisdictions so that various development strategies are expected to survive;[92] (3) policies will vary within a country due to citizens' differences in their tastes for local public goods as well as due to differences in their capability of paying for them; and (4) sub-national governance structures may be different, implying that policies that are efficient in some jurisdictions are, for example, politically not feasible in others.[93]

Eventually, as Parikh and Weingast (1997) point out, the axiomatic approach to MPF also provides the tools of a comparative theory of federalism in the sense that it allows the political and economic consequences of federal systems that violate one or more of the conditions that constitute MPF to be identified. If, for example, all conditions except for C4 are satisfied, it is likely that those subordinated jurisdictions, that would be harmed by the competitive pressures of a common market, will introduce trade barriers. This implies that, while some jurisdictions may continue to enhance market activities, others will not. In the latter case, political interference in markets will not only adversely affect the overall economic performance of the national economy, but will also be conducive to political patronage and corruption. It may be presumed that, especially in LDCs, a violation of C4 is more likely in a newly established federal system than in a mature one, because a possibly existing '(l)imited exposure to markets naturally generates suspicion of them and of their potential for generating dependence on outsiders' (ibid.: 1605). Therefore, demonstration effects of other jurisdictions that may successfully promote markets are critically important to overcome those concerns and to check protectionist tendencies.

Alternatively, if all axioms are fulfilled except C5, serious growth-impeding effects are to be expected. If, for example, the authority to provide credit remains in part in the hands of sub-national governments, inflation will be comparatively higher as each lower government has the incentive to overgraze the commons and overall money supply will increase more than is desirable. What is more, decentralized credit creation softens the budget constraints of lower governments and triggers moral hazard behavior, because jurisdictions may be inclined to subsidize ailing companies and to borrow more in order to finance an increasing number of investments, which would not be sufficiently profitable without access to (subsidized) credit.

Finally, violations of the axioms C2, C3, or C5 entail the national government being powerful enough to make lower government dependent on its will. Any political system that violates one or more of these conditions may be *de jure* a federal system, but *de facto* it is unlikely to exhibit any sustainable market-preserving qualities. In the extreme case, sub-national governments may degenerate into mere administrative units of the national government. If any of these conditions is not satisfied, the federal governance structure cannot provide institutional safeguards that make political commitments credible and ensure the predictability of policy making over time.

In what follows, we apply the theory of MPF to three large economies in transition. In doing so, we will argue that MPF, Chinese style, has significantly contributed to the remarkable growth record of China. In contrast, severe deficiencies in the federal systems of India and Russia have constituted serious obstacles to development in these countries.

China

Note the following political-economy puzzles relating to China: (1) Market-oriented reforms have been effectively conducted without any major political reforms; (2) the national government has been perceived to exert substantial political discretion and to have the power suddenly to reverse the policy reforms; (3) only a few attempts have been made to establish secure private property rights, and the authorities neither developed a commercial law nor established an independent judiciary; and (4) reforms, so far, have succeeded without large-scale privatization and complete liberalization of markets (that is, factors emphatically stressed by mainstream economists as being crucial for economic transition) (Montinola *et al.* 1995; Qian 1999).

At first glance, governance appears to be highly ineffective in China. Given the political monopoly of the Chinese Communist Party (CCP), economic returns are threatened by political arbitrariness and predation. This potential threat, in turn, seems to imply that there are no institutional safeguards that can hinder the government from reversing the reforms. This also means that a potential turnover in leadership could allow a new (less reform-minded) government to confiscate (private) wealth and to impose penalties on those whose businesses succeeded under the economic reforms. Facing these political threats, why should private economic agents put any effort or resources into long-term investments?

But note the actual performance of the Chinese economy since the beginning of the reforms in 1978: within two decades, the country has moved from a centrally planned to a dynamically emerging market economy. Over the same period, GDP per capita has quadrupled, and living standards of ordinary people have substantially improved. Moreover, this outstanding economic performance has been accompanied by significant improvements in social indicators. Not only has the number of people living in absolute poverty declined by 80 percent, but life expectancy has also increased from less than 65 years to almost 71 years and infant mortality has fallen by over 40 percent (Qian 1999).

Recent research on the institutional underpinnings of the Chinese policy reforms suggests several important pointers which help us to understand this seeming contradiction between (perceived) weak governance and fast economic growth. Conceding that the quality of the institutional matrix in China is far from meeting the standards of advanced economies in the West and recognizing that property rights are not as clearly defined and secure as they should be, various scholars persuasively argue that political reforms have been much more pronounced than usually perceived and have in fact placed substantial limits on the potentially discretionary behavior of the national government.[94] In this context, Montinola *et al.* (1995: 51) conclude that '(t)hese limits, in turn, provide the beginnings of a strong and credible political foundation for many market-oriented enterprises throughout the successful regions of China'.

In fact, political reforms in China have neither opened the door for the emergence of a democratic order nor have they sought to separate the CCP and the state. Today's China lacks almost all of the formal characteristics of a democracy. Nevertheless, several critical political changes have occurred over the last 20 years: (1) political decentralization has shifted considerable powers to lower governments and altered the relations between the central government and sub-national jurisdictions in ways that cannot be easily reversed; (2) with the CCP having increasingly favored a pragmatic, market-based policy approach, a significant ideological shift in political thinking has taken place which has underpinned and fostered economic reforms; and (3) the government has significantly increased the degree of openness of its economy (Shirk 1993; Montinola *et al.* 1995).

The systemic reforms realized so far can be interpreted as a process with two stages. During the first phase (1978–1993), both the economic and the political system were reformed through a combination of conventional and unconventional measures. These essentially included political decentralization, entry as well as expansion of private but particularly of local government enterprises, a subtle dual-track strategy for market liberalization, and enhancement of financial stability by using the means of 'financial dualism'.[95] During the second phase (since 1994), increased efforts have been undertaken to replace the old socialist economic system with a rule-based, market-oriented economy that increasingly exhibits best-practice institutions that have proved to be effective in advanced economies. Until the end of the 1990s, major progress could be achieved regarding exchange rate unification and current account convertibility, tax and fiscal reforms, reorganizing the central bank, downsizing the public administration as well as the restructuring and privatization of state-owned enterprises (SOEs). Remaining challenges which need to be addressed by future reforms mainly relate to the transformation of the financial system, restructuring of the SOE sector, reforming corporate governance, and the enforcement of the rule of law (Qian 1999).

A major change of policy making was the increased openness of the Chinese economy. However, while international competition can basically play a critical role in disciplining governments, enhancing markets, and fostering structural adjustment, the benefits associated with foreign trade and FDI usually play a much greater role for relatively small countries than for a large economy like China's. More important for a previously closed economy may be the access to new technology and new ideas as well as increased competition. Their effects, however, are eventually contingent on internal factors, including policy and institutional changes. The latter will be the focus of this section.

Particularly during the first stage of reforms, critical improvements of the country's governance structure as well as unorthodox policy choices attributing a significant and active role to the state in the transition process were essential for economic progress. The most important step towards more effective governance was the regional decentralization of government. Although China is *de jure* still a unitary state, *de facto* it is not. Montinola *et al.* (1995: 53) among others show convincingly that the political changes mentioned above have brought about a new quality of the political system, which they call 'federalism, Chinese style'. This kind of federalism differs substantially from federal systems in Western countries in so far as it lacks the commitment to political freedom, individual rights, and, hence, democracy. Moreover, it lacks an explicit constitutional embodiment. But several essential factors have been realized that are crucial in order to take advantage of the economic benefits of a federal system. As will be argued below, the current federal system in China satisfies (at least in part) all the conditions constituting MPF. More specifically, conditions C1 and C3 are completely satisfied, whereas the system fulfills C2, C4, and C5 at least partially.

Fiscal decentralization started as early as 1977 as an experiment and has been reinforced and complemented by political decentralization since 1979, when political authorities recognized that the previous centralized system of policy making was incompatible with the new market-oriented reforms.[96] The devolution of government authority to lower levels affected not only provinces but also prefectures, counties as well as townships and villages. As a consequence, lower-level governments assumed major responsibility over public-fixed investments and supervised more than 70 percent of public enterprises in the industrial sector (in output terms). Governments of villages and townships were assigned to control so-called township-village enterprises (TVEs) directly. Furthermore, sub-national governments gained considerable regulatory influence over the local economy by being responsible for issuing business licenses, coordinating business development, resolving business disputes, and influencing tax policies. Lower governments were also authorized to decide upon local expenditures and to provide local public goods (for example, price subsidies, utilities, schools, and health care). Finally, and of major importance, provincial governments were allowed to establish their own foreign trade corporations, and local authorities were encouraged to attract FDI and form joint ventures with foreign investors.[97]

The assignment of an increasing number of responsibilities to lower-level governments was accompanied by fiscal reforms that provided sub-national jurisdictions with stronger incentives for prudent fiscal management and for fostering the development of their local economies. In 1980, the old 'unified revenue collection and unified spending' system (which had been nicknamed 'eating from one big pot') was replaced by the 'fiscal contracting system' (nicknamed 'eating from separate kitchens') (Qian 1999: 9). The new revenue-sharing scheme has been based on medium-term contracts between adjacent governmental levels. Although the details of the scheme vary across regions as well as time, the common concept is that lower-level governments contract with the respective upper-level governments on the amounts of revenues which must be transferred. The rest is kept by the lower-level governments, making them residual claimants (in numerous instances, the marginal retention rate has been 100 percent). In turn, lower governments had strong interests in increasing revenues and hence promoting economic growth in their jurisdictions. In the mid-1980s, these incentives were even strengthened by the expansion of extra-budgetary funds which did not have to be shared with the central government and could be used more flexibly than regular funds.[98]

In this context, an Achilles' heel of decentralization must be mentioned: while the tax system and the limitations of intergovernmental transfers *per se* ensure relatively hard budget constraints at all governmental levels, the decentralization of the state banking system in the mid-1980s undermined this accomplishment. As a consequence of financial decentralization, provincial, municipal, and county governments gained considerable control over credit allocation. While this financial decentralization strengthened the influence of lower governments, it had adverse macroeconomic effects, because it softened the budget constraints of both SOEs and sub-national governments and eventually fed inflation (World Bank 1995b). Note, however, that the lowest-level jurisdictions – the township and village governments – were not affected by this financial decentralization. On the contrary: since the decentralization only reached down to the county level, township and village governments have very limited access to credit and are hence subject to hard budget constraints. The same applies to the TVEs owned by the village and township communities and controlled by the respective governments, which are also entitled to claim the residuals of these enterprises. Unlike SOEs, which are controlled by higher-level governments, TVEs may lay off employees and face the risk of bankruptcy. Moreover, township and village governments do not have the means continually to bail out loss-making TVEs or to shield them from competition by protectionist measures. As a consequence of this mixture of incentives and constraints, the

TVEs have become a driving force of economic growth, and their output accounted for some 30 percent of total industrial production in 1993.[99]

Another most noteworthy feature triggered by decentralization was regional experimentation and imitation which reduced adjustment costs for economic and political agents by allowing for gradual and structured learning. For example, the so-called household responsibility system that was a key feature of agricultural reforms originated in initiatives by local governments. This system was gradually imitated by other jurisdictions before the national government started to promote it. Eventually, the old collective farming system was replaced across the country. Another well-known example concerns the establishment of special economic zones, the first of which already came into existence in 1980 when the overall Chinese economy was still subject to central planning. Within these zones, foreign investments and business practices played the primary role, private ownership dominated, and market mechanisms were allowed to coordinate the allocation of resources. At a later stage, numerous new practices (such as marketing techniques, employment practices, and accounting methods) which had been successfully used in these zones, were adopted in other parts of the economy (Qian 1999). Several similar examples are reported by Montinola *et al.* (1995), and all of them appear to be in line with the theoretical predictions following from the concept of MPF. Thus, while at the early stages of the decentralization process a great number of diverse policy choices had been made by lower governments (ranging from highly interventionist to free-market approaches), in the course of time many jurisdictions that had pursued inferior policies imitated (sometimes due to increasing pressure of the people) those that had been proved superior elsewhere. In general, the intense inter-jurisdictional competition and substantial political freedom over local economies have encouraged learning, experimentation as well as adaptation and eventually have promoted economic growth.

Hence, from a governance perspective, federalism, Chinese style has a number of crucial benefits:[100]

1. A critically important advantage of decentralization was that it represented a feasible means of overcoming political opposition to economic reforms that existed within the national government. Given the relative strength of conservative, anti-reform forces in the 1970s and at the beginning of the 1980s and the weak chances for a consensus on policy reforms at that time, decentralization proved to be effective in overcoming political deadlock. In association with a gradual reform strategy, the devolution of political power also helped to create coalitions supporting reform policies from below. Especially in the fast growing regions of the southern coastal areas, the farmers as well as the political authorities, enterprises, and

households at the township and village level emphatically supported market-based reforms.

2. Decentralization and the growing pressures for reform by lower-level governments have helped to make market-oriented reforms more durable and sustainable by limiting discretionary interventions of the central government. This means that a potential reversal has become more costly or even impossible. Hence, decentralization has indirectly and informally enhanced the credibility of political commitments to an increased market orientation. Several more recent events illustrate this point: first, following the tragedy in Tiananmen Square in 1989, conservative forces in the central government assumed greater influence and attempted to recentralize financial and investment powers. The push for recentralization was even reinforced by the collapse of socialism in CEE and the Soviet Union that brought about a loss of power of the communist parties in these countries. But eventually the conservatives failed (Shirk 1993). The reasons for this not only included the effective resistance of a number of provincial governors and the increased (technical) problems of centrally monitoring and controlling the vast new market-based sectors of the economy, but also the fact that a potential reversal of reforms had become costly in financial terms. Recentralization of economic and political powers would have halted economic reforms and eventually caused production losses and unemployment. This, in turn, would have substantially increased demands on the national government and increased its financial problems.

Moreover, central authorities recognized that their political legitimacy was contingent on further economic growth and hence a continuation of market-oriented reforms; the more so as large segments of society including workers, farmers, and most bureaucrats had benefited considerably from marketization. Another factor that contributed to the failure to recentralize was the significant change in the incentive structure within the political apparatus.. Due to the increased political and financial autonomy of subordinated jurisdictions, public and party officials were no longer interested in promotion to posts at higher political levels. Especially in economically advanced regions, officials had increasingly substituted their previous devotion to the central government for a new loyalty *vis-à-vis* local authorities. Another event then gave the reform process new momentum. Deng Xiaoping's now famous journey to the economically advanced regions of the south crucially helped to end the political deadlock. By using the support of regional authorities for ongoing reforms, he tipped the fragile political balance within the central government in favor of strengthening the reform process. This, after all, revealed that the reform process was in fact protected by a relatively high degree of sustainability.

3. Another governance-related benefit of decentralization was that it created inter-jurisdictional competition and allowed for a great variety of experiments at the regional levels. This not only improved the policy adaptability across regions and fostered a high degree of pragmatic flexibility in policy making, it also encouraged the acceptance of reforms as well as the adaptive efficiency of the whole institutional matrix of the country.

4. Finally, decentralization combined with a so-called dual-track approach to price liberalization allowed the government to pursue the principle of conducting economic reforms without creating losers, thus developing a shared-growth strategy, Chinese style.[101] While decentralization-cum-marketization played a crucial role in promoting economic growth, reform-minded Chinese policy makers could not rely solely on market mechanisms for several reasons: first of all, as mentioned above, there was initially no broadly based consensus in favor of market-oriented reforms; secondly and related to the first, in order to maintain political power dismantling the old planning system at one stroke was politically infeasible; and thirdly, during systemic transformation there is always a need to prevent the emergence of political coalitions that seek to reverse the transition and to compensate those who will be hurt by policy reforms. Initially, this essentially held for numerous bureaucrats and other government employees, workers as well as consumers who were used to receiving large implicit subsidies under the planning system. For these reasons, a dual-track approach was pursued in China. Qian (1999: 17) succinctly summarizes how the system worked:

> Under the plan track, economic agents were assigned rights to and obligations for fixed quantities of goods at fixed plan prices as specified in the pre-existing plan. In addition, a market track was introduced under which economic agents participated in the market at free market prices, provided that they fulfilled their obligations under the pre-existing plan. With this approach, real market prices and markets as a resource allocation institution were created in China in the very early stages of reform.

Although this approach was frequently criticized by neoclassical economists for being incomplete and distorting resource allocation, theoretical reasoning and the practical experiences in China showed that the dual-track liberalization can be and in fact was efficient *and* provided the means to compensate potential losers from market reforms.[102] While the market track provided participating economic agents with the opportunity to increase their welfare, the plan track implicitly provided transfers that compensated potential losers from marketization by delivering the previous rents, which continued to exist under the maintained plan arrangements. Eventually, the dual-track liberalization served to reduce opposition to economic reforms *ex ante* (because it temporarily protected status-quo rents) and increased the opposition to reform reversal *ex post* (because an increasing number of agents benefited from the reforms in the course of time).[103]

In sum, these four sets of arguments suggest that political and economic decentralization has been the single most important factor in initiating market-oriented economic reforms in the late 1970s and early 1980s and in improving the country's governance structure so that the emerging markets became increasingly secure and the reforms durable, that is increasingly costly, if not impossible, to reverse. Decentralization has created a particular form of MPF that has aligned local politicians' interests with the economic prosperity of their jurisdiction. It has also brought into existence a number of new rival power centers at lower governmental levels which counterbalance the power of the national government. This means that the agenda of economic reforms is no longer dictated by the national government. The increased political and economic autonomy of sub-national governments thus confirms that not only condition C1 but also condition C3 is completely satisfied in China.

This does not, however, hold for the three other conditions constituting MPF, all of which are only partially satisfied. Although factor and goods mobility has developed substantially throughout the country, it remains imperfect. In particular, the mobility of goods has been limited. Decentralization has not only led to more competition between jurisdictions, but has also increased the incentives and the political means of lower-level governments at and above the county level to undertake protectionist policies. This option seemed to be especially attractive for those governments that were hostile or hesitant with respect to market-based reforms and led to so-called dukedom economies that are plagued by patronage and corruption.[104] Thus, the common market condition C4 is completely satisfied only at the township and village level and partially satisfied at higher levels of government. A similar conclusion holds for C5 (the hard budget condition). While both enterprises and governments at the township and village level face hard budget constraints, this does not hold for higher-level governments and SOEs which are controlled by them. Although the system of fiscal federalism does not provide significant channels for receiving rents or subsidies, it has been chiefly the deficits of the decentralized banking system that helped to soften these actors' budget constraints. Finally, condition C2 is insufficiently satisfied. While all lower-level governments have achieved a relatively high degree of autonomy which cannot be easily compromised by central government discretion, this autonomy has not been effectively institutionalized. Despite the introduction of a formalized system of fiscal federalism in 1994, there is still a considerable lack of rule-based decentralization that would constitutionally guarantee the independence of lower-level governments and provide transparent mechanisms of conflict resolution.

This incomplete satisfaction of all conditions indicates pressure for future reform in order to protect the benefits of decentralization and to make the system sustainable. It is of major importance to strengthen the central government without eroding the institutions that have limited its discretion. In particular, the capacity of the national government to provide critical public goods (including a unified monetary system under control of a single central authority, a common market, an independent judiciary, and law enforcement) needs to be enhanced. Furthermore, the *ad hoc* approach to developing a decentralized system was probably the only politically feasible way to proceed. But in the course of time, the drawbacks of an *ad hoc* approach have begun to outweigh the advantages. While the initiation of economic reforms and decentralization had greatly benefited from Deng Xiaoping's commitment, personality, and vision – in short, the existence of a charismatic leader – the consolidation of reforms requires institutionalization, especially in a time when the leader has passed his powers to succeeding politicians. The most important advantages of a rule-based governance framework, especially in a system that is still dominated by a single political party that has a quasi monopoly to control political power, are that it enhances the accountability, predictability, the transparency, and the uniformity of policy making. This, in turn, will reduce economic risks, corruption, and rent-seeking and thus the transaction costs of economic exchange.

Summing up, we recognize that the success of China's reforms must be essentially attributed to a number of unconventional policy measures and institutional reforms. In contrast to policy prescriptions following economics textbooks, the Chinese experience allows some distinct conclusions to be drawn: (1) it demonstrates that effective reforms do not require a theoretically optimal but rather a pragmatic and politically feasible sequencing of reform steps; (2) the maintenance of some old institutions during the first stage of transition may be more effective than the rapid 'import' of new formal institutions according to international best practice,[105] (3) 'economic laws', which focus on the beneficial effects of performance-related incentive structures, competition, and hard budget constraints, not only apply to enterprises but also to governmental organizations; (4) systemic economic reforms can actually be implemented and enforced without creating big or numerous losers; and (5) the Chinese experience clearly indicates that an 'incomplete' system of MPF can nevertheless represent a relatively pronounced MEGS which, in spite of still existing institutional weaknesses, is suitable to initiate an economic take-off at an early stage of development and to stimulate both participation (in this case of lower-level governments) in policy making and accountability in policy reforms (again of lower-level governments *vis-à-vis* the citizens in their jurisdiction).

Whether or not the momentum of economic progress and policy reforms will be sustained in the future critically depends on further institutional reforms and especially on the capability of the political leadership to further the transition from personal to impersonal rule and to enforce the existing laws and regulations. The second phase of economic reforms which began in 1994 indicates that China is on the right track. Already in the early 1990s, a new official government strategy gradually began to emerge, the objective of which was eventually to establish a full market system. Subsequently, a number of reform challenges that had been neglected or postponed were explicitly addressed. These essentially concerned the creation of key economic institutions that constitute a market economy. Besides exchange rate unification and the introduction of current account convertibility, the tax and fiscal systems became increasingly rule-based, international best practices (including more prudential regulation) and competition were introduced in the banking sector, the government administration was downsized by trimming the number of ministries in the national government from 45 to only 29 and by cutting the number of bureaucrats by 50 percent. Furthermore, political authorities started to privatize SOEs and to lay off state workers.[106] While it is still too early to make a final assessment of the Chinese reform process, it nevertheless seems to be evident that the country's gradual, partial reform strategy has worked well – in contrast to the experiences of other countries (notably in CEE before 1989) that had also pursued piecemeal reforms but eventually failed. Qian (1999) identifies three reasons underlying the success: first, although reforms have been partial in China, they created relatively strong competition between public and non-public enterprises and between (lower-level) governments. This means that partial reforms did not create huge rents for some actors and make others worse off. This helped to overcome the resistance to reforms which may have arisen among old vested interests or interim beneficiaries of reform. Secondly, potential future gains expected from market growth were thought by many economic agents likely to exceed their previous rents and hence motivated them to support further reform. Thirdly, old as well as newly emerged vested interests which could have an interest in blocking reforms were to some extent compensated for actual or potential losses. Thus, the first two decades of reforms in China illustrate that a partial reform trap is not the necessary outcome of an incremental approach to policy reform and economic transition. And most importantly, the Chinese experience clearly supports our hypothesis that a politico-institutional foundation is a *conditio sine qua non* for economic reforms and development and that an adequate, even if imperfect, MEGS can be politically crafted.

India

In 1991, the Indian government gradually launched an effective set of policy reforms which has brought about a significant increase in economic growth. Following a program of macroeconomic stabilization, the government substantially liberalized the investment regime, opened virtually all sectors to foreign competition, limited the scope for state intervention, liberalized capital and money markets, introduced prudential regulations in the financial sector and reduced entry restrictions, started a tax reform, established full convertibility for current account transactions, and considerably reduced tariffs. Since 1995 the economy has been growing on average by 6.8 percent per annum. The curtailed economic role of the public sector has been a critical structural change towards a more market-oriented economy. Previously dominant domains of the public sector such as banking, heavy manufacturing, and telecommunications are now open to private-sector investment. Efforts aimed at liberalizing the economy have considerably reduced microeconomic distortions and increased competition.[107]

Through these comprehensive reforms, the Indian government began managing the transition from the Nehruvian Socialist model of state-led industrialization (which had been inspired by the Soviet development model) towards a competitive market economy. However, the design of a suitable reform program is a necessary, but not a sufficient condition for ensuring sustainable development. India, like many other LDCs, has largely suffered from impeding prevailing institutions and lacks the institutional arrangements that have proved to work well in other (industrialized) countries. A major reason for this institutional shortcoming is that the state[108] has been a soft state in Myrdal's (1968) sense.[109] State actors have not been able to precommit themselves credibly to particular policies and have merely reacted to demands and actions by private actors, pressure groups, and political parties. The success of current and future reform programs will therefore critically depend on improvements in the country's governance structure, the problems and reform options of which are discussed in this section.

The macroeconomic crisis in 1991 which eventually triggered the ultimate rejection of the old development path, emphatically helped legitimize the new bold market-oriented reforms. Contrary to earlier reform efforts under Indira and Rajiv Gandhi, recent reforms were unambiguous in their intention, gained momentum and kept the opposition off balance. Prime Minister Rao's government (1991–1996) actively supported the reform process, which changed the perceptions of the country's economic prospects and ended a long period of neglect by foreign investors. The credibility of these reforms has been much greater than that of their predecessors.[110] The government was capable of signaling its commitment to sustainable economic development, the more so as it began explicitly addressing the problems of primary education, health care, rural employment, and India's most important challenge, that of poverty. The fact that the recent stabilization program did not cause a J-curve effect in overall production additionally contributes to raise support for the ongoing economic change. Nevertheless, maintaining credibility strongly depends on the pace and magnitude of reforms, and Indian authorities may put their newly earned credibility at stake if they cannot overcome the still numerous shortcomings of present reforms. Notably, these include serious problems regarding the fiscal imbalances at the central and sub-national levels, the legal and regulatory framework, a deepening of the capital market and further financial sector reform, the provision of public infrastructure as well as agricultural sector and public enterprise reform (ADB 1999c). Moreover, even if recent surveys showed that the business elite have substantial confidence in the general economic situation, credible commitment by the government is difficult in the Indian parliamentary system, because both government and parliament are controlled by the political parties in power. Even if regulatory interference is rejected by the courts, the executive can introduce new procedures or legislation. Thus, administrative discretion may easily destroy confidence among private actors. Making government's commitments credible requires specific institutional devices that complement the basic institutions of a parliamentary system.[111]

Furthermore, the fact that India is a democratic society burdened not only with severe economic problems, but with numerous vast disparities regarding regional, caste, ethnic, and religious issues,[112] implies that gaining broad political support for public policies is much more difficult than in more homogeneous societies and that the central government's legitimacy does not solely depend on economic progress. Bhalla (1995) has already recognized a slowdown of reforms due to growing political instability. Following defeats in several State elections, the Congress Party also lost the parliamentary elections in 1996, in which the Bharatiya Janata Party (BJP), representing Hindu nationalism, won the majority of seats. The succeeding United Front (UF) government, a coalition of 13 different parties, proved to be quite fragile and was toppled after less than two years in office. In the course of the general elections in February 1998, the BJP eventually hobbled to power by winning 179 of the 539 seats in Parliament and leading the new government, a fragile 19-party coalition, which barely survived a confidence vote in March 1998 and was, due to the defection of one coalition party, again toppled in April 1999. But the BJP-led National Democratic Alliance managed to retain power in the subsequent general elections in September and October 1999. The adopted national agenda for reform aims at continuing economic liberalization. But the government also plans to maintain the protection of the domestic industry and to curb direct foreign investment in consumer goods. The government's policy guidelines emphasize *swadeshi* (economic nationalism), but generally remain deliberately vague – a reflection of conflicting views between the BJP and its coalition partners.[113]

Yet a drastic reversal of economic reforms is hardly to be expected. The economic reform program was not a central issue in recent elections. Rather, political issues, particularly corruption, were more important in the failure of the incumbent political parties.[114] Moreover, even the BJP has notable records of economic reforms at the State level, showing its commitment to economic restructuring and modernization.[115] And indeed, within a short time after assuming power in 1998, the BJP promoted foreign trade liberalization by lifting quantitative restrictions on 340 import products, sought to take politics out of electricity pricing by creating regulatory bodies responsible for fixing electricity tariffs, and announced that foreign companies will be allowed to invest in the insurance sector – measures that the party had objected to when it had been in opposition. Having been newly re-elected in 1999, the government promised to continue the outward-oriented reforms and especially to create a less intrusive, more effective state apparatus. With the relatively liberal Atal Behari Vajpayee as Prime Minister, the BJP seeks to establish a more moderate and responsible image, and many businesspeople seem to trust that the government will prove to be more pragmatic than ideological. After all, the BJP's quest for political power has made it increasingly dependent on a number of allies pursuing significantly different agendas. This may have a disciplining effect on the party's hard-liners.[116]

A greater impediment to further promoting economic reforms than a potential lack of BJP's commitment appears to be the fragile nature of the coalition government, which puts the survival of the BJP in power at the mercy of its small though influential allies. The coalition partners, most of them regional parties, have substantial leverage to topple the government and do not hesitate to blackmail the new government. For example, threatening to withdraw political support, Jayaram Jayalalitha, leader of a Tamil regional party, demanded the dismissal of the State government of Tamil Nadu (which was prosecuting her in several criminal charges) and the Samata Party demanded that the Bihar government be dismissed and grant Bihar some US$ 12.6 billion. Such characteristics of coalition politics seriously challenge political stability and make a coherent economic reform program an infeasible policy choice.

India's diversity and persisting disparities will require constant compromise in policy making and may involve the continuation of fragile party politics, regardless of whether the government is led by the BJP, the Congress Party or the United Front. This makes muddling-through politics the most likely outcome of political bargaining, tactics, and constraints. Against this background, predictable economic policy making based on transparent rules instead of arbitrary discretion can hardly be expected. Moreover, the next stage of economic reform, including restructuring of public-sector enterprises (PSEs) (by reducing employment, imposing hard budget constraints, and closing plants), privatization of PSEs, revision of fertilizer and food subsidies, and labor-law reform, needs to be even more radical and will be politically more challenging than the initial ones, because it will involve short-term discomfort for most parts of the population and may appear to betray the traditional Indian commitment to social justice and equity. Unlike the first phase of reform, which involved limited public awareness, the next wave of reforms will require a broad political consensus and a secure and transparent institutional foundation.[117] The necessary political commitment to these reforms will be extremely difficult for the central government to accomplish under the current conditions. One might still agree with Bhalla's (1995: 572) conclusion 'that the future of economic reforms will be much more at the mercy of political forces than has been the case in the past'.

Hence, most if not all present reform challenges are related to serious governance problems. The recent political topsy-turvy and the current reform pressures underscore the need for the state to strengthen and reform itself and to redefine its role in economic development. In general, these problems have been recognized by all major political forces and some progress has been made. For example, recent accomplishments in the governance realm include measures to depoliticize the reform process, foster competition, promote private investment, and reduce discretionary government interventions. The predictability and transparency of policy making have been increased in some areas through newly created independent commissions, for example, in the insurance, telecommunications, gas, and power sectors. Finally, the need to restructure and enhance public sector management has been broadly recognized (ADB 1999c). Despite these achievements, there remains a substantial unfinished reform agenda, which from a governance perspective is vital for the implementation of badly needed structural reforms and their sustainability. This holds with regard to the creation of key economic institutions that guide the liberalization of industry and foreign trade, corporate governance reforms, and the improvement of the regulatory framework of the financial sector. Even more important, however, is the implementation of a secure political foundation of policy reforms needed to craft a flexible MEGS. In this context, the two most serious obstacles to effective policy reform include the inefficient public administration and the conflict-ridden relations between the political center and the sub-national jurisdictions.[118]

Taking the Weberian ideal-type as a reference point, an analysis of the current state of the public administration in India reveals a number of weaknesses which may prove to be impediments to successful policy reform. Certainly, India's bureaucracy has an eminent tradition. The old Indian Civil Service 'had provided "the steel frame of empire," serving as a model not just for other colonial administrations but for England's own civil service as well' (Evans 1995: 66). Its successor, the Indian Administrative Service (IAS), tried to continue this tradition. Entry into the IAS is meritocratic and highly competitive. Recruitment, however, has been almost exclusively reserved for the middle classes and shows an upper-caste bias.[119] Obligatory nationwide examinations have rewarded those applicants with a sound general, humanistic education resulting in a discrepancy between civil servants' educational background and the rather technical skills required by their jobs. Furthermore, since job rotation within the bureaucracy has been quite intense, bureaucrats have hardly had sufficient time to acquire necessary skills. Also, administrative institutions have been gradually eroded over the past decades. Both redeployment and promotion have mostly been subject to arbitrary decisions by politicians and seniority rules, respectively, than based on performance. This has undermined bureaucrats' efforts and work ethic and their affinity to the political objectives of the government. Moreover, real wages for civil servants have declined at the federal and the subordinated levels of government over the last 20 years. This has been one important factor in corruption[120] and rent-seeking, which have been regularly found (even within the IAS though presumably not widespread), as well as in the increasing propensity of skilled graduates to take jobs in the private sector. Finally, rigid bureaucratic structures and practices in combination with significant political interventions in the economy still cause extremely high transaction costs for private businesses.[121]

During the 1980s, a consensus emerged among scholars that the bureaucracy had an independent, strong, and self-serving nature, making it one of the dominant classes in society. Bureaucrats were considered to be chiefly interested in maintaining the public sector, expanding public employment, and enhancing administrative activities for the appropriation of economic resources. Pedersen (1992) challenges this view and shows that the expansion of public employment took place at predominantly subordinated levels of government, reflected interests of local public employees and local politicians as well as political patronage at the local level. Moreover, the increase in local public employment reflected additional developmental tasks that had been delegated to State governments. He concludes that 'the uniform picture of an influential, powerful and indeed dominant social class capable of independently deciding over the allocation of public resources' is not justified and that there is an 'increasing penetration of the state apparatus by powerful economic interests, primarily private industrialists' (ibid.: 627). Finally, the perception of a dominant, self-interested, and powerful bureaucracy is obviously exaggerated in view of the recent liberalization and deregulation measures, which delimit the scope for rent-seeking and, after all, had been originally initiated by parts of the bureaucracy itself.

At present, the Indian public administration still constitutes a relatively homogeneous and privileged entity. Despite its deficits, it shows basic attributes of a Weberian-type bureaucracy with respect to a functional definition of duties, meritocratic appointment, and full-time devotion to administrative tasks. In particular, IAS officers are said to basically 'exhibit (...) attitudes of servants of the state rather than that of independent masters' (Pedersen 1992: 628). However, substantial changes in the structure of class relations during the last decades induced an erosion of political institutions. The strengthening of both the 'new agrarian bourgeoisie' and the 'modern, high-tech oriented factions' in industry as well as the increasing fusion of agrarian and industrial interests reduce the requirement of bureaucratic intermediation and eventually delimit the scope of independent administrative actions. Pedersen (1992: 634–5) concludes that '(w)hile political sources of economic problems will continue to be important, they will to a lesser degree emanate from within the state and increasingly originate from "disturbances" in the wider society in the form of struggles between heterogeneous, often culturally defined social groups'. This observation calls for a future strengthening of the bureaucracy in the Weberian sense. At present, the public administration is neither sufficiently independent of political discretion or vested private interests nor adequately accountable for its actions. Given the new pattern of class relations and dominance, one might follow Evans' (1995) consideration that the main problem is the way the administration defined its relations to dominant groups of society.

In this context, some scholars raised the question of whether the governance of the Indian economy can be improved by drawing lessons from the HPAEs, and more specifically whether the concept of embedded autonomy can be made to work in the Indian case.[122] In general, two basic arguments question the suitability of this model for India: first, as long as the public administration is not independent of political discretion and direct influence by private firms, the model is unlikely to work, because developmental commitment of the government cannot be credibly ensured, collusion between public officials and private firms is conceivable, and incentives for rent-seeking and corruption persist. Thus, a reform of the bureaucracy towards the Weberian ideal is indispensable and becomes even more important in the course of the new market-oriented reforms, which put new kinds of demands on the bureaucracy.

Secondly, and even more important, the heterogeneous nature of Indian society makes collective action for the formulation of cohesive and consistent developmental objectives and public policies particularly difficult (Bardhan 1995); the more so if one considers the technical difficulties of governing a subcontinent of more than 900 million people. At present, the bureaucracy cannot rely on private business either as a source of providing information on what type of industrial policy may yield positive development results or as an instrument for implementing industrial policy. The bureaucracy's inability to provide organizational coherence concerning development projects still hinders private investment. Also, unselective state interventions and particularly the great number of inefficient PSEs placed a burden on the administrative capacity, limiting the scope for effective governance (Evans 1995). Bardhan (1995) argues that in India, where no social group is strong enough to capture the state, the democratic process leads to scrupulous rules for sharing the spoils among different elite groups, all of which seek particularistic advantages, and that there is (also due to the institutional legacy of the former colonial power) widespread suspicion of the state's internal organization. In this context, installing a system of embedded autonomy seems to be very difficult, the more so as close relations and a fusion of interests between public officials and private agents would raise strong political animosity among other social groups, whose electoral support is important for Indian politicians.

These considerations permit the following provisional conclusion to be drawn: in general, the state apparatus is rather weak, allowing distributional conflicts and rent taking to persist, and rendering the state unable unambiguously to determine a developmental agenda. Strengthening the executive requires administrative reforms towards the Weberian ideal, which might prove to be difficult as long as the central government and its administration are unselectively involved in too many interventions. In this regard, the recent liberalization and deregulation efforts might help to redefine and restructure the tasks of the bureaucracy and its relations to business elites and other social groups.

But the issues of how to limit entrenched government strength and to gain broad support for developmental policies are more difficult to handle. The establishment of bureaucratic embeddedness is impeded by contending interests of pressure groups and widespread suspicion of centrally-devised institutional arrangements. Neither policy makers nor private interest groups are powerful enough to determine the parameters of action unilaterally. Since the outcome of emerging bargaining games depends on the bargaining strengths of the parties involved, it is of utmost importance to improve the accountability of all actors at all levels of government.[123] Furthermore, the traditional top-down approach to policy making in India with the central government taking the lead and collaborating with the private sector, has proved to be counterproductive for a number of reasons. These not only concern the weight of non-economic issues in the political debate, the geographical size of the country, and the significance of the informal sector. It is also the political importance of rural regions, the specific characteristics of party politics (which have been considerably shaped by regional concerns and constituencies), and the political culture that delimit the chances of establishing an effective *centralized* governance structure. In order to lay down an adequate institutional foundation for current and future policy reforms, the hitherto overly centralized governance structure needs to be modified and complemented by institutions taking country-specific characteristics and problems into account. In the Indian case, therefore, a bottom-up approach promises to serve better as an appropriate institutional solution.

This brings us to the question of political and economic decentralization. In the heterogeneous and conflict-ridden Indian society, a unitary state, even if administratively decentralized, is hardly able to solve collective-action problems and to ensure political stability. Also, the rejection of the state-led development strategy and the implementation of structural market-oriented reforms are inconsistent with the centralized nature of the Indian state. Moreover, as already indicated above, increasing trends of regionalism and the alienation and marginalization of large segments of society have shown that excessive concentration and centralization of political powers in governmental structures and the major political parties have undermined democratic processes. Therefore, the following considerations focus on the suitability of the current federal structure in India to provide a secure political foundation for policy reforms. Taking the concept of MPF as a reference point, the strengths and weaknesses of the current system will be analysed in order to identify feasible options for creating a strong but limited government and hence to improve the overall governance structure of the country.

India consists of 25 States and 7 Union Territories. These are diverse entities, particularly regarding population, natural resources, administrative capacity, social and economic performance, and ethnic composition.[124] The constitution prescribes a division of power between the central government and the States. The responsibilities assigned to the central government essentially encompass national defense, foreign affairs, national infrastructure, communication, legislation concerning agricultural land that belongs to the Union (although State Legislatures have exclusive jurisdiction over those areas), monetary policy, foreign trade, insurance and banking, inter-State trade, and all those responsibilities not explicitly specified. Policy areas which are the exclusive provenance of State governments encompass public order and police, local government, public health and sanitation, local public goods, agriculture, water supply and irrigation, and legislation on markets. State Legislatures have exclusive power over intra-State trade, unless it is related to products of those industries that the Union controls due to expedient public interest. In these cases, the legislative power is concurrent. Finally, a concurrent list contains all those responsibilities and powers that are to be shared between the center and the States. These include social security, education, social and economic planning, electric power, bankruptcy and insolvency, as well as industrial and labor disputes (Basu 1988).

The basic importance of the States for successfully implementing the economic reforms is clearly revealed by the constitutional assignments of responsibilities and their share in public expenditure. In the mid-1990s, State governments have paid for 85 percent and 56 percent of the overall expenditures on economic and social services, respectively. Moreover, after almost one decade of economic reforms, it turns out that reform measures of the central government alone are insufficient to improve the economic environment profoundly. Further progress crucially depends on reforms in those areas for which the responsibilities have been assigned to the States or are to be shared between the central and the sub-national governments (particularly road transport, irrigation, education, and power). However, institutional weaknesses and the precarious condition of State finances are major constraints on the provision of social services, infrastructure, and other local public goods (World Bank 1995c).

Most taxes are assigned to the central government. The States essentially receive the sales tax on intra-State trade, land revenue and agricultural income tax, taxes on motor vehicles, and excise duty on alcoholic beverages (Basu 1988). About 60 percent of total State revenues is received from tax receipts. Almost 20 percent of total revenue consists of grants from the central government. Between 1986 and 1994, recurrent expenditure (exceeding capital expenditure by four times) and interest payments increased steadily relative to GDP, while capital and development expenditures decreased. This is essentially an outcome of an inappropriate expenditure composition and the States' failure to improve revenue efforts (World Bank 1995c and Shah 1994).

Intergovernmental transfers are a critical source of State revenues. The current transfer system (reflecting the constitutional mismatch in the assignment of revenues and responsibilities to central and subordinated governments as well as the need to deal with the great differences among the States) comprises three basic elements. First, the Finance Commission appointed by the president arbitrates upon fiscal center–State conflicts and makes recommendations for transferring grants and shared taxes from the center to the States. Its objective is to match the various governments' constitutional responsibilities and their revenues better. Secondly, the Planning Commission authorizes tied and untied transfers, which are partly related to centrally sponsored development and central plan schemes. The third source is loans by the center in order to finance the budget deficits of the States. In past years, these loans have covered around 50 percent of States' deficits. Moreover, the center also controls how the remainder of those deficits is financed (Krishnaswamy *et al.* 1992).

The system of intergovernmental transfers involves severe problems. Discretionary transfers (including grants and loans for any purpose) exceed 50 percent of total transfers and are often not allocated due to objective criteria. Project-related transfers by the Planning Commission are partly spent to finance recurrent expenditure. This means an erosion of growth-promoting investment expenditures and postpones structural budgetary reforms. By subsidizing incremental programs, the Planning Commission creates incentives for the States to start new projects, although additional necessary State revenues may not be available. This spurs the growth of expenditures and weakens fiscal discipline. Repetitious refinancing without conditionality and loan forgiveness by the central government have undermined States' efforts towards proper fiscal management. Regarding the revenue sharing mechanism, formulas to allocate tax revenues do not account for States' fiscal capacity. Moreover, the current system provides States with incentives to compete for private investment by transferring resources to the investor and to shift the burden of financing this transfer partly to the center and other States. Finally, requirements for revenue-sharing created weak incentives for the center to collect shared taxes effectively.[125]

Furthermore, many States have relied on federal transfers as solutions to their fiscal problems (the more so as the intergovernmental transfer system provides a mechanism to partly finance States' budget deficits), and sub-national governments have chosen opportunistic approaches to maximize transfers without worrying about their fundamental budgetary problems. Since lower-level governments are not sufficiently responsible for raising their own revenues, they have limited incentives to provide public services cost-effectively.[126] Soft budget constraints badly affect the decisions and commitment of sub-national governments, because benefits of regional policies are basically garnered within States, whereas costs are externalized.

Apart from this intergovernmental revenue distribution scheme, States have only limited access to sources of finance. According to the constitution, States face constraints in borrowing from the market as long as they owe loans to the center. As a consequence, States have built up a substantial debt position *vis-à-vis* the center, which makes them heavily reliant on decisions by the national government (Parikh and Weingast 1997).

De facto, the federal system meets neither the conditions of dual federalism nor those of MPF. Conditions C2, C3, and C5 are not met in the Indian case. The central government determines most of the major decisions about economic issues and prevents competition among States. Thus condition C3 fails. Centrally appointed agencies and boards control industrial policies through licensing and regulation. Despite some deregulation and decentralization measures initiated by recent governments, this *License Raj* system still reserves the prerogative for the central government to determine major policy changes (Bhagwati 1993). Furthermore, the central government sets most economic regulations and laws, controls political priorities of the States by approving capital expenditures and virtually all channels of resource-transfer, and it can exercise discretion over transfers without being sufficiently accountable to subordinated governments. The violation of C5 implies that States face no incentives for conducting prudent and accountable fiscal policies. In contradiction to condition C2, the constitution includes mechanisms which further enhance the center's control over the States. A simple parliamentary majority, for example, is sufficient to redraw the boundaries of States. Moreover, the president reserves the right to dissolve a State government if national security is threatened by external forces, a State's constitution breaks down, or a financial crisis occurs. Since the beginning of the 1960s, the usage of this provision has increased and has become more and more politicized. By declaring presidential rule, the central government can take over a State government, thereby undermining the autonomy and authority of State governments and any credible commitment to the federal system (Parikh and Weingast 1997). These institutional arrangements jeopardize the beneficial relations between a federal structure, economic reforms, and sustainable development, because the central government's discretion considerably compromises the market-creating and market-preserving qualities of the federal system.

The asymmetric division of economic control has produced a system of 'bogus federalism' (Williamson 1995: 186), which is essentially a direct result of historical factors, including the formerly dominating economic planning system and Nehru's view that the people had to show devotion and loyalty to national objectives and reconstruction. Power-sharing devices had been subordinated to the imperatives of state building, security, and stability. Diversity had been considered as inherently divisive (Mukarji and Arora

1992). Nehru and his followers implemented the system of central planning in order to protect emerging domestic industries, to foster the creation of a strong industrial base, and to prevent disparities between poor and rich States from increasing. However, economic centralization did not lead to greater equality among States. Between the 1950s and the 1980s, per capita transfers to high-income States were significantly higher than to low- and middle-income States (Krishnaswamy *et al.* 1992).

Neglecting the diverse nature of the economy and the society implied a non-coherent policy frame, that was neither suitable to promote economic reforms effectively nor to integrate the society. Facing the legacy of these political institutions for today's India and the fact that there is a widening gap between the fast-track segment of the Indian economy reflecting the characteristics of the high-tech age and the rest of society which consists of the vast majority of constituents, political reforms are to be regarded as a necessary complement to economic reforms. Reform-minded politicians would be well advised to use the momentum of recent reforms and to implement the political institutions that are necessary for sustainable development. Recent political developments seem to be favorable to political decentralization. The fragmentation of political power, highlighted by the parliamentary elections in 1996, 1998, and 1999, may represent a unique opportunity for decentralization. The new Parliament is more representative of the persistent divisions in Indian society. The election results further suggest that political power is gradually devolving to the States and that local discontents, interests, and issues play an important role in Indian politics. After all, the new central government is strongly dependent on regional parties, which are more responsive to regional and local demands than former Congress governments.

Summing up, political institutions constituting a strong but limited government are the key for successful economic development. Analysing the institutional conditions in today's India reveals substantial failures in the former British colony. Political institutions have been largely undermined by the growing demands of numerous social groups and distributional conflicts, political leaders being primarily instruments of their parties. The bureaucracy, subject to political discretion and vested interests, is not adequately accountable for its actions, and cannot rely on private business as a source of information. Political authorities have undertaken a wide range of unselective interventions in the economy thereby overburdening the organizational capacity of the state, and a transparent policy dialogue between the public and private sector does not exist. Corruption and collusion are endemic, and the vast majority of the population has lost its confidence in politics.

Nevertheless, the Indian government successfully launched comprehensive reforms. Whether these reforms will be sustainable not only depends on a reform of the bureaucracy and its external relations, but also on center–State relations; the more so as remaining reforms strongly require the involvement of State governments. But as yet, the central government imposes its will on the States, and these, in turn, dictate to local authorities. At present, there is no *de facto* federalism in India, let alone the MPF that is necessary to limit a strong government and to preserve thriving markets. Given the weaknesses of India's political institutions, the country's prospects for continuing its economic reforms effectively are limited. Policy reforms are only sustainable if they are accompanied by institutional reforms that create the foundations of economic development.

The challenge facing the Indian government is complicated. It is not simply designing a suitable economic reform program and decentralizing political powers. The central problem to be addressed is how to establish a set of political institutions in practice, which is appropriate to create and to sustain strong but limited governments at all federal levels. Political authorities need to take demands of subordinated governments and constituents seriously, and institutionalized channels must be implemented which ensure their active political participation. If India is able to overcome her institutional deficits, Bhagwati's (1993: 98) hope may be eventually fulfilled, that '(t)he energy, talents, and worldly ambitions of India's many millions, captured so well in V. S. Naipaul's latest work ... need merely an appropriate policy framework to produce the economic magic that Jawaharlal Nehru wished for his compatriots but which, like many well-meaning intellectuals of his time, he mistakenly sought in now discredited economic doctrines'.

Russia

From a governance perspective, the systemic transformation in Russia shows a striking difference from the economic transitions in China and India. While policy reforms in the two latter countries could not and cannot be effectively undertaken without some kinds of political reforms, notably decentralization, the Russian transformation process has been distinguished from its very beginning in 1992 by the explicit objective of pursuing a *twofold transition* towards both a market economy and a democracy. Moreover, due to strong interdependencies of all societal subsystems, restructuring the economic and political system must be accompanied by fundamental changes in the legal system, the administration, and the socio-cultural system. Thus, the transition process especially includes

- substituting the socialist command economy by a market economy;
- displacing the totalitarian political system by a liberal-democratic order;
- creating a constitutional state, based on a legal framework focusing on the individual; providing comprehensive legal protection, and meeting the principles of a market economy;
- establishing a public administration that does not serve privileged elites but the people; and
- overcoming individual disorientation and helplessness by creating a cognizant framework that encourages individual initiatives and self-responsibility.

Confronting these adjustment necessities, the systemic change could not and cannot be realized by either a pure pragmatic-constructive or a pure organic-evolutionary strategy. Policy makers have to recognize that the transformation represents a complex phenomenon of two overlapping processes: the deliberate destruction of old, and construction of new, institutions, accompanied by a spontaneous evolution of a new political and economic order. Furthermore, the transformation requires the development of a political vision, based on a broadly accepted fabric of formal and informal institutions. This section argues that ineffective governance-related reforms are the single most important factor that has rendered economic policy reforms fruitless and caused the continuing economic and social crisis. Given the current balance of political power in Russia and other country-specific characteristics such as the vast geographical size of the economy which prevent the central government from becoming a regulating power for the transition process, the most promising, politically feasible solution for overcoming the systemic crisis appears to be political and economic decentralization.

The twofold transformation involves a problem of simultaneousness which has been aggravated by a radical upheaval of the socio-cultural order, the breakdown of the USSR, and Russia's search for a new statehood. Due to an unstable political, economic, social, international, and psychological framework, it has been hardly possible properly to predict the effects of bold policy reforms. In addition, it has become increasingly evident that economic transformation steps cannot be efficient unless they are complemented by suitable measures addressing the restructuring of other subsystems and vice versa. Close interrelations between single sub-transformations have exacerbated prevailing problems and caused severe effects of obstruction. Yet there has been and still is a strong need for pragmatic action and implementation of a comprehensive and consistent transformation strategy.

Risk-taking political pioneers need to introduce new constituent elements into all social subsystems simultaneously.

Since the beginning of the transformation, the economic situation has continued to deteriorate drastically. Due to a controversial assignment of powers, different perceptions concerning the design of economic reforms, and the massive influence of pressure groups, the disposing capacity of Russian executive organs has been strongly restricted. Moreover, increasing economic disintegration of the Russian market has occurred as a consequence of regional protectionism, ethnic conflicts, and an insufficient enforcement of laws and decrees.

In the course of transition, massive inflation paralyzed public and private investment. Both domestic and foreign trade broke down. Inter-enterprise arrears rose substantially. Between 1992 and 1998, production losses have accelerated in almost all industries. During this period, total agricultural output declined by more than 40 percent and industrial production by roughly 50 percent, even exceeding the United States' losses during the Great Depression. However, due to continuing subsidization, state enterprises were hardly forced to adjust. The necessary structural change has not started yet. Few bankruptcies occurred and unemployment remained at a relatively low level until the mid-1990s. Only in 1998, in the course of the recent financial crisis, did unemployment figures increase more significantly toward an unemployment rate of 12.4 percent in 1999. The poverty ratio reached a record high in 1999 with about 35.3 percent of all Russians living below the poverty line (DIW *et al.* 1999).

While some considerable progress in macroeconomic stabilization could have been achieved between 1994 and 1997, the Russian economy experienced another major set-back in the aftermath of the 1998 crisis. The central causes that have impeded policy reforms throughout the 1990s and eventually triggered the recent crisis are to be attributed to the inability of the government to implement and enforce a functioning market-oriented economic order. At first glance, this is due to the lack of key economic institutions such as secure private property rights, a prudently regulated financial sector, an effective tax system, and a modern market-oriented legal framework. The deeper source of the ongoing transformation crisis, however, is the lack of an effective MEGS. It was not the lack of a reform-minded central government but the political constraints it faced and the flawed economic advice it received which doomed the transition policies to failure.

Regarding the latter aspect, recall that in the 1980s and early 1990s a distinct school of thought dominated the international academic discourse as well as the debates within policy making circles. This was largely based on neoclassical theory and its policy prescriptions culminated in the so-called Washington Consensus.[127] This school of thought essentially consisted of macroeconomists and organizations such as the IMF with a strong faith in market forces but with little appreciation of the numerous subtle conditions that are required to make markets work effectively. These economists not only had little knowledge of Russia's economic history and the country-specific problems relating to the systemic transformation, but they did not believe that they needed that knowledge. By relying on the seemingly universal rules of neoclassical reasoning, they simply assumed that neither history, nor institutions, nor variables such as income distribution matter. This caused most of these economists to believe that so-called shock therapy would lead to rapid economic recovery and to sustained economic growth (Stiglitz 2000).

This school of thought not only dominated the academic debate in the West until the mid-1990s but also gained significant influence on the reform-minded Russian government. Thus under the guidance of Boris Yeltsin and then-prime minister Jegor Gaidar, the government introduced a so-called shock therapy in 1992. The two main elements of the economic reforms included a comprehensive price liberalization and a quick mass privatization of SOEs essentially based on a voucher program. Although formally relatively successful, the rapid privatization allowed a relatively small group of new oligarchs to take over the control of former state assets and to exploit these by taking advantage of persistent economic monopolies and their close connections to the ruling political elite. Competitive structures did not emerge in the wake of privatization, nor did investments take off. On the contrary, the level of gross fixed investment (a more important sign of a striving market economy) has fallen dramatically over the last decade (EBRD 1998). Moreover, necessary structural and institutional reforms were neglected, postponed, or conducted only half-heartedly. As a consequence, the institutional preconditions of market-oriented policy making are still insufficient in today's Russia. Government policy making is still erratic and inconsistent, and populist pressures threaten to stall any progress in transformation.

Both the policy recommendations of Western advisors and the IMF and hitherto pursued transformation policies have been sharply criticized from a second, initially less influential school of thought. This group consists of well-known scholars including Joseph Stiglitz (the former Chief Economist of the World Bank), the Nobel Prize winners Kenneth Arrow and Douglass North, numerous adherents to institutional and evolutionary approaches to economic development as well as a number of experts on CEE and the former USSR.[128] These scholars have criticized the neoclassical approach to economic transition from a variety of perspectives. In particular, they not only blamed the Russian reform policies for ignoring the importance of informal institutions such as social and organizational capital but also for neglecting economic fundamentals including financial sector reforms, competition policy, and problems relating to corporate governance. Critics further stressed the urgent need for an active state especially with respect to crafting a market-oriented institutional infrastructure and a social safety net. Furthermore, Amsden *et al.* (1994) argue that particularly in PSCs, where market integration is weak and market imperfections exist, market-enhancing government intervention and possibly industrial policies that complement and facilitate private-sector coordination are critical.

One major reason why neoclassical policy prescriptions were misguided has been that the state was viewed as the primary source of economic problems whereas the (emerging) private sector was seen through rose-colored glasses. For example, Shleifer and Vishny (1998: 11), two key advisors to the Russian government on privatization, argued: 'The architects of the Russian privatization were aware of the dangers of poor enforcement of property rights. Yet because of the emphasis on politics, the reformers predicted that institutions would follow private property rather than the other way around.'

Most remarkably, these authors not only believed that corporate governance and regulatory institutions would evolve automatically in Russia, they even saw this process actually happening. 'Institutions supporting corporate governance, such as the banking sector and capital markets, are also developing rapidly in part because of the profit opportunities made available by the privatized firms' (ibid.: 254). But, in fact, this observation seems to reflect wishful thinking. The present economic landscape looks quite different and is dominated by financial instability, rent-seeking and corruption, disorganization, and economic oligarchy. Stiglitz (1999) describes the situation aptly when he writes that

> the resulting program of transferring assets to the private sector without regulatory safeguards (...) has only succeeded in putting the 'grabbing hand' [of the state; J.A.] into the 'velvet glove' of privatization. The 'grabbing hand' keeps on grabbing with even less hope of public restraint. The rapid liberalization of capital accounts allowed the (...) 'banking sector' to spirit tens of billions of dollars of loot out of Russia each year while the architects of capital account liberalization negotiated more billions of international debt. Economic and political forces – incentives – are at play, with far different outcomes than predicted by the proponents of the grabbing hand theory (some of whom are still arguing that, ten years after the beginning of the process, with output plummeting and inequality soaring, we are being too hasty in reaching a judgment). And why should we be surprised? It is not the first time that strong vested interests have used political processes to maintain and strengthen their economic interests. What is remarkable about this episode is that economists, who should have known better, had a hand in helping create these interests, believing somehow – in spite of the long history to the contrary – that Coasian forces would lead to efficient social outcomes.

Of course, even some radical market reformers and their advisors clearly acknowledge the failure of so-called shock therapy reforms, but they essentially attribute it to ongoing rent-seeking and corruption (Aslund 1999) without recognizing that 'the institutional blitzkrieg in destroying but not replacing the old social norms – and thus in removing the last restraints against society-threatening levels of corruption' (Stiglitz 1999) was a major cause of the current problems. Privatization and liberalization alone can not overcome the problems associated with irresponsible power, private or public. That is the reason why critics of the Washington Consensus in general and of the Russian reform policies in particular have repeatedly emphasized the need for strengthening the state, institution building, and decentralizing economic decision making to lower levels at which people can rely on local institutions and organizations to protect their assets and interests and to use their resources in order gradually to re(invigorate) functioning institutional arrangements.

However, it would be wrong to put the blame regarding the unsuccessful Russian transition solely on misguided policy advice or incomplete reform policies. This brings us to the first aspect mentioned above. Even if a more gradual transition strategy with a stronger emphasis on institution building and competition policy had been pursued, it is unlikely that it would have been much more successful. The reason for this assumption is that it was chiefly the political constraints faced by the executive branch of government that critically limited any market-oriented reforms. Given the initial vacuum of political power in 1991–92 and the subsequently evolving power of a parliament that was dominated by communist and nationalist parties and proved to be hostile to economic reforms, the primary objective of the executive was to create a *fait accompli* as quickly as possible in order to make the nascent transition process irreversible. Thus, a bold liberalization-cum-mass privatization program seemed to be essential in order to depoliticize the process of economic transition rapidly. Furthermore, due to the parliament's refusal to pass market-oriented legislation, the President largely relied on policy making through decrees. On the one hand, this allowed him to use his discretionary power to design reform packages and helped circumvent veto points that threatened to block reform, on the other hand, these reform programs were not credible because they could also be undone by decree. What is more, however, many reform steps could not be properly implemented due to a shortage of adequate administrative skills and further resistance to reforms on the part of the bureaucracy at both the central and lower levels of government (Ahrens 1994 and Schleifer and Treisman 1998). In order to understand better the politico-institutional side-conditions of economic reforms, let us briefly look at some milestones of Russia's recent political history.[129]

The first two years after the breakdown of the Soviet Union witnessed chaos in the political landscape of Russia (as in most of the successor states of the USSR). Due to a power vacuum and the lack of mechanisms to resolve conflict, a systematic and determined transformation policy could not be realized. Government, parliament as well as the constitutional court lost their credibility, and parts of the internal sovereignty of the state were claimed by the mafia and the nomenclatura. Separation of powers existed only formally. Actually, executive and legislative organs struggled for power and blocked each other in all respects. Lack of (democratic) traditions and unclear responsibilities hindered the evolution of an actual independence of the judiciary. The Congress of People's Deputies and the Supreme Soviet, both elected in socialist times and dominated by reactionary forces, offered fierce resistance against the transformation policies favored by the government and President Yeltsin.

In October 1993, Russia was on the eve of a civil war. Yeltsin brought the struggle for power to an end by dissolving parliament and having military forces storm the White House (the location of the parliament) by assault. At this time, the dualism of executive and legislative powers seemed to have been overcome. The parliamentary elections and the adoption of a new constitution in December 1993 represented necessary preconditions for stabilizing the political system. According to the constitution, the new form of government is to be interpreted as a representative presidential democracy, also showing elements of a parliamentary democracy. The parliament has no power to overthrow the government, whose continuance completely depends on the president. Based on the constitution, the president is provided with considerable formal powers, which should basically allow him to conduct radical and resolute transformation policies.

However, Yeltsin was hardly capable of using his formal powers effectively and of becoming a regulating power for systemic change. First of all, parliament could delimit presidential powers due to its numerous legislative competences, and there was no united action by the government and the parliamentary majority; secondly, since the October crisis and in the course of the wars in Chechnya the army became more independent and influential. This not only affects Russia's defense, foreign, and internal policies, but also the economic transformation. In particular, this has aggravated the conversion of the military-industrial complex and hence the reallocation of resources; thirdly, as of the summer of 1993, a steadily growing loss of Yeltsin's authority and popularity could be recognized; and, fourthly, after the parliamentary elections in 1995, the president and the government again faced a State Duma dominated by communist and nationalist forces. The Russian democratic forces failed to organize themselves and actually became losers in the elections. The realization of radical transformation policies in the face of strong reactionary forces dominating the parliament proved to be extremely difficult, especially under the side-condition of maintaining social peace.

In 1996, insecurity regarding the continuance of economic reforms seemed to decrease somewhat, because the majority of Russian voters again supported Yeltsin in the presidential elections. He, in turn, appointed some transformation-minded politicians to the central government's cabinet and made Anatoly Chubais, a well-known radical reformer, chief of staff in the Kremlin. However, the political topsy-turvy continued nevertheless because the parliament remained hostile to any constructive reform policies and none of the four prime ministers appointed by the president within the next three years proved to be powerful enough to form adequate parliamentary coalitions to support his policies. The privatization of large companies and banks made things even worse, as this helped new oligarchs with close relations to the inner circles of the Kremlin to gain substantial economic power and political influence, which they used to redirect reform policies in their interests. Eventually, a glimmer of hope emerged when the parliamentary elections in December 1999 brought about an allegedly far less anti-reform parliament. Since the parliamentary party of the communists grew smaller by 25 percent, and that of the nationalists by more than 60 percent, the new State Duma is politically less polarized than its predecessor. This basically represents favorable starting conditions for Vladimir Putin, the new Russian president, to overcome the antagonism between the Kremlin and the parliament. Whether or not Putin will be able to do so, can hardly be predicted. However, Putin has already harmed himself by supporting a coalition between the Kremlin-backed political forces and the communists in the elections of the new chairman of the Duma. Whether or not this arrangement was an *ad hoc* agreement following tactical considerations prior to the presidential elections is still unclear. In any case, Putin has been celebrated in Russia as the new, badly needed, strong leader who appeals to patriotic sentiments and promises to establish law and order. However, most outside observers remain skeptical regarding the chances of further democratic and market reforms in Russia. Heinrich Vogel (2000), an outstanding expert of Russian politics, summarized his thoughts on governance in Russia in the aftermath of the recent presidential elections, as follows:

> The development of the political system in Russia is of key importance. In the light of current experience it is not to be expected that the necessary institutional framework for good governance can be brought about in the short term. Political traditions, customs and forms of political behaviour (paternalism, the power of the clans, secondary centres of power, nepotism, etc.) will in all probability continue for a long time. In the next five to ten years the position of today's administrative-

economic elite is not really under threat. A strengthening of the functioning structures of a fully fledged society and the assumption of relevant social and political functions by this society is not really to be expected given still widespread resignation, persistent influence of powerful lobbies, and the obvious lack of operative strategies.

This seems to be the more likely as Putin's economic strategy, although he has not yet made any clear statements, seems to favor a protectionist, state-led approach. In Vogel's (2000) words:

> Putin (...) seems to envisage an alternative scenario of modernisation by mobilisation ('begin with restoration of moral values, not with taxes') linked to protectionism, partial renationalisation, state-centered industrial policy, and a tendency for the 'strong state' – with a distinct possibility of turning authoritarian. His confidence rests on stable windfalls, Western creditors' largesse, traditional myths, and a technocratic understanding of economic policy as interventionism in a constitutional system of checks without balances. This may be a realistic way in the short term out of the malaise inherited from Yeltsin's dream teams. In the longer run, however, the concept of modernisation by mobilisation is unrealistic in its visionary fixation on repositioning Russia as a great power. The ensuing frustration over predictable failure may well cause new uncertainties about the future political orientation of Russia as a partner in the management of international relations.

Hence, the starting conditions for an evolving democracy in Russia, the institutions of which could provide a stable foundation for a functioning market economy, have been extraordinarily bad, even compared to other CEE countries. Given the recent political developments in Russia, one can hardly expect a stable, functioning, and enduring democracy based on a free-market economy to evolve in the short or medium run. Actually, Yeltsin's political triumph proved to be a Pyrrhic victory. Numerous conflicts between radical reformers, nationalists, communists, and strong interest groups have occurred and continue to dominate the political stage, impeding political stabilization and yielding at best half-hearted political compromises. If, however, political elites, economic actors, and social groups do not coordinate their activities in order to minimize destructive effects, neither democratic consolidation nor economic restructuring can succeed. Rent-seeking and a continuing struggle for political and economic power, accompanied by naïve social wishful thinking, badly affect the development of a functioning multiparty system, the enhancement of the government's capacity to rule, and the implementation of a comprehensive and consistent transformation program. Contrary to constitutional prescriptions, the Russian government and the presidential apparatus are weak rather than strong. At present, the executive is neither able to protect property rights nor to implement and enforce reform policies, legislation, and private contracts. Authorities have been unable to collect taxes and to control expenditures effectively. Spontaneous insider privatization strengthened vested interests and jeopardized the restructuring of the capital stock. State interventions into economic processes have not been based on transparent rules, but on executive or administrative discretion. This, in turn, resulted in opportunism and corruption, not in prudent supervision. Also, since the state is too weak to control its own officials, public agents act independently of one another. This implies inconsistent, discretionary, and nontransparent public policies. The inability to enforce rules paralyzes private business activities and investment. The weak government is not capable of enforcing the minimal conditions to create and maintain markets. Instead, private individuals and narrow, but powerful interest groups have established special connections to political representatives in order to sustain production and trade. This, inevitably, leads to collusion, corruption, and a private extraction of the country's resources. This way, the weak Russian state has become a predatory state.

So far, the transformation policy has proved to be only effective with respect to the destruction of old institutions. Regarding the central task to create new competitive economic structures and institutional safeguards, it has shown substantial deficits. Contradicting a widespread perception, there was no real shock therapy in Russia. Single shock elements such as price liberalization were implemented, but their effects were undermined by gradual measures and half-hearted stabilization efforts. Transformation policy resembled rather an inconsistent and nontransparent muddling-through approach. The most important causes of the 'transformational recession'[130] include an insufficient institutional restructuring of the economic order, the lack of horizontal and vertical mechanisms of coordination and conflict resolution, and a weak state that allowed massive rent-seeking of old and new vested interests to take place. This increased the misallocation of resources and fueled inflation. Moreover, ill-conceived economic policies, an inconsistent assignment of political powers as well as political conflicts aggravated the economic crisis. In this context, factors such as the central bank's actual dependency on political bodies (especially during the first half of the 1990s), the unstable banking and financial sector, deficits of the legal system, which has not been in line with real market conditions, and the deficient sense of policy makers regarding the importance of a proper legal framework have played an important role. Moreover, lasting conflicts between federal political institutions (especially between the executive and the legislative branch of government) on the one hand and between Moscow and subordinated regional and local authorities on the other hand have been major causes of the economic crisis. These conflicts have prevented the necessary consensus concerning the elaboration and implementation of a comprehensive and credible transformation strategy as well as the enforcement of agreed measures at lower levels of the public administration.[131]

At present, the most important measures to overcome the prevailing economic crisis include:[132]

- stabilizing the economy by tight fiscal and monetary policies and implementing an effective tax system;
- creating a basic network of market-oriented institutions and enforcing them by an independent judiciary;
- introducing and enforcing private property rights (including the property of land);
- stabilizing and restructuring the banking and financial sector;
- introducing hard budget constraints for state enterprises and enforcing the bankruptcy law;
- promoting competition by reducing public subsidies, thoroughly eliminating barriers to market entry (especially for foreign investors), and opening up the economy;
- implementing a social safety net for the inevitable losers from transformation; and
- streamlining and restructuring the economic bureaucracy at all levels of government.[133]

Most of these measures, however, will only materialize in the medium or the long run. And eventually, their success will strongly depend on the ability of policy makers to overcome the deeper roots of the crisis which mainly concern politico-institutional factors. The political system has to be stabilized, state institutions must be reinforced, an effective system of incentives and sanctions needs to be implemented, and responsibilities must be clearly assigned.

Yet another major impediment to effective policy and institutional reform is that the nascent democracy is confronted with several historical and socio-cultural factors obstructing both its own development and economic restructuring. The persistent informal institutions that have been shaped by individual experiences and perceptions, induce a hysteresis in individual behavior and negatively affect the progress of reforms. The country has never experienced a democracy in its history. Communist rule, having lasted for almost 70 years, was preceded by the autocratic regime of the Tsars. Both systems suppressed individual freedom as well as political initiatives and promoted individual passivity and social atomization. As a consequence, a conscious and organized pattern of collective action and, accordingly, a developed civil society do not exist in today's Russia. A civil society, however, with its numerous political, economic, and social organizations represents a system that could create checks and balances, manifest the autonomy of non-public organizations against the state, and sustainably support the development of a democratic political culture. Hence, an integral part and a catalyst of democracy has not evolved yet. Also due to history, potential democratic leaders having sufficient experience in practical policy making are thin on the ground. Not surprisingly, most leading positions in politics and administration are still occupied by formerly communist functionaries.

At present, most people are tired of confusing politics and do not show any political initiatives. All recently-founded parties lack a broad social basis. High inflation, the danger of unemployment, and the deprivation of formerly state-guaranteed securities have led to individual disorientation and helplessness. Most parts of the population give priority to surviving economically and to finding a new position in society rather than to engaging in politics. Individual fears and the complexity of the systemic change tempt people to trust simple and radical political programs offered by populists, nationalists or other demagogues. This sort of a nostalgia trap does not only hamper democratic development but also efficient economic restructuring. Finally, socialist paradigms and ideals are still present in people's minds and often dominate individual thinking and acting. Not only have solidarity and social justice been maintained as values and norms, but also the perception of a paternalistic duty of the state to take care of individual needs. The demand for a strong political leader still characterizes the behavior and the attitude of many Russians. In that sense, too, the past is a factor determining the present and the future and obstructing the process of democratization.

Summarizing the preceding stocktaking of the Russian transformation process from a governance perspective, we may conclude as follows: during the first decade of the systemic change, the quality of governance has dramatically deteriorated. The central government has not only been extremely weak in formulating, implementing, and enforcing market-oriented reforms, it has also been increasingly captured by newly emerged vested interests seeking to maintain a partial reform equilibrium. As yet, there are no effective institutional safeguards that could enhance the predictability and transparency of policy making and serve as counterweights to the predatory behavior of state actors. Institutions that hold the government accountable for its public policies are lacking, as are those that ensure a transparent participation of economic actors, civic organizations, and sub-national governments in economic policy making. The overall capacity of the Russian state apparatus (including that of regional and local administrations) to implement policies and enforce laws and regulations is extremely weak. Most of the key economic institutions that constitute a functioning market economy are either non-existent or not enforced. And finally, the persistent fabric of informal institutions seems to be another factor that impedes the consolidation of democracy and further market-based reforms.

Therefore, the crucial question is how a flexible MEGS can be gradually created that is not only conducive to improving the economic prospects of the country but that is, above all, politically feasible. Since political instability and a controversial assignment of powers between the central government and subordinated authorities have proved to be crucial factors hampering the transformation process and threatening total political paralysis and anarchy, it is of the utmost importance to create the necessary preconditions for restoring the government's capacity to rule effectively and for enforcing transformation measures at all administrative levels throughout the country. In this context, it has to be guaranteed that prevailing political instabilities are eliminated, political decision-makers protected against pressure groups, and conflicts between the central government and lower-level public entities overcome.

In order to improve the country's overall governance structure, institution and capacity building needs to become the primary concern of both domestic policy makers and the international community which seeks to support Russia in its transition. From an economist's standpoint, this primarily requires the creation and enforcement of key economic institutions such as private property rights, commercial laws, financial sector regulation, and anti-trust legislation to ensure the proper functioning of a market system. But in order to put the political authorities in a position to do so, it is of even greater importance to enhance the capabilities and capacities of the state. The most urgent task, then, is to a create a strong but limited central government, capable of effectively pursuing stabilization, structural adjustment, and institutional policies. An obvious starting point to this is the adoption of a constitution that guarantees human rights and freedom of the press and establishes a strong executive and an independent judiciary power. Such an institutional foundation should be basically conducive to implementing a bold program of economic restructuring. At the same time, the basis for continuing democratization would also be created. By adopting the new constitution in 1993, a restricted democracy has been founded in Russia. Thus, one important precondition for stabilizing the political system has been at least partly realized. However, the formal implementation of the new political order does not automatically ensure a successful systemic change, the more so as even the new system shows considerable weak points. Despite the formal powers assigned to the executive, the Russian state is not strong, but weak. Neither the government nor the bureaucracy is insulated or accountable for its actions. In fact, both have been captured by narrow interest groups. Although formally a Federation, the present system is not in tune with truly federal concepts, but rather represents a type of bogus federalism. Finally, politics is not rule- or institution-based, but still depends on the personal power of the president and his administrative apparatus.

In order to strengthen the government and simultaneously limit its potential discretionary and opportunistic behavior, the constitution needs to be complemented by a set of further institutional arrangements. The government must face incentives to avoid discretionary interventions and closed decision making, which lead to corruption, a waste of resources, patronage, and poor transformation management. Therefore, public sector reform deserves particular attention. More specifically, this concerns the introduction of modern accounting and auditing systems, legal and regulatory reform, and the establishment of an independent judiciary. These and other micro-level reforms represent an essential precondition for effective public sector management and will help to improve the administrative ability to provide public goods and services. They are also necessary in order to modernize the tax system, to reduce rent-seeking, and to enhance the accountability of the public sector. Furthermore, public sector reform requires the implementation of a public bureaucracy insulated from old and new vested interests. For this reason, priority should be given to building new administrative structures, to training administrative skills, and to introducing a meritocratic recruitment and promotion system based on objective rules for bureaucratic activities and appointments. In addition, independent personnel agencies can help to reduce external pressure on appointments and patronage. This way, corruption could be fought, expectations stabilized, and private economic activities promoted. Further, an introduction of hard budget constraints in the public sector may help also to delimit the influence of interest groups on government expenditures and can additionally measure bureaucrats' ability in macroeconomic management. Similarly, statutory boards can also be used to help monitor civil servants' performance. As far as public sector reform is concerned, Russia can draw on the experiences of the HPAEs as well as the more advanced market economies in the West. This does not mean that it would be useful simply to imitate systems that have been effective elsewhere. It rather suggests that it would be advisable to identify general principles of public sector management and to apply them to the country-specific characteristics of the Russian Federation.[134]

However, progress in public sector management alone cannot ensure a successful transition as long as paralyzing power struggles continue in Moscow and laws, regulations, and policies are not implemented at lower levels of government. This raises the question of what factor can become a driving force to strengthen governance. In heterogeneous and conflict-ridden Russia, governance structures based on centrally-devised institutions are inadequate, particularly because different overlapping economic, political, social, regional, and ethnic divisions exist which make collective action at the political center and a consensual policy dialogue extremely difficult. In this case, it is almost impossible for political authorities to precommit themselves to policies that are consistent with the interests of society as a whole. A stable political regime with functioning executive powers requires a clear, consistent, and broadly accepted assignment of political powers. The new constitution fulfills this precondition only partly. In particular, the regional and local authorities do not accept the reduction of their powers in favor of the central government.

During the past years, growing political and economic demands for power by regional and local authorities have undermined many transformation efforts by the central elites. Decrees and laws have often not been enforced at lower administrative levels. Subordinated governments pursue their own goals and strategies and have different priorities regarding the timing and sequencing of certain transformation steps. At present, there is neither effective cooperation nor a coordination of policy measures. Some regions intend to maintain elements of the traditional socialist economic system, whereas others elaborate their own concepts of economic restructuring. These problems as well as regional protectionism, conflicts between different federal levels concerning property rights of natural resources, and the assignment of state expenditures and revenues result in an economic disintegration of the country. In connection with separatist movements, these problems also imply the danger of political disintegration as the case of Chechnya clearly demonstrates.[135]

In the light of these still prevailing weaknesses of the political system as well as the lack of vertical coordination mechanisms, the center can hardly be expected to become sufficiently strong and an effective power capable of meeting all challenges of the systemic change. Since the Kremlin's capacity to act is extremely limited, it is essential not to overburden the center. Therefore, a realistic, efficient, and credible restructuring of the political-administrative order must primarily address the conflicts between the central government and the subordinated territorial authorities; the more so as these conflicts proved to be a major cause of the past failures in transition (Wallich 1994 and Ahrens 1995).

As in China, therefore, political and economic decentralization appears to be not only a necessary but, in fact, the only politically feasible way to establish an effective governance structure. But whereas in China decentralization proved to be the only practicable way for the political elites to maintain their power and simultaneously to foster economic development, in Russia it is the only way for the central policy makers to regain authority and credibility and to overcome the deep systemic crisis. Hence, the starting conditions for decentralization in Russia differ greatly from those in China; the more so as China had already gathered some experiences in decentralization before the inception of its economic reforms and could rely on the existence of a central policy-making authority that has been able to control critical realms of the economic transition.

Nevertheless, replacing the old political-administrative order is an unalterable prerequisite to enforcing resolute transformation policies, overcoming ethnic-territorial conflicts, and stopping economic and political disintegration. When building a new order, authorities have to recognize the integrative function of federalism. The new federal structure must ensure that regions participate in the political decision-making process and that a consistent assignment of responsibilities as well as a vertical separation of powers are realized. This way, stable mechanisms could be implemented which take the economic and cultural heterogeneity of Russian regions into account. In view of Moscow's loss of authority and control, the variety of regional living conditions and regionally different political preferences, successful systemic change can succeed only if all subjects of the Russian Federation are given greater autonomy. Decentralization will not only yield positive economic effects, but also protect regions against the political topsy-turvy in Moscow. Moreover, the authority of the central government could be enhanced by delegating power to sub-national levels, because this helps to balance presidential powers and the potential strength of the central government and necessitates greater accountability. This would increase the credibility of policy makers in Moscow, help to overcome persistent conflicts between the political center and lower-level governments, and improve the ability of the political center to assume the classical functions of a central government and to manage the remaining transformation policies in which it has a comparative advantage.

But what are the chances for federalism in Russia? Looking again at the model of market-preserving federalism, only condition C1 is fulfilled at present in Russia. Though formally a federation, the Russian system neither shows a market-preserving character nor the ability to limit a strong central government. The current federal structure is an extremely complex system consisting of 89 federal elements that have been inherited from the Soviet Union. Its overall structure, as well as the existence of autonomous republics, *oblasts*, and *krajs* still reflect the arbitrary politico-administrative decisions made by Stalin during the heyday of Moscow's power politics. At present, administrative and ethnic boundaries are not congruent in one single case. Formally, the Russian Federation consists of republics, territories, regions, federal cities, an autonomous region, and autonomous areas. Although the constitution declares that all federal elements shall have equal rights, in fact they do not, because the republics are ranked higher than other federal elements.[136] Another discrepancy between the constitutional prescriptions and reality relates to the so-called autonomous areas. While they should have the same rights as the other regions, in fact they are subordinated to other lower-level governments (the *krajs*) in the jurisdictions where they are geographically located. Furthermore, most constitutions of the republics include provisions which contradict the Federal Constitution. Finally, given the contradictory economic, ethnic, and (geo)political interests between various Russian regions and between them and the central government, a considerable, clear and present danger exists for the disintegration of Russia. This, above all, holds for the northern parts of the Caucasus (including Chechnya), the regions in the Ural and along the Volga (including Tatarstan), and the regions in the south of Siberia. Such a tendency towards fragmentation can only be halted if the central government is able to improve the overall social and economic situation and to craft a universally acceptable federal structure (which possibly needs to incorporate certain confederative elements) (Schneider 1999).

Thus, the present attributes of the federal system not only impede economic transition but essentially threaten the political survival of the federation *per se*. This fact should help to align the interests of central and sub-national policy makers and provide a feasible channel to restructure the political and economic relations between Moscow and the subordinated jurisdictions. The two most urgent reform tasks are the restructuring and the institutionalization of the fiscal relations between different levels of government and a clear assignment of responsibilities to reduce the discretionary intervention of the central government in sub-national affairs. So far, Russian authorities have been unable to agree upon either a clear assignment of public expenditures and revenues to different federal levels or on a functioning and transparent division of labor and power. The relations between Moscow and the regions are regulated by nontransparent bilateral or multilateral negotiations, which led to inconsistent and unstable agreements (Zhuravskaya 2000). Revenue-sharing schemes between different levels of government are renegotiated frequently. Treisman (1996) shows that grants from the central government have been distributed only according to political bargaining and are not guided by economic objectives. He further provides evidence that frequent negotiations between the central and sub-national governments concerning sharing schemes have given regional governments incentives to promote separatist movements as well as other types of political revolt against the central government. Moreover, Zhuravskaya (2000) argues persuasively that the effects of fiscal bargaining between regional and local governments have been impeding private business and economic growth. Neither transfers nor shared taxes are determined according to a fixed formula, but depend on political negotiations (and hence political bargaining power) between regional and local government officials; they vary over time as well as across smaller jurisdictions within a single region. Her empirical analysis strongly indicates that the current revenue-sharing schemes provide lower-level governments with virtually no incentives to promote tax collection or to provide local public goods. This is because any changes in the revenues of lower-level governments are almost completely offset by automatic changes in the revenues that are to be shared. This, in turn, not only leads to predatory political behavior towards local businesses, but also undermines the efficiency of public expenditure policies. Reforms of the revenue-sharing schemes need to institutionalize the intergovernmental fiscal relations according to predetermined economic objectives and aim at hardening the budget constraints of all lower-level governments. This is necessary to overcome moral hazard behavior of sub-national governments and to create incentives for prudent financial management at lower levels.

Moreover, local and regional governments need to be granted autonomy over policy making regarding their jurisdictions in order to allow for experimentation and local learning processes which take advantage of locally available information and are guided by local preferences. Pushing decision making down to local levels will also enable people to control policy makers and other agents more directly without the more elaborate institutional arrangements of central monitoring and enforcement which would take a long time to develop. At present, the constitution opens several channels for the central government to encroach on local markets and on the policy making of lower-level governments. For example, according to articles 71 and 72, the policies assigned to the central government and concurrent responsibilities essentially encompass all areas of public policies, giving the political center the right to intervene in virtually any policy issue. Article 77 postulates a system of executive authority consisting of central and regional executive bodies and does not clearly stipulate whether or not regional executive bodies can be held solely accountable to regional legislatures. Article 85 delimits regional autonomy, provides the president with substantial intervening powers, and blurs the vertical separation of powers. Article 96 enables central authorities substantially to influence the election of regional representatives to the Federation Council and the national legislature in general.[137] Given these constitutional constraints, a more suitable assignment of powers and responsibilities to the various members of the federation will require either a different interpretation of the constitutional prescriptions or (much better) an amendment of the constitution itself.

The task of replacing the current market-hampering federalism with a market-preserving (or better: enhancing) federal structure is complex but not insurmountable. In fact, given the power struggles and political deadlock in Moscow, the reform of the federal system towards a system of MPF will be the only politically feasible way to enhance the quality of governance in Russia and to make the political and economic transformation durable. In this context, it has been encouraging to observe that sub-national concerns have been increasingly recognized in the more recent past. The growing importance of sub-national jurisdictions became most evident when the former Prime Minister Primakow allowed several regional leaders to take an active part in the policy making of the central government in 1998. Most importantly, incorporating these regional leaders into the government presidium demonstrated the central government's acceptance of specific regional demands (Schneider 1999).

Necessary and sufficient? Market-preserving federalism reconsidered

The preceding sections on governance in large and heterogeneous transition countries have made clear that political and economic decentralization may be the single most important constitutive factor towards creating an effective MEGS. The model of market-preserving federalism has been taken as a reference to assess current federal systems in China, India, and Russia, to identify possible avenues of reform for these countries' politico-institutional structures and to make them more conducive to the implementation of policy reforms and eventually to economic and social development.

However, restructuring federal systems towards the MPF ideal may be a necessary, but not sufficient condition for achieving a secure political foundation for economic development.[138] MPF is an appropriate device to limit a strong government and basically to protect and promote thriving markets, but it does not automatically guarantee the existence of a strong government, either at the center or at sub-national levels. Potentially weak center or sub-national governments may be captured by vested interests and can hardly implement governance structures that decisively promote economic reforms. Therefore, the concept of *Participatory Market-Preserving Federalism* (PMPF), a feasible approach to address these problems, is developed here. This approach and the architects of the MPF theory agree that there is no logical link between the general nature of a federal system and governmental preservation or enhancement of markets, but that MPF as one particular type of federalism incorporates the self-enforcing institutional characteristics which are necessary to promote markets. However, we will argue that MPF alone is insufficient to preserve and promote thriving markets. This type of federalism is limited because it neglects the question of how institutionally to secure the existence of strong but accountable governments at sub-national levels.

PMPF seeks to combine the elementary qualities of an embedded-autonomy approach and those of MPF. Its objective is to create the preconditions for strong but limited governments at all federal levels. PMPF requires the realization of all conditions defining MPF. This limits a potentially strong central government, engenders competition among the different jurisdictions, and enables sub-national governments to conduct (economic) policies that meet the needs of their constituencies, thereby promoting regional and eventually overall economic development. But MPF *per se* does not guarantee strong but limited governments at sub-national levels, even if a common national market is ensured. Lower-level governments may be either too weak to protect legal rights and to enforce contracts or too strong (that is predatory) in their own demands. Even in a system of MPF, subordinated governments may be controlled by special-interest groups, which do not have an encompassing interest. These groups may pursue specific economic or non-economic interests, but even the latter may harm the regional economy (for example, if entry into certain businesses is restricted to specific groups of society). Therefore, political institutions are required which create independent but accountable executive bodies at sub-national levels. Thus, in a system of MPF the problem of balancing government independence and accountability is partly shifted to sub-national levels.[139] Also and particularly at these levels, governments have to be shielded from vested interests, and public officials must be responsible for their behavior and responsive to citizens' needs. Creating regional Weberian-type bureaucracies serves the first purpose,[140] and realizing a government–business interface by delegating authority, promoting the exchange of information, and involving private agents in the political decision-making process helps to constitute accountability of subordinated governments. Moreover, the regional implementation of embedded-autonomy institutions (in the form of industry-specific and community-specific deliberation councils) makes regional policies more transparent and predictable and strongly underpins governments' credible commitment.

But the picture of PMPF is still incomplete. Two basic questions have yet to be answered. First, which responsibilities and powers should be decentralized? Secondly, should the federal system be limited to two levels of government, leaving the local levels as pure extensions of Chinese provinces, Indian States, and Russian Republics? Regarding the first question, several economic theories of federalism[141] (the implications of which are inherent to MPF) provide a convincing rationale for decentralized political decision making. It is argued that this will result in efficiency gains, better accountability and manageability and enhance political autonomy.[142] The practical policy guidance provided by these theories is consistent with the guidance that emanates from the *principle of subsidiarity*. Following that principle, all public responsibilities and powers are to be allocated according to the problem-solving capabilities of the actors at different federal levels. This implies a federal system in which each political decision-making unit is only responsible for those tasks and functions which cannot be (efficiently) assumed by subordinated governments or private actors. Moreover, higher levels of government need to acknowledge the creative and organizational capabilities of subordinated units and to enable them to act independently.[143] MPF represents an appropriate institutional arrangement to realize the principle of subsidiarity.

In general, the allocation of responsibilities and powers should precede tax assignments, because tax needs are guided by spending needs. An efficient provision of public services requires political jurisdictions in which the sets of beneficiaries and tax payers overlap, so that the costs and benefits of providing public services are internalized. This reduces financing illusions and helps to overcome free-riding. Furthermore, it promotes competition among jurisdictions, makes regional and local decision makers responsive to their constituencies, and increases their accountability.[144] According to economic theories on federalism, the central government's role should be restricted to defense policies, foreign affairs, enforcing federal rights, national infrastructure, monetary policy, and policing the common market. Remaining responsibilities should be assigned to sub-national governments and private agents, depending on their problem-solving capabilities, unless spatial externalities or economies of scale in the provision of public services exist. Taxing power has to be suitably assigned to regional and local governments in order to prevent the central government (or higher levels of government in general) from manipulating (sub-national) economic activity and in order to create proper incentives for subordinated authorities. In this regard, even personal income taxes and corporate taxes should be assigned to sub-national governments, or regional authorities should have access to these tax bases through piggybacking on federal taxes. Since lower-level governments should undertake most economic policies (including redistribution policies), the access to income taxes is justified. Levying (supplementary) regional tax rates would foster competition among regions and strengthen the autonomy of sub-national governments.[145]

By establishing the principle of subsidiarity, economic freedoms will be manifested, inequities reduced, and citizens will recognize that their individual rights are guaranteed. Private initiative will be strengthened and comparative advantages of single social units can be used to manage public operations and private business. The devolution of responsibilities and control rights improves the economy's flexibility of restructuring and reduces transaction costs, because rigid bureaucratic structures are dissolved in favor of more adaptable administrative units at subordinated levels. If the central government and other superior decision-making units are obliged to enable subordinate social units to help themselves, regional and local interests will yield considerable economic efficiency gains. Moreover, by decentralizing political powers, the credibility of economic reforms as well as the responsibility for failures are expected to increase, thereby promoting people's backing for reforms.

But the principle of subsidiarity involves more than decentralizing economic responsibilities to lower-level governments. It also promotes democratization by creating equality of opportunity for different social units and individuals and the active involvement of all federal levels and all groups of society in political decision-making processes. It contributes to overcoming prevailing (non-economic) conflicts among regions, and between them and the central authorities, and creates the instrumental and institutional framework necessary for maintaining political unity. Finally, it helps to make MPF sustainable. Historical examples show that realizing condition C2, in particular, depends on both formal and informal institutions. While formal institutionalization, which is necessary once the political initiators of MPF pass power to their maybe less reform-minded successors, can be implemented by a constitutional embodiment, the latter are more difficult to realize. But the limitation of a government also depends on how constituents react to potential violations of governments' constraints. In 18th-century England and 19th-century United States, creating and maintaining MPF were the outcome of a historical process, which resulted in a broad consensus over rules and procedures and about the appropriate limits of the government's authority (Weingast 1995). Since the principle of subsidiarity assigns comprehensive participatory rights to rather homogeneous groups and individuals, it is a suitable device to develop informal norms. Formal institutions can serve as a focal point that contributes to the alignment and coordination of informal views and, therefore, to the emergence of such a consensus.[146]

Hence the notion of PMPF is based on three pillars which are mutually reinforcing; the concept of MPF, the idea of embedded autonomy, and the principle of subsidiarity. The combination of these components is expected to create strong but limited governments at all federal levels, prevent higher-level governments from overwhelming lower-level ones and from confiscating private wealth. PMPF fosters economic reforms and stimulates regional as well as overall development.[147] Government–business–society relations at all federal levels associated with the principle of subsidiarity establish the 'participatory' component of PMPF. This implies an active political participation of all groups of society and constituents, promotes the emergence of a civil society, ensures the governments' accountability, and explicitly links economic progress and political development.[148] Participation of beneficiaries in the design and implementation of projects and policies will mobilize their commitment and cooperation to a greater extent than the exogenous imposition of policy directives. In addition, it makes policies and projects more responsive to actual needs. Finally, participation can ensure control from below to keep bureaucrats in check if they are seen to serve vested interests.

However, participation is no panacea. As Streeten (1997) persuasively argues, there are basic rights which set limits on participation, and in particular cases authorities may – with some well-founded justification – not want communities to choose according to their long-time preferences, but to acquire different ones. For example, governments may seek to overcome habits and customs such as child marriage, excluding women and girls from education, child labor, and slavery, or also try to break down rigid institutional structures such as India's caste system. Moreover, if projects are highly technical in nature, experts must be involved in assisting participatory organizations in design and implementation.[149]

For participation to be effective it is necessary to thoroughly design a politico-institutional structure that can be used to guide an effective implementation of a strategy. In order to prevent local power elites from taking over decentralized participatory associations, countervailing powers at superior levels of administration are required to support participation. Of particular importance is to clarify who should be responsible for different decisions, at what federal level, and what sequence of decision-making needs to be followed (Streeten 1997). Furthermore, the effects of participation may be limited unless individuals and social groups have instruments to monitor superior decision-making units and to punish the violation of rules. Formal and informal networks like community- and industry-specific deliberation councils, watchdog committees and so on can serve as monitoring devices. Additionally, individuals and groups should have the right to appeal to the courts if rules are violated, and different forms of direct democracy (particularly the rights of referendum and initiative) should be introduced in order to give constituents flexible instruments to influence political outcomes directly. Since the system of PMPF creates effective checks and balances through a subtle system of political institutions, it also alleviates common-pool problems, where distinct social groups seize their shares of the pool of available rents until the pool is exhausted (Persson *et al.* 1997). The rule of law and democratic institutions that give social groups veto rights over rent appropriation by other groups, help to overcome the problem of interest group polarization. This in turn reduces rent-seeking behavior and fosters a consensus for public goods, thereby avoiding long-run growth tragedies (Easterly and Levine 1997).

The preceding considerations have also implicitly answered the question of whether the federal system should be limited to two levels of government. The principle of subsidiarity requires the federal system to comprise at least three levels of government (center, regions, local communities) and that local governments, various social groups, and individuals are given the opportunity to participate independently in political processes. In China, some progress in this direction has already been achieved as the experiences in policy making of the township and village governments illustrate. Also, India recently began to enhance the status of political entities at the local level. According to the 73rd Amendment of the Indian constitution, a third stratum of government (the *panchayati raj)* is now a requirement at and below the district level. This institution may become an effective means of exchanging information and fostering local autonomy and self-government, if *panchayati raj* actually get the freedom to devise their own instrumentalities. However, the 73rd Amendment does not sufficiently clarify how its provisions should be enforced. Essentially, it is within the competence of State legislatures to decide which powers will be devolved to the *panchayats.* At present, the only State having effective political *panchayats* is West Bengal. In this context, Indian States need to realize that their claims to be treated as partners by the central government are only justified if they are also willing to devolve responsibilities to *panchayats* and to acknowledge their autonomy (Mukarji 1993).

The general attributes of PMPF promise to be beneficial for regional and overall development in all three countries and supportive for continuing current economic reforms. More specifically, PMPF will improve these societies' organizational capability and governments' policy adaptability, that is the ability to collect reliable and relevant information and to adjust public policies according to new information. Furthermore, these attributes can serve as safeguards against corruption through an open participation of private business in the process of rule-making. Eventually, PMPF promises to increase the transparency, predictability, and accountability of public policies and, hence, helps to create a MEGS.

The preceding considerations illustrate again that a universal MEGS does not exist, but that lessons can be learned from successful cases. Whereas in the HPAEs centralized governance structures proved relatively effective, large and heterogeneous economies in transition need to rely on decentralized frameworks for policy making. But the ultimate objective is the same in both groups of countries, namely to establish strong but limited governments that are embedded in institutional structures that are conducive to promoting the quality of the core dimensions of effective governance. While the notion of embedded autonomy proved to be a critical factor in the small East Asian countries, it can hardly be transferred to large countries. Nevertheless, the benefits of a Weberian-type bureaucracy, for example, are obvious, and in this respect even China, India, and Russia can usefully draw on the experiences of the HPAEs. Similarly, this also holds for establishing transparent consultation and cooperation mechanisms linking the public and the private sector. In large countries, however, such mechanisms will prove to be much more effective if introduced at lower levels of government and if they are viewed as critical components of a bottom-up strategy of institution building and development.

6.3.2 EU accession candidates: the Visegrád countries

While the preceding case studies focused on the role of distinct political and economic institutions and especially on countries' *domestic capacities* to transform these institutions into an effective governance structure, this section examines yet another critical variable that may help to enhance the quality of governance sustainably – that is, the *external factor*. Notwithstanding the fact that international competition or relations have also played significant roles in shaping the governance structures in the HPAEs and other countries, the following considerations suggest that the influence of international organizations such as the IMF and particularly the existence of an external anchor (in this case the EU) for reforms can become a key driving force for institutional change. More specifically, it will be argued that for a subgroup of transition economies in CEE the prospect of EU membership has helped to form a societal consensus for market-oriented policy reform, facilitated the implementation of structural and institutional reforms, and promoted the consolidation of the overall reform process.

These hypotheses will be scrutinized with the use of examples, especially of four transition economies, namely the Visegrád countries including the Czech and Slovak Republics, Hungary, and Poland, all of which (except Slovakia) belong to the first echelon of countries with which the EU has recently started accession negotiations.[150] These countries share several important similarities constituting a similar context of policy reform. These include, for example, the pre-communist legacies, the commitment to economic transition, the functioning of the public sector, the absence of ethnic tensions, the victory of non-communist opposition parties in the first free elections (the so-called founding elections), and the prospect of relatively early EU membership. On the other hand, a number of other political and economic conditions which may influence the feasibility of market-oriented reforms vary between these countries: this particularly holds for differences in political mandates for the newly elected democratic governments, the fiscal and overall economic situation at the early stage of transformation, the authority and strength of the executive branch of government as well as the power of economic reformers within the governments (Bönker 2000). Taking these similarities and differences as a starting point, this section in a first step discusses briefly the political-economy aspects of the reforms in these countries. In a second step, the role of the EU as an outside anchor for the consolidation of the reform process is analysed.

Ex ante and ex post constraints to economic reforms

Frequently, political constraints are so binding in the process of policy reform that they hinder the implementation of theoretically efficient reform measures. From a governance perspective, it is useful to distinguish *ex ante* and *ex post* political constraints (Roland 1994 and 1997). While the former play a crucial role in the *initiation* of a reform program, the latter determine the prospects for its *consolidation*. At the beginning of the transition, political conditions were favorable for the implementation of radical market-oriented reforms in all Visegrád countries. In fact, the simultaneity of the political and economic transformation initially proved to be a clear advantage in these cases. The revolutionary political change allowed the initiation of reform measures which would have had little chance of being implemented in such a radical way either under the old socialist regime or in a fully-fledged democracy. In the nascent democracies, the new governments could take considerable advantage of honeymoon effects and enjoyed a period in which extraordinary politics were suddenly possible.

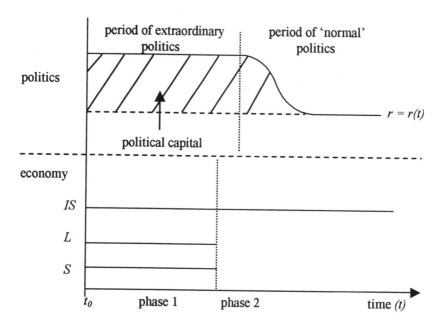

Note: Reprinted with permission by the Massachusetts Institute of Technology (The MIT Press).
Source: Balcerowicz *et al.* (1997); modified

Figure 6.23: Political and economic dynamics of the transition process

After 40 years of communism, the old regimes were lastingly discredited, and – given the economic stagnation in the 1970s and 1980s – the necessity for reform was undisputed. Moreover, there was not only a *consensus of termination* regarding the old system but also a *consensus of destination*. After two decades of partial reforms, arguments for a 'third way' played no considerable role. The clear-cut objectives of political and economic transformation were to build a competitive, outward-looking market economy and a democracy and, eventually, to return to Europe. The marginalization of the old communist parties in the founding elections confirmed the discredit of the previous regime and illustrated the broad consensus regarding the direction of economic reforms.[151] Another advantage for the reformers was that initially public and political debates focused on constitutional and political problems. Moreover, due to the election results, the new governments had been provided with a high degree of legitimacy. These factors considerably facilitated the introduction of economic reforms. Finally, the executive authority of the new governments was strengthened through the absence of organized interest groups that would have been able to resist economic reforms effectively.[152] This scarcity of organized actors was also favorable for the implementation of radical reforms, because it even constrained anti-reform forces within the new governments: on the one hand, there was little leverage for the critics to mobilize opposition or resistance within their parties, and on the other hand, they could not use any organizational alternatives outside government (Bönker 1995).

Figure 6.23 shows the window of opportunity that was available to most Central European economies in transition and illustrates the essence of the reform programs pursued, particularly in Poland and former Czechoslovakia.[153] The lower part of the diagram reflects a big-bang approach to economic reforms, with its main components macroeconomic stabilization (S), price and trade liberalization (L), as well as institutional and structural transformation (IS). The radical nature of the economic strategy is symbolized by the position and the length of the lines IS, L, and S. Alternative, more gradual strategies would be represented by longer lines or by lines that would be located farther right.[154] The upper part of the figure represents the political situation. The function $r = r(t)$ expresses the degree of public readiness to agree to and support a radical economic approach; t_0 is a point in time just after a clear and significant discontinuity in a given country's history, for example, a regime change, the collapse of the previous institutional order, the liberation from outside political dependence, or a deep economic crisis. The underlying assumption is that such phenomena can lead to a political breakthrough that produces 'a special state of mass psychology and a corresponding state of political system which are reflected in an abnormally high level of r; this can only be maintained for a relatively short time' (Balcerowicz *et al.* 1997: 136–7). The temporary surplus of *r* over its 'normal' level creates a special form of political capital, a precious resource provided by history, which can be exploited by determined political leaders to implement radical reforms. In such a situation, the political structures tend to be fluid, and there is often a lack of experienced professional politicians because the old elite has been discredited and policy makers who represent the new order have not yet entered the political stage in large numbers. But as Balcerowicz (1994: 177) argues, policy making may become highly effective in such a case, because 'the period of extraordinary politics' not only calls for but actually creates the conditions conducive for the emergence of so-called *technopols*, that is, economic technocrats who assume key positions of considerable political responsibility.[155]

This political capital provided governments with the opportunity to quickly undertake drastic and bold policy programs. A delay in reforms would entail a higher risk of resistance and social protest and eventually reduce their acceptance. Figure 6.23 also suggests that two phases of a radical approach to economic reforms need to be distinguished. The first phase should include all those measures which can be quickly implemented and work faster, such as *S*, *L*, and, for example, small-scale privatization. This is necessary in order to use the full potential of the political capital, before it starts to deplete, and to make the systemic change irreversible. In the second phase, more time-consuming structural and institutional reforms are to be undertaken. These usually face more political resistance because it is chiefly these reforms that provoke fierce distributional conflicts and because potential losers from these reforms will be better organized in the meantime. Thus, the second phase is a phase of 'normal' politics, that is, politics dominated by various well-established political parties and organized interest groups, as is, for example, assumed in Public Choice theory (Buchanan and Tullock 1962).

As mentioned above, *ex ante* political constraints to economic transformation were not particularly binding in the Visegrád countries and thus allowed for a period of extraordinary politics, in which policy makers could take advantage of the temporarily available political capital in order to implement necessary reforms. However, the window of opportunity was differently wide in these countries. The degree of the societal break following the political upheaval in 1989/90 was perceived differently by the populations in the Visegrád countries so that the new governments could gain from honeymoon effects to different extents. Furthermore, economic starting conditions differed substantially, so that economic reforms were more urgent in some countries than in others. Overall, the political conditions prior to reforms were far more favorable in Poland and Czechoslovakia than in Hungary (Bönker 1995). In the former countries, the political break in

1989/90 was perceived as more radical and far-reaching than in the latter, where economic reforms had already started in 1968, relatively liberal political conditions had already emerged under the old regime, and the transition toward a democratic order had taken place in a rather evolutionary way. Consequently, the new Hungarian government was given a significantly smaller credit than the governments in the other two countries (Batt 1991).

In addition, the long history of partial reforms in Hungary had not only resulted in a certain reform fatigue, but also in the perception that the country had already left behind the most painful part of economic restructuring. This viewpoint made many Hungarians believe that their economy was in a comparatively good starting position *vis-à-vis* their neighbors and that they could afford a slower and more piecemeal approach to reform. In contrast, only half-hearted reforms had been pursued under the old regime in Poland, and in Czechoslovakia virtually no major reforms had been introduced. Therefore, the election of the first non-communist government was perceived as a significant break in both countries. Moreover, economic reforms were considered far more necessary in these countries than in Hungary. In 1989, Poland experienced an acute macroeconomic crisis with an inflation rate of 640 percent at the end of the year. Although the macroeconomic situation was far better in Czechoslovakia, the need for bold reforms was acute here, too, because they were perceived as indispensable to catching up with the reform progress in their neighboring countries. Yet another factor that caused a more gradual reform approach in Hungary was that the process of forming political parties had progressed much further than in the other two countries due to Hungary's earlier political liberalization. Hence, the campaign prior to the founding elections in Hungary was not dominated by a competition between old communists and one broad opposition alliance, but by two non-communist parties. In this case, the dynamics of the party competition placed a stronger focus on the potential costs of the economic transformation (Bönker 1995).

In sum, it can be argued that the *ex ante* political restrictions to policy and institutional reforms were relatively low in the Visegrád countries. Particularly in Czechoslovakia and Poland, governments were provided with a strong mandate to pursue radical market-oriented reforms, the politico-institutional conditions granted reformers a high degree of autonomy, and enabled effective political-change teams under the guidance of determined and powerful politicians such as Leszek Balcerowicz in Poland and Václav Klaus in Czechoslovakia to rapidly implement some key economic policies and institutions which are indispensable for the emergence of a functioning market economy.

However, the continuation and consolidation of economic reforms in the second phase of transition has proved to be much more difficult than their initiation.[156] On the one hand, early reform measures did not materialize as quickly as expected, and on the other hand, several factors that had facilitated the introduction of reforms became gradually less significant. Hence, in the course of transition, the readiness of the populations to attribute the costs of the systemic change to the old regime and to grant premature praise to the new governments decreased. Given the transformational recession in all countries, large segments of the populations found themselves in a nostalgia trap. The sobering recognition that 'the transition process was a crude awakening that capitalism is not merely about being rich' (Pejovich 1994: 522) paved the way for an idealized transfiguration of the virtues of the old regime. Moreover, many people saw 'the gains from exchange as a redistribution of wealth within the community rather than as rewards for creating new value' (ibid.: 520). They did not perceive capitalism as a system based on self-responsibility, self-determination, and competition, but rather as a system automatically providing a great variety of goods and large incomes, the realization of which would neither require reducing 'socialist' welfare benefits nor changing the traditional work ethos. These factors made the transformation process path dependent and induced hysteresis effects, so that capitalist behavioral norms as postulated by neoclassical reasoning could not emerge in the short run. In addition, the gradual emergence of organized interest groups and political parties brought a higher number of influential actors onto the political stage, thus providing possibilities for effectively articulating discontents and constraining the autonomy of economic policy making.

The politico-institutional conditions in the Czech Republic remained reasonably favorable for continued reforms due to relatively weak trade unions and a high degree of government autonomy which was strengthened by a secure parliamentary majority of the governing party and its strong local basis and organization. But even in the Czech Republic, structural and institutional reforms were not always pursued in a determined and effective way and were subject to *ex post* constraints as serious problems in privatization and corporate governance as well as delays in price liberalization in certain areas illustrate (Piazolo 1998).

Basically, the politico-institutional conditions in Hungary were also favorable for the implementation of reforms, because the election law helped to form stable governments. Moreover, as in the Czech Republic, trade unions suffered from relative weakness due to organizational fragmentation and internal conflict. However, due to the decentralization of economic decision making under the old regime, interest groups existed at the enterprise level, whose interests conflicted with the transformation objectives of privatization as well as genuine marketization. Furthermore, the system of indicative planning that had been introduced since 1968, made it difficult for the government to control and monitor key policy issues in the transition process. This holds, for example, for privatization. Since earlier reforms had created a set of diffuse ownership rights, spontaneous privatization in the 1990s was probably an unavoidable consequence in the transfer of property rights. Unlike in the Czech Republic, where a strictly centralized governance structure enabled the government to overcome this problem, the Hungarian government was hardly able to regain control of the privatization process. Yet another major problem of implementing reforms policies proved to be the lack of a coherent change team which would have been able to formulate and guide determined reform programs. In addition, the key positions in government, such as that of the finance minister, were increasingly occupied by party politicians who lacked economic expertise.

In contrast, conceivably unfavorable *ex post* conditions existed in Poland, where two strong trade unions were able effectively to constrain economic policy making. Moreover, the structure of the political system and the conduct of numerous political elections contributed to frequent changes in governments and political instability. Fragile political coalitions and conflicts between the president Lech Walesa, the government, and parliament impeded the government's ability to act effectively and to implement reforms. The constitutional rights granted to the president to veto proposals of the parliament further complicated the need to win parliamentary approval for badly needed structural reforms, especially for mass privatization, which only commenced in 1995. Lastly, while the Polish transition, like the Czech reform program, was initially driven by a coherent change team under the guidance of the then-finance minister Balcerowicz, the position of determined reformers was somewhat weakened in the course of time, when especially the appointment of the finance minister became increasingly dependent on political rivalries.

Finally, the politico-institutional conditions in Slovakia, after its separation from the Czech Republic in 1993, worsened considerably from a governance perspective. Although the government managed to implement a stabilization program (including strict monetary and fiscal policies and a prudent incomes policy) which led to a fast macroeconomic recovery, structural and institutional reforms were postponed time and again or even cancelled. This was most obvious regarding privatization. The divestiture of SOEs underwent substantial politicization under the past administrations, who abandoned the previous voucher privatization and opted for direct sales of assets. In turn, privatization became increasingly subject to political patronage. In a rather obscure and opaque way, the government sold SOEs to the enterprises' ruling management at prices far below market values. Consequently, the privatization process did not succeed in enhancing the performance of the majority of old enterprises. Instead, the old management was able to maintain control, and the enterprises remained heavily indebted and unattractive to new strategic investors. In addition, the state-owned banks continued to subsidize unprofitable enterprises which resulted in an increasing number of bad loans in their portfolios. The reversal of the privatization policies and the delay in structural, institutional, and administrative reforms reflected the desire of the Slovak authorities under the leadership of Vladimir Meciar to pursue a more gradual, populist, and nationalistic transition strategy.

The increasingly authoritarian direction of policy making in Slovakia since 1994 seriously impeded any determined effort to implement policies and institutions that are indispensable for a functioning market economy. Furthermore, the shortcomings in establishing genuine democratic structures and processes as well as in modernizing the public administration, the continued violation of human rights, and the discrimination of the Hungarian and Roma minorities led the EU in 1997 to exclude Slovakia from the first-round candidates of CEE countries with which accession negotiations are being conducted. In 1998, however, the prospects for an improvement in the politico-institutional conditions were significantly improved. The parliamentary elections in September brought about a drastic turn in the political situation of the Slovak Republic. Four democratically-oriented, former opposition parties together won a three-fifths majority in parliament that is necessary for constitutional revisions. These elections not only meant a change in government but a regime change. Whether or not, however, the political system will eventually stabilize and become more democratic is far from clear. Meciar is *ante portas* again. His populist-authoritarian party won the majority of seats in parliament and hence is the strongest opposition power.

This brief stocktaking of the politico-institutional conditions in the Visegrád countries leads to the provisional conclusion that the pursued transition policies made the transformation process irreversible in all countries. Even the return of old communists in several governments did not result in a return to communism. But it is also clear that the transition has not been completed in any of these countries. In particular, the gradual depletion of the initially available political capital and the increasingly binding *ex post* constraints on economic policy making have aggravated badly needed structural, institutional, and administrative reforms. At the end of the 1990s, it showed that the transition policies that had initially followed most of the policy prescriptions inherent in the Washington Consensus were incomplete. What was overlooked or consciously ignored in the early phases of the transformation was that a functioning market economy requires an adequate institutional infrastructure providing market-preserving and market-enhancing incentives to both policy makers and private business. There is broad evidence that in most transition countries insufficient attention and resources were devoted to building new institutions and to rendering policy making more efficient, effective, and accountable. Based on the alleged dichotomy of states and markets, policy makers, foreign advisers, and international organizations advocated a minimalist state and aimed at a drastic reduction in the size and scope of government (Amsden *et al.* 1994; Hare 1997). A recent UNDP report concludes that 'the "shrinking state" (...) in many parts of the region has contributed to worrying trends in human development, including high rates of poverty, rapidly growing economic and social inequality amounting to socio-economic fragmentation, deterioration in public health and public education, and worrying trends in culture and the long-term health of the environment'.[157]

Initially, governance problems were viewed as part of a secondary reform agenda or were expected to be overcome automatically through getting the prices and macroeconomic fundamentals right. The neglect of governance issues may have also been caused by a surge of anti-statism resulting from the demise of the communist state and the policy prescriptions of neoclassical economics. The Washington Consensus, in particular, disregarded the question of how state institutions can be effectively reformed in order to help policy makers perform their new roles in a market-oriented environment (Kolodko 1999). And yet, a small subgroup of CEE transition economies managed to implement institutional reforms relatively well. This group includes all those countries in which a broad consensus has existed from the very beginning of the transformation process to return to Europe, that is to strive for a rapid integration into Western (European) structures and membership in organizations such as NATO and especially the EU. The Visegrád countries belong to the frontrunners of this subgroup of economies in transition, the transformation process of which has already greatly benefited from the realistic prospects of becoming EU members in the short or medium term.

The importance of future EU membership

Transformation and international integration are mutually dependent processes. There is broad evidence that successful transformation policies facilitate the integration of the PSCs into the international division of labor and create the necessary preconditions for membership in international organizations such as the WTO.[158] But the direction of causality is in fact two-way. Actual and even potential progress in international integration may substantially reinforce transformation policies, strengthen the political power of reformers, and improve domestic governance structures. The Visegrád countries are a case in point illustrating this hypothesis.

Despite the existence of *ex post* constraints on the implementation of market-oriented policies and institutions, all Visegrád countries have performed comparatively well in terms of policy and institutional reforms. Together with Estonia, Lithuania, and Slovenia they have achieved the greatest progress in institutional reform and the fastest growth in real GDP (see Tables 6.9 and 6.10). To a great extent, this progress can be attributed to the desire of these countries to become fully integrated into international structures and organizations. In order to foster integration into the world economy, the Visegrád countries renewed, tightened, or established new relations with international organizations such as the IMF, the World Bank, the WTO, and the OECD (see Table 6.11). Particularly, Poland, Hungary, and Slovakia needed IMF support to overcome macroeconomic instabilities.

But the key external driving force of domestic transformation policies was the vision of gaining access to the European Union. The peaceful revolution in many CEE countries in 1989/90 went hand in hand with a broad societal consensus and the political vision to gain membership in the EU. In particular, in Central European countries, potential EU membership has dominated the political agenda from the very beginning of the transition and has played a significant role in domestic political and economic debates (Wagener 1999). It is also obvious that internal political divisions in these countries have been temporarily less important, as different political forces have cooperated in their efforts to fulfill the requirements for EU membership (Berglöf and Roland 1997). Actually, the most important motive underlying the Visegrád declaration of Czechoslovakia, Hungary, and Poland in 1991 was to increase their bargaining power in negotiations with the former European Communities (EC) and NATO. In particular, these countries shared an interest in replacing their trade agreements with the European Economic Community and the European Coal and Steel Community with EC Association Agreements (Hoen 1998). The common objective of these countries was defined in the Visegrád declaration as 'the restoration of each state's independence, democracy and freedom, and the dismantling of the structures of the totalitarian regimes, as well as the total integration into the Western European political, economic, security, and legislative order' (De Weydenthal 1991: 29). Therefore, regional cooperation was mainly motivated by external considerations at that time.

This cooperation proved to be quite successful with respect to the negotiations for the Association Agreements with the EC in 1991 (the so-called Europe Agreements), in which the EC treated the Visegrád countries more or less alike.[159] Moreover, the EC announced that all countries with which Agreements have been signed, are to be considered as potential candidates for future EU membership. At the following EU summit in Copenhagen in 1993, accession of these countries was on the political agenda

Table 6.9: Growth in real GDP in CEE, the Baltic States and the CIS

	1999	2000	2001	estimated level of real GDP in 2000 (1989=100)	average growth p.a. in percent (1990–2001)
Albania	7.3	7.8	7.0	103	0.8
Bulgaria	2.4	5.8	4.0	71	-2.5
Croatia	-0.4	3.7	3.8	80	-1.5
Czech Republic	-0.8	3.1	3.5	98	0.1
Estonia	-0.7	6.9	4.5	83	-1.2
FYR Macedonia	2.7	5.1	-4.0	77	-2.5
Hungary	4.2	5.2	4.5	104	0.7
Latvia	1.1	6.6	6.5	64	-3.1
Lithuania	-3.9	3.9	4.0	65	-3.2
Poland	4.1	4.0	2.0	127	2.2
Romania	-3.2	1.6	4.0	77	-1.8
Slovak Republic	1.9	2.2	3.0	103	0.5
Slovenia	5.2	4.6	2.2	114	1.3
Armenia	3.3	6.0	6.0	63	-3.3
Azerbaijan	7.4	11.1	8.0	52	-4.7
Belarus	3.4	5.8	2.5	85	-1.1
Georgia	3.0	1.9	3.0	34	-8.4
Kazakhstan	2.7	9.6	10.0	69	-2.3
Kyrgyzstan	3.7	5.1	5.0	66	-3.0
Moldova	-4.4	1.9	5.0	33	-8.5
Russia	5.4	8.3	5.5	63	-3.3
Tajikistan	3.7	8.3	6.0	47	-5.6
Turkmenistan	16.0	17.6	10.0	75	-1.6
Ukraine	-0.2	5.8	7.0	42	-6.4
Uzbekistan	4.1	4.0	3.0	98	0.1

Source: EBRD (2001), own calculations.
Data for 1998–99 represent most recent official estimates. Data for 2000 are preliminary actuals. Data for 2001 are EBRD projections.

Table 6.10: Progress in institutional change in CEE and the CIS for the year 2001

Countries	Enterprises			Markets and trade			Financial institutions		Legal reform		indicator of institutional change
	large-scale privatization	small-scale privatization	governance & enterprise restructuring	price liberalization	trade & foreign exchange system	competition policy	banking reform & interest rate liberalization	securities markets & nonbank financial institutions	extensiveness of legal rules	effectiveness on investment	
CEE											
Hungary	4	4.33	3.33	3.33	4.33	3	4	3.67	3,67	3.67	37.33
Estonia	4	4.33	3,33	3	4,33	2.67	3.67	3	3.33	4	35.66
Poland	3.33	4.33	3,33	3.33	4.33	3	3.33	3.67	3,67	3	35.32
Czech Republic	4	4.33	3.33	3	4.33	3	3.67	3	3	3	34.66
Slovenia	3	4.33	2.67	3,33	4.33	2,67	3.33	2.67	3,67	4	34.00
Lithuania	3,33	4.33	2.67	3	4,33	3	3	3	3,67	3,67	34.00
Slovak Republic	4	4.33	3	3	4.33	3	3,33	2.33	3.33	3,33	33.98
Latvia	3	4,33	2.67	3	4.33	2.33	3,33	2.33	3.67	4	32.99
Croatia	3	4.33	2.67	3	4,33	2,33	3,33	2.33	3,67	3.67	32.66
Bulgaria	3,67	3.67	2.33	3	4.33	2,33	3	2	4	3.67	32.00
Romania	3,33	3.67	2	3,33	4	2,33	2.67	2	4	4	31.33
FYR Macedonia	3	4	2,33	3	4	2	3	1.67	3,33	3,67	30.00
Albania	2,33	4	2	3	4,33	1,67	2,33	1.67	2,33	2	25.66
Bosnia/ Herzegovina	2,33	2,67	1.67	3	3	1	2.33	1	1,33	2	20.33

CIS	large-scale privatization	small-scale privatization	governance & enterprise restructuring	price liberalization	trade & foreign exchange system	competition policy	banking reform & interest rate liberalization	securities markets & nonbank financial institutions	extensiveness of legal rules	effectiveness on investment	indicator of institutional change
Kazakhstan	3	4	2	3	3,33	2	2.67	2,33	4	4	30.33
Moldova	3	3.33	2	3,33	4,33	2	2.33	2	3,33	3,67	29.32
Georgia	3.33	4	2	3,33	4,33	2	2.33	1,67	3	3	28.99
Kyrgyzstan	3	4	2	3	4	2	2.33	2	3,33	3	28.66
Russian Federation	3.33	4	2,33	3	2.67	2.33	1.67	1.67	3	3,67	27.67
Ukraine	3	3.33	2	3	3	2,33	2	2	3,33	3	26.99
Armenia	3	3.67	2	3	4	2	2.33	2	2,67	2	26.67
Azerbaijan	2	3,33	2	3	3.33	2	2,33	1,67	3	2	24.66
Uzbekistan	2.67	3	1,67	2	1,67	2	1.67	2	3	3	22.68
Tajikistan	2.33	3,67	1.67	3	3,33	1,67	1	1	2	2	21.67
Belarus	1	2	1	2	2	2	1	2	3	3	19.00
Turkmenistan	1	2	1	2	1	1	1	1	2	3	15.00

Notes: Progress in institutional change is estimated by the EBRD for ten areas and valued on a scale from 1 (little progress) to 4+ (standards and performance comparable to advanced industrial countries). The figures in the table represent the achieved level in 2001. For legal reforms in Kyrgyzstan, indicators represent the achieved level in 2000. Pluses (+) and minuses (-) from the figures, respectively. Indicators were transformed into numerical values by adding or subtracting 0.33 from the figures, respectively.

Source: EBRD (2001), own calculations.

Table 6.11: Relations of the Visegrád countries with Western economic and political organizations (month/year)

	Czech Republic	Hungary	Poland	Slovakia
European Union				
Association Agreement				
- signed*	10/1993	12/1991	12/1991	10/1993
- in force	2/1995	2/1994	2/1994	2/1995
Interim Agreement on trade aspects				
- in force**	3/1992	3/1992	3/1992	3/1992
application for membership	1/1996	4/1994	4/1994	6/1995
GATT partnership**	1/1948	9/1973	19/1967	1/1948
WTO membership	12/1994	12/1994	7/1995	12/1994
IMF membership**	1945–54	—	1945–50	1945–50
	10/1990	5/1982	6/1986	10/1990
World Bank membership**	1945–54	—	1945–50	1945–54
	10/1990	7/1982	7/1986	10/1990
OECD membership	11/1995	3/1996	7/1996	—

Notes: * Regarding the Czech and Slovak Republics, the data refer to a replacement of the previous Agreement with former Czechoslovakia, signed 12/1991.
** Regarding the Czech and Slovak Republics, data refer to former Czechoslovakia.

Source: Hoen (1998)

for the first time. At this summit, the preconditions for negotiations for membership were stipulated. These so-called *Copenhagen Criteria* require that any candidate country must achieve:

- 'stability of institutions guaranteeing democracy, the rule of law, human rights and respect for and protection of minorities';
- 'the existence of a functioning market economy as well as the capacity to cope with competitive pressure and market forces within the Union';
- 'the ability to take on the obligations of membership including adherence to the aims of political, economic and monetary union';

and they must create 'the conditions for its integration through the adjustment of its administrative structures, so that European Community legislation transposed into national legislations [is; J.A.] implemented effectively through appropriate administrative and judicial structures' (EU 2000).

Thus, since the Copenhagen European Council meeting, EU enlargement has no longer been a question of 'if' but 'when'. At least since the Copenhagen summit, the broad vision of returning to Europe has been complemented and reinforced by the concrete prospects and challenges of EU membership. Consequently, all Visegrád countries applied for membership in the EU; Hungary and Poland in 1994, Slovakia in 1995, and the Czech Republic in 1996. The process of EU enlargement was launched on 30 March 1998. At present, negotiations are being held with the Visegrád countries, the Baltic states, Bulgaria, Romania, and Slovenia and with two non-transition countries, Malta and Cyprus. The fundamental principle of the negotiations is that the applicant countries have to accept existing EU law, adopt the complete *acquis communautaire*, and completely fulfill the Copenhagen criteria.

From a governance perspective, membership in international organizations such as the IMF and the WTO, or in supranational organizations such as the EU can play a significant role in relieving both *ex ante* and *ex post* constraints to economic policy making. As has been well documented in the literature on policy reform (for example, Berglöf and Roland 1997 as well as Dhonte and Kapur 1997), such organizations may serve as agencies of restraint or outside anchors which help to enhance the credibility of political commitments in their member states or can exert pressure on anti-reformist governments to implement badly needed policy and institutional reforms. They can also serve as a means of increasing domestic support for reform programs. As Leszek Balcerowicz (1994: 175) put it with respect to the IMF support of the radical Polish transformation program in the early 1990s, which was chiefly designed by himself when he was finance minister:

> Within the government and in parliamentary debates, I used conditionality only as [an; J.A.] additional argument in favor of the economic program. In other words, I stressed that the program was motivated by our internal considerations, but in addition, its implementation meant the support of the IMF (and of other international organizations), and this support was needed to make the program internationally credible and to obtain sizable debt reduction. This was not only truthful but also probably politically more effective than trying to push through tough measures on the pretext that the IMF had imposed them.

Another instructive example is Slovakia, where the Meciar government proposed to slow down reforms after the split from the Czech Republic. But already six months after independence, a rather pragmatic view had emerged among policy makers. The IMF and the EU, in particular, exerted severe pressure on Slovakian authorities not to allow the transformation process to fall behind that in its neighboring countries. Recall that after the break-up of Czechoslovakia the Association Agreements with the EC had to be renegotiated. A new Agreement was concluded with the Slovakian government in October 1993. This Agreement resembled the former one with Czechoslovakia, but additionally included institutional safeguards for democratization and the protection of human rights. Thus, Slovakia was externally forced to make firm commitments not only to the implementation of market-oriented economic institutions, but also regarding the transition to a genuine democratic system (Hoen 1998). These contractual safeguards actually proved to be effective. Due to political reasons and persisting institutional deficits, the Slovak Republic was in fact excluded in 1997 from the group of countries that were primarily eligible for negotiating EU membership. This strongly reduced the likelihood of rapid accession to the EU. The European Commission recognized that only if the economic and political conditions improve significantly, will there be a possibility of the country being reconsidered for EU membership.[160]

Perhaps equally important for the continuation of *economic* transition policies was the role of the IMF. Negotiations with the Fund had already started in early 1993, but they were quickly abandoned when the policies proposed by the IMF were rejected by the government. Finally, an agreement was made in mid-1993 which granted Slovakia access to a systemic-transformation facility. This credit facility not only entailed that the Fund exert great influence on fiscal policies, but it also placed the country in a backward position *vis-à-vis* the other three Visegrád countries. None of the latter had to use the systemic-transformation facility, but could rely on regular stand-by loans. Hence, the IMF seemed to have more confidence in these countries' abilities to use market-conforming policy instruments to overcome balance-of-payments problems. In addition, since the IMF's policies are frequently interpreted by private investors as a 'stamp of approval', the kind of facility chosen may have dissuaded international investors from becoming active in Slovakia. Eventually, the conditionality imposed by the IMF caused the Meciar government to undertake a significant policy switch. At least in the realm of macroeconomic stabilization, the intention to slow down reforms was actually reversed (Hoen 1998).

It is precisely the mixture of imposed conditionality and external financial support (or other economic benefits) that helps to overcome political constraints to reform. *Ex ante* constraints can be more easily overcome because the external pressure for reforms comes with loans (for example from the IMF) which may help reduce the social costs of reforms. This may enhance the acceptance of bold transition policies and reduce the influence of vested interests which seek to slow down the transition process. Similarly, *ex post* constraints may be attenuated because the reversal of reforms and the breach of imposed conditionality invokes high costs in terms of the loss of financial assistance or other economic benefits. In particular, the EU has served as an external anchor to reforms in the Visegrád countries. The leverage induced by the prospects of EU accession is of particular importance in an international environment in which financial constraints are relatively soft. Note that even relatively poor performers in the transition have had relatively easy access to international capital markets in the recent past so that the Bretton Woods organizations seem to have a decreasing leverage. Berglöf and Roland (1997), for example, report that a eurobond issued by Moldova (a modest reformer according to Table 6.10) was five times oversubscribed. Therefore, for a distinct group of CEE countries, the European Union may be the only organization that is able to impose serious, credible, and effective policy conditionality. This is because membership in the EU promises substantial economic and political benefits which are expected to outweigh the potential costs associated with the bold policy and institutional reforms that are necessary to gain entry into the Union. These benefits include:[161]

- the gains from increased trade and the import of modern technological and managerial know-how;
- full access to EU markets;
- a more predictable business environment and hence reduced uncertainty for both foreign and domestic investors;
- the prospects of substantial resource transfers from the EU through its regional and structural funds as well as its Common Agricultural Policy;[162]
- a potential export of workers (which may help to reduce unemployment);
- the participation in the Union's political decision-making process;
- further external pressure to modernize the economies and public administrations; and
- a more predictable political and security framework in which the candidate countries will be embedded.

Anticipating these benefits, the people and governments particularly in the Visegrád countries were willing and able to accept the political and economic conditions imposed by the EU as a prerequisite for future membership and to rapidly improve their political and economic governance structures in order to bring them in line with EU standards and rules. However, EU membership may also entail considerable risks for the transition economies. These comprise, for example:

- increased competitive pressures on domestic markets from the 'old' EU members;
- a reduced number of policy instruments which will be available to governments in order to overcome economic shocks, disequilibria, and differences in the level of development;
- a massive inflow of foreign capital which may mean a reduced autonomy in economic policy making;
- a brain-drain resulting from labor migration because most potential emigrants will be high-skilled workers; and
- a potential overburdening of the absorption capacity of transition countries with respect to financial transfers; this may not only lead to an inefficient allocation of resources but also to a slowdown of further reforms.

Most importantly, the candidate countries must recognize that the distribution of benefits and costs (in size and in time) will depend on their own reform policies aiming at a rapid and effective adjustment to EU rules. If they are well-designed, domestic policies can considerably enhance benefits and reduce costs even before full membership is achieved. In fact, the prospects of EU accession have not only determined the direction of reforms in the Visegrád countries (that is, the establishment of an economic and legal order according to the Western European model), but also their speed (Wagener 1999). Moreover, the sequencing of approaching the EU especially in the case of the more advanced accession candidates has differed considerably from that pursued by less advanced member countries in the 1980s. Spain, Portugal, and Greece first became full EC members and then, as a consequence of institutional integration, began to develop stronger intra-industry and microeconomic linkages to the most developed countries of the Communities. In contrast, the Czech Republic, Hungary, Poland, and Slovenia had already established such links to the EU in the recent past. This leads Inotai (1999: 3) to conclude that

(d)ue to rapid economic and trade liberalization, quick (...) privatization, the inflow of foreign direct capital and a skilled and mostly flexible labour [force; J.A.], their integration into EU (...) production networks is today not only deeper than that of the Mediterranean countries a few years before their accession to the EU, but even in comparison with their present position.

These observations clearly support the hypothesis that the EU has in fact served as an effective anchor for transition reforms in CEE and most notably in the Visegrád countries.

Last but not least, it is noteworthy in this context that the prospects of membership will help further relieve domestic political constraints to continuing transition reforms. For the mentioned benefits will only materialize if the candidate countries completely fulfill the Copenhagen criteria. And actually the EU has a strong interest not to allow for an overly early entry, because this could overburden the financial capacities and the economic adjustment capabilities of the present EU members. Only if the EU can ensure that the accession candidates have achieved a certain degree of economic and political maturity, will the costs of enlargement be economically manageable and politically acceptable. By setting clear-cut entrance criteria, therefore, the EU can exercise leverage and possibly postpone the accession of new members until they have fulfilled these criteria. This, in turn, will help to overcome potential resistance to reforms of vested interests in the applicant countries and further enhance the quality of their governance structures (Berglöf and Roland 1997).

Table 6.10 displays the differences in institutional progress achieved so far in all transition countries of CEE and the Commonwealth of Independent States (CIS). It supports the hypothesis that the EU has in fact served as an effective outside anchor to transition reforms in most countries of Central Europe. The top performers for improving economic governance structures have been those countries which have the best prospects for early EU membership. A striking feature is the difference in institutional reforms between the CEE countries on the one hand, and the members of the CIS on the other. This may be attributed to differences in historical legacies as well as economic and political conditions at the onset of the transformation process. However, the lack of a vision concerning international integration and of an external anchor to transition reforms is very likely to have made policy and institutional reforms comparatively more difficult in all successor states of the former Soviet Union, except for the Baltic countries where the prospects for EU entry are relatively good. A similar argument may hold for the differences in reform progress between the Visegrád countries and the Balkan countries (except for Slovenia). The differences in reform records between these countries have surely been influenced by the differences in the chances of EU accession (Berglöf and Roland 1997). This hypothesis is further supported by the fact that at the beginning of the systemic transformation in 1989, most of today's top performers faced relatively unfavorable institutional starting conditions. According to the liberalization index computed by de Melo *et al.* (1996) (an indicator measuring structural and institutional reforms),[163] the best institutional starting conditions existed in the successor states of former Yugoslavia, which even outperformed Hungary and Poland. The Baltic states were near the bottom of the country ranking, which includes 26 transition economies in CEE and the CIS, and

Czechoslovakia was even categorized as a completely unreformed economy. All Visegrád countries, however, managed to catch up and surpass the early reform leaders within two years and further promoted reforms vigorously during the 1990s.

To date, most CEE countries have achieved substantial progress in institutional reforms concerning the trade and foreign exchange regime, privatization, and the legal system, while reform progress in areas such as corporate governance, competition policy, and financial markets has been modest or diverse (Table 6.10). Furthermore, Nunberg (1999) found in her cross-country analysis, that the restructuring of the core institutions of government has been moderate and reforms have been slow to materialize even in the Visegrád countries. Both governments and donor agencies have been hesitant in initiating and supporting programs aimed at enhancing administrative efficiency and making public–private cooperation and coordination more effective. More recently, however, especially governments of the most promising candidates for EU entry have begun energetically to address highly politicized problems of administrative reform. Nunberg (1999), for example, reports that public-sector and bureaucratic restructuring were substantially boosted and received high-level political support. Particularly in Poland, this was mainly spurred by the rapid pace of the country's preparations for EU membership. The Polish government clearly recognized that bureaucratic capacity is a critical step towards completing the political and economic agenda of transition and pushed a package of major reform measures through Parliament. This quick action reflected the increasing awareness that the country's hopes of gaining full EU membership actually depend to a large extent on the existence of a modern bureaucracy that is capable of easing the process of adjusting to Western European norms and standards. In Poland, as in other CEE countries, the common desire to return to Europe has helped to overcome the political impasse which had impeded administrative reform in the early stages of transition. As in the area of public-sector reform, the challenge of fulfilling the Copenhagen criteria is also very likely to further boost reforms in other areas in which progress has been limited.

To conclude this section, we will summarize the main points of the preceding arguments. With respect to relaxing *ex ante* political constraints, the vision of EU membership has helped reformers in the early phase of transition to take advantage of the window of opportunity and to make radical reforms acceptable for the population. More important, however, is the prospect of EU accession for overcoming *ex post* constraints. A slowdown of reforms in any given candidate country would incur high economic and political costs because it means the rejection, or at least a postponement, of membership and would hence place the country in a significantly backward position *vis-à-vis* successful candidates. This may be one critical factor that explains why even the return of (former) communists in responsible government positions in several countries has not led to a reversal of reforms.

Eventually, institutional reforms requested by the Copenhagen criteria have enhanced, and will continue to enhance, the credibility of transition policies in the Visegrád countries and other accession candidates. More specifically, governments increase their credibility through institution building by signaling commitment, changing governmental incentives, as well as reducing the scope of discretionary policy making. First, EU integration involves governments signaling their determination to achieve their own goals as well as committing themselves to institutional integration. Secondly, the obligations created by the new institutional arrangements reduce opportunistic behavior and the propensity to arbitrary policy changes. Thirdly, these obligations as well as the potential sanctions imposed for non-compliance alter the incentive structures of governments. The adoption of institutional arrangements that are consistent with EU standards, implies that governments tie their own hands and commit themselves to pursuing sound institutional and economic policies (like maintaining open domestic markets for all economic actors from the EU). This eventually helps to delimit the influence of national vested interest groups (Piazolo 1998). In sum, the Association Agreements as well as the actual negotiations for entry into the EU significantly enhance the credible commitment to policy and institutional reform and make public policies more transparent and predictable. Non-compliance may mean a loss of benefits resulting from the Europe Agreements and potential postponement or even denial of EU membership, as the Slovakian example clearly demonstrates. Finally, increased credibility will further accelerate the pace and the efficacy of reforms, because investors will have a stronger trust in political announcements and adjust accordingly. The EU and prospect of membership in the Union will continue to play a key role as an external anchor to improving the quality of governance further and overcoming *ex post* constraints to structural and institutional reforms, especially at a time when more and more civic associations emerge and vested interests are increasingly better organized and hence able to articulate their opposition to reforms which they fear will mean a loss of rents and privileges. The experiences of the Visegrád countries clearly illustrate that favorable geopolitical factors can reinforce transformation policies (once *ex post* constraints are increasingly binding), help to enhance government capacities, and support the emergence of strong but limited states. Hence, the existence of an external anchor to transition policies can considerably support the emergence of flexible market-enhancing governance structures.[164]

NOTES

1. In this context, see also Campos and Nugent (1999) who find in their empirical study that different institutional characteristics can play prominent roles in enhancing development performance. They observe that in East Asia the quality of the economic bureaucracy was critical for performance, whereas in Latin America the efficacy of the rule of law was the most important factor.

2. Of course, it would be worthwhile to include countries from other regions such as Latin America and sub-Saharan Africa in our analysis. This has been done implicitly in the cross-country regressions to be discussed in Section 6.1. But since we subsequently analyse particular case studies, a broader regional focus would have been beyond the scope of this study, the more so as, for example, in much of sub-Saharan Africa problems of nation-building and ethnic conflicts dominate the governance agenda – problems which are not directly accessible by our governance framework. For specific discussions on governance-related problems in sub-Saharan Africa, see, for example, the contributions in Hýden and Bratton (1992) as well as Wohlmuth (1998); regarding these problems as they concern Latin American countries, see, for example, Burki and Perry (1998) and Santiso (1999).

3. See, however, Reynolds (1983) and Morris and Adelman (1988 and 1989).

4. *Subjective* indicators of institutional quality essentially reflect the perceptions of those analysts who compile the data sets as well as of the respondents to country survey questionnaires. The most widely used subjective indicators have been distilled from surveys of domestic and international investors (Brunetti *et al.* 1997a, b, and c), from the data sets compiled by international consultant firms such as the *Political Risk Group* (see the Internet Webpage: http://www.prsgroup.com), or from nonprofit organizations such as *Freedom House* (see the Internet Webpage: http://www.freedomhouse.org) which continually investigate the business and investment climate of a great variety of countries. Most of the studies listed in Table 6.1 are based on such subjective indicators, in particular on the International Country Risk Guide (ICRG) compiled by the *Political Risk Group*. In contrast, *objective* indicators seek to assess whether or not certain formal rules, regulations, and legal provisions are in place in a given country in order to develop a broad measure concerning the overall institutional quality of a country's economy or polity. La Porta *et al.* (1997a) and Levine (1997), listed in Table 6.1, belong to the relatively few studies that use this type of indicator.

5. They form indicators of 'predictability of rules', 'political stability', 'property rights security', 'reliability of the judiciary', 'lack of corruption', and 'credibility' from respondents' experiences in doing business.

6. Rodrik's country sample includes all HPAEs (except for Hong Kong) and also Japan and the Philippines.

7. In this context, Brunetti, Kisunko, and Weder (1997c) emphasize the problem of insufficient reliability of investment data.

8. Usually, investment as percentage of GDP is taken. From their theoretical approach, per capita values are justified and, instead of GDP, population might also perform well as a proxy for market size.

9. In many cases, the variables are significant at a 1 percent level in either one or both of the two equations.

10. This comes close to the governance clusters in Kaufmann, Kraay, and Zoido-Lobatón (1999).

11. Note that although the diagrams are similar to those presented by Burki and Perry (1998), the figures are not directly comparable due to different country samples.

12. See Annexes 1 and 2 for the definitions of the ICRG indicators as well as for the list of countries included in each regional group. Information on the rating system underlying the ICRG indicators can be found on the Internet Website: http://www.prsgroup.com/icrg/icrg.html.

13. With respect to economic reforms in LAC and East Asia since the 1980s, see Burki and Perry (1998) and World Bank (1993), respectively.

14. Regarding the growth performance of the East Asian countries see Table 6.2 and Figure 6.22.

15. Note that for reasons of clarity, only a few countries are considered in Figure 6.8, the transformation policies of most of which are also explicitly discussed in the subsequent sections of this study.

16. For a comprehensive discussion of the economic reforms in the USSR under Gorbachev and in Russia under Yeltsin during its first phase of transition, see Ahrens (1994).

17. Between 1989 and 1998, Russian GDP fell by 45 percent in real terms. Life expectancy decreased from 69.2 to 66.9 years; see EBRD (1999) and also Table 6.9.

18. Regarding the growth records of transition countries see Table 6.9, and for a documentation of structural reform efforts in transition economies, see EBRD (1999 and 2001).

19. Note in this context that these institutional indicators reflect only partially the institutional requirements which must be fulfilled to become eligible for EU membership. In several other respects, the EU candidates, although they have experienced improvements over time, still show considerable deficiencies; see EBRD (1999 and 2001) as well as Table 6.10.

20. The rule-of-law index reflects the soundness of political institutions, the strength of the court system, and the willingness of individuals to accept the established institutions to make and implement laws and adjudicate disputes; for the definition of the other institutional variables, see Annex 2.

21. For a similar conclusion see Campos and Nugent (1999).

22. See Annex 2 for the definitions of the ICRG indicators.

23. This problem arises with respect to virtually all available data sets including those provided by Freedom House or distilled from the ICRG or BERI.

24. For a comprehensive and instructive discussion of problems related to empirical analyses of the relationship between institutions and economic performance, see, for example, Dethier (1999a), Klitgaard (1994), and Fedderke and Klitgaard (1998).

25. In this context, see, for example, the instructive studies by Morris and Adelman (1988) and Lindenberg (1993).

26. The poorly performing economies in East Asia include Cambodia, Laos, Mongolia, Myanmar, North Korea, the Philippines, and Vietnam. Although Vietnam (since 1986) and more recently also the Philippines have entered a promising track, their growth records must yet prove to be sustainable.

27. A direct comparison of China with the HPAEs is problematic due to its different ownership structures, mechanisms of corporate and overall governance, and methods of policy making that guide market development.

28 The following arguments in this and the next two subsections essentially draw on Ahrens (1998a), from which some parts of these subsections are reprinted with permission from Elsevier Science.

29. Note that foreign trade policies as well as the openness to FDI significantly varied across countries: Hong Kong established a *laissez-faire* trade regime and had virtually no restrictions on FDI. In contrast, trade liberalization was, for example, limited in South Korea and Taiwan until the 1980s, where governments sought actively to foster exports and established significant restrictions on imports. In both countries, FDI has been heavily restricted or subject to government control (Rodrik 1996).

30. Economic policy making in Hong Kong came relatively close to the ideal of *laissez-faire*, although there was substantial intervention in the housing market; see Root (1996).

31. See, for example, Pack and Westphal (1986), Amsden (1989), Wade (1990), Johnson (1982), Lall (1995), Rodrik (1995), and Aoki *et al.* (1997a). For a review of the controversy between neoclassical and revisionist explanations of the East Asian Miracle, see Baer *et al.* (1999).

32. To be sure, a number of policy mistakes occurred and not all government interventions materialized as expected. But governments were relatively well prepared to correct failures and to revise policies. For example, both the Malaysian and the South Korean governments

reduced the promotion of chemical as well as heavy industries when rising fiscal costs and financial-sector tensions threatened to undermine macroeconomic stability; Indonesian authorities relinquished interest rate and capital markets controls when they turned out to be ineffective; and Singaporean wage policy gradually shifted from one repressing wages, to one fostering rapid wage increases, to one that coordinates wage growth with productivity increases; see World Bank (1993) which discusses the HPAE governments' pragmatic flexibility in policy making at some length.

33. See Stiglitz (1996) and the literature referred to therein.
34. Regarding a more detailed analysis of the foregoing arguments see Stiglitz (1996) and Rodrik (1995).
35. See Aoki *et al.* (1997b), who also present several instructive examples of how governments can improve private sector coordination.
36. See Stiglitz and Uy (1996) as well as Aoki *et al.* (1997a) for a theoretical analysis and more examples of contingent rents. Note, however, that contingent rents as well as other interventionist measures require a competent and disciplined bureaucracy. Also, the government must be able credibly to precommit to its policy principle not to collude with individual private actors; regarding these aspects see Section 6.2.2.
37. See Campos and Root (1996) and the contributions in Aoki *et al.* (1997a). For a discussion of how these policy instruments relate to the governance frameworks in the HPAEs, see Ahrens (2002).
38. See Aoki *et al.* (1997b); this approach concedes, however, that the boundary for state activism may depend on a country's level of development. At an early stage of development, the number of intermediating organizations is limited, capabilities of private enterprises are modest, and the efficiency of resource allocation through markets may be hampered by insufficient property rights and poor market integration. Under these conditions, there is considerable scope for government activism. During the course of development, less government intervention is necessary and desirable, although it is not expected to disappear completely.
39. See, for example, World Bank (1993), Evans (1995), Root (1996), and Campos and Root (1996).
40. The change in inequity was much lower in Korea and Taiwan, which started their growth process with highly equal distributions of income; see World Bank (1993).
41. See World Bank (1993); poverty rates, in the region as a whole, dropped from approximately 60 percent in 1975 to some 20 percent in 1995 (Furman and Stiglitz 1998).
42. For a more detailed discussion of these points see Rodrik (1996) and Aoki *et al.* (1997a).
43. South Korea was threatened by North Korea, Taiwan by mainland China, and Thailand by North Vietnam as well as Cambodia. Indonesia, Malaysia, Singapore, and Thailand had to face internal insurgencies of communist forces, and the former two countries additionally had to cope with problems resulting from ethnic diversity; see Campos and Root (1996) and the references therein.
44. Of course, it makes a difference whether or not one finds shared growth a desirable development strategy and whether or not political authorities have the incentives and the means to implement such a strategy. While in the HPAEs, shared growth was widely perceived as being critical for the political survival of governments, this was not the case in the Philippines, where no government, for example, was capable of implementing an effective land reform. The fact that Philippine authorities saw no need to take politically difficult decisions which would have been required by a shared-growth strategy, has been attributed to historical circumstances and especially to the financial and military support by the United States. In order to maintain its two largest military bases outside the US, the United States government had a great interest in supporting the local Philippine elite, the wealth of which had been traditionally based on the ownership of land. Therefore, Philippine governments could reliably count on the US to help to combat potential communist insurgencies and hence neglect redistribution policies; see Campos and Root (1996) and more specifically Karnow (1990).

45. The importance of government intervention in basic education is reconfirmed by the experiences of Thailand. Since Thai authorities had neglected post-primary education, income distribution significantly deteriorated during the 1980s when economic activity gradually became more skill intensive; see Campos and Root (1996).

46. While the importance of the SME sector for the Taiwanese economy has been widely acknowledged, in Japan SMEs have also played a significant role in manufacturing thus making the widespread subcontracting system linking the large trading houses and enterprises with the small-scale industry more effective. Even in South Korea, the industrial structure of which has been dominated by the *chaebols*, the SME sector started to grow quickly in the 1980s not least as a result of financial public support programs; see Itoh and Urata (1994), Kim and Nugent (1994), and Campos and Root (1996).

47. For South Korea, see, for example, the assessment by Adelman and Robinson (1978).

48. In addition, it must be noted that authorities in Taiwan, Singapore, South Korea, and Japan politically disabled labor by establishing state-controlled unions preventing the labor force from effective lobbying, striking, and other disruptive activities and meaning that companies demanded fewer government subsidies. Nevertheless, the economic needs of labor were essentially met as documented by the average increase in real earnings, which rose several times faster in East Asia than in South Asia or Latin America. Also, the example of Singapore documents that, despite politically-controlled trade unions, the labor force was not excluded from political processes, but – in order to maintain industrial peace – was institutionally incorporated into wage bargaining; see World Bank (1993), Campos and Root (1996), and Root (1996), as well as the literature referred to by these authors, for instructive analyses of how these wealth-sharing mechanisms actually worked in the HPAEs.

49. Rent-seeking is reduced, because shared growth is based on a broad social consensus. If a government relies on the support of narrow interests, it is hardly able to reject the demand of pressure groups. In the case of a government whose legitimacy is broadly based, the gains from lobbying are expected to be lower, because authorities' power does not crucially depend on the support of interest groups. Decreasing lobbying makes more resources available for investment and reduces the uncertainty of political decisions.

50. Campos and Root (1996: 138–9); with respect to the empirical evidence of the actual effects of this Weberian-type bureaucracy on economic growth see ibid.

51. A professional bureaucracy that is characterized by internal promotion instead of political appointments allows for a lengthening of the time period which public officials are willing to wait before the benefits of their policies are realized. This increases the share of public resources devoted to long-term investment projects such as infrastructure and eventually leads to higher economic growth (Evans and Rauch 1995). Also, note that in all HPAEs the bureaucracy was given primacy over legislature with respect to drafting laws. The latter had simply to approve the laws that the former prepares. Thus, the administration considerably controlled the agenda and was able to minimize political pressure (World Bank 1993).

52. Additionally, as mentioned earlier in Chapter 5, Section 5.3.5, informal networks are indispensable to the administration's coherence and autonomy. In most HPAEs, impersonal institutional relations reinforced by informal peer relations within the bureaucratic elite promoted a corporate identity that could not emerge through meritocracy alone (Evans 1992).

53. Of course, performance criteria are not the only mechanism that determines professional promotion; seniority still counts, especially in Japan and South Korea.

54. The recruitment systems applied in Taiwan and Malaysia are similar to those institutionalized in South Korea and Japan, but entry exams are less stringent. In Taiwan, this is partly offset by recruiting graduates from leading universities and providing them with fixed-term appointments (Wade 1990). In Malaysia, exams have been difficult, but performance criteria are somehow attenuated due to affirmative action requirements favoring the ethnic Malays.

55. Reprinted with permission by the Brookings Institution Press. The following examples illustrate how political power vested in persons can be used to reform bureaucratic

structures effectively and to craft new, stable institutional arrangements. Of course, these examples do not provide a blueprint that can, or should, be easily emulated by governments elsewhere, the more so as all measures described were realized under authoritarian regimes. What these cases, however, document is that in the absence of stable and transparent political institutions, individual policy makers can and possibly must play a critical role in guiding reforms. But the more recent experiences of these countries also show (especially Indonesia's crisis at the end of the Suharto era) that this kind of personalized policy making can backfire unless political authorities are capable of managing the transition from rule by political authority vested in persons to rule by impersonal institutions.

56. The extent of corruption has been very different across the HPAEs. While governments in Singapore and Hong Kong have been very successful in fighting extra-legal activities of bureaucrats through anti-corruption agencies, other countries, especially Indonesia, Thailand, and South Korea, have largely failed in reducing corruptive practices. In the most recent corruption ranking by Transparency International, ranging from 0 (maximum corruption) to 10 (no corruption), Singapore and Hong Kong achieved values of 9.1 and 7.7, respectively, while Indonesia and Thailand scored 1.7 and 3.2, respectively. In general, however, the rankings achieved by the HPAEs are still significantly higher than those of most other LDCs in Latin America, sub-Saharan Africa, and Eastern Europe; see Transparency International (1999).

57. With regard to the preceding remarks see the more detailed considerations in Campos and Root (1996).

58. For a theoretical and empirical analysis of how information problems may impede economic growth and development see Klitgaard (1991).

59. In this respect, also recall the use of contingent rents, discussed earlier, which induced competition among Schumpeterian entrepreneurs which would not have evolved without government intervention. With respect to examples of how governments provided and received information and implemented specific sectoral interventions (for example, regarding the Korean automobile, shipbuilding, or steel industries) see the instructive analyses of Wade (1990) and Amsden (1989).

60. See Stiglitz (1996), Campos and Root (1996), and World Bank (1993).

61. Note that once governments allow such deliberation councils to permeate the economy, the incentives of political authorities to act opportunistically or to renege on agreements *ex post* will be weak. This is because the value of deliberation councils will be undermined for *all* business and social groups, if a government unilaterally imposes unwarranted pressure on *any* sector or industry. Such behavior would threaten the whole system of consultative and cooperative decision-making. Moreover, a unilateral termination of these cooperation devices on the part of the government would increase the transaction costs of policy making and possibly retard economic growth, something that in turn might undermine government's legitimacy (Root 1998a).

62. Note that the accountability of the government has also been enhanced by other institutions; in South Korea, for example, the relatively independent media and civil society organizations in association with student movements that represented *social* interests played an important role in this regard.

63. Note in this context that in Taiwan and Indonesia governments did not create formal deliberation councils for the coordination of public and private sector activities. Due to historical, ethnic, and socio-cultural circumstances, they rather relied on indirect and informal mechanisms in order to include politically marginal groups (the native Taiwanese in Taiwan and the Chinese business elite in Indonesia) in their shared-growth strategy. Particularly in Indonesia, political factors and the influence of the military also played an essential role in the reliance on rather informal and opaque mechanisms guiding public–private relations; see Sautter (1990), Wade (1990), and Root (1996).

64. Note, however, that such embeddedness increases state capacity at the initial stages of development, but later it may become an impediment to growth (Evans 1992). This, in fact, has caused serious problems in recent policy making in the HPAEs; especially in South Korea.

65. For comprehensive analyses and controversial discussions of the causes of the Asian Crisis, policy implications, and the actual responses of the IMF and governments of crisis-affected countries see, for example, Goldstein (1998), IMF (1998a and b), Feldstein (1998), Furman and Stiglitz (1998), Radelet and Sachs (1998a and b), Wade (1998 and 1999), ADB (1999a and b), and Yoshimoto and Ohno (1999). Regarding political aspects associated with the crisis, see Haggard (2000) and the contributions in Pempel (1999b). The probably most comprehensive and detailed chronology of the Asian crisis as well as numerous further references can be found on Roubini's *Asian Crisis Homepage* on the Internet at: http://www.stern.nyu.edu/globalmacro/.

66. For a more detailed discussion of these warning indicators see Hesse and Auria (1998) and Bosworth and Collins (1999).

67. For example, in Thailand the ratio of bank credits to GDP increased from 100 percent in 1995 to 122 percent in 1996. The development in Hong Kong, Malaysia, the Philippines, and South Korea was similarly dynamic (Hesse and Auria 1998).

68. See 'Asia's Economic Crisis. How Far is Down', *The Economist*, 15 November, 1997.

69. Note that debt-to-equity ratios have been relatively high in these countries due to the underdevelopment of capital and securities markets. This also helps to explain the rapid expansion of the ratio of broad money (M2) to GDP; see IMF (1998b).

70. This phrase is attributed to Alan Greenspan, quoted in 'Of Bears and Tigers', *Financial Times*, 29 October, 1997.

71. Regarding the role of the IMF in the Indonesian crisis, see, for example, Radelet (1998) and Radelet and Sachs (1998b).

72. Alan Greenspan put it most eloquently in a testimony to the Foreign Relations committee of the US Senate in February 1998 by stating: 'What we have here is a very dramatic event towards a consensus of the type of market system which *we have in this country*' (quoted in Wade 1998: 1536; original italics).

73. Large black economies are said to have emerged, not because of high taxes, but due to excessive red tape and corruption.

74. Note, however, that this hypothesis is still actively debated; for an overview of the controversy, see Felipe (1999).

75. See Emmerson (1998), Wade (1998), and Baer *et al.* (1999). Note that while the economic problems relating to the large conglomerates, for example, in South Korea did not trigger the crisis, they certainly aggravated the financial troubles. Due to the large variety of essentially unconnected businesses in which the *chaebols* have been involved, they were highly leveraged after the eruption of the crisis. When the country was getting into turmoil, these conglomerates were blamed for suppressing the entrepreneurship which results from having numerous small competitors (Baer *et al.* 1999).

76. Quoted in Wade (1998: 1537)

77. 'How to fix the Asian economies', *New York Times*, 31 October, 1997.

78. Note in this context that, for example, actual growth in South Korea in 1999 even exceeded the most optimistic forecasts. As the Bank of Korea reported on 22 March, 2000, GDP growth accounted for 10.7 percent and was boosted not only by rising exports but also by strong domestic demand. This development signals the Korean economy's full recovery from the previous severe recession; see 'Korea's GDP surged 10.7% in 1999', *The Korea Herald*, 23 March, 2000.

79. The following arguments essentially draw on, and are further elaborated in, World Bank (1993), Hesse and Auria (1998), Krugman (1998), Baer *et al.* (1999), Bosworth and Collins (1999), Corsetti *et al.* (1999), and Yoshimoto and Ohno (1999).

80. The IMF's motivation to do so was explained by Jagdish Bhagwati, a strong adherent of free trade. When he was asked why the Fund sought to open up financial markets, he responded: 'Wall Street has become a very powerful influence in terms of seeking markets everywhere. Morgan Stanley and all these gigantic firms want to be able to get into other markets and essentially see capital account convertibility as what will enable them to operate everywhere (...) nowadays there is a "Wall Street-Treasury complex" because Secretaries of State like Rubin come from Wall Street. (...) So today, Wall Street views are

very dominant in terms of the kind of world you want to see. They want the ability to take capital in and out freely. It also ties into the IMF's own desires, which is to act as a lender of last resort. They see themselves as the apex body which will manage this whole system. So the IMF finally gets a role for itself, which is underpinned by maintaining complete freedom on the capital account' (quoted in Wade (1998: 1546)).

81. The ADB estimates that GDP growth in Vietnam was 4.4 percent in 1998 and 4.3 percent in the first half of 1999. China's growth rates are estimated at 7.8 and 7.0 percent in 1998 and 1999, respectively; see the most recent ADB *Country Assistance Plans* of both countries available on the Internet Website: http://www.adb.org/Work/Country/Assistance Plans/caps.asp.

82. The term *federalism* denotes a state that is broken up into several provinces (and the provinces possibly into a number of other lower-level jurisdictions). In general, political powers are divided between the various levels of government. While some powers may be shared between sub-national jurisdictions and the national government, each lower-level entity is able to make distinct decisions autonomously; see Riker (1964).

83. The following considerations are essentially based on Weingast (1995), and Qian and Weingast (1996 and 1997b).

84. An overview of the most important arguments in this realm has been provided by Rubinfeld (1987).

85. See Oates (1972) for the classic argument. Note, however, that the economic theories of federalism have not adequately addressed some critical, governance-related problems. As has been argued by political economists and political scientists, for example, the problems relating to local corruption have usually been ignored, and the often (implicitly) made assumption of governments being benevolent does not reflect reality (Rose-Ackerman 1978 and Buchanan 1995).

86. Important works in this strand of the literature include McKinnon (1995), Montinola *et al.* (1995), Weingast (1995), Bednar *et al.* (1996), Qian and Weingast (1996 and 1997b), Bednar (1997), and Figueiredo and Weingast (1998).

87. See Weingast (1995) and Montinola *et al.* (1995).

88. Note that C5 does not *a priori* preclude revenue sharing mechanisms among different (levels of) government(s). In fact, hard budget constraints are conceived to limit in a transparent way the channels through which revenues are to be shared. Particularly, these constraints avoid an open-ended subsidization of lower governments that show an increasingly poor performance, and they effectively limit the access of these lower governments to the capital market and loans from the central bank.

89. For a detailed analysis see McKinnon (1995).

90. Regarding the following considerations see Montinola *et al.* (1995) and the classical work of Oates (1972). An overview of the economic benefits of federalism is provided by Rubinfeld (1987).

91. Another institutional arrangement to reduce governmental arbitrariness in legislation is proposed in Hayek (1979). In a parliamentary system, in which the horizontal separation of powers is *de facto* not established, because the executive and the legislature are based on the same political majority, the legislature is strongly influenced by vested interests. Hayek's radical statement suggests a two-chamber system including a genuine legislature and a governmental assembly. While the latter would be responsible for public law and mediate group interests, the former – elected independently and composed of different individuals – would be responsible for legislation proper which is not to be governed by special interests 'but by opinion, i.e. by views about what *kind* of action is right or wrong – not as an instrument for the achievement of particular ends but as a permanent rule and irrespective of the effect on particular individuals or groups' (p. 112; original italics). Hence, the legislature would be capable of limiting a strong government and help to reduce rent-seeking.

92. Regarding this point, see the instructive study by Krugman (1991).

93. With respect to the preceding arguments, see Parikh and Weingast (1997). Note, however, that the fourth aspect concerning sub-national governance structures has been neglected by

the theory of MPF. Ineffective governance at the lower level, however, may seriously impede economic and social development not only in the respective jurisdiction but in the whole federal system, through gradual negative spill-over effects; this problem will be addressed at the end of this section.

94. Studies that explicitly analyse the institutional foundations of economic performance in China include, for example, Burns (1993), Qian and Xu (1993), Shirk (1993), Montinola *et al.* (1995), Lau (1997), Qian and Weingast (1997a), Dethier (1999b), Qian (1999), and Lau *et al.* (2000).

95. While it was essentially the interplay of these measures that accounted for successful economic reforms and rapid growth, this study explicitly addresses only the aspect of decentralization because of its overwhelming importance for governance. For a knowledgeable discussion of the overall reform process in China, with a particular emphasis on institutional reforms, see Qian (1999).

96. Note that the Chinese economy had never been as centralized as the economy of the former Soviet Union. Already under Mao's rule, a number of decentralization measures had been conducted that mainly concerned the delegation of SOEs to lower governments and the involvement of local political units in central-planning procedures; for a detailed account of these measures, see Qian and Weingast (1996). What distinguished the decentralization that started in 1979 from previous efforts is that it also substantially transferred authority to lower governments as well as to enterprises and households and that it was accompanied by market-oriented policies and an opening up of the economy.

97. See Qian and Weingast (1996), Qian (1999), and Lin and Liu (2000). Regarding the latter point, note that foreign investment increased from US$ 4.5 billion in 1985 to US$ 19.2 billion in 1992 and that the share that was administered by provincial governments increased from 35 to 68 percent during the same period (Montinola *et al.* 1995).

98. For details of the revenue-sharing scheme, see Montinola *et al.* (1995). Moreover, note that while the extra-budgetary funds clearly reduce the transparency of the fiscal system, during transition they played a critical role, because they made local governments more autonomous and self-reliant. With respect to further modifications of the 1980s reforms, see Qian and Weingast (1996) and Lin and Liu (2000). The latter study as well as an investigation by Jin *et al.* (1999) empirically support the thesis that strong fiscal incentives resulting from political decentralization have fostered economic growth in sub-national jurisdictions.

99. See Byrd and Qingsong (1990) and Qian and Weingast (1997a). Note that these limits on governments and enterprises are considerably weaker at higher levels of government which explains the significant performance differentials of TVEs and SOEs, although both types of enterprises are considered as so-called public enterprises (Qian and Weingast 1996 and 1997a).

100. For more details regarding the following arguments, see Montinola *et al.* (1995) and Qian and Weingast (1996).

101. Note that this does not imply a reduction in income inequality. In fact, inequality across regions is reported to have been increased in the course of decentralization *inter alia* due to the failure of the central government to ensure a common market. Inequalities within regions, however, have been significantly reduced; see Montinola *et al* (1995).

102. See, for example, Lau *et al.* (1997 and 2000). Note that a single-track or big-bang liberalization as it was essentially pursued in CEE including Russia can lead to efficiency but cannot avoid a transformational recession due to persisting market imperfections (Kornai 1994, Li 1999, and Roland and Verdier 1999).

103. For a detailed discussion of the dual-track approach, see Lau *et al.* (2000).

104. Protectionist measures have been mainly undertaken to restrict free trade of high profit-margin manufacturing goods and raw materials that are in short supply (Montinola *et al.* 1995).

105. In general, this is because path dependence matters in institution building, and, more specifically, this is because new institutions that remove actual distortions in one area, may nevertheless prove to be counterproductive if other distortions persist.

106. See Qian (1999) for an instructive and comprehensive discussion of the most recent reform steps. With regard to the benefits and drawbacks of administrative reforms, see Burns (1993).
107. See Ahrens (1997). An overview and an evaluation of the Indian economic reforms are given in ADB (1999c), World Bank (1995c), and Bhagwati (1993).
108. In this section, the term *state* is used for the whole of public authorities, while the term *State* refers to the Indian federation's constituent units.
109. Of course, India's central government is powerful in the sense that it is able to impose crippling regulations on the private sector, to grant favors to special interest groups, or to compromise the independence of State governments. However, it is weak in the sense that it is not insulated from the pressures of vested interests and not capable of conducting and implementing coherent developmental policies, which benefit the economy as a whole.
110. See Bhagwati (1993). Also, the fact that India has recently attracted considerable inflows of foreign capital and direct foreign investment indicates that reforms are regarded as credible by international investors.
111. With respect to the separation of powers and the problem of political accountability in parliamentary systems see Persson *et al.* (1997) as well as Przeworski (1995).
112. See, for example, Varshney (1993) and the contributions in Kohli (1988).
113. See 'India's begrudging voters', *Economist*, October 9, 1999 and 'India. A tiger or a dodo?', *Economist*, 4 December, 1999 as well as the survey of India's economy in *The Economist*, 4 March, 2000.
114. See 'India's Election. Greater Expectations', *Economist*, 4 September, 1999.
115. See 'All Change in India', *Economist*, 18 May, 1996.
116. See 'India. A tiger or a dodo?', *Economist*, 4 December, 1999.
117. A well-known example of how policy reform can be contested politically when it lacks a secure institutional foundation is the State government's reluctance in Maharashta to accept a business deal with Enron. The previous government, which had consummated the deal, introduced liberal economic reforms but did not create necessary institutions and tender procedures to ensure transparent and accountable outcomes. This aroused the suspicions of the political opposition even in the absence of evident malfeasance by public officials (Root 1998b).
118. The following arguments essentially draw on Ahrens (1997).
119. See Pedersen (1992). Increasing demands by lower castes for guaranteed quotas concerning government jobs encountered strong resistance from higher castes indicating the difficulty in eliminating caste-specific privileges in India; see Andersen (1995).
120. According to a corruption ranking by Transparency International (1999), India achieved a value of 2.9 on a scale from 0 to 10, placing the country close to the bottom of the ranking that comprised 99 developing and industrial countries. Regarding an instructive analysis of corruption in India see Root (1998b).
121. See, for example, Evans (1995) and ADB (1999c).
122. See, for example, Bardhan (1995) and Evans (1995).
123. See Bardhan (1995). The problem of how to reinforce accountability at the regional and local level will be discussed in greater detail below.
124. See World Bank (1995c). Regarding the difference in status between the Union Territories and the States see Basu (1988).
125. See Krishnaswamy *et al.* (1992), World Bank (1995c), and Shah (1994).
126. Mehta (1997), for example, reports that the government of Madhya Pradesh, unable to resist populist pressures, recently decided to provide free electricity to large parts of its rural population.
127. See Williamson (1990) as well as Chapter 2 of this study.
128. See, for example, Stiglitz (1999 and 2000), North (1995a and b), Poznanski (1995), Amsden et al. (1994), and Murrell (1991).
129. The following arguments are essentially based on Beyme (1994), Voigt and Kiwit (1995), Ahrens (1998b), and Merkel (1999).
130. The term is due to Kornai (1994: 39).

131. See DIW *et al.* (1999), Thanner (1999), and Ahrens (1998b).
132. For a more detailed discussion, see EBRD (1999), DIW *et al.* (1999), and Götz (2000).
133. According to a recent estimate of a Russian author, the bureaucracy employs approximately 18 million people which corresponds to roughly 25 percent of the total labor force. Real and financial assets that are used or controlled by the administration are estimated to account for some 13 billion US$ (Khaitun 2000).
134. It would be beyond the scope of this study to discuss comprehensively the current bottlenecks of, and the feasible road to, administrative reform in Russia; for a well-informed and instructive discussion of these issues, see Nunberg (1999) and Kralinski (1999).
135. See Ahrens (1998b) as well as 'Stones from the sticks?', *Economist*, 31 August, 1996.
136. The Russian constitution in full-text is available on the Internet at: http://www.departments.bucknell.edu/russian/const/constit.html.
137. For more details see Ordeshook (1995).
138 The following arguments essentially draw on Ahrens (1997).
139. Regarding these potential dangers of decentralization see the instructive discussions in Bardhan (1997a) and Prud'homme (1995).
140. Civil service reform may be easier at sub-national levels, because the executive is directly responsive to constituents, and, given a system of transparent decision making, residents and businesses can more easily implement effective monitoring devices.
141. See, for example, Olson (1969), Oates (1972), and Tiebout (1956) as well as the excellent survey by Rubinfeld (1987).
142. See an overview in Shah (1994).
143. Decentralizing responsibilities can be supported by strengthening local institutional capacities. Higher-level governments can offer training programs and technical assistance, facilitate staff transfers, provide guidance on management issues and organizational structure.
144. Particularly in diversified and large economies, regional and local fiscal autonomy can be instrumental in mobilizing revenues from regional and local sources; see Shah (1994).
145. See Shah (1994), Montinola *et al.* (1995), and McKinnon (1995). In this context, for example, India's intergovernmental transfer system has to be reduced to a *rudimentary* system of *conditional* transfers. This is necessary to ensure *minimum standards* of public services across the country and to support backward regions. Minimum standards (especially for social services and infrastructure) are also necessary for preserving a common market; see Shah (1994).
146. In this regard, see Knack and Keefer (1997a) who show in their cross-country investigation that formal institutional rules which constrain authorities from acting arbitrarily are based on the development of trust and cooperative norms.
147. PMPF also offers an appropriate institutional framework to deal with the problem of inefficient SOEs. If large-scale privatization is limited due to underdeveloped capital markets, SOEs could be made more efficient by subordinating them to the exclusive jurisdiction of sub-national authorities following the example of China's Township-and-Village Enterprises; see Qian and Weingast (1997a).
148. Experiences of the World Bank confirm the benefits of participation, which have been found in LDCs (including India) to be an efficient means to promote the success of projects and policies economically, socially, and environmentally; see World Bank (1992). An example where embedded autonomy may also work in a large, heterogeneous, and conflict-ridden country is given by Kerala, an Indian State, where social mobilization and participation are intense and social welfare standards largely exceed those of the rest of India though per-capita income is significantly lower than the country's average. In Kerala, participation and administrative State capacity helped to construct institutions which implied highly consensual and effective social policies. This case shows that successful embeddedness is not restricted to state–business relations and reinforces the notion that successful embeddedness implies encompassing participation.
149. For a detailed discussion of participation and local empowerment see Streeten (1997).

150. The term *Visegrád countries* comes from a declaration signed by the leaders of Czechoslovakia, Hungary, and Poland in Visegrád (a Hungarian city) in early 1991. The declaration included statements concerning a potentially closer economic and political cooperation, the relations with the USSR, and common efforts to join West European organizations. While the summit's declaration was rather vague with respect to the first two issues, it was most explicit and determined regarding external economic and political relations. Motivated by each country's aspirations to accede to Western organizations, the main idea was to cooperate regionally in order to raise their bargaining power in negotiations with the European Communities and NATO; for a detailed discussion of the Visegrád declaration and subsequent political and economic developments, see Hoen (1998).

151. In Poland, *Solidarnosc* were able to win almost all freely elected mandates in both the Sejm and the Senate in 1989; in Hungary and Czechoslovakia, the old communist parties won less than 15 percent of the votes in the first free elections; see Bönker (1995).

152. In this context, Poland was an important exception. But *Solidarnosc* was initially a key player in the new government.

153. Comprehensive discussions of the economic reforms in the Visegrád countries can be found in Balcerowicz (1994), Balcerowicz *et al.* (1997), Zecchini (1997), Hoen (1998), and EBRD (1999).

154. For example, if *S* were located farther right, this would represent a delay in stabilizing the macro-economy as in Russia.

155. See Williamson (1994) for a discussion of the role of *technopols* in the design and implementation of policy reforms in LDCs and PSCs.

156. The following stocktaking of the politico-institutional conditions in the Visegrád countries essentially draws on Bönker (1995), Hoen (1998), Nunberg (1999), Schneider (1999), and Lang (2000).

157. UNDP (1997: 1). This study provides a comprehensive stocktaking of institutional and political reforms that have been undertaken in the transition countries in the 1990s.

158. See, for example, Hoen (1998) and the contributions in Zecchini (1997).

159. Aside from the Visegrád countries, Association Agreements were endorsed with Bulgaria (1993), Estonia (1995), Latvia (1995), Lithuania (1995), Romania (1993), and Slovenia (1996). The most important short-term component of these bilateral agreements is the establishment of a free-trade area between the EU and the respective associated country. In the course of the 1990s, all of these countries have officially applied for EU membership.

160 Due to the progress of political and institutional reforms after the 1998 parliamentary elections, the EU actually started membership negotiations with the Slovak government at the end of 1999.

161. With respect to the potential benefits and costs of EU membership from the viewpoint of the candidate countries, see Wagener and Fritz (1998) as well as Inotai (1999).

162. Of course, the EU will not be able to afford a maintenance of the current system of transfers. But even after a reform of the Union's Common Agricultural Policy and its structural funds, new members from CEE will be eligible for considerable transfer payments.

163. This liberalization index is a weighted average of an economy's liberalization in the areas of internal and external markets and of private sector development. It was computed for the period 1989–1994 and is somewhat less comprehensive than the EBRD's transition indicators which are used in Table 6.10. Unfortunately, the latter are only available as of 1994.

164. Note that the estimated growth bonuses from further institutional and policy reforms are substantial. Piazolo (1998) estimates that a complete adoption of the *acquis communautaire* will yield a static growth bonus accounting for 9 percent of GDP in the advanced candidate countries. An additional dynamic bonus resulting from adjustments in the countries' capital stocks may account for another 18 percent of GDP. Even if these estimates are very rough approximations, they may serve to strongly reinforce the efforts of these countries to fulfill the Copenhagen criteria as soon as possible and to eventually join the EU.

7. Rethinking effective governance: politico-institutional structures and economic development in comparative perspective

Today, it is not a spectacular or path breaking deduction to conclude that institutions matter. Due to the theoretical insights provided by the NIE and the NPE and numerous disappointing experiences with policy reforms in LDCs and PSCs, the importance of formal and informal institutions for effective economic policy making and development has been widely acknowledged among scholars of economic development and transition, development practitioners, policy makers, and international organizations. Especially since the beginning of the 1990s, the re-discovery of institutions meant that almost no speech on economic reform could be held, no policy paper written without a fashionable reference to the importance of institution building. Obviously, it has become particularly obligatory to emphasize the need to strengthen institutional arrangements which are critical for establishing effective rule-of-law systems, sound regulatory frameworks, as well as improving education and health care for the poor. Unfortunately, however, only a small number of these papers and speeches offer useful pointers on how these institutional reforms can be implemented, and an even smaller number of publications and statements have analysed the politico-institutional underpinnings of such reforms.

This study has sought to help overcome this deficiency by providing theoretical insights and empirical evidence regarding institutional change that may assist in the formulation, implementation, and enforcement of policy and institutional reforms in LDCs and PSCs. In Part I, we argued that, especially due to collective action problems, efficient institutional change that benefits society at large will rarely emerge if it is left to market forces. The state has been and remains a central actor which is needed to initiate, foster, and safeguard the emergence of formal economic and political institutions. State involvement, however, is no panacea. Political markets are usually even more inefficient than economic ones. Nevertheless, reforms will only be successful if they are based on a secure politico-institutional foundation that enhances the adaptive efficiency of both the polity and the economy. Thus the arguments in Part I laid the groundwork for developing a broad conceptual approach that focuses on the questions of what are the constituting principles and components of such a foundation and how it can be developed. Subsequently, Part II introduced the notion of flexible market-enhancing governance structures (MEGS). This is a useful analytical approach that helps to identify and fulfill critical institutional and political preconditions for successful economic reforms. The conceptual map presented in Part II is a comprehensive framework for assessing the factors that affect the capacity and the capability of governments to undertake reforms effectively. The subsequently discussed case studies indicate that this framework is a useful tool for sorting out where the most binding governance-related constraints and, maybe more important, the most promising starting points are for creating more capable states. They also indicate that both constraints to, and institutions that support, effective governance are interrelated within countries and vary considerably among countries and over time. As a result of these considerations, the developed governance concept and the case studies have helped to answer the leading question of this study, namely what are the institutional mechanisms that create a political system where market-oriented economic reforms and hence a viable market economy are stable policy choices. The major findings of the preceding chapters have been that

- the postulate for a minimal state common to both neoclassical theory and the original Washington Consensus is misleading and fails to recognize that the state and its political institutions are integral parts of the economy which, after all, not only determine the existence and efficacy of numerous economic institutions such as private property rights, but also the design and effectiveness of development strategies and policy reforms. In other words: government interventions are not only necessary to overcome market and coordination failures and to enhance the proper functioning of markets. Government action is also indispensable to improve the quality of governance, which is defined as the capacity of a country's institutional matrix to implement and enforce public policies and to improve private-sector coordination;

- a MEGS represents one particular type of governance structure that shows the essential characteristics that enhance the credibility of commitments made by political and economic actors and especially by government members and agencies. The four dimensions of governance (accountability, participation, predictability, and transparency) can be seen as necessary preconditions for sound development management, as measured in terms of the formulation, implementation, and enforcement of policies that support and complement private sector activities and enhance the adaptive efficiency of the political and economic order. The better these principles are implemented the stronger the probability of effective governance;

• there are basically four factors which together have a positive impact on the core dimensions of governance and hence reinforce the credibility of political commitments and constitute a MEGS: (1) enhancing the strength of governments to protect property rights, enforce contracts, and limit the influence of vested interests; (2) posing limits on government strength in order to reduce arbitrary and discretionary governmental behavior. If no institutional safeguards are in place that hinder policy makers from altering rights, laws, and regulations at will and from undertaking confiscatory policies, it is hardly conceivable that credible commitments could be made to the private sector; (3) capacity building (including institution building, organizational reforms, and human resource development) in order to create the institutional means necessary to implement and enforce political decisions, public policies, and regulations; and (4) establishing formal economic institutions that constitute a functioning market economy;

• the fifth component that shapes the quality of governance in a given country relates to informal institutions. Social norms, moral values, or ideologies do not necessarily reinforce formal rules and regulations. In fact they frequently impede economic reforms. Conflicts between informal and formal institutions presuppose that the normative contents of these rules contradict each other. Hence, a conflict is more likely with respect to formal task-oriented institutions because they define specific objectives or prescribe particular actions that economic actors have to perform in order to accomplish these objectives. Regarding formal market order-oriented institutions, conflicts are less likely because economic actors are allowed to act as they wish unless they violate or harm the rights of others. Since informal institutions tend to change only slowly over time and cannot be directly altered by political decisions, reformers need to be aware of the limits of political interference and economic reforms. Therefore, a MEGS ought to be perceived as a nexus of relational contracts, the efficacy of which depends on the interplay between formal and informal institutions and the gradual change in informal constraints during the course of development. In order to cope with the problems associated with path dependence, a flexible MEGS needs to be adaptively efficient;

• governance structures are basically subject to political design as far as formal rules are concerned. This implies that government and market institutions can be consciously altered in order better to achieve policy goals. The effectiveness of governance structures in general, and of political institutions in particular, however, is essentially shaped by the incentive structures they provide, resulting from the structural characteristics of states, including their administrative organization, their connections to societal groups, as well as the international relations in which these states are embedded;

- policy reform and high economic growth rates cannot be sustained without continuing institutional change. Therefore, effective governance needs to be interpreted as a dynamic process. New institutions will only survive and unfold their positive developmental impact if they are supported by individuals and organizations that have a stake in their survival. This presupposes that a MEGS needs to be sufficiently flexible in order to enhance the adaptive efficiency of a country's institutional matrix and to ensure a high degree of incentive-compatibility of government policies and economic performance;

- the latter argument suggests that a definitive model of effective governance, which prescribes an institutional matrix that can be universally applied, cannot exist. This is not possible for the seemingly banal but important reason that the conditions for adaptive efficiency and economic progress – and hence for the success of policy reforms that need to be undertaken – differ across countries and change over time;

- the case studies illustrate that a flexible MEGS is necessarily associated with comparatively high degrees of accountability, participation, predictability, and transparency in political and economic decision making. These studies also indicate that there is a great variety of institutional opportunities to build an effective governance structure. After all, it is different country-, context- and time-specific circumstances which determine what kinds of formal institutions are most conducive to improve governance quality.

The analysis of governance structures involves the question of how to improve the practice of policy reform and the conditions determining that effort. The question of how politico-institutional structures can be altered to strengthen the contribution that politics makes to economic development is of particular significance at a time when more and more countries are in the process of establishing open market-based economies, that is when a great variety of countries are looking for alternative modes and directions of policy making. It is of the utmost importance after the collapse of the socialist regimes in Central and Eastern Europe, that is in a situation in which political, economic, and civic structures, institutions, and organizations are to be simultaneously (re)invigorated. The real test of governance structures occurs in situations where regime changes or major policy shifts are required to cope with new problems or to meet new societal demands. As Hydén (1992: 14–15) puts it:

> The uncertainty or conflict that such demands or problems create generates pressures among governors or governed, or both, to change the rules of the game. Regime changes [and major policy shifts; J.A.] are more difficult, and often more painful, than ordinary policy alterations. The former imply more or less far-reaching shifts in the basic rules of how society conducts its public affairs or how governors and governed relate to each other. The study of governance, then, involves the identification of the conditions that facilitate good governance and, by implication, effective problem solving.

This means that governance work must not be assigned to so-called second generation reforms, although this has typically been done by numerous policy makers, economic advisors, and international organizations. It is actually a key task and an unalterable precondition to most, if not all, policy components of economic reforms, above all in PSCs, but also in most LDCs.

This study has provided a useful conceptual framework for how to analyse and improve governance structures in LDCs and PSCs. But it does not offer a how-to manual that can direct policy makers through the complicated terrain of institution building. Thus, easy answers are not on the cards with respect to answering the leading questions which direct the research on institutional change and effective governance. Much more research at the country level is needed to understand the factors better that impede or promote the emergence of a flexible MEGS.

In order to conclude this study, this chapter will subsequently discuss potential lessons for LDCs and PSCs that can be derived from the conceptual considerations and empirical observations made in the preceding chapters. In addition, the analysis will be extended to examining key factors that are crucial to explain how effective governance structures may evolve over time. Subsequently, we will ask how external actors such as international organizations may help LDCs and PSCs to craft a flexible MEGS. Finally, we will close the chapter with a brief reprise highlighting the overall contribution of this study to the possible emergence of a Post-Washington Consensus.

7.1 THE EVOLUTION OF EFFECTIVE GOVERNANCE

The 1980s and 1990s experienced numerous market-oriented reforms in developing and transitional economies which have been unprecedented in scale and scope. But most of these reforms are far from being sustainable or completed. This raises the question of whether there are any helpful lessons from success cases in economic reform and development which may give guidance to political leaders regarding the design and implementation of policy and institutional reforms. Suitable policies to overcome underdevelopment and poverty are well known, but the mechanisms that are required to implement these policies and to gain the political support of all those parts of society whose cooperation is an unalterable prerequisite for successful reforms are less well-understood. The conceptual framework developed in this study as well as the case studies discussed do not offer a manual on how to proceed, but they provide an appropriate set of rules to guide specific solutions for other LDCs and transition economies.

The implementation, enforcement, and monitoring of reform policies requires the enhancement of governance capacity through which new forms of conflict resolution are created, principal–agent problems mitigated, and participation as well as political feasibility ensured.[1] Governments need to avoid uncertain and variable policy frameworks and closed decision making, which lead to corruption, patronage, a waste of resources, and poor development management. Institutional change and innovation have to be regarded as a decisive part of the economic and political development agenda. In this context, improving government capacity, including accounting and auditing systems, legal reform, and restructuring the civil service deserve particular attention. Micro-level reforms represent an essential precondition for effective public sector management and improve the administrative capability of providing public goods and services. In most LDCs and PSCs, they are also necessary in order to modernize the tax system, to reduce corruption and rent-seeking, to enhance the accountability of the public sector, and hence to increase the credibility of reform measures.

Basically, caution is advised if one seeks to draw policy conclusions for other countries. To some extent, institutional and organizational structures constitute organic wholes: then it proves difficult to effectively transplant one piece without transferring the complete system. Nonetheless, there are several implications resulting from our conceptual considerations as well as some general lessons that can be drawn from the preceding cases – lessons that underscore the critical importance of strengthening political and economic institutions as a key component of economic reform processes. This is a component that must not be postponed to late stages of reform. In what follows, the most important key points will be briefly summarized.

The initiation and consolidation of economic reforms
At first glance, policy and institutional reforms appear to be politically 'unlikely' events, because they are usually associated with (at least in the short run) severe political risks and relatively high short-term social costs. Nevertheless, economic reforms have been pursued in a wide range of

countries. However, only a small number of reform programs materialized as expected. The major obstacles and impediments to effective policy reform parallel those that also aggravate institutional change.[2] They relate to problems of collective action, redistribution, and social costs. Most policy and institutional reforms seek to provide public goods. Since in most cases nobody can be excluded from the benefits of these reforms, rational actors may find it not in their interest to invest resources in order to ensure the success of reform programs. Moreover, fiscal and structural reforms as well as institutional change tend to provoke strong distributional conflicts. Even if the overall reform program promises to yield substantial efficiency gains, some groups in society may turn out to be losers, for example if subsidies are lifted or protective trade regulations eliminated. If compensation is infeasible or not credible, potential losers will resist reforms. A slowdown of reform is then more likely to result, the better that potential losers are organized and the better their institutional access is to veto positions that provide them with disproportionate bargaining power in political decision-making processes (Bönker 2000). Two other factors can make these distributional conflicts even more severe. First, such conflicts may entail unstable political coalitions (especially if redistribution is a zero-sum game), because losers could bribe members of the dominant majority coalition (Tullock 1959). Secondly, if the identity of losers and winners is uncertain *ex ante*, the adoption of reform programs may be blocked, even if a majority of the population would support them *ex post* (Fernandez and Rodrik 1991). Similarly, distributional conflicts may be intensified and lead to a 'war of attrition' if different societal groups are uncertain about the willingness of other groups to bear the costs of reforms (Alesina and Drazen 1991; Drazen 1996). Finally, and related to the foregoing, major reform programs may be impeded because they often necessarily include a stabilization component that may induce considerable transitory costs. For example, the well-known transformational recession in CEE implied a J-curve effect on production figures and led to a substantial decline in GDP in virtually all transition economies before a lasting recovery could be realized. Consequently, reformers face the politically formidable challenge of leading the population 'through a "valley of tears" before benefits may start to materialise' (Bönker 2000: 4).

Notwithstanding these obstacles, economic reforms have been successfully implemented in a number of countries. This raises the question of what the political and economic conditions are that are conducive for both the initiation and consolidation of such reforms. This question has been central to the literature on the political economy of policy reforms that has appeared over the last 15 years.[3] This body of research has identified a number of critical conditions which are confirmed and complemented by studies by institutional economists.

Important factors that facilitate the *initiation* of reforms include a fiscal or economic crisis, a government that enjoys broad political legitimacy and has a strong mandate, and the existence of a visionary leader who is supported by a powerful and coherent change team (Williamson and Haggard 1994; Bönker 2000). Especially, the juxtaposition of economic crisis and strong political mandates can help to overcome impediments to reforms, because this grants reformers 'a temporary autonomy from the push and pull of short-term political pressures' (Rodrik 1994: 212). In fact, this factor played a crucial role in most case studies discussed in the preceding chapters. Recall, for example, the 'window of opportunity' that was temporarily opened for most CEE countries after the fall of the Berlin Wall and that even allowed radical reformers in Russia to initiate bold stabilization measures in 1992 after the demise of the Soviet Union. Also, economic crises as well as external and internal political threats were important factors that helped to launch reform programs in the HPAEs in the 1960s, most notably in South Korea. Similarly, the fiscal crisis in India in 1991 enabled the government to start a bold stabilization-cum-adjustment program. Moreover, regime or electoral changes (principally but not exclusively in a time of crisis) often enhance the standing of the new government with respect to its supporters and possibly also to the opposition. This is especially the case if the new government enjoys a broad societal legitimacy and is able to blame its predecessors for social hardships and economic problems (Bönker 2000).

However, while strong political mandates, broad legitimacy, and economic crises may bring about viable starting points for comprehensive reforms, these factors cannot guarantee their adoption. This is the point at which political leadership and the political power of reformist forces within the government apparatus play a key role. In this context, the existence of a coherent and able change team, which is capable of designing and implementing a consistent reform program is necessary to seize the available opportunity for policy changes. Of particular importance, however, is the presence of a determined and courageous leader with a long-term view; a political entrepreneur, who is able to initiate the reforms, to develop a vision of future development, and to articulate the need for and the expected effects of policy changes *vis-à-vis* different groups in society. These 'heroes of the economics profession' (Rodrik 1996: 9) have been critical actors in most, if not all, successful reform episodes in less developed countries. With respect to policy reforms, for example, in Latin America, Arnold Harberger, a leading expert on the economies in that region, summarized his experiences, observations, and research results by stating that 'in every case about which I have close knowledge, the policy would in all likelihood have failed (or never got started) but for the efforts of a key group of individuals, and within that group, one or two outstanding leaders'.[4] Similar insights were gained by

Williamson and Haggard (1994) who surveyed the political and economic conditions of successful episodes of policy reform in a sample of 13 countries (including OECD members, transition economies, and LDCs from different regions of the world). In all cases, leadership played a critical role in the initiation of reforms. Additionally, in all cases effective leadership was reinforced by strong legislative and social support. Moreover, it is to be noted that it is not necessarily the head of state or the head of government who assumed the strongest leadership position regarding economic reforms. In many cases, it has been a minister of a key ministry, such as the ministry of finance, or a senior government official, who was the leader of the economic change team. Especially in these latter cases, the strength of the leader critically depends on his backing by the chief executive.

The pivotal importance of leadership is also evident in the case studies discussed in the preceding chapters. Most of the HPAEs had strong political leaders at the beginning of their economic catch-up processes: Park Chung Hee and Chun Doo Hwan in South Korea, Lee Kuan Yew in Singapore, Suharto in Indonesia, and Mahathir Mohamad in Malaysia. All had strong mandates and the capacity to give a new direction to their countries' development policies. However much distaste one may have, for example, for Park's or Suharto's rule, they undoubtedly had a clear development scheme and a vision of their countries' fundamental transformation, and they were willing to pursue their policies regardless of the costs. In China, Deng Xiaoping forcefully introduced the shift to more decentralized, market-oriented economic policy making. In India, it was Prime Minister Rao and especially the remarkable Finance Minister, Manmohan Singh who seized the day in 1991 and successfully launched a bold stabilization-cum-adjustment program. In particular Singh has 'taken India on what Jawaharlal Nehru would have called her "tryst with destiny"' (Bhagwati 1993: 4). Also in the transition economies in CEE, the determination of individual leaders facilitated the initiation of transformation policies. In Poland, Lech Walesa played a crucial role in fostering the political regime change, and Leszek Balcerowicz as finance minister has become well-known for the implementation of his big-bang approach to transition. In Czechoslovakia and subsequently in the Czech Republic, Vaclav Klaus successfully articulated his notion of a market economy without attributes and hence set the seal on the ultimate break of the country with its economic past. Furthermore, Mikhail Gorbachev triggered the end of the communist dictatorship in the Soviet Union by promoting his policies of *glasnost* and *perestroika*. Subsequently, it was Boris Yeltsin and his first Prime Minister Jegor Gaidar, who brought the market economy to Russia. Although their economic transformation policies were not as successful as desired, they made the systemic change irreversible. Finally, the Slovak Republic under Meciar represents an example of how strong and determined leadership may also have counterproductive effects on a country's economic prospects. For it was not only institutional but mainly political reasons which led the EU to exclude Slovakia from the group of countries that are primary candidates for EU accession.[5]

All these examples illustrate the importance of political leaders especially at the early stages of economic development and transition, that is at a time when in most countries a MEGS was not institutionalized yet. In such a situation, rule vested in persons who have an *encompassing* or *national interest* (Bardhan 1995; Olson 1993) can serve as a substitute for a lack of institutions and as an effective trigger for radical economic change.[6] This argument also fits well with the findings of Grindle and Thomas (1991: xiv) who conclude that 'public officials make a critical difference in the introduction, scope, and pursuit of policy reform. (...) People do change policy, and they do it from motivations and perspectives that are imbued with personal and professional values and that frequently include serious concern for the public interest and public welfare in their societies.' Most notable, however, is that in almost all success cases discussed in this study strong leadership coincided with what Eucken (1990/1952: 251) called the 'historische Moment' (the historical moment), which proved to be favorable for a significant policy or regime change. This means that distinct (historical) circumstances often play a critical role in explaining why, how, and when political decisions are made. In most countries economic crisis or stagnation represented such a moment; an opportunity that allows significant changes in public policy making to be brought about. Then, it usually depends on the existence of political entrepreneurs to seize this opportunity, to initiate institutional change, and to lay the foundation of what may eventually become a MEGS.[7]

However, once started, policy reforms must be *consolidated*. The political economy literature on economic reforms as well as the NIE indicate that conditions that are conducive for the consolidation of reforms differ remarkably from those that favor their initiation. Of major importance is to strengthen the executive authority of governments as well as the capacity and capability of the public administration to implement follow-up reform steps, particularly those relating to structural and institutional reform. Especially when the short-term costs of policy reforms become evident, initially strong political mandates can be easily eroded. To stay on course, the government must be capable of overcoming reform fatigue and resisting the emerging pressure of particularistic interests. This involves the difficult task of shielding policy making and implementation against anti-reform influences and, at the same time, establishing a system of checks and balances which helps to limit a strong government. Thus while the initiation of economic reforms may be facilitated by the discretionary authority of political entrepreneurs and political institutions that insulate policy making from the one-sided claims of interest groups, their consolidation requires a consistent and coherent institutionalization of political and economic processes which stabilize the expectations of political and economic actors regarding a new set of incentive structures and create confidence that these cannot be altered by discretion. What may happen if formal institutionalization fails, has been documented by the recent economic and political turmoil in Indonesia, which ended the Suharto era. Similarly, what may happen if policy makers fail to adjust a country's governance structure continually to changing international, economic, and political environments could be observed in South Korea where the recent Asian Crisis revealed substantial weaknesses in corporate governance, financial sector regulation, and government–business relations.

Furthermore, since public sector and policy reform is a political process, its consolidation requires the broad support of various social groups. In order to prevent potential losers from economic reforms blocking new policy initiatives, reform-minded governments need to create a coalition supporting change. In the HPAEs, the lack of a dominant class in society at the beginning of reforms (especially in Northeast Asia) and credible strategies of shared growth ensured that broad social coalitions evolved, whose members expected that economic reforms could be successfully implemented and that everyone would share in future benefits. This perception was even supported by the participatory character of the policy making process. Similarly, the dual-track approach pursued in China since 1978 helped to implement economic reforms without creating a large number of losers. Moreover, the vision or expectation that institutional and policy reforms will yield substantial productivity gains and income growth may not only help to initiate policy changes but also to form a broad coalition that supports reforms. This was certainly the case in those PSCs that have desired EU accession from the very beginning of the transformation process and that have subsequently become eligible for first-round membership negotiations. The importance of a vision for the initiation *and* consolidation of reforms has also been clearly demonstrated by South Korea's early reform experience in the 1960s. As Root (1996: 18) observes:

> [President Park Chung Hee; J.A.] appreciated the need for leadership to have a vision that had meaning for all levels of society, as well as the need for institutions to make leadership accountable for that vision. (...) Capitalism did not have deep roots in 1960s Korean society. To foster a consensus in favor of capitalist development, President Park introduced a nationalistic element that is captured in the slogan 'Modernization of the Fatherland'. This seemingly benign phrase aroused strong sentiment among Koreans who had once lost their fatherland. (...) By making opposition to reform seem unpatriotic, the theme 'Modernization of the

Fatherland' prevented the polarization of society into winners and losers. Modernization became everyone's responsibility.

Furthermore, strengthening civil society brings government closer to its constituents and facilitates the solution of social problems; a dense government–society interface as well as political and economic decentralization and empowerment of local government may be regarded as promising steps in this direction. Last but not least, poverty reduction remains one of the most important issues in East and South Asia and in other regions of the world. The strategy of *shared growth* in most HPAEs with its main component of giving real assets to people (especially fostering rural development) did not only reduce poverty and increase political support of reforms, but also reduced hidden lobbying and enabled governments to resist pressures from vested interests and to concentrate more on policies that provide widespread, long-term benefits.

The experiences of the HPAEs suggesting a significant positive correlation between income equality and growth have been empirically supported by Alesina and Rodrik (1994), who found in their cross-country analysis (comprising numerous LDCs) a significant inverse relationship between initial levels of wealth and income inequality and subsequent economic growth. This implies a strong argument in favor of shared-growth approaches and in particular of those policies that seek to improve income and wealth distribution at the beginning of reforms. In this regard, land reform may be considered as an appropriate instrument to lay the basis for shared growth, especially in Latin America, but also in Asian countries such as the Philippines. However, if past failures of numerous land reform programs are to be avoided, policy makers need to care about persistent social conditions and political market realities. In particular, a soft state in the sense of Myrdal (1968), based on nepotism and personal connection, and weak bureaucracies will yield negative consequences. Also, reformers may learn from analytical errors underlying past programs. Recent studies have revealed that agricultural production in low-wage LDCs is associated with constant or decreasing returns to scale, even with cash crops, and that share tenancy may result in the same efficient resource allocation as owner farming or fixed-rent contracts.[8] This calls for rethinking and redesigning reform programs allowing for small-scale farming and encouraging a broad variety of organizational forms. If properly planned and implemented, land reforms can enhance both efficiency and equity.

Shared-growth strategies may also be appropriate and feasible for the transformation in CEE and possibly some CIS countries due to favorable initial conditions in terms of high educational levels and equal income distribution relative to living standards throughout the region.[9] Giving a large part of the population access to productive resources may significantly reduce distributive struggles that threaten to impede transformation, and facilitate growth and adjustment policies. Unalterable preconditions for productive asset transfers, however, include (besides political commitment) considerable investments in the *maintenance* of the region's human capital and its *adjustment* to the new demands of competitive markets.[10] In this regard, it is of major importance to invest in human capital as early as possible during the transition, because otherwise a vicious circle may evolve: overall investment would be initially blocked by political instability and subsequently by deteriorating human capital, which may become (prohibitively) costly to reverse (Overland and Spagat 1996). In addition, investment in public infrastructure and health-care systems, and enhancing marketable business skills (for example, marketing and accounting skills, which were essentially unimportant and neglected under socialism) should be regarded as complementary measures to support human-capital development, to reduce (latent) unemployment, and to lay the basis for growth.

Moreover, a one-time redistribution of assets such as land reform may be also considered by those transition countries with vast agricultural resources such as Russia. With the privatization of SOEs, however, it may be more appropriate to give broad parts of the population a stake in the economy. Small-scale privatization is of utmost importance for providing the breeding ground for new entrepreneurs and promoting a capitalist exchange culture. Large-scale privatization is more problematic for economic and political reasons. In this respect, the voucher method is preferable to selling companies one-by-one to investors, because it involves all citizens equally and helps to depoliticize the economy rapidly by eliminating political control over enterprises.[11] But such a procedure will only succeed if effective corporate-control structures, functioning capital markets, and hard budget constraints can be established. If these preconditions are not satisfied, citizens may not benefit from large-scale privatization as expected, as the experiences of both the Czech Republic and Russia have clearly demonstrated.

However, shared-growth strategies will only be successful if policy makers can credibly ensure that future benefits will accrue to all groups of society *and* that potential future losses will be shared, too. This is of particular importance for some successor countries of the former USSR, in which the decline in production figures may still not have bottomed out (EBRD 1999). Therefore, introducing competition and transferring assets to citizens is essential, but not on its own sufficient, to increase the equality of opportunity and a willingness to take individual risks. Additionally, corruption, rent-seeking of political power groups, and collusion between public officials and private business have to be fought decisively. This requires an independent judiciary, a stable and transparent legal framework as well as inclusionary, non-discretionary policies.

Another problem, related to large-scale privatization, concerns enterprise restructuring and building up competitive industrial structures. There are two major obstacles to this transition. First, due to the politically-devised monopolistic production structure under socialism, industries neither reflect comparative advantages nor will they automatically become competitive under world-market conditions. Radical trade liberalization has basically a disciplining effect on domestic enterprises, but also carries the danger that some industries, which would be viable after restructuring, might show a negative value added when shifting to world-market prices. Though it is hardly possible for governments to determine *a priori* those enterprises that will be profitable after adjusting to world-market conditions, they may be capable of creating winners by temporarily protecting domestic industries through transparent, differentiated, gradually decreasing and converging tariff rates, as suggested by McKinnon (1992). Secondly, since the transformation has rendered much of the physical capital stock obsolete, transition countries are relatively poorly endowed with physical capital, whereas they possess a relatively skilled labor force. This human-capital advantage implies a high latent return on private investment creating a similar coordination problem as in South Korea and Taiwan. Overcoming market imperfections, improving private sector coordination, and hence preparing the economies for take-off requires government action to coordinate and subsidize private investment through tax incentives, credit subsidies, public investment, and administrative guidance. Additionally, similar measures may be necessary to promote small- and medium-sized firms and labor-intensive manufacturing as long as functioning capital markets do not exist. To overcome these obstacles functional and selective interventions, the nature of which depends on national circumstances, are indispensable. This necessity confronts authorities with the paradox that during transition the state is required to reduce its role in the economy, while adjustment problems may require it to promote interventionist measures. To solve this problem, effective and transparent governance structures need to be established that strengthen state capacity and enhance the reputation and competence of both the government and the bureaucracy.

The market-enhancing role of governments
The broad framework suggested in this study maintains that an active role of the state is essential to foster economic development and transition. Sound macroeconomic and structural policies are necessary for promoting economic progress and social change. But they are insufficient if problems of institutional design and implementation are neglected. In contrast to some of

the rent-seeking literature that maintains that the public sector is necessarily debilitating to the economy, there is broad evidence that the state can and needs to play a central role in facilitating the successful organization of markets without supplanting those markets in favor of a system of centralized control. Besides the need to strengthen key political and economic institutions, the quality of a country's governance structure can be further enhanced by government action that seeks to overcome market imperfections and to support private sector development and coordination.

Recent research by development and institutional economists has persuasively suggested that *market-enhancing* government activism is critical to economic development.[12] But theory and evidence also suggest that, if badly designed and implemented, interventions can severely impede development. In order to overcome the dichotomy of government action and market coordination which has dominated the viewpoints of neoclassical scholars on the one hand and structuralists and revisionists on the other, Aoki *et al.* (1997b: 2) propose a market-enhancing view that 'stresses the mechanisms whereby government policy is directed at improving the ability of the private sector to solve coordination problems and overcome other market imperfections', which evolve due to the incompleteness of markets, bounded rationality, information asymmetry, and limited knowledge. Since government behavior is constrained by a limited capacity to process information and governments' incentives are influenced by its institutions and interrelations with private agents, the government is to 'be regarded as an endogenous player interacting with the economic system as a coherent cluster of institutions rather than a neutral, omnipotent agent exogenously attached to the economic system with the mission of resolving its coordination failures' (ibid.).

Advocates of the market-enhancing view identify complementaries between private coordination within a firm or across firms and the design of the institutional environment. Therefore, governments' role is not to substitute for private agents' coordination, but to create a complementary institutional environment that supports private coordination and increases the capabilities of private sector institutions.[13] For example, a central point of government intervention in most HPAEs was that it – contrary to common perception – did not imply extensive rent-seeking behavior. The reason is that interventions did not create rents, but policy-induced *rent opportunities* (contingent rents) for private agents, whose exploitation depended on their own efforts to conduct business and to meet objective and transparent rules under, for example, an export contest. In contrast to unconditional subsidies, contingent rents foster competition and facilitate the resolution of coordination problems in the private sector.

Another channel through which governments can effectively promote private sector coordination is by fostering the development of private intermediaries. Coordination problems basically justify government action, but not necessarily the replacing of market-based coordination with a government-led one. Due to information problems, governments are often at a disadvantage *vis-à-vis* private institutions in resolving coordination failures. Instead, institutional arrangements beyond the market may evolve in the non-public sector, including industry and trade associations, farmers' organizations, financial intermediaries, and chambers of commerce, which may be in a better position to address these problems. Then, governments' primary role is to support the development of these organizations and to constructively interact with them.[14]

According to the market-enhancing view, public policies need to show a bias towards private-sector institutions whenever feasible, because these institutions are basically more appropriate in solving coordination problems due to their built-in self-regulating properties like competition and their more suitable responsiveness to local information. This approach concedes, however, that the boundary for state activism may depend on a country's level of development. At an early stage of development, the number of intermediating organizations is limited, capabilities of private enterprises are modest, and the efficiency of resource allocation through markets may be hampered by insufficient property rights and poor market integration. Under these conditions, one may expect considerable scope for government activism. During the course of development, less government intervention is necessary and desirable, although it is not expected to disappear completely.

Thus the scope and nature of market-enhancing government activities is contingent on a country's stage of development, its institutional matrix, the scale and type of market failures, and government capacity. Initially, as long as capabilities are weak and capacities low, governments may prefer initiatives that match their limited capabilities. Experiences from East Asia suggest that at early stages of economic development policy makers should seek gradually to improve capabilities through fostering education and institution building.[15] Selective interventions should be limited in number and focus on strategic industries (for example, low-skill manufacturing industries, resource extraction, and agriculture) that contribute to accumulating know-how and capabilities that are critical for the pursuit of more sophisticated policies. This approach provides political authorities with the opportunity to improve their understanding of how to craft sectoral policies and to learn what kind of incentives work under various conditions (Akyüz *et al.* 1998). Subsequently, given a more competent bureaucracy and institutions facilitating cooperation between the government and private actors, policy making can increasingly rely on more sophisticated activities which require specialized skills and more information. But high-intensity government action (for example, creating or picking winners and investment coordination) should only be taken if the development of public and private institutions is well advanced, the business sector is competitive, and stable mechanisms are in place through which governments can credibly precommit themselves to developmental policies, which restrain arbitrary public action, and which ensure policy flexibility in case of failure.

Governance, transition, and informal institutions

The main lesson from the case studies is that governance matters. Besides selecting the right policies (aimed at macroeconomic stability and possibly including microeconomic interventions to overcome market imperfections), governments need to focus on the policy environment. Crafting and adopting institutions that make decision-making procedures more transparent and predictable, ensure a broad representation of interests, delimit the authority of government, and enhance leadership accountability, have to be regarded as essential ingredients of development and transformation management. East Asian governments secured the broad support of ordinary people and economic elites without compromising their sound policies by establishing checks and balances against their authority. They ensured that they would not confiscate private assets by trading authority for private information, and hence tied their own hands by creating institutions that reduced leaders' opportunity for arbitrary actions. In much of Eastern Europe and elsewhere, self-enforcing constitutional safeguards still need to be established that prevent governments from transgressing against citizens' rights. This means that the government itself is subject to transition. For example, a major weakness of Russian transformation has been the lack of political restructuring. Although Russia adopted economic reforms similar to those of Poland, its economic performance has been significantly worse. The transition of government towards a nexus of institutions that represents the political foundation of a market economy is as important as the proper sequencing and timing of transformation policies. Contrary to the Central European countries, Russia still lacks a radical change in its government apparatus regarding both personnel and structure, particularly at sub-national levels. Eliminating political appointments at the mercy of Moscow and accelerating regional and local elections is critical for a turnover of political elites and the replacement of obsolete human capital in politics. This would increase political accountability and responsiveness to business. In addition to reforming the electoral system, restructuring fiscal federalism is critical. Introducing hard budget constraints for lower-level jurisdictions and strengthening their tax bases would encourage prudent budget management and improve the incentive-compatibility of public policies and economic performance. After all, institutional reforms need to continue, especially legal reforms, and functional and meritocratic bureaucracies must be created at sub-national levels in order to implement and enforce reform policies effectively (Shleifer 1997).

But whether a society is driven by the rule-of-law does not only depend on its political institutions. Since rules can be politically ignored, mechanisms must be put in place that allow for the policing of deviations. Weingast's (1993 and 1995) analyses suggest that the effectiveness and maintenance of political institutions defining the legitimate boundaries of the state crucially depend on a societal consensus among citizens about the limits of government. This consensus, in turn, depends on the interaction of informal and formal institutions. In order to create a societal consensus during the transformation process, promoting the emergence of a civil society is of the utmost importance. Formal institutions may become a focal point to help to coordinate and align citizens' informal attitudes, so that (new) formal institutions of policy making and representation can be sustained. Thereafter, the constituency is better prepared to police government behavior and to react in concert against the government if it is perceived to transgress its legitimate boundaries.[16]

Conflicts between formal and informal institutions do occur in both LDCs and PSCs, but it is likely that these conflicts are more severe in transition economies, because the transformation process implies a bold, sudden, and large-scale replacement of formal institutions, whereas in most LDCs formal institutional change takes place in a more piecemeal and gradual manner. In fact, the transition towards capitalism in CEE and the CIS has been impeded by informal institutions which evolved in the region before and during socialist rule and which have aggravated the emergence of a societal consensus about the new economic role of government and its limits (Raiser 1997). These include, for example, widespread pro-collectivist attitudes, nationalism, communalism, political alienation, and habituation to political hierarchy (including paternalistic-authoritarian expectations *vis-à-vis* the state). The philosophical heritage has neither been conducive to individualism, to performance-contingent rewards nor to a constitutional state. This factor made the transformation process path dependent and induced hysteresis effects, so that capitalist behavioral norms as postulated by neoclassical reasoning could not emerge in the short run. This also means that creating capitalist institutions by fiat following textbook models will not yield the intended effects and will entail acceptance problems as the resurgence of pro-collectivist political parties indicates. Instead, policy makers should seek citizens' compliance with transformation policies by allowing them to experiment with alternative institutions and to adopt those arrangements that succeed in the market test. A market for institutions (for example, regarding the choice of contractual agreements and the design of property-rights structures)[17] in association with the transfer of productive assets to non-elites would provide the underprivileged with upward mobility, contribute to overcome hysteresis effects, and encourage a consensus for the support of economic reforms. Eventually, this would help to increase the adaptive efficiency of both the political and economic order and hence enhance the flexibility of a country's governance structure.

Strong but limited governments

In most HPAEs, strong but limited governments emerged based on a relatively autonomous bureaucracy embedded in a complex set of external relations to society. Basically a broadly-defined concept of embedded autonomy involving ties to multiple social groups can offer a robust basis for policy reform.[18] But whether this concept is effectively transferable to other countries depends on national circumstances. Especially, the efficacy of deliberation councils depends on the size of the private sector, on which economic actors are involved, on their societal acceptance, and on an economy's stage of development. If the private sector is too small, councils may degenerate into fora that breed collusion and rent-seeking. If these councils are perceived to be closed shops of non-transparent policy making and cozy relations between government and (parts of) the business sector, they would lack societal legitimacy and undermine the trust of broader segments of society in government policies (World Bank 1997). Moreover, as Lipsey (2002) argues by drawing on East Asian experiences, consultative processes which pooled knowledge and financial means from the public and the private sector worked well in the catch-up phase and reduced inefficient duplication of research. But with respect to cutting-edge industries, the existence of considerable uncertainties requires multiple, cost-effective investigations which can be better ensured by uncoordinated experimentation rather than by concentrating efforts. Furthermore, in more heterogeneous or culturally diverse societies such as Russia or India, governance structures in the form of centrally-devised councils may be inadequate, particularly if countries lack coherent, meritocratic administrative structures or if different overlapping economic, political, social, or ethnic divisions exist that make collective action and a consensual policy dialogue more difficult. This is also conceivable if income and wealth distribution is less equal at the beginning of reforms than it was in the HPAEs. In these instances, it may be more difficult for political leaderships to make shared growth credible and to precommit themselves to policies that are consistent with the interests of society. Then, alternative mechanisms need to be created in order to limit a strong government. If embeddedness, as realized in the HPAEs, is not feasible, introducing institutions such as market-preserving federalism as in China, functional, overlapping, and competing jurisdictions,[19] the principle of subsidiarity, or elements of direct democracy may prove to be a more appropriate means, all of which ensure considerable participation of the people, a factor necessary for political leaders to make informed choices and to allow citizens to protect individual rights.

Key actors of change

Although critical parts of a MEGS can be politically drafted, the emergence of effective governance is necessarily an evolutionary process. Institution building is a time-consuming endeavor which is shaped by a great variety of players on the politico-economic stage. The efficacy of the interaction of these players essentially depends on a country's formal and informal institutions and the capability of the different actors to initiate and facilitate institutional change. The key player determining alterations of governance mechanisms is naturally the state with its different branches of government, decision-making bodies at different jurisdictional levels, and its numerous public agencies.

Implementing policy reforms not only requires clear objectives and credible commitment on the part of the government but, equally important, a well-designed, competent, and meritocratic bureaucracy that is closely related to the business sector but yet that can act sufficiently independently of vested interests. It often also requires the ability of the government to balance on a knife-edge. This holds, in particular, with respect to selective interventions and high-intensity government action as well as establishing adequate government–business relations. Of utmost importance is that governments seek to rely on the private sector as much as possible and to assume a genuine market-enhancing role. Moreover, governments need to recognize that crafting effective governance structures should be their primary concern. But they must also recognize that institution building is an open-ended process. Due to a continual changing economic, political, technological, and international environment, governance structures that were once effective may gradually become impediments to economic development. In some instances, particularly in the case of 'exogenous shocks' caused, for example, by radical liberalization programs, a country's accession to the WTO, or the Asian Crisis, governance structures may be abruptly rendered ineffective or even counterproductive, or latent weaknesses of governance structures may suddenly become visible. In some cases, these shocks may trigger institutional change that (although economically necessary for years) had been postponed for political reasons.[20] In other cases, economies may be prepared to adapt to exogenous shocks with relatively low adjustment costs if the economic structure of the country and its governance structure proved to be sufficiently flexible.[21]

However, not all actions needed for establishing a MEGS will be necessarily taken by governments; be it due to lack of information or capacity, a lack of political interest, or the fear that governance-related policies (especially if they aim at altering political institutions) will affect the balance of political power at the expense of (parts of) the incumbent government. This implies that non-governmental actors (such as private economic agents, intermediary organizations like trade unions or employers' associations, NGOs, and international organizations) can and need to support the development of effective governance structures. Thus political leaders and representatives of the national government are not the only key agents for change. Although the emergence of effective governance structures always presupposes political commitment and leadership at the national level or at least at local/regional levels of policy making, strong intermediary associations and dynamic economic and institutional entrepreneurs can reinforce public policies and possibly also compensate (at least temporarily) for policy failures or help gradually to remove rigid governance mechanisms which impede innovative activities. Important roles can and ought to be assumed by business associations, private firms, and local governments in order to enhance the quality of governance from below. If, for example, the national government is not willing or capable of undertaking economic and institutional reforms for some reason, local governments may proceed along their own lines and seek to pursue their own strategies within the overall institutional framework in which they are embedded. This can bring about substantial economic progress at the regional and local level as the example of the Chinese township and village governments illustrates. There may also be cases in which domestic firms can effectively cooperate with local governments.[22] Moreover, private ordering (possibly supported by local governments) can considerably improve a country's governance structure in a specific policy area. For example, with respect to technology policy in LDCs, business associations may play important roles in establishing communication channels between technology institutions and firms and in moderating and facilitating potential conflicts that may arise in the course of inter-firm cooperation. As experiences from Latin America and East Asia illustrate, business associations (possibly in collaboration with local governments) may be able to create new (sector-specific) institutions, to improve governance structures by using a step-by-step approach, and to help overcome problems relating to asymmetric, imperfect, or incomplete information, which become more severe if economies shift to increasingly complex modes of production.[23] Note in this context that bottom-up and participatory approaches to guiding technology development (for example, through industrial districts) as well as horizontal policy interventions which seek to involve the private sector directly (for example, through deliberation councils or more informal institutional arrangements) may enhance the legitimacy and acceptance of public policies over time and hence strengthen the overall governance structure.

Finally, international organizations such as the multilateral development banks or the IMF can play crucial roles in reforming and modernizing national governance structures. Especially in countries which are dependent on external financial assistance, these organizations may have considerable leverage in shaping the quality of key economic and legal institutions.

7.2 HOW TO PROMOTE EFFECTIVE GOVERNANCE? THE ROLE OF INTERNATIONAL ORGANIZATIONS[24]

Recently, governance has emerged as a leitmotiv of numerous bilateral aid programs and as a pivotal concern of multilateral development agencies. It owes its current relevance to several factors including the misuse of aid funds by recipients, a growing awareness of the growth-impeding effects of corruption, the resurgence of ethnic conflicts in many countries, and the sobering experience with structural adjustment programs in LDCs that have not brought about the expected outcomes. Eventually, the growing focus on governance issues has been given new impetus by the collapse of the totalitarian states in CEE and the CIS and by the popular call for multiparty democracy in Africa and Latin America.

Since numerous LDCs and PSCs have unstable polities and poor systems of governance and also face severe resource constraints, the major donor agencies may possibly become key players on the politico-economic stage, as they are able to provide considerable assistance and to exert significant influence. In addressing governance issues, however, these external actors need to go beyond criticizing particular economic reform programs or development projects. They call into question the capacity and the capability of political authorities to govern effectively in the collective interest (Landell-Mills and Serageldin 1992). Consequently, in practical and operational terms, governance work always touches politically sensitive areas, even if donors seek to confine themselves to the economic and social dimensions of governance because of the inherent political implications.

Nevertheless, governance-related reforms may be in the interests of both the donor community and the recipient countries' governments. On the one hand, governments in LDCs and PSCs may be eager to ask international development agencies for technical and financial support in order to enhance the quality of their countries' governance framework. This is particularly conceivable when the government is reform-minded and explicitly concerned about governance-related problems, when it faces domestic political constraints which impede the implementation of policy and institutional reforms, or when it lacks the capacity, capability, and experience to (re)invigorate political and economic institutions in an effective way.[25] In these cases, external support by a development agency can serve as a catalyst and facilitator of institutional reform. On the other hand, it may be in the interest of international donor organizations to promote effective governance in their member countries in order to improve the efficiency of using program and sector loans as well as development aid, to ensure a purposive implementation of structural adjustment policies and sector-specific projects, and eventually to fight corruption in recipient countries. If the interests of international donor agencies and recipient governments are congruent, a governance-related reform program can be relatively easily developed. Extremely problematic, however, is the case in which the recipient government is not receptive to governance issues. Then, the external agency faces the dilemma that continued financial assistance will mean a further waste of resources and possibly slow down any serious efforts at policy reforms. At the same time, however, a suspension of external assistance may not be possible as long as the recipient government does not explicitly violate the terms of agreements with the donor agency. But as will be argued below, even in such a case it is not entirely impossible for international development agencies to promote effective governance. In order to achieve sustainable results, however, external actors need to develop indirect and subtle approaches to reform that are acceptable for the recipient government.

Since international development and financial organizations are to be considered as key actors who can critically help to improve the quality of policy making in LDCs and PSCs, the following considerations briefly review the current approaches of several international organizations for promoting effective governance in their member countries and discuss novel ways to incorporate governance issues in these organizations' strategies and operations.

Governance policies of international organizations

While some multilateral donors (such as the UNDP) and many bilateral donor agencies, most notably the USAID, address governance problems in a normative and positive manner and also include political objectives such as democratization and the improvement of human rights on their governance agendas, most multilateral development and financial organizations are not allowed to interfere in the sovereignty of the member countries. Nevertheless, the World Bank, the IMF, the EBRD, and the ADB – which are among the major donor agencies in CEE, the CIS, and Asia – have all recognized that orthodox adjustment programs and technical solutions are not sufficient to promote economic growth and development and that governance plays a crucial role in the transition toward open market-oriented economies and for effective policy reforms. They view governance as a means to an end and have begun to give governance issues heightened prominence on their operational agendas (for an overview of these organizations' governance policies see Boxes 7.1–7.4).

The World Bank had already started at the end of the 1980s to focus on governance problems and their inherent constraints to policy reform (World Bank 1989). The Asian Development Bank (ADB), however, was the first of the multilateral development banks (MDBs), that adopted an official governance policy in 1995. The ADB (1995) proposed to integrate governance-related issues into its country operations through the inclusion of suitable policy measures, project components, and technical assistance projects. Today, most multilateral and bilateral donor organizations take the problem of fighting corruption and creating effective governance structures into consideration.

All MDBs claim that they have been involved in promoting 'good' governance for a long time. This has certainly been true with respect to governance issues related to specific projects.[26] But essentially, governance work has been carried out in an *ad hoc* manner. The World Bank (1994), for example, concedes that in its *Country Assistance Strategies*, which are a primary vehicle for the review of the Bank's lending strategy in each country, governance issues have been largely neglected or, if taken into consideration, mainly concerned problems of public sector management. So far, most MDBs have lacked a consistent and systematic approach to addressing key governance issues. To date, none of them has provided a coherent analytical and operational concept that is suitable to establish an *overall* governance strategy for a particular country.

Taking the example of the World Bank, this failure may be attributed to several factors: (1) the Bank's definition of governance is vague and provides only few pointers for analysts or development practitioners as to the nature of governance or the factors affecting its quality (see Box 7.1). (2) As discussed in this study, the key components of effective governance include accountability, participation, predictability, and transparency. These represent highly abstract concepts, the real-world manifestations of which are differentiated, diverse, and may partially conflict each other. Neither the World Bank nor the IMF provides sufficient guidance about how to unravel and clarify the broad concepts. This, however, would be necessary to gain a better understanding of how different variants, mechanisms, and degrees of them interact with each other and may be practical and beneficial in different country-specific circumstances.[27] (3) Governance work, even if it is confined to its economic dimensions, is always a politically sensitive issue (Lancaster 1993). The World Bank, like the IMF and the ADB, is neither legitimized to

Box 7.1: Governance policies of the World Bank

The World Bank was the first of the multilateral donor agencies that *expressis verbis* gave prominence to governance issues in economic development (World Bank 1989). Since the beginning of the 1990s, the volume of its governance-related activities has increased substantially. The main geographical focus has been on Africa, Latin America, and the Caribbean. Governance work relating to CEE and the CIS, however, is still at an early stage.

The Bank identified three dimensions of governance: (i) the form of the political regime; (ii) the processes by which authority is exercised in the management of a country's economic and social resources; and (iii) the capacity of government to formulate and implement policies and discharge government functions. Concerning its operations, the first dimension is beyond the Bank's mandate. Hence, for the purposes of the Bank's business, governance has been defined as 'the manner in which power is exercised in the management of a country's economic and social resources for development' (World Bank 1992: 1). The Bank's governance activities concern its lending operations, economic and sector work, research, and policy dialogue. Four components of governance have been identified, which are relevant for the Bank's work given its mandate and resource constraints. These include public sector management, accountability of public officials, predictability and the legal framework for development, and transparency and information.

Since a functioning government apparatus is perceived to be a key issue of effective development management, the main thrust of governance-related activities has been public sector management including reform of state-owned enterprises, financial management, and administrative reform. With respect to enhancing public-sector accountability, Bank support has concentrated on fiscal decentralization, improving auditing and accounting mechanisms, implementing financial management standards, and promoting competition in service delivery and beneficiary participation in project work. In order to enhance transparency and the flow of information, the Bank has helped to improve public financial management, budgeting systems, and procurement procedures. The Bank also organized training programs for journalists from LDCs in order to increase public awareness and to stimulate public debate on policy reform. In the area of legal and regulatory reform, the World Bank has supported member countries, especially economies in transition, in developing a legal framework conducive for private economic activity. Additionally, support for judicial infrastructure and legal training has been provided. Finally, the Bank has started to explore and to mainstream participatory approaches concerning project design and implementation.

Only recently, the World Bank and particularly the World Bank Institute have begun preparations to conduct National Institutional Reviews (NIR) as well as governance and anticorruption diagnostic surveys in member countries. These new 'products' are intended to help assess the institutional foundation of policy reform and project work. Their objective is an analysis of key institutions that are critical for effective governance. Based on discussions with, and inputs from, policy makers, legislators as well as representatives from non-governmental organizations, academia, the media, and other organizations, the NIR and the diagnostic surveys are supposed to yield comprehensive assessments of the institutional environment of the respective country including its political situation. Hence, these tools should help to identify priorities for institutional reform, which are to be incorporated in the Country Assistance Strategy and lending programs.

Box 7.2: Governance policies of the International Monetary Fund

Given its mandate, the IMF is, like the World Bank, strictly confined to the economic dimensions of governance. In 1997, the Executive Board promulgated guidelines specifying the Fund's role in governance issues. While suggesting that 'it is legitimate (...) to seek information about the political situation in member countries as an essential element in judging the prospects for policy implementation', these guidelines also adhere to the nonpolitical mandate of the organization, requiring the Fund's judgments not to be affected 'by the nature of the political regime of a country' (IMF 1997: 4–5). Particularly, the guidelines specify that 'the IMF should not act on behalf of a member country in influencing another country's political orientation or behavior' (ibid.).

Based on a pragmatic, rather than a systematic approach, the IMF seeks to address governance-related problems mainly through policy advice and technical assistance. For the Fund, areas of major concern include capacity building at the Treasury, reform of budget management procedures, accounting and auditing practices, tax and customs administration, economic data management, central bank operations as well as financial sector reform including related legal reforms. By encouraging the liberalization of the price, exchange, and trade systems and the abolition of direct credit allocation, the Fund has sought to assist member countries in establishing institutions that limit *ad hoc* decision making, rent-seeking, and corruption. Technical assistance projects have been aimed at enhancing member countries' capacity to formulate and implement economic reforms, establishing market-oriented institutions, and enhancing the accountability of policy makers. The Fund has also promoted transparency in the public sector, particularly with respect to financial transactions in the central bank and the government budget. It intends to increase its involvement in governance issues through a more extensive treatment in Article IV consultations and a more comprehensive consideration of those governance-related aspects, that are within the organization's mandate and expertise, in its lending activities. Furthermore, the Fund seeks to treat governance issues in all member countries evenhandedly and to improve the collaboration with other multilateral donors. From the IMF's perspective, its primary contribution to enhancing governance lies in its support for economic reforms that reduce opportunities for rent-seeking and for strengthening institutional and administrative capacity.

Governance-related conditionality in the form of prior actions, structural benchmarks or performance criteria may be attached to policy measures if economic aspects of governance will have a direct macroeconomic impact. Moreover, financial support could be suspended in case of weak governance structures, which are conceived to have negative macroeconomic implications, threaten the effective implementation of an IMF-supported program, or facilitate the misuse of funds. Corrective measures to improve governance may be required as a precondition for the resumption of support.

---

interfere in the internal political affairs of a sovereign country nor is it capable of ensuring political stability in their member countries.[28] But occasionally it is difficult to draw a distinct boundary between economic conditionality and political interference. For example, the call for greater transparency and accountability in policy making may implicitly require freedom of the media and free political elections. Therefore, governance work, which is intended to promote economic adjustment and development, turns out to be a difficult balancing act. This political sensitiveness may have

Box 7.3: Governance policies of the European Bank for Reconstruction and Development

Basically, the EBRD is concerned with both economic and political aspects of governance. The former comprise *inter alia* administrative reform, tax collection and budget management, central–local government relations, legal, regulatory, and financial-sector reform, labor market reform, private property rights and corporate governance. The latter include member countries' commitment to multiparty democracy, pluralism, and human rights. In 1991, the Board of Directors approved procedures which the Bank should adopt in order to implement the political aspects of its mandate (EBRD 1992). Particularly, it was proposed to assess economic and political progress annually in member countries in respective country strategy papers (CSPs) and not on a project-by-project basis. EBRD activities are guided by the CSPs which contain an assessment of the member countries' political situation. If a country's political orientation is not appropriate or if a country is implementing policies that are inconsistent with the Bank's purpose (that is, the transition to open market-oriented economies), the EBRD can postpone proposed operations, restrict them or suspend the operations altogether. This, however, does not amount to political conditionality attached to any individual project. Besides this punitive measure, the Bank may emphasize political aspects such as the conduct of free elections, the accountability of the executive *vis-à-vis* the legislature and the constituency, the separation of the state and political parties, the rights of free speech and association as well as freedom of the press and coalition building in its technical advice and assistance activities.

With respect to administrative and participatory aspects of governance, the Bank has provided technical assistance aimed at strengthening institutional arrangements of the executive and judicial branches of government. It has also promoted public consultation and participation in the preparation of sector-specific projects. Most governance work, however, concerns the economic issues of governance, which are predominantly addressed in the context of sector-specific projects. Conditionality is applied to project lending and has prescribed passing laws on accounting procedures, privatization of utilities as well as establishing a market-oriented regulatory framework.

Given the EBRD's mandate, a key feature of its operations is support for the private sector. Operating as both a development bank and a merchant, the Bank provides direct financing for the private sector, enterprise restructuring, and privatization. Its investments also contribute funding for strengthening institutions and realizing financial and physical infrastructure projects that support private sector development. Since the Bank's operational purview is microeconomic and most of its clients are private companies or state-owned enterprises which operate in a competitive environment or which are assigned for privatization, overall policy reform issues, though important side conditions, play a minor role in the Bank's operations. This implies that the EBRD is more concerned with economic aspects of governance relating to private business transactions and less concerned with governance issues relating to overall policy reform.

prompted the Bank (as well as other international organizations) to adopt a rather loose definition of governance and hindered the organization from elucidating and specifying its broad and abstract approach. However, the exploration of modes of intervention that are politically feasible, justifiable, and promising is a necessary undertaking if the notion of effective

Box 7.4: Governance policies of the Asian Development Bank

The importance of governance quality for economic development was formally recognized by the ADB in 1995 when the organization's Board adopted an official governance policy (ADB 1995). Ever since the Bank has emphasized that – due to its Charter – its governance work will be restricted to the economic and social dimensions of governance and that any operations will be avoided that include political activities or considerations. The broad approach to governance taken by the ADB is quite similar to the concept developed in this study. The Bank identified the same basic components of effective governance including accountability, participation, predictability, and transparency. Today, effective governance is viewed by the Bank's management as essential for achieving the organization's objectives; especially for poverty reduction. The ADB stresses that governance problems need to be clearly distinguished from policy mistakes. Hence, similar to the conceptual standpoint taken in this study, the Bank states that 'governance has to do with the **manner** in which policies and decisions are formulated and implemented, and not with the policies or the decisions **themselves'** (ADB 1998: 1–2; emphasis in original). Stimulated by the experience with economic development in the Asian and Pacific region and especially in East Asia, the ADB recognizes that successful development is independent of the nature of political systems. Instead, policy stability, flexibility in reacting to market signals, as well as discipline in maintaining policy measures that are necessary to achieve long-term objectives, in spite of short-term costs, are viewed as hallmarks of effective governance (ADB 1995).

In order to make the elements of its governance framework operationally relevant, the Bank seeks to translate these abstract components into specific realms of its programming and sector work; including public sector management and reform, legal and regulatory reform, economic decentralization, and private sector development. In 1997, the Bank created a *Governance and Capacity Building Resource Group* within the *Strategy and Policy Office* to serve as the institutional focal point for these issues (Nishimoto 1997). Moreover, the ADB proposes to design its country programs and sectoral projects such that the quality of governance will be raised in the sectors that are targeted by its operations. In fact, the Bank has done so in almost all of its developing member countries through the inclusion of suitable policy measures in its programming activities, specific components in the design of individual projects, and comprehensive technical assistance activities. Additionally, advisory technical assistance is provided for distinct policy studies, training, and seminars. In 1999, the Bank started to produce and publish a series of country reports that, similar to the NIR of the World Bank, are supposed to provide a general overview of major governance-related issues, challenges, and bottlenecks in the Bank's developing member countries.

The guiding principle underlying any governance-related operations is that the ADB will only become active upon the explicit request of governments in its member countries. The possible consideration of governance issues with respect to loan conditionality has not played a significant role (ADB 1995).

governance is to become a leading and broadly accepted principle in the organization's operations. (4) The Bank itself concedes that it lacks adequate expertise in public sector management, institution building, and participatory approaches and, one needs to add, in political science and sociology (World Bank 1994). This represents a serious bottleneck to handling the complexity inherent in the governance issue effectively, to translating governance concerns suitably into the Bank's operations, and to improving the Bank management's understanding of country-specific political, social, cultural, and ethnic side conditions of economic policy making.

More recently, however, the Bank has begun – under the guidance of the World Bank Institute (WBI) – to pursue governance policies more systematically. The Governance group of the WBI was established to facilitate participatory and action-oriented programs to enhance the quality of economic and institutional reform and to fight corruption in member countries. By providing courses on corporate governance, corruption control, and investigative journalism, raising public awareness, conducting programs on strengthening judicial reform as well as government accountability, participation, and parliamentary oversight, and producing governance and anticorruption diagnostic surveys, the WBI seeks to improve governance in collaboration with other operations of the World Bank and with other international organizations. This integrated approach to foster capacity building, improve governance, and fight corruption promises to become a critical tool for improving the quality of the Bank's operations in the future.[29]

The IMF's envisaged approach to governance, which still lacks a proper definition of the term, is restricted to governance-related problems in public sector management and (financial) market regulation. From the Fund's perspective and given its traditional purview and expertise, economic liberalizing-cum-related institution building is the best way to curb rent-seeking, corruption, and preferential treatment of privileged elites and hence to improve governance (IMF 1997). The call for leaner and more effective government, the application of neoclassical policy prescriptions, and the evenhanded treatment of member countries, however, ignore country-specific circumstances, informal institutions and historical factors.

This omission may turn out to be counterproductive, because non-economic factors may have a significant impact on the efficacy of policy reforms. If these are neglected and if future political and social consequences resulting from recommended policy adjustment packages are not taken into account, policy reform may be doomed to fail, especially if existing governance structures are weak. Therefore, international donor organizations need to explore suitable ways to reduce the number of cases in which anticipated reform success evolves into unexpected and expensive failures.

The treatment of the Indonesian crisis in 1997/98 by the IMF is a case in point. Through the imposition of an orthodox austerity approach-cum-financial sector restructuring, the Fund unintentionally contributed to a worsening of the crisis. Regardless of whether or not the recommended policies were appropriate from a theoretical point of view, it must be argued that potential country-specific social and political reactions to policy reforms need to be taken into consideration in order to ensure the feasibility of reforms and not to jeopardize political stability.[30] Policy actions that do not reflect the views of broad societal groups can cause social and political disruptions which seriously interfere with the functioning of the economy.[31] Therefore, both domestic experts in policy making and international organizations need to take the costs of those disruptions into consideration, even if the social and political ramifications may not be explicit parts of their objective functions. From a governance perspective, the application of standard adjustment programs based on allegedly even-handed policies cannot be effective. The Fund's envisaged approach to governance still lacks a proper theoretical basis. Instead of seeking a conceptual foundation and applying it to country-specific circumstances, the IMF is looking for best practices as a basis for developing new standards to be evenly applied across countries. Notwithstanding the importance of standards in technical areas such as data dissemination as well as fiscal and banking codes, macro- and microeconomic policy recommendations need to be tailored to the needs, capacities, and capabilities of individual countries. If these requirements cannot be fulfilled by the Fund, be it for a lack of expertise or a restricted mandate of the organization, then the IMF should consult and cooperate more closely with the regional development banks and other international organizations, when it designs adjustment programs.

The European Bank for Reconstruction and Development (EBRD) is the first multilateral financial organization in the Charter of which political goals have been incorporated.[32] In accordance with its founding agreement, the EBRD is supposed to work only in countries committed to and applying the principles of multiparty democracy, pluralism, and market economics. Adherence to these principles is monitored closely and the political situation is regularly reviewed for the Bank's country strategies. The Bank uses information on the political situation in its member countries as a yardstick to judge countries regarding their eligibility for external assistance. In a recent *Transition Report*, the EBRD (1998: 3) states that

> (t)here remain (...) a number of authoritarian regimes, particularly in Belarus and in most countries of Central Asia, where effective multi-party democracy has not taken root. The experience of transition to date has shown that the reliance of these regimes on manipulation and control undermines sound economic decision-making and prevents an effective response to economic difficulties once they have arisen.

Consequently, in several cases operations have been slowed down or halted. This underscores that the volume of lending is significantly influenced by a country's governance capacity. In none of these countries, however, have operations been suspended.

The Bank has been most explicit with respect to Belarus. In this case, it distinguishes three scenarios. Given a base case that reflects current political conditions, the Bank would focus its operations on private sector development. In an intermediate case reflecting progress in the political sphere, two public-sector projects, the preparatory work on which has been halted, would be promoted. The high-case scenario requires substantial progress in both overall economic and political reform. In that case, the Bank would see a viable opportunity to expand its program. With regard to the Central Asian countries, which do not meet democratic political standards, no public information is currently available concerning the influence of the political situation on the Bank's future operational program.[33]

Despite its mandate, the EBRD does not actively pursue political changes in its member countries. It has not interpreted its mandate in a pro-active way, but rather in a conservative manner. Political reforms appear to be regarded as preconditions for the promotion of state-sector projects, but the Bank does not provide significant assistance to improve the overall governance structure of a country. Institutional reforms that are supported mainly focus on the economic dimension of governance such as legal and regulatory reform aimed at enhancing the management of a specific sector in the economy. Since most of its operations focus on the micro-level and the Bank is not involved in structural adjustment at the state level, no conditionality exists in terms of policy-related lending and basically no prior policy actions are required for financing private sector projects.[34] At the macro level, governance work is restricted to a policy dialogue at the ministerial level. With respect to re-orientating and restructuring the government apparatuses in recipient countries, the Bank is involved in a very limited way, especially focusing on the legal transition.

Last but not least, the ADB's approach to governance is similar to that of the World Bank. Although the World Bank has started explicitly to address governance-related issues much earlier and has meanwhile gained substantial experience, the ADB has been somewhat more explicit about developing a coherent conceptual approach. Also, its analytical framework seeks to distinguish clearly between the components that constitute effective governance and the distinct realms of action. The ADB's lead *vis-à-vis* the World Bank in developing a more consistent governance framework which is supposed to guide the organization's policies and operations may be attributed to its smaller size, relatively flat organizational hierarchy, and limited geographical focus. These factors may have been quite conducive to modifying the thrust of the Bank's policies and to finding a sufficient internal consensus that is supportive of such a modification.

However, developing governance policies and translating them into appropriate actions has not been easy for the ADB either. Its governance work has been considerably shaped by the particular traditions and specific institutional context in which it has been embedded. The increasing importance of governance issues in the ADB's lending operations represents a new challenge that reflects the Bank's more general shift towards becoming a fully-fledged development agency. Historically, the ADB concentrated its activities on financing large engineering projects including roads, dams as well as irrigation projects. Consequently, governance issues have been addressed narrowly and usually as an afterthought, and project designers have been chiefly concerned with aspects relating to training in order to ensure that local staff in member countries were able to maintain and operate new equipment properly. In contrast, governance work at the World Bank has been *inter alia* influenced by the experience with stabilization-cum-adjustment programs in the 1980s and (initially) mainly focused on efforts to contain public expenditures. Hence, initially most governance-related support provided by the ADB focused on the sectoral level, and only minor efforts were undertaken to reform central government functions and mechanisms. More recently, the Bank has begun to strengthen its focus on issues such as public sector reform, private sector development, and strengthening structures of an emerging civil society. But the number of technical assistance projects and loans primarily addressing these concerns is still relatively small. Moreover, similar to the other three international organizations, only very limited progress has been achieved in developing a strategy that seeks to improve the overall politico-institutional structure that underlies and determines economic policy making in its developing member countries.

In short, a stocktaking of governance work conducted by the multilateral financial organizations draws attention to eight important facts: (1) the incorporation of governance issues in these organizations' activities is still at its very beginning, and governance issues have not been fully mainstreamed in their operations; (2) although donor agencies have been involved in numerous governance-related activities, their governance work has been largely carried out in an *ad hoc* manner and does not follow a systematic approach, let alone a consistent and coherent strategy; (3) the highly abstract components constituting effective governance are at times used in formalistic and legalistic terms and occasionally in more specific ways; (4) the importance of government credibility and commitment to policy reform has been essentially neglected as a pivotal precondition for effective economic reforms; (5) governance work, to date, has been mainly technical in character (especially with respect to sector-specific projects and public sector management), that is it addresses the machinery of a given sector, but not automatically the sources of poor performance; (6) there is a lack of expertise to move the governance agenda forward. If governance issues are to be taken seriously, staff skills need to be upgraded and new skills acquired particularly in the areas of institution building, public sector management, participatory approaches, and public–private partnerships. A related aspect concerns the need to adjust the organizational culture relating to habits of thought and behavior, that is the informal institutions within these organizations. This not only includes reforms of the organizational structures and work processes, but also the need to enhance the awareness of staff regarding the importance of governance issues; (7) governance-related activities are always politically sensitive and may in some cases collide with the international organizations' mandate. The elaboration of a feasible governance agenda represents a balancing act between the consideration of economic necessities and the acknowledgement of political constraints; and (8) while recipient governments remain the primary partners regarding communication, negotiation, and particular operations, international organizations do have the right to initiate a dialogue with other political, economic, and social actors in the country concerned. This does not call the sovereignty of recipient countries into question, but gives the donor agency some latitude to overcome restrictions by governments. Donors need to intensify and institutionalize such dialogue in order to gather information, to form an independent judgment in deciding on assistance programs, and to identify the politically feasible and economically effective ingredients of policy reform.

Toward a new kind of conditionality in international lending operations?
Today, it is uncontroversial that the politico-institutional environment in a borrowing country plays a major role in shaping the country's economic and social development, the efficacy of policy reform, and the effectiveness of external aid. Therefore, it is only reasonable that donor organizations take the issue of sound development management into consideration in their lending decisions. The crucial question, however, is how this ought to be done given the restricted mandate of most organizations and the political sensitiveness of the issue. Should the provision of development assistance be made contingent on political reforms and improving governance structures in recipient countries? Political conditionality, that is promoting democratic reform and improving human rights, clearly falls outside the mandate of most multilateral financial organizations. But is there a political or economic rationale to impose governance-related conditionality, that is to make program and project lending conditional on reforms concerning the *economic* dimensions of governance?

Sometimes multilateral organizations can fulfill the function of agencies of restraint by imposing conditionalities that help governments to implement economically necessary policies that are domestically disputed by political opposition. But conditionality based on key governance issues will be associated with several problems: (1) it may, rightly or wrongly, be interpreted by recipient governments as interference in their internal political affairs or as neoliberal imperialism by the donor agency, which may seek to impose Western-type values in the hope of restraining potential competitors.[35] (2) Policies and projects can often be substituted for one another, opening channels for evading conditions that are included in program loans (Streeten 1996). (3) Conditionality may be reluctantly accepted, but not implemented as desired. Instead imposed policies threaten to reinforce hierarchical political relationships and hence exclude particular segments of society that are critical for successful development (Stiglitz 1998c). (4) The impact of informal institutions on the efficacy of policy making, persisting ideologies, social structures, and external security threats contribute to the complexity of the governance issue and may affect the quality of a country's governance structure regardless of the nature of the political regime. To date, it is not sufficiently understood what kinds of political and institutional problems are crucial to effective lending operations in a particular country and which are not. (5) Governance-related conditionality is also confronted with a traditional dilemma of external assistance. Loans or grants of whatever form will not yield the desired outcomes unless the recipients are credibly committed to institutional reforms and the implementation of policies that are indispensable for sustained social and economic development. External support has all too often failed to offset a lack of local ownership of policy reforms (Killick 1996; Nunnenkamp 1995).

Governance-related conditionality will inevitably represent a balancing act between an economic rationale and political interference. Furthermore, it is extremely difficult to apply evenhanded criteria to measure country performance in terms of governance. Landell-Mills and Serageldin (1992: 305) argue that

> in practice country situations are never identical. Moreover, significant improvements in some areas may be accompanied by failures in others. The 'acceptable' level of deviance from an ideal remains a subjective matter (...). Conceptually, it is almost impossible to reduce the complex social, cultural, political, legal, and economic interactions that make up a modern society to a single measure of good governance.

Individual country circumstances make judgmental approaches inescapable. Therefore, a pragmatic, though consistent and coherent, approach to promoting governance is highly desirable. Besides the punitive form of conditionality (a reduction, redirection or suspension of development assistance in the case of non-compliance), there are two positive forms of assistance which provide the opportunity to proceed accordingly. These include an increase of external funds to reward efforts at improving governance capacity and specialized forms of support in the form of technical assistance projects and policy dialogue.

In applying the different forms of assistance available to multilateral donors, they would be well advised to distinguish between different categories of governments, not with respect to regime type, but regarding their willingness to overcome governance-related bottlenecks to policy reform and project management. First of all, there are countries whose governments are reform-minded, willing to improve governance structures, and request the donor organization to provide assistance. Secondly, a number of countries exist in which (parts of) the government opposes major steps toward governance reform, and thirdly, there are countries whose governments significantly violate human rights. The governance work by multilateral donors, which can be effectively and feasibly pursued, crucially depends on which category a particular country belongs to. While countries belonging to the first category may be reasonably responsive to comprehensive reforms of their governance structure, those of the second group are not. If the multilateral development agencies choose to pursue governance work in these countries, they need to decide in favor of a more gradual, piecemeal approach. Countries belonging to the last group may still be eligible for foreign assistance by multilaterals beyond humanitarian and emergency aid, if they fulfill the economic preconditions required to implement an economic adjustment program (Stevens and Gnanaselvam 1995). However, if lending is eliminated for any reason, the only remaining option is to seek to improve the government's understanding of governance issues through a continuing policy dialogue.

In all cases, government ownership is the all-embracing issue. Even if international donor organizations seek to base their governance work or possibly emerging governance strategies on a 'depoliticized' concept, key governance issues will almost always address sensitive political areas of policy reform, at least in the perception of recipient governments. This is the main reason why governance-related adjustment programs or projects need to be elaborated in cooperation between donors and recipient countries. Governments need to take full ownership of broad scale governance programs and also single projects, if they relate to critical areas of policy making, for example, the establishing of a national audit office.

In most LDCs and PSCs, there is an urgent need to clarify priorities and phasing of governance-related policies and projects. Basically, there are two ways to improve the overall governance structure of a country: (1) through a frontal, system-wide, big-bang approach or (2) through an incremental, long-term strategy. Given the political sensitivity and reluctance on the part of government authorities to discuss governance issues openly, a frontal, bold, and comprehensive attack to improve governance structures is not feasible in most countries, except for those PSCs that strive for EU membership. In most cases, only an indirect and gradual approach to improving the overall governance structure will be effective and sustainable and also acceptable to governments, so that they can assume ownership of the reform process.

However, experiences in numerous LDCs indicate that the gradualist approach (the work with specific sectors and institutions and the hope that gradually the change will spread into other areas of the system) has been defeated by systemic ineffectiveness and has produced only 'islands of excellence'. There are no blueprints to overcome this dilemma. Appropriate ways of how to proceed will depend on country-specific characteristics. From a conceptual perspective, however, a *focal-point approach* would be suitable to gradually enhancing the overall governance structure in countries whose governments are reluctant to adopt bold reforms or whose informal institutions would be in conflict with an institutional big-bang approach. Focal points can be already existing or newly created institutions or organizations that perform core governance functions. The strengthening of focal points (supported by external assistance) will yield spill-over effects to other institutions in the system through their demonstration function or through induced changes in the incentive structures underlying the behavior of individuals and the activities of agencies. Focal points are strategic entry points for reform that can be used to address key governance issues. These include improving the public administration, strengthening mechanisms and institutional arrangements which facilitate the flow of information, improving actual service delivery in order to encourage user feedback and discipline the line ministries, and assuring a minimum of genuine user participation in order to improve implementation. Focal points of high priority may include organizational and procedural reforms of central banks, Ministries of Finance, national audit offices, Ministries of Education, core governance agencies that are responsible for public administration reform and for translating the broad guidelines on reform into action plans, core agencies of the executive branch of government at sub-national levels, privatization and anti-trust agencies, and schools and training centers for administration and management.[36]

These focal points indicate some of the key organizations which are of critical importance for the effectiveness of the overall governance structure in a given country. A major problem of the focal-point approach, which is inherent to external support programs in general, is that of identifying the most appropriate local counterparts of the donor agency. The implementation of the World Bank's programs, for example, is essentially conducted by sectoral departments, which have as their counterparts the corresponding ministries of the recipient government. This involves two problems: (1) in some cases, the objective of policy reform may be to abolish these ministries or particular departments therein; they would in turn oppose reforms. (2) Even if the survival of the relevant client itself is not at stake, the counterpart may be hostile to the proposed policy or project and endeavor to block or slow down its implementation. These problems are particularly acute if the recipient country has a badly divided government.[37] In several PSCs, notably in Russia, the government has been formed as a coalition of individuals or political parties who represent sharply different interests, political convictions, and loyalties. Governments often include both reformist and anti-reformist forces. The latter usually represent interests of industrial, agricultural, or military pressure groups which strive to maintain the strongholds of the former communist system or seek to preserve the current partial reform equilibrium which allows them to capture massive rents resulting from a non-competitive market environment. When governments are badly divided, a bold and coherent reform program can hardly be implemented even if reformist forces belong to the leaders of government. Often ministries opposed to reform are still able to pursue their own agendas and, hence, anti-reformist policies. In this case, the pursuit of first-best economic reform policies may be counterproductive, because anti-reformist forces may be in charge of making the relevant decisions.[38] Moreover, the existence of a deeply divided government may imply that external financial assistance is channeled precisely to those ministries or agencies that oppose policy reform. Boycko et al. (1996) report that in 1994 the World Bank approved a loan on land reform in Russia, the administration of which was assigned to the State Committee on Land. This committee, however, opposed land privatization and used the loan to impede land reform. Multilateral development agencies need to take these political side conditions into account when they design structural adjustment programs, and to distinguish between economically efficient and politically feasible measures. Furthermore, external support needs to be strategically targeted toward those focal points that are controlled by reform-minded policy makers.

In sum, the conceptual framework presented in this study in combination with the available policy tools discussed above represent a roadmap for multilateral donor agencies to address those governance issues that are pivotal for sustained policy reform in LDCs and PSCs. Given the problems and options associated with the reform of governance structures, the following policy conclusions can be drawn for multilateral development agencies, who intend to enhance sound development management in their member countries:

- anticipate the social and political consequences of program lending, project aid and attached conditionality;

- ensure that recommended policies are not only economically sound but feasible, that is that the institutional and political preconditions exist that are necessary for implementation and enforcement; in particular, this concerns credible government commitment including its willingness to reform, its capability to implement, and the political institutions' suitability to sustain reforms beyond government changes and exogenous shocks;
- refrain from standardized governance policies and pursue country-specific approaches taking the recipient country's history and social and political conditions into account;
- make sure that governments assume full ownership of any governance-related program or project;
- in case of a divided government, strengthen the parts of government that are committed to policy reform against the government ministries or agencies that oppose reforms;
- devote a high proportion of external assistance to support human resource development in order to ensure the effective functioning of an improved politico-institutional environment;
- involve sub-national governments in governance programs, for example, by selecting pilot regions eligible for assistance, which could create demonstration effects;
- encourage consensus-building mechanisms in the recipient country in order to increase the acceptance of reforms and involve segments of civil society in debates about governance reforms;
- be cautious regarding governance-related conditionality due to political sensitiveness and the traditional dilemmas of making conditionality work effectively;
- ham-fisted conditionality imposed on grudging governments should be replaced by quiet signaling or a premium approach, which rewards reform efforts by increasing external assistance;[39]
- intensify country dialogue on key governance issues at a senior minister or head of government level.

Governance-related constraints are usually interrelated within countries, and their nature varies considerably from place to place. Domestic institution building and its external support, therefore, must be strategic. No blueprints or how-to manuals can be offered. Crafting effective governance structures involves a long gestation period and requires continuous fine tuning and adjustment to changing economic, political, social, and international circumstances. The road to effective governance is also mapped out by cultural and historical factors which vary substantially across countries. This is why externally devised standard models for (re)invigorating governance structures, which do not sufficiently take into consideration the complexity of persisting state–society relations, may produce unanticipated negative effects. Moreover, explicit conditionality may be incompatible with the notion of local ownership of reforms. Hence, one may agree with Martin (1992) that effective governance cannot be introduced by external actors. However, one needs to add that there are strong arguments that external assistance will be necessary and suitable to support the creation of effective governance structures which are initiated by local policy makers.

7.3 TOWARDS A POST-WASHINGTON CONSENSUS?

During the 1990s, the view that the politico-institutional environment has been the primary source of obstacles for sustained economic change, has come to reflect the failures of structural adjustment programs. Problems concerning the adequate institutional design for the formation, implementation, and enforcement of policy reform programs have gradually become seriously analysed issues in both scholarly debates and the work of international organizations (including the multilateral development banks[40]). Moreover, in the light of growing public concern about corruption, misuse of funds, and poor policy making, international organizations have been increasingly urged to give governance issues a higher priority on the agenda of policy reforms. And, in fact, international organizations, most of which have usually demanded that LDCs and PSCs radically implement a package of clear and simple adjustment recipes as a precondition to further lending, have come to realize that their policy recommendations have been deficient – but that the necessary change in their programming policies would threaten to overrun their own agenda. Given the governance dimension of policy reform, the MDBs face a dilemma: improving adjustment programs means that these organizations will have to take into account that the nature of political orders of sovereign countries is now at stake – but any consideration of this, on the other hand, would not only exceed their technical expertise but also their mandate. Nevertheless, governance issues and the need to strengthen institutional reforms in LDCs and PSCs have received considerable attention in different fora (Ahrens 2000):

- LDC and PSC governments themselves have been expressing growing concern with various aspects of poor development management;
- bilateral development agencies have been devoting growing attention to using aid effectively, especially to reverse the signs of aid fatigue resulting from the misuse of funds;

- facing the challenge of aid effectiveness, the MDBs are increasingly taking the promotion of effective governance into consideration;
- United Nation agencies, especially the UNDP, are increasingly addressing the problem of how to improve governance structures;
- in 1989, the World Bank was the first of the MDBs that explicitly addressed governance issues;
- the ADB was the first of the MDBs that adopted an official governance policy in 1995;
- in 1995, the European Union added the promotion of 'good governance' as a central principle for the Union's development policies;
- at the Halifax Summit in 1995 and the Lyon Summit, the G7 countries declared 'good governance' as the foundation of sustainable development;
- in 1996, the World Trade Organization Ministerial Conference declared the establishment of a working group to prepare an agreement to improve transparency in government procurement practices;
- in 1996, the Ministers of the Intergovernmental Group of Twenty-Four also discussed governance issues, although they emphasized that the Bretton Woods Institutions should proceed with great caution in applying conditionality in the area of governance;
- in 1997, the ad hoc working group on participatory development and good governance established by the Development Assistance Committee of the OECD viewed 'good governance' and democratization as unalterable prerequisites for sustainable development; it emphasized the role of civil society and the importance of country-level policy dialogue and adequate aid management as central factors in a long-term strategic framework;
- in 1997, the Executive Board of the IMF adopted guidelines for the role of the Fund in governance issues;
- during the last ten years, virtually all international organizations and bilateral development agencies called for decisive measures to combat bribery and to fight corruption in international and domestic business transactions; notably Transparency International, a non-governmental organization dedicated to increasing government accountability and curbing both international and national corruption, has stimulated the international discussion on corruption in international business transactions since 1995 by annually publishing an international corruption index covering more than 80 countries.[41]

Furthermore, leading policy makers and economists have recently begun to call for a new coherent paradigm for economic and social development. Within the donor community, the most prominent proponents of a *Post-*

Washington Consensus have been James Wolfensohn, President of the World Bank, and Joseph Stiglitz, the Bank's former Senior Vice President and Chief Economist. The *World Development Report 1997* was a milestone in revising the political paradigm for development of the World Bank, the starting point of a new, more productive dialogue between the Bank, other political decision makers, academics, and civil society.[42] Stiglitz (1996, 1998a), in particular, advocates developing and using more policy instruments to pursue broader objectives of development, including sustainable, egalitarian, and democratic development. He argues that the new paradigm for development should seek to explore ways to achieve an overall transformation of society effectively. A new development strategy should be less prescriptive, though more comprehensive than the original Washington Consensus. It needs to give key development issues comprising education, health and living standards as well as the environment the same priority as GDP growth and capital allocation. Processes and consensus for policy reform need to evolve at all levels of society and should not be imposed in the form of abstract prescriptions by outside donor organizations.

Nevertheless, the debate on a Post-Washington Consensus is still at the very beginning regarding a discussion on how governments, social groups, and local non-governmental organizations can be supported in developing and improving the capabilities and institutional capacities needed to pursue policy reform successfully. Stiglitz (1998b) identifies five promising propositions in this regard:

- government interventions should be restricted in areas that are subject to a significant and systematic influence of special interest groups;
- a crucial government role is to promote competition and to act as a referee in a market economy;
- in order to improve government performance, political decision-making processes need to become more open and less subject to secrecy;
- governments need to encourage the provision of public goods by the private sector in order to discipline itself and to convey voice; and
- political authorities should aim to achieve a balance between the technical expertise of policy making on the one hand and accountability and democratic representativeness on the other hand.

These propositions clearly point to the importance of governance. Greater openness, a public–private partnership, and an increasing number of participants providing inputs on policy making are central factors in bringing about more balanced signals reflecting societal preferences. They are also critical to ensure that the government and the private sector act in a complementary fashion. Moreover, inclusionary policy making based on consensual processes shows a higher degree of permanence and enhances the feasibility and efficacy of policy reforms. Competitive advocacy processes represent an appropriate means to discuss opposing arguments openly. They advance the consideration of costs and benefits related to specific policies in a more balanced manner.

Of course, notions of how to redefine the role of government in economic development and how to make it more effective and accountable need to be incorporated in a new paradigm for development. But how should governance issues be coherently and consistently included in the emerging new paradigm? In this regard, neither the literature on policy reform and development nor discussions among development practitioners have provided an answer. Besides the political sensitiveness of the issue, it is the difficulty of operationalizing any concept of governance which imposes new challenges on the development community. Turning good intentions into action and developing new adjustment programs that may eventually lead to a Post-Washington Consensus are associated with serious problems and challenges (Ahrens 2000):

- governance is a politically sensitive area, and donor organizations need to ensure that LDC and PSC governments can assume full ownership of governance-related programs;
- in order to formulate a consistent governance strategy tailored to the needs of a borrowing country, the MDBs must establish internal consensus-building mechanisms to deal with persisting diverse interests and convictions within their management; in addition, they need to find rules and procedures to overcome external political and commercial pressures on their programming activities;
- international development organizations such as the World Bank or the regional development banks need to develop a coherent governance policy on which their operations will be based;
- in order to implement this policy, these organizations must develop adequate technical expertise;
- since development agencies perform different roles and have different mandates, a concerted action of multilateral and bilateral agencies seems to be necessary to develop coherent program strategies and to achieve the desired results.

Experiences show that institutions and policies as well as the design of the economic and political order are of utmost importance for effective economic reforms. This fact is encouraging in so far as it allows the conclusion that less successful countries should be basically capable of overcoming the impediments to development. But this requires that the governments of these economies as well as authorities of industrialized countries and multilateral financial organizations are ready to take advantage of existing options to development. However, in designing new adjustment programs, policy makers should bear in mind that

> it is entirely possible that neither interest-based explanations nor institutional ones will be entirely satisfactory for explaining how societies cope with the challenges of policy reform and consolidation. Particularly within a democratic framework, consolidation may also require what Kahler calls social learning; the evolution of a broader ideational consensus among leaders, interest groups, party elites and attentive publics that sets some boundaries on the range of economic debate. Such a consensus does not imply stasis or the absence of conflict (...). Nonetheless, it is possible that the long-term sustainability of policy choices will depend on a convergence of thinking about fundamental means–ends relationships in the economy. If so, then the formation of elite preferences, ideas, and ideology, as well as the evolution of public opinion, are potentially important explanatory variables. (Haggard and Kaufman 1992b: 36)

These arguments again emphasize that, although external actors such as international organizations may play critical roles as catalysts and advisors, eventually governance structures must be home-grown in order to be effective. The conceptual approach to establishing a flexible MEGS developed in this study represents a modest but useful starting point to incorporate governance issues systematically into country-specific development strategies and policies; the more so as this governance concept does not presuppose the existence of a distinct political regime and emphasizes the adaptive efficiency of a country's politico-institutional structure. With its implications for formulating and implementing policy reforms in LDCs and PSCs, it may also help to re-assess the policies of international organizations and hence contribute to the emergence of a Post-Washington Consensus that fosters the development of economically effective *and* politically feasible reform policies.

Before concluding, I would like to discuss briefly some of the limits and possible extensions of this study. First, the case studies discussed in the preceding chapters indicate useful pointers for identifying the constituent pillars of effective governance structures and how they can be crafted. However, in order to understand better how governance structures actually evolve over time and how their development is shaped by the dialectic relationships between different political and economic actors, the cases need to be analysed in much greater detail; secondly, in order to empirically test the usefulness of the four core dimensions of governance – accountability, participation, predictability, and transparency – and to identify adequate channels for their realization in different country settings, more country studies (and especially those which include economies of other regions) need to be conducted; thirdly, while the importance of information institutions such as cultural factors has been emphasized in this study, more research is needed at the country level in order to understand better their impact on the efficacy of policy and institutional reform; and fourthly, although the openness of economies has been stressed as a factor that promotes the emergence of effective governance, the challenges relating to globalization in general have not been addressed. Current and future processes of globalization, however, will open up new options for development, but may also threaten to erode indigenous structures and traditions and potentially to limit the capability of governments from independently pursuing particular development strategies. In addressing these challenges, national governance structures will inevitably come under adjustment pressure. Moreover, the issues of global governance have been entirely omitted in this study. But as the recent financial crisis in East Asia and its contagion effects in Eastern Europe and Latin America clearly indicate, there is a strong need to strengthen institutional structures at the supra-national level. As a matter of fact, this not only holds for reforming the international financial architecture, but also with respect to environmental problems, social and labor standards, and human rights issues, among others.

The wave of transformation that has evolved throughout the world since the 1980s has burdened numerous countries with the problem of parallel development, the simultaneous transition towards democratic rule and a market economy. The pathways to democratic capitalism, however, are manifold, and neither governments, social elites, constituencies nor international organizations have a blueprint at their disposal of how to avoid dead-end roads or roundabouts. All emerging market economies and democracies need to overcome the tension between the necessity for bold and fast executive decision-making and the tenets of participation. In this regard, the cases discussed in this study provide valuable lessons on the consolidation of democratic rule and economic reforms. They have clearly demonstrated that the rules of policy making matter. Of utmost importance for the twofold transformation to succeed is (1) a credible commitment to broadly shared, future growth dividends; (2) fostering the emergence of open economies and open societies; (3) the development of political institutions that create credible limits on governments' authority, effectively mediate debates on policy reform, and facilitate coordination between contending economic and social interests; and (4) the reduction of executive discretion and the enhancement of accountability by political authorities. These are fundamental preconditions for building effective governance structures, based on a strong but limited government. This type of government is one in which political leadership is balanced by political and economic institutions, one that ensures participation, and in which bureaucratic autonomy is balanced by accountability. After all, governance ought to be interpreted as a dynamic process. Policy makers have to ensure that policies match institutions and vice versa. Effective governance requires constant fine tuning and the adjusting of institutions and policy solutions to changing technological, social, economic, and political environments. In this sense, effective governance will significantly contribute to improving the adaptive efficiency of an economy and a polity, a factor that is needed to lay a secure foundation for effective policy reform and sustained economic development and transition. Note, however, that the simultaneous pursuit of market-oriented and democratic reforms is not a *conditio sine qua non* for economic progress. Eventually, the emergence and continuous fine tuning and adjustment of a MEGS may (and most likely will) lead to significant progress in democratization, but it should also be clear that a fully-fledged democracy following the model of Western Europe or the US is not an indispensable prerequisite for successfully implementing policy reform at the early stages of development.

Difficulties relating to policy reforms in LDCs and PSCs do not result from a lack of understanding of how markets work, but from difficulties in understanding how to move to a higher trajectory of economic and social development from the specific situation of particular countries. The most important challenge is not to identify an adequate target design for new institutions and organizations, but to frame the process of development and transition that helps to achieve those targets. In this context, one should bear in mind that the assumption of the superiority of a particular model of economic development – the Washington Consensus approach, say – in fact excludes other strategies of development that have actually worked well in the past, as well as others that promise to be economically effective and politically feasible in the future. This consideration led Rodrik (1999) to conclude that

> It is telling that when South Korea recently came under IMF conditionality, the IMF asked the country to undertake an ambitious range of reforms in trade and capital accounts, government–business relations, and labor-market institutions that entailed remolding the Korean economy in the image of a Washington economist's idea of a free-market economy. (...) If Korea, a country with an exemplary development record, is subject to pressures of this kind, one can imagine what is in store for small countries with more checkered economic histories. (...) an approach that presumes the superiority of a particular model of a capitalist economy is quite restrictive in terms of the range of institutional variation that market economies can (and do) admit.

Thus, neither international organizations nor LDC and PSC governments should seek to follow seemingly ideal theoretical models strictly. Although lessons can and ought to be learnt from the experience of other countries and theoretical models can and should guide policy making, national governments, societal groups, and external actors must refrain from relying on dogmatic approaches. Institutional experimentation has been and remains a critical factor in finding the most promising way to overcome problems of underdevelopment and systemic transformation. The development and lasting improvement of flexible market-enhancing governance structures, which promote the adaptive efficiency of all societal suborders, is a fruitful approach to enhancing the quality of policy making and to helping different stakeholders in development and transition to protect and effectively to pursue their own interests. In sum, there is no single path to effective governance that fits every country. But some major, instructive principles exist which underlie successful-country experiences. Given the context-specificity of effective governance structures, the main conclusion of this study is that crafting a flexible MEGS is an evolutionary process in which policy tools and institutional arrangements need to be designed, scrutinized, re-designed, and implemented to help realize those principles and to fit institutions to local conditions. Essentially, as Meier (1995: 63–64) stresses, '(t)he very essence of policy making is to practice the art of the possible and to institute the feasible. The objective is not simply to replicate the development of another country in an earlier period.' The notion of a MEGS as an integral component of a Post-Washington Consensus can help to achieve this objective.

NOTES

1. Experiences show that even if political leaders are reform-minded and try to commit themselves to suitable adjustment policies, they may be hindered in doing so due to existing institutional deficits, which, instead, may create strong incentives for more populist policies. Note that reforms aiming at curtailing the scope of state intervention (like privatization, liberalization, and deregulation) actually require the enhancement of the governance capacity of the state; see World Bank (1992). In this context, participation plays a crucial role, because it might help to overcome possible stagnation of reforms. Fernandez and Rodrik (1991) show that a rational electorate might reject reforms that would benefit a majority of the constituents and that political systems basically show a bias toward maintaining the status quo, even if that situation is inefficient and economic subjects are risk neutral. The reason is that the losers and the gainers from reform cannot sufficiently be identified *ex ante*. But it is conceivable that participation and giving real assets to people can change that kind of reasoning.
2. See Chapter 4, Sections 4.1 and 4.2 in Part I of this study.
3. See, for example, Haggard and Webb (1993), Williamson (1994), and Rodrik (1996).
4. Harberger (1993: 343).
5. For more specific arguments relating to the importance of political leaders in the countries mentioned in the text, see Root (1996), Campos and Root (1996), Ahrens (1994), Hoen (1998), Williamson (1994), and Qian (1999).

6. Even if institutional constraints exist, they 'tend to be less binding in times of crises and "honeymoons". This is simply to say that potential veto-players often do not dare to challenge a government with a strong mandate or behave acquiescently if a crisis prevails' (Bönker 2000: 5).

7. This is not to say that major shifts in policy making only occur in times of crisis. Note, however, that 'certain kinds of policies – a devaluation, say – tend to get on decision makers' agendas only when crisis conditions exist. Other kinds of policies – to decentralize, for example – emerge almost uniquely under politics-as-usual circumstances' (Grindle and Thomas 1991: 73). Regarding the different dynamics of agenda setting and political decision making in crisis and non-crisis situations, see ibid.

8. See Hayami (1991), who analyses the failure of past land reforms and suggests how to redesign future reform programs.

9. Note, however, that income inequality has been significantly rising since the beginning of the transformation, notably in Russia, Bulgaria, Estonia, and the Kyrgyz Republic (World Bank 1996). On the one hand, this may be a natural process associated with the transition towards capitalism. On the other hand, it may induce severe social and political tensions, especially if rising inequality results from an increasing division of society into two classes: privileged and underprivileged. Therefore, authorities, if committed to effective transformation, have to establish social safety nets and to take care that increasing inequality results from economic competition rather than from social or political power struggles.

10. Human capital inheritance is a basic asset for economies in transition. However, considerable portions of the human-capital stock have been rendered obsolete by the large-scale reallocation of the factors of production. This requires a reform of the education system in order to transform specific skills to more flexible and broader skills able to meet the challenges of a market economy. Replacing obsolete human capital in both the economy and in politics is a critical problem of transformation.

11. See, for example, Boycko, Shleifer, and Vishny (1995) regarding Russian privatization, and Hoen (1996) regarding privatization in the Czech and Slovak Republics.

12. See, for example, Aoki *et al.* (1997a), Olson (1997), and World Bank (1997).

13. See Aoki *et al.* (1997b), who also present several instructive examples of how governments can improve private sector coordination.

14. See, for example, Aoki *et al.* (1997a) as well as Ahrens (2002), who discusses several instructive cases in which LDC governments have promoted the development of and the collaboration with intermediary organizations in order to implement technology policies better.

15. Note in this context that problems and policy requirements substantially vary among catch-up economies that are mainly concerned with diffusion and cutting-edge economies that prefer to rely on path-breaking innovations and novel discoveries. Thus it should be clear that priorities in education policies and regarding the establishment of (intellectual) property rights as well as other policy requirements need to vary according to the stage of a country's development (Lipsey 2002).

16. Regarding the interaction of ideology, formal and informal institutions, and economic performance in Western market economies, LDCs, and socialist economies see North (1992) and Chapter 4, Section 4.3 in Part I of this study.

17. See Pejovich (1994); preconditions for a market for institutions to work effectively comprise a stable and credible legal system, equal protection of all property rights, and the freedom of exchange and law of contract.

18. This does not only hold for countries in East Asia, but also for economies as diverse as those of Austria and Kerala (a State of India); see Evans (1995).

19. Regarding the concept underlying the notion of functional, overlapping, competing jurisdictions and its applicability to LDCs, see Frey (1997) and Frey and Eichenberger (1995).

20. See, for example, Altenburg and Meyer-Stamer (1999) and Borner (1999) regarding the economic and institutional consequences of recent liberalization policies in Brazil and

Argentina, respectively, as well as Root *et al.* (1999) with respect to long-neglected institutional and economic reforms in South Korea in the aftermath of the Asian Crisis.

21. This was in fact the case in Taiwan, which was relatively little affected by the Asian Crisis. In particular, the country had run significantly positive current account surpluses, had virtually no foreign debt, and had accumulated huge currency reserves. These factors made the economy far less vulnerable to the Asian Crisis than its neighboring countries. Moreover, Taiwan's political leadership had not only pursued very conservative fiscal and monetary policies, but also emphasized prudent financial regulation and preferred *domestic* financial liberalization to internationalization of the financial and banking sector. Regarding the political economy aspects that helped shield Taiwan from the crisis, see the excellent studies by Chu (1999) and Haggard (2000). In this context, note also that key institutions of governance, especially relatively autonomous economic bureaucracies, had substantially helped East Asian countries in earlier periods (in particular in the 1970s and 1980s) to respond successfully to external shocks (Akyüz *et al.* 1998).

22. See, for example, the cases of public–private cooperation and institution building in the Cholla region in South Korea and in the Third Italy, which are discussed in Ahrens (2002).

23. With respect to concrete experiences in Latin America and East Asia, see Altenburg and Meyer-Stamer (1999) and Akyüz *et al.* (1998) as well as Evans (1998), respectively.

24 Arguments in this and the subsequent section essentially draw on Ahrens (2001).

25. An instructive example, in this context, is the government of Sri Lanka which requested the ADB in 1996 to help the government in designing and implementing governance and public administration reform; see Jayawardena (1997).

26. This essentially relates to the institutional strengthening of, and capacity building at, a particular ministry or agency as one component of a specific project in a particular sector.

27. See Moore (1993), who provides an instructive and comprehensive critique of the World Bank's approach to governance.

28. Article IV, Section 10 of the *World Bank's Articles of Agreement* states that 'the Bank and its officers shall not interfere in the political affairs of any member; nor shall they be influenced in their decisions by the political character of the member or members concerned'. However, the World Bank indirectly touches on the political dimensions of governance through its policy dialogues with governments and through its position as chairperson of the Consultative Group meetings between recipient governments and donor agencies.

Article IV, Section 3 of the *IMF's Articles of Agreement*, for example, reads: '(a) The Fund shall oversee the international monetary system in order to ensure its effective operation, and shall oversee the compliance of each member with its obligations under Section 1 of this Article.

(b) In order to fulfill its functions under (a) above, the Fund shall exercise firm surveillance over the exchange rate policies of members, and shall adopt specific principles for the guidance of all members with respect to those policies. Each member shall provide the Fund with the information necessary for such surveillance, and, when requested by the Fund, shall consult with it on the member's exchange rate policies. The principles adopted by the Fund shall be consistent with cooperative arrangements by which members maintain the value of their currencies in relation to the value of the currency or currencies of other members, as well as with other exchange arrangements of a member's choice consistent with the purposes of the Fund and Section 1 of this Article. These principles shall respect the domestic social and political policies of members, and in applying these principles the Fund shall pay due regard to the circumstances of members.'

Article 36(2) of the *ADB's Charter* reads: 'The Bank, its President, Vice President(s), officers, and staff shall not interfere in the political affairs of any member, nor shall they be influenced in their decisions by the political character of the member concerned. Only economic considerations shall be relevant to their decisions. Such considerations shall be weighed impartially in order to achieve and carry out the purpose and functions of the Bank.'

29 For more information on these governance policies, see the WBI's website on the Internet at http://www.worldbank.org/wbi/governance/overview.htm.

30. Regarding the role of the IMF in the Indonesian crisis see, for example, Radelet (1998) and Radelet and Sachs (1998b).

31. In this context, it should be noted that the IMF has recently begun to improve its dialogue with members of civil society. The information provided by civic organizations is now used by some IMF staff to make an assessment of the political effects of IMF policies. To date, however, the dialogue between the Fund and civil society has been poorly institutionalized, haphazardly sustained, and the initiatives have been improvised and reactive (see Scholte 1998).

32. The author is indebted to Joel S. Hellman for helpful information on the Bank's approach to governance.

33. Regarding country-specific information on the Bank's operations, visit the EBRD's website on the Internet at http://www.ebrd.com/english/opera/Country/index.htm.

34. Note that according to its Articles of Agreement, at least 60 per cent of the EBRD's financing should be targeted at the private sector. In 1997, private sector commitments accounted for 76 per cent by volume (EBRD 1998).

35. This is a criticism often voiced, for example, by Mahathir Mohamad, the Prime Minister of Malaysia.

36. Regarding the concept of focal points and other novel instruments that may be used by international organizations to promote governance quality in their member countries, see Ahrens (2001).

37. For a detailed analysis of the implications of a divided government for policy reforms in PSCs, see Boycko *et al.* (1996).

38. In Russia, for example, attempts at an economically efficient pre-privatization restructuring of state-owned enterprises were counterproductive, because sectoral ministries sought to increase rather than decrease monopoly power and industrial concentration. This called for a rapid mass privatization program as a feasible, though theoretically second-best policy, in order to depoliticize the privatization process (see Boycko *et al.* 1995 and 1996).

39. Regarding the premium approach see the instructive study by Hiemenz (1989).

40. In this context, the MDBs include the World Bank, the Asian Development Bank, the Inter-American Development Bank, the African Development Bank, and the European Bank for Reconstruction and Development.

41. For information about Transparency International and its activities visit the organization's Internet website at http://www.transparency.org/ as well as the website of the University of Göttingen's Internet Center for Corruption Research at http://www.gwdg.de/~uwvw/.

42. Although it is difficult to assess the actual impact of the World Development Reports on the World Bank's operations and policies, it is conceivable that the new tone of the 1997 Report represents the beginning of a newly emerging policy stand. If its conclusions (partly) percolate into the actual Bank operations, its influence on sectoral programs and Country Assistance Strategies will be significant.

Appendix

ANNEX 1: COUNTRIES INCLUDED IN THE SAMPLE USED FOR FIGURES 6.5–6.10 IN CHAPTER 6[†]

HPAEs	CEE	LAC	SSA	OECD[1]
Hong Kong	Albania	Argentina	Angola	Australia
Indonesia	Bulgaria	Bolivia	Botswana	Austria
Malaysia	Czech Republic[2]	Brazil	Burkina Faso	Belgium
Singapore	Hungary	Chile	Cameroon	Canada
South Korea	Poland	Colombia	Congo	Denmark
Taiwan	Romania	Costa Rica	Ethiopia	Finland
Thailand	Russian Fed.[3]	Dominican Rep.	Gabon	France
	Yugoslavia[4]	Ecuador	Gambia	Germany
		El Salvador	Ghana	Greece
		Guatemala	Guinea	Iceland
		Guyana	Guinea-Bissau	Ireland
		Haiti	Ivory Coast	Italy
		Honduras	Kenya	Japan
		Jamaica	Liberia	Luxemburg
		Mexico	Madagascar	Netherlands
		Nicaragua	Malawi	New Zealand
		Panama	Mali	Norway
		Paraguay	Mozambique	Portugal
		Peru	Niger	Spain
		Trinidad/Tobago	Nigeria	Sweden
		Surinam	Senegal	Switzerland
		Uruguay	Sierra Leone	Turkey
		Venezuela	Somalia	United Kingdom
			Sudan	United States
			Tanzania, Togo	
			Uganda, Zaire[5]	
			Zambia, Zimbabwe	

Notes:

[†] High-performing Asian economies (HPAEs); Central and Eastern Europe (CEE); Latin America and the Caribbean (LAC); sub-Saharan Africa (SSA); Organization for Economic Co-operation and Development (OECD).

[1] Included are all current OECD member countries except the Czech Republic, Hungary, Mexico, Poland, South Korea, and Turkey, all of which are included in other categories.

[2] The data refer to Czechoslovakia until its dissolution in 1993 and to the Czech Republic afterwards.

[3] Before 1992, the data refer to the USSR.

[4] Before 1992, the data refer to the former Socialist Federal Republic of Yugoslavia; since 1992 they relate to the Federal Republic of Yugoslavia (including Serbia and Montenegro).

[5] The data refer to the Rep. of Zaire before 1997, to the Democratic Rep. of Congo afterwards.

ANNEX 2: INSTITUTIONAL INDICATORS USED IN FIGURES
6.1–6.20 IN CHAPTER 6

The data used in Figures 6.1–6.20 in Chapter 6, Section 6.1 and for the
calculation of the 'composite institutional index' were obtained from a data
set that had been compiled by the *Center for Institutional Reform and the
Informal Sector (IRIS)*, at the University of Maryland. Stephen Knack and the
IRIS Center had assembled the data set from hard copies of the *International
Country Risk Guide (ICRG)*, a monthly publication of the Political Risk
Services (PRS) Group, a private investment risk service company. The data
set was designed to analyse the quality of governance of the countries
covered by the ICRG. Each variable's value for a given country and year is a
simple average of the two values for the months April and October (for 1995,
only April was used; for 1982, the first year, no observations were available
prior to September). Originally, these data were used in the following IRIS
Working Paper: Knack, Stephen and Keefer, Philip (1994), 'Institutions and
Economic Performance: Cross Country Tests Using Alternative Institutional
Measures', IRIS Working Paper No. 109, University of Maryland at College
Park.

The IRIS data set definitions are as follows:

Government repudiation of contracts is the indicator that addresses the
possibility that foreign businesses, contractors, and consultants face the risk
of a modification in a contract taking the form of repudiation, postponement,
or scaling down. A country may initiate contract modification with a foreign
business because of an income drop, budget cuts, indiginized pressure, a
change in government, or a change in government economic and social
priorities. Low point totals signify a greater likelihood that a country will
modify or repudiate a contract with a foreign business.

Risk of expropriation of private foreign investments encompasses outright
confiscation and forced nationalization. The risk of expropriation may vary
by type of business or by the investor's country of domicile. However, for
simplification of country comparisons, the ICRG expropriation risk indicator
does not make these distinctions. The low risk ratings are given to countries
where expropriation of foreign investment is a likely event.

Corruption, measured on a scale from zero to six, is a measure of corruption
within the political system. Such corruption is a threat to foreign investment
for several reasons: it distorts the economic and financial environment, it
reduces the efficiency of government and business by enabling people to
assume positions of power through patronage rather than ability, and last but
not least, introduces an inherent instability into the political process. The

most common form of corruption met directly by business is financial corruption in the form of demands for special payments and bribes connected with import and export licenses, exchange controls, tax assessments, police protection, or loans. Such corruption can make it difficult to conduct business effectively, and in some cases may force the withdrawal or withholding of an investment.

Rule of law: A country with an established law and order tradition has sound political institutions, a strong court system, and provisions for an orderly succession of power. This indicator reflects the degree to which the citizens of a country are willing to accept the established institutions to make and implement laws and adjudicate disputes. A high risk point total means that there is a strong law and order tradition, while a low risk point total means there is a tradition of depending on physical force or illegal means to settle claims. In countries with poorly developed law and order traditions, governments may be less likely to accept the obligations of the previous regime.

Bureaucratic quality: The institutional strength and quality of the bureaucracy is a shock absorber which tends to minimize revisions of policy when governments change. Therefore high risk points are given to countries where the bureaucracy has the strength and expertise to govern without drastic changes in policy or interruption in government services. In these low-risk countries, the bureaucracy tends to be somewhat autonomous, and independent of political pressure, and to have an established mechanism for recruitment and training. Countries that lack the cushioning effect of a strong bureaucracy receive low risk rating points because a change in government tends to be traumatic in terms of policy formulation and day-to-day administrative functions.

References

Organizations are usually cited in the text by acronym (for example EBRD, IMF), but are alphabetized here by their full name (for example European Bank for Reconstruction and Development, International Monetary Fund). In case of difficulty, the reader should check the list of acronyms at the beginning of the book.

Aberbach, Joel D. and Bert A. Rockman (1992), 'Does Governance Matter – And If So, How? Process, Performance, and Outcomes', *Governance: An International Journal of Policy and Administration*, 5(2), pp. 135–53.

Adelman, Irma and Cynthia Taft Morris, (1967), *Society, Politics, and Economic Development*, Baltimore: Johns Hopkins University Press.

Adelman, Irma and Sherman Robinson (1978), *Income Distribution Policy in Developing Countries: A Case Study of Korea*, Oxford: Oxford University Press.

Ahrens, Joachim (1994), *Der russische Systemwandel: Reform und Transformation des (post)sowjetischen Wirtschaftssystems*, Frankfurt/Main: Peter Lang.

Ahrens, Joachim (1995), 'Systemtransformation von unten. Über die Bedeutung der national-staatlichen Ordnung für den russischen Systemwandel', *Osteuropa-Wirtschaft*, 40(1), pp. 24–37.

Ahrens, Joachim (1997), 'Prospects of institutional and policy reform in India: toward a model of the developmental state?', *Asian Development Review*, 15(1), pp. 111–46.

Ahrens, Joachim (1998a), 'Economic Development, the State, and the Importance of Governance in East Asia', *Economic Systems*, 22(1), pp. 23–51.

Ahrens, Joachim (1998b), 'The Political Economy of Policy Reform in Russia: In Search of Developmental Institutions', *Baltic Journal of Economics*, 1(1), pp. 59–86.

Ahrens, Joachim (2000), 'Toward a Post-Washington Consensus: The Importance of Governance Structures in Less Developed Countries and Economies in Transition', *Journal for Institutional Innovation, Development and Transition*, 4, pp. 78–96

Ahrens, Joachim (2001), 'Governance, Conditionality and Transformation in Post-socialist Countries', in: Herman W. Hoen (ed.), Good Governance in Central and Eastern Europe. The Puzzle of Capitalism by Design, Cheltenham; UK and Northampton, US: Edward Elgar, pp. 54–90.

Ahrens, Joachim (2002), 'Governance and the Implementation of Technology Policy in Less Developed Countries', *Economics of Innovation and New Technology*, 11(4-5), pp. 441-76.

Ahrens, Joachim and Martin Meurers (2000), 'Institutions, Governance, and Economic Performance in Post-Socialist Countries: A Conceptual and Empirical Approach', paper presented at the Annual ASSA/ACES Meeting in Boston, MA, 7–9 January, 2000.

Akerlof, George A. (1976), 'The Economics of Caste and of the Rat Race and Other Woeful Tales', *Quarterly Journal of Economics*, 90, pp. 599–617.

Akyüz, Yilmaz, Ha-Joon Chang and Richard Kozul-Wright (1998), 'New Perspectives on East Asian Development, *Journal of Development Studies*, 34(6), pp. 4–36.

Alchian, Armen A. (1961), *Some Economics of Property*, Santa Monica, CA: RAND D-2316.

Alesina, Alberto and Allan Drazen (1991), 'Why Are Stabilizations Delayed?', *American Economic Review*, 81(5), pp. 1170–88.

Alesina, Alberto and Dani Rodrik (1994), 'Distributive Politics and Economic Growth', *Quarterly Journal of Economics*, CIX, pp. 465–90.

Altenburg, Tilman and Jörg Meyer-Stamer (1999), 'How to Promote Clusters: Policy Experiences from Latin America, *World Development*, 27(9), pp. 1693–1713.

Amsden, Alice H. (1989), *Asia's Next Giant: South Korea and Late Industrialization*, New York: Oxford University Press.

Amsden, Alice H., Jacek Kochanowicz and Lance Taylor (1994), *The Market Meets Its Match. Restructuring the Economies of Eastern Europe*, Cambridge, MA: Harvard University Press.

Andersen, W. K. (1995) 'India in 1994. Economics to the Fore', *Asian Survey*, XXXV(2), pp. 127–39.

Aoki, Masahiko, Hyung-Ki, Kim and Masahiro Okuno-Fujiwara (eds) (1997a), *The Role of Government in East Asian Economic Development. Comparative Institutional Analysis*, Oxford: Clarendon Press.

Aoki, Masahiko, Kevin Murdock and Masahiro Okuno-Fujiwara (1997b), 'Beyond *The East Asian Miracle*: Introducing the Market-Enhancing View', in: Masahiko Aoki, Hyung-Ki Kim and Masahiro Okuno-Fujiwara (eds) (1997), *The Role of Government in East Asian Economic Development. Comparative Institutional Analysis*, Oxford: Clarendon Press, pp. 1–37.

Aranson, Peter H. (1998), 'The New Institutional Analysis of Politics', *Journal of Institutional and Theoretical Economics*, 154(4), pp. 744–53.

Arthur, W. Brian (1988), 'Self–Reinforcing Mechanisms in Economics', in: Philip Anderson, Kenneth Arrow and David Pines (eds), *The Economy as an Evolving, Complex System*, Reading, MA: Addison-Wesley, pp. 9–31.

Arthur, W. Brian (1989), 'Competing Technologies, Increasing Returns, and Lock–In by Historical Small Events', *Economic Journal*, 99, pp. 116–31.

Asian Development Bank (1995), 'Governance: Sound Development Management, Internet Website: http://www.adb.org/Work/Policies/Governance/.

Asian Development Bank (1998), 'Governance at the ADB. Early Results and an Agenda for the Medium Term' (Strategy and Policy Office Working Paper), Manila: The Asian Development Bank.

Asian Development Bank (1999a), *Asian Development Outlook*, Hong Kong: Oxford University Press.

Asian Development Bank (1999b), *Asian Development Outlook Update*, Manila: The Asian Development Bank.

Asian Development Bank (1999c), Country Assistance Plan (2000–2002) India, Internet Website: http://www.adb.org/Work/Country/Assistance_Plans/caps/ind.PDF.

Asian Development Bank (2001), *Asian Development Outlook*, Hong Kong: Oxford University Press.

Aslund, Anders (1999), 'Why Has Russia's Economic Transformation Been So Arduous?' Paper prepared for the Annual World Bank Conference on Development Economics, Washington, DC, 28–30 April, 1999, Internet Website: http://www.worldbank.org/research/abcde/washington_11/pdfs/aslund.pdf.

Auroi, Claude (ed.) (1992), *The Role of the State in Development Processes*, London: Frank Cass.

Azarya, Victor (1988), 'Reordering State–Society Relations: Incorporation and Disengagement', in: Donald Rothchild and Naomi Chazan (eds), *The Precarious Balance: State and Society in Africa*, Boulder, CO: Westview Press.

Aziz, Jahangir and Robert F. Wescott (1997), 'Policy Complementarities and the Washington Consensus', IMF Working Paper 97/118. Washington, DC.

Baer, Werner, William R. Miles and Allen B. Moran (1999), 'The end of the Asian Myth: Why were the Experts Fooled?', *World Development*, 27(10), pp. 1735–47.

Balcerowicz, Leszek (1994), 'Poland', in: John Williamson (ed.), *The Political Economy of Policy Reform*, Washington, DC: Institute for International Economics, pp. 153–77.

Balcerowicz, Leszek, Barbara Blaszczyk and Marek Dabrowski (1997), 'The Polish Way to the Market Economy 1989–1995', in: Wing Thye Woo, Stephan Parker and Jeffrey D. Sachs (eds), *Economies in Transition: Comparing Asia and Eastern Europe*, Cambridge, MA: The MIT Press, pp. 131–60.

Bardhan, Pranab (1989), 'The New Institutional Economics and Development Theory', *World Development*, 17(9), pp. 1389–95.

Bardhan, Pranab (1993), 'Introduction: Symposium on Democracy and Development', *Journal of Economic Perspectives*, 7(3), pp. 45–9.

Bardhan, Pranab (1995), 'The Nature of Institutional Impediments to Economic Development', unpublished manuscript, University of California at Berkeley.

Bardhan, Pranab (1997a), *The Role of Governance in Economic Development. A Political Economy Approach*, Paris: OECD Development Centre Studies.

Bardhan, Pranab (1997b), 'Corruption and Development: A Review of Issues', *Journal of Economic Literature*, XXXV(3), pp. 1320–46.

Barro, Robert J. (1991), 'Economic Growth in a Cross Section of Countries', *Quarterly Journal of Economics*, CVI(2), pp. 407–43.

Barro, Robert J. (1994), 'Democracy and Growth', NBER Working Paper No. 4909, Cambridge, MA.

Barzel, Yoram (1989), *Economic Analysis of Property Rights*, Cambridge: Cambridge University Press.

Basu, D.D. (1988), *Shorter Constitution of India*, New Delhi: Prentice Hall.

Bates, Robert H. (1981), *Markets and States in Tropical Africa. The Political Basis of Agricultural Policies*, Berkeley, CA: University of California Press.

Bates, Robert H. (1999), 'Institutions and Economic Performance', paper prepared for delivery at the IMF Conference on Second Generation Reforms, Internet Website: http://www.imf.org/external/pubs/ft/seminar/1999/reforms/index.htm.

Bates, Robert H. and Krueger, Anne O. (eds) (1993), *Political and economic interactions in economic policy reform*, Oxford: Blackwell.

Batt, Judy (1991), *East Central Europe from Reform to Transformation*, London: Pinter.

Bednar, Jenna (1997), 'Federalism: Unstable by Design', unpublished manuscript, Stanford University.

Bednar, Jenna, William N. Eskridge and John Ferejohn (1996), 'A Political Theory of Federalism', unpublished manuscript, Stanford University.

Berglöf, Erik and Gérard Roland (1997), 'The EU as an "Outside Anchor" for Transition Reforms' (SITE Working Paper No. 132), Stockholm: Stockholm Institute of Transition Economics and East European Economies, Internet Website: http://www.hhs.se/site/Publications/workingpapers/132-web.PDF.

Berglöf, Erik and Ernst–Ludwig von Thadden (1999), 'The Changing Corporate Governance Paradigm: Implications for Transition and Developing Countries', Annual Bank Conference on Development Economics, the World Bank, Internet Website http://www.worldbank.org/research/abcde/papers.html.

Bernholz, Peter (1993), 'Constitutions as Governance Structures: The Political Foundations of Secure Markets. Comment', *Journal of Institutional and Theoretical Economics*, 149(1), pp. 312–20.

Beyme, Klaus von (1994), *Systemwechsel in Osteuropa*, Frankfurt/Main: Suhrkamp.

Bhagwati, Jagdish N. (1982), 'Directly Unproductive, Profit-Seeking (DUP) Activities', *Journal of Political Economy*, 90, pp. 988–1002.

Bhagwati, Jagdish N. (1993), *India in Transition. Freeing the Economy*, Oxford: Clarendon Press.

Bhalla, A. S. (1995), 'Recent Economic Reforms in China and India', *Asian Survey*, XXXV(6), pp. 555–72.

Bhatnagar, Pradip (1999), 'Electronic Commerce, Trade and Development', *Development Policy Review*, 17(3), pp. 281–91.

Boeninger, Edgardo (1992), 'Governance and Development: Issues and Constraints', *Proceedings of the World Bank Annual Conference on Development Economics 1991*, pp. 267–87.

Böhm, Franz (1950), *Wirtschaftsordnung und Staatsverfassung*, Tübingen: Mohr.

Bönker, Frank (1995), 'The Dog That Did Not Bark? Politische Restriktionen und ökonomische Reformen in den Visegrád–Ländern', in: Hellmut Wollmann, Helmut Wiesenthal and Frank Bönker (eds), *Transformation sozialistischer Gesellschaften: Am Ende des Anfangs*, Opladen: Westdeutscher Verlag, pp. 180–206.

Bönker, Frank (2000), 'Initiating and Consolidating Economic Reform: A Comparative Analysis of Fiscal Reform in Hungary, Poland and the Czech Republic, 1989–1999', forthcoming in: Jürgen Beyer, Jan Wielgohs and Helmut Wiesenthal (eds), *Successful Transitions: Political Factors of Socio–Economic Progress in Post–Socialist Countries*, Baden–Baden: Nomos.

Borner, Silvio (1999), 'Strength and Commitment of the State: It Takes Two to Tango. A Case Study of Economic Reforms in Argentina in the 1990s', unpublished manuscript, University of Basle and Instituto Torcuato Di Tella.

Borner, Silvio, Aymo Brunetti and Beatrice Weder (1995), *Political Credibility and Economic Development*, New York: St. Martin's Press.

Bosworth, Barry and Susan M. Collins (1999), 'From Boom to Crisis and Back Again: What Have We Learned?' (Paper presented at the Workshop on Development Paradigms, Asian Development Bank Institute, Tokyo, 10 December, 1999), Internet Website: http://www.adbi.org/Calendar/ ws991210/papers/bosworth.pdf.

Boycko, Maxim, Andrei Shleifer and Robert W. Vishny (1995), *Privatizing Russia*, Cambridge, MA: MIT Press.

Boycko, Maxim, Andrei Shleifer and Robert W. Vishny (1996), 'Second–best economic policy for a divided government', *European Economic Review*, 40, pp. 767–74.

Bradford, Jr., Colin I. (ed.) (1994), *Redefining the State in Latin America*, Paris: Organization for Economic Co-Operation and Development.

Bratton, Michael and Nicholas van der Walle (1992), 'Toward Governance in Africa: Popular Demands and State Responses', in: Göran Hydén and Michael Bratton (eds), *Governance and Politics in Africa*, Boulder, CO: Lynne Rienner, pp. 27–55.

Brautigam, Deborah (1992), 'Governance, Economy and Foreign Aid', *Studies in Comparative International Development*, 27(3), pp. 3–25.

Brücker, Herbert (1995), *Privatisierung in Ostdeutschland: eine institutionenökonomische Analyse*, Frankfurt/Main: Campus Verlag.

Brunetti, Aymo, Gregory Kisunko and Beatrice Weder (1997a), 'Institutional Obstacles to Doing Business: Region-by-Region Results from a Worldwide Survey of the Private Sector', World Bank Policy Research Working Paper No. 1759, Washington, DC: The World Bank.

Brunetti, Aymo, Gregory Kisunko and Beatrice Weder (1997b), 'Credibility of Rules and Economic Growth', World Bank Policy Research Working Paper No. 1760, Washington, DC: The World Bank.

Brunetti, Aymo, Gregory Kisunko and Beatrice Weder (1997c), 'Institutions in Transition. Reliability of Rules and Economic Performance in Former Socialist Countries', World Bank Policy Research Working Paper No. 1809, Washington, DC: The World Bank.

Buchanan, James M. (1980), 'Rent-Seeking and Profit-Seeking', in: James M. Buchanan, Robert D. Tollison and Gordon Tullock (eds), *Toward a Theory of the Rent-Seeking Society*, College Station: Texas A & M University Press.

Buchanan, James M. (1995), 'Federalism as an Ideal Political Order and an Objective for Constitutional Reform', *Publius*, Spring 1995.

Buchanan, James M. and Gordon Tullock (1962), *The Calculus of Consent: Logical Foundations of Constitutional Democracy*, Ann Arbor: University of Michigan Press.

Burki, Shahid Javed and Guillermo E. Perry (1998), *Beyond the Washington Consensus. Institutions Matter*, World Bank Latin American and Caribbean Studies, Washington, DC.

Burns, John P. (1993), 'China's administrative reforms for a market economy', *Public Administration and Development*, 13, pp. 345–60.

Byrd, William A. and Lin Qingsong (eds) (1990), *China's Rural Industry: Structure, Development, and Reform*, Oxford: Oxford University Press.

Calabresi, G. (1961), 'Some Thoughts on Risk Distribution and the Law of Torts', *Yale Law Journal*, 70, pp. 517–19.

Callaghy, Thomas (1984), *The State–Society Struggle: Zaire in Comparative Perspective*, New York: Columbia University Press.

Camdessus, Michel (1999), 'Opening Remarks', presented at the IMF Institute Conference on 'Second Generation Reforms: Reflections and New Challenges', Washington, DC, 8 November, 1999, Internet Website: http://www.imf.org/external/pubs/ft/seminar/1999/reforms/index.htm.

Campos, Jose Edgardo and Sanjay Pradhan (1996), 'Budgetary Institutions and Expenditure Outcomes: Binding Governments to Fiscal Performance', Policy Research Working Paper No. 1646, Washington, DC: World Bank.

Campos, Jose Edgardo and Hilton L. Root (1996), *The Key to the Asian Miracle: Making Shared Growth Credible*, Washington, DC: The Brookings Institution.

Campos, Jose Edgardo, Margaret Levi and Richard Sherman (1994), 'Rationalized Bureaucracy and Rational Compliance' (IRIS Working Paper No. 105), University of Maryland, College Park.

Campos, Nauro F. and Jeffrey B. Nugent (1999), 'Development Performance and the Institutions of Governance: Evidence from East Asia and Latin America', *World Development*, 27(3), pp. 439–52.

Chalker, L. (1991), *Good Governance and the Aid Programme*, London: Overseas Development Administration.

Chang, Ha-Joon (1999), 'The Economic Theory of the Developmental State', in: Meredith Woo-Cumings (ed.), *The Developmental State*, Ithaca and London: Cornell University Press, pp. 182–99.

Chang, Ha-Joon and Ali Cheema (2002), 'Conditions for Successful Technology Policy in Developing Countries–Learning Rents, State Structures, and Institutions', *Economics of Innovation and New Technology*, 11(4-5), pp. 369–98.

Chazan, Naomi (1992), 'Liberalization, Governance and Political Space in Ghana', in: Göran Hydén and Michael Bratton (eds), *Governance and politics in Africa,* Boulder, CO: Lynne Rienner, pp. 121–42.

Che, Jiahua and Yingyi Qian (1998), 'Institutional Environment, Community Government, and Corporate Governance: Understanding China's Township-Village Enterprises', *Journal of Law, Economics, and Organization,* 14(1), pp. 1–23.

Cheng, Tun-Jen, Stephan Haggard and David Kang (1998), 'Institutions and Growth in Korea and Taiwan: The Bureaucracy', *Journal of Development Studies,* 34(6), pp. 87–111.

Chong, Alberto and Cesar Calderón (1997a), 'Empirical Tests on the Causality of and Feedback Between Institutional Measures and Economic Growth', unpublished manuscript. Washington, DC: The World Bank.

Chong, Alberto and Cesar Calderón (1997b), 'Institutional Change and Poverty, or Why is it Worth it to Reform the State?', unpublished manuscript. Washington, DC: The World Bank.

Chong, Alberto and Cesar Calderón (1998), 'Institutional Efficiency and Income Inequality. Cross Country Empirical Evidence', unpublished manuscript. Washington, DC: The World Bank.

Chu, Yun-han (1999), 'Surviving the East Asian Financial Storm: The Political Foundation of Taiwan's Economic Resilience', in: T. J. Pempel (ed.), *The Politics of the Asian Economic Crisis,* Ithaca, NY and London: Cornell University Press, pp. 184–202.

Clague, Christopher (ed.) (1997), *Institutions and Economic Development. Growth and Governance in Less-Developed and Post-Socialist Countries,* Baltimore and London: The Johns Hopkins University Press.

Coase, Ronald H. (1937), 'The Nature of the Firm', *Economica,* 4, pp. 386–405.

Coase, Ronald H. (1960), 'The Problem of Social Cost', *Journal of Law and Economics,* 3, pp. 1–44.

Coleman, James S. (1988), 'Social Capital in the Creation of Human Capital', *American Journal of Sociology* (Supplement), 94, pp. S95–S120.

Coleman, James S. (1990), *Foundations of Social Theory,* Cambridge, MA: Harvard University Press.

Cooter, Robert D. (1997), 'The Rule of State Law and the Rule-of-Law State: Economic Analysis of the Legal Foundations of Development', in: Michael Bruno and Boris Pleskovich (eds), *Annual World Bank Conference on Development Economics 1996,* Washington, DC: The World Bank, pp. 191–217.

Corbo, Vittorio and Stanley Fischer (1995), 'Structural Adjustment, Stabilization and Policy Reform: Domestic and International Finance', in:

Jere Behrman and T.N. Srinivasan (eds) (1995), *Handbook of Development Economics, Vol. III B*, Amsterdam: Elsevier Science, pp. 2845–2924.

Corsetti, Giancarlo, Paolo Pesenti and Nouriel Roubini (1999), 'Paper Tigers? A Model of the Asian crisis', *European Economic Review*, 43, pp. 1211–36.

Cox, Gary W. and Mathew D. McCubbins (1997), 'Political Structure and Economic Policy: The Institutional Determinants of Policy Outcomes', unpublished manuscript, University of California, San Diego.

Cull, Robert (1998), 'How Deposit Insurance Affects Financial Depth', World Bank Policy Research Working Paper No. 1875, Washington, DC: The World Bank.

David, Paul A. (1985), 'Clio and the Economics of QWERTY', *American Economic Review*, 75(2) (Papers and Proceedings), pp. 332–7.

Davis, Lance and Douglass C. North (1971), *Institutional Change and American Economic Growth*, New York: Cambridge University Press.

de Melo, Martha, Cevdet Denizer and Alan Gelb (1996), 'From Plan to Market: Patterns of Transition', World Bank Policy Research Working Paper No. 1564, Washington, DC: The World Bank.

Demirgüc-Kunt, Asli and Enrica Detragiache (1998), 'Financial Liberalization and Financial Fragility', World Bank Policy Research Working Paper No. 1917, Washington, DC: The World Bank.

Demsetz, Harold (1967), 'Toward a Theory of Property Rights', *American Economic Review. Papers and Proceedings*, 57(2), pp. 347–59.

Demsetz, Harold (1969), 'Information and Efficiency: Another Viewpoint', *Journal of Law and Economics*, 12, pp. 1–22.

Denzau, Arthur T. and Douglass C. North (1994), 'Shared Mental Models: Ideologies and Institutions', *Kyklos*, 47, pp. 3–31.

Dethier, Jean-Jacques (1999a), 'Governance and Economic Performance: A Survey' (ZEF Discussion Paper on Development Policy 5), Bonn.

Dethier, Jean-Jacques (1999b), 'Governance Reforms in China, India and Russia', paper presented at the Global Development Network (GDN) Conference, Bonn/Germany, 5–8 December, 1999.

Deutsches Institut für Wirtschaftsforschung Institut für Weltwirtschaft and Institut für Wirtschaftsforschung (1999), 'Die wirtschaftliche Lage Rußlands. Wachstumsperspektive fehlt weiterhin – Schuldenerlaß keine Lösung', *DIW–Wochenbericht*, 49/99.

De Weydenthal, J.B. (1991), 'The Visegrád Summit', *Report on Eastern Europe*, 2, pp. 28–32.

Dhonte, Pierre and Ishan Kapur (1997), 'Towards a Market Economy: Structures of Governance', International Monetary Fund Working Paper WP/97/11, Washington, DC.

Dia, Mamadou (1996), *Africa's Management in the 1990s and Beyond. Reconciling Indigenous and Transplanted Institutions,* Washington, DC: The World Bank.

Diamond, Larry and Marc F. Plattner (eds) (1995), *Economic Reform and Democracy,* Baltimore and London: The Johns Hopkins University Press.

Dietl, Helmut (1993), *Institutionen und Zeit,* Tübingen: J.C.B. Mohr (Paul Siebeck).

Dillinger, William and Marianne Fay (1999), 'From Centralized to Decentralized Governance', *Finance & Development,* 36(4).

Dixit, Avinash (1996), *The Making of Economic Policy: A Transaction-Cost Perspective,* Cambridge, MA: MIT Press.

Dollar, David and Jakob Svensson (1998), 'What Explains the Success or Failure of Structural Adjustment Programs?' Policy Research Working Paper Series, No. 1938, Washington, DC: The World Bank.

Doner, Richard F. (1992), 'Limits of State Strength. Toward an Institutionalist View of Economic Development', *World Politics,* 44, pp. 398–431.

Doornbos, Martin (1995), 'State Formation Processes under External Supervision: Reflections on "Good Governance"', in: Olav Stokke (ed.), *Aid and Political Conditionality,* London: Frank Cass, pp. 377–91.

Dornbusch, Rudiger (1998), 'Asian Crisis Themes', unpublished manuscript, Massachusetts Institute of Technology, Cambridge, MA.

Downs, Anthony (1957), *An Economic Theory of Democracy,* New York: Harper and Row.

Downs, Anthony (1962), 'The public interest: its meaning in a democracy', *Social Research,* 29, pp. 1–36.

Drazen, Allan (1996), 'The Political Economy of Delayed Reform', *Journal of Policy Reform,* 1(1), pp. 25–46.

Durkheim, Emile (1960/1933), *The Division of Labor in Society* (4th print), New York: The Free Press.

Dutt, Amitava Krishna, Kwan S. Kim and Ajit Singh (1994), 'The state, markets and development', in: Amitava Krishna Dutt, Kwan S. Kim and Ajit Singh (eds), *The State, Markets and Development, Beyond the Neoclassical Dichotomy,* Aldershot, UK and Brookfield, US: Edward Elgar, pp. 3–21.

Easterly, William and Ross Levine (1997), 'Africa's Growth Tragedy: Policies and Ethnic Divisions', *Quarterly Journal of Economics,* 112(4), pp. 1203–50.

Edwards, Sebastian (1984), *The Order of Liberalization in Developing Countries,* Princeton, NJ: Princeton Essays in International Finance.

Edwards, Sebastian (1989), 'On the sequencing of structural reforms', NBER Working Paper No. 3138.

Eggertsson, Thráinn (1990), *Economic behavior and institutions*, Cambridge: Cambridge University Press.

Eggertsson, Thráinn (1997), 'The Old Theory of Economic Policy and the New Institutionalism', *World Development*, 25(8), pp. 1187–1203.

Eggertsson, Thráinn (1998a), 'Limits to Institutional Reforms' (Max Planck Institute for Research into Economic Systems Working Paper 08/98), Jena.

Eggertsson, Thráinn (1998b), 'Comments on "Institutions, markets, and development outcomes" by Nugent', in: Robert Picciotto and Eduardo Wiesner (eds), *Evaluation & Development. The Institutional Dimension*, New Brunswick and London: Transaction Publishers, pp. 24–9.

Eisen, Andreas and Hellmut Wollmann (1996), *Institutionenbildung in Ostdeutschland: zwischen externer Steuerung und Eigendynamik*, Opladen: Leske + Budrich.

Elsenhans, Hartmut (1996), *State, Class and Development*, London: Sangam Books.

Emmerson, Donald K. (1998), 'Americanizing Asia?', *Foreign Affairs*, 77(3), pp. 46–56.

Enelow, James M. and Melvin J. Hinich (1984), *The Spatial Theory of Voting*, New York: Cambridge University Press.

Ensminger, Jean (1992), *Making a Market. The institutional transformation of an African society*, Cambridge: Cambridge University Press.

Ergas, Henry (1987), 'Does Technology Policy Matter?' in: Bruce R. Guile and Harvey Brooks (eds), *Technology and Global Industry. Companies and Nations in the World Economy*, Washington, DC: National Academy Press, pp. 191–245.

Eucken, Walter (1990/1952), *Grundsätze der Wirtschaftspolitik* (6th edition), Tübingen: J.C.B. Mohr (Paul Siebeck).

European Bank for Reconstruction and Development (1992), *The Political Aspects of the Mandate of the EBRD*, London: EBRD.

European Bank for Reconstruction and Development (1996), *Transition Report 1996. Commercial infrastructure and contractual savings institutions*, London: EBRD.

European Bank for Reconstruction and Development (1998), *Transition Report 1998. Financial sector in transition*, London: EBRD.

European Bank for Reconstruction and Development (1999), *Transition Report 1999. Ten years of transition*, London: EBRD.

European Bank for Reconstruction and Development (2001), *Transition Report 2001. Energy in transition*, London: EBRD.

European Union (2000), 'EU Enlargement – A Historic Opportunity', Internet Website: http://europa.eu.int/comm/enlargement/intro/criteria. htm.

Evans, Peter (1989), 'Predatory, Developmental and Other Apparatuses: A Comparative Political Economy Perspective on the Third World State', *Sociological Forum*, 4(4), pp. 561–87.

Evans, Peter (1992), 'The State as Problem and Solution: Predation, Embedded Autonomy, and Structural Change', in: Stephan Haggard and Robert R. Kaufman (eds) (1992), *The Politics of Economic Adjustment. International Constraints, Distributive Conflicts, and the State,* Princeton, NJ: Princeton University Press.

Evans, Peter (1995), *Embedded Autonomy. States & Industrial Transformation,* Princeton, NJ: Princeton University Press.

Evans, Peter (ed.) (1997), *State–Society Synergy: Government Action and Social Capital in Development,* Berkeley, CA: UC Berkeley, International and Area Studies Publications.

Evans, Peter (1998), 'Transferable Lessons? Re-examining the Institutional Prerequisites of East Asian Economic Policies', *Journal of Development Studies*, 34(6), pp. 66–86.

Evans, Peter B. and James E. Rauch (1995), 'Bureaucratic Structures and Economic Performance in Less Developed Countries' (IRIS Working Paper No. 175), University of Maryland, College Park.

Evans, Peter, Dietrich Rueschemeyer and Theda Skocpol (eds) (1985), *Bringing the State Back In,* New York: Cambridge University Press.

Evenson, Robert E. and Larry E. Westphal (1995), 'Technological Change and Technology Strategy', in Jere Behrman and T.N. Srinivasan (eds), *Handbook of Development Economics, Vol. III A,* Amsterdam: Elsevier, pp. 2209–99.

Fedderke, Johannes and Robert Klitgaard (1998), 'Economic Growth and Social Indicators: An Exploratory Analysis', *Economic Development and Cultural Change*, 46(3), pp. 455–89.

Feeny, David (1989), 'The Decline of Property Rights in Thailand, 1800–1913', *Journal of Economic History*, 49, pp. 285–96.

Feeny, David (1993), 'The Demand for and Supply of Institutional Arrangements', in: Vincent Ostrom, David Feeny and Hartmut Picht (eds) (1993), *Rethinking Institutional Analysis and Development,* San Francisco: ICS Press.

Feldstein, Martin (1998), 'Refocusing the IMF', *Foreign Affairs*, 77(2), pp. 20–33.

Felipe, Jesus (1999), 'Total Factor Productivity Growth in East Asia: A Critical Survey', *Journal of Development Studies*, 35(4), pp. 1–41.

Fernandez, Raquel and Dani Rodrik (1991), 'Resistance to Reform: Status Quo Bias in the Presence of Individual–Specific Uncertainty', *American Economic Review*, 85(5), pp. 1146–55.

Ferree, Myra Marx (1992), 'The Political Context of Rationality: Rational Choice Theory and Resource Mobilization', in: Aldon D. Morris and Carol McClurg Mueller (eds), *Frontiers on Social Movement Theory*, New Haven, CT: Yale University Press.

Figueiredo, Rui de and Barry R. Weingast (1998), 'Self-enforcing Federalism: Solving the Two Fundamental Dilemmas', unpublished manuscript, Hoover Institution/Stanford University.

Fischer, Stanley (1993), 'The role of macroeconomic factors in growth', *Journal of Monetary Economics*, 32, pp. 485–512.

Fischer, Stanley, Ratna Sahay and Carlos A. Végh (1996), 'Stabilization and Growth in Transition Economies: The Early Experience', *Journal of Economic Perspectives*, 10(2), pp. 45–66.

Fishlow, Albert, Catherine Gwin, Stephan Haggard, Dani Rodrik and Robert Wade (1994), *Miracle or Design? Lessons from the East Asian Experience*, Washington, DC: Overseas Development Council.

Foster, John, John Greer and Erick Thorbecke (1984), 'A Class of Decomposable Poverty Measures', *Econometrica*, 52(3), pp. 761–5.

Frey, Bruno S. (1988), 'Political Economy and Institutional Choice', *European Journal*, 4(3), pp. 349–66.

Frey, Bruno S. (1997), *Ein neuer Föderalismus für Europa: Die Idee der FOCJ* (Beiträge zur Ordnungstheorie und Ordnungspolitik), Freiburg/Breisgau: Walter Eucken Institut.

Frey, Bruno S. and Reiner Eichenberger (1995), 'Competition among Jurisdictions: The Idea of FOCJ', in: Lüder Gerken (ed.), *Competition among Institutions*, Basingstoke: Macmillan Press and New York: St. Martin's Press, pp. 209–29.

Frey, Bruno S. and Gebhard Kirchgässner (1994), *Demokratische Wirtschaftspolitik: Theorie und Anwendung*, München: Vahlen.

Frischtak, Leila L. (1994), 'Governance Capacity and Economic Reform in Developing Countries', World Bank Technical Paper No. 254, Washington, DC.

Fukuyama, Francis (1995), *Trust. The Social Virtues & the Creation of Prosperity*, New York: The Free Press.

Fukuyama, Francis (1999), 'Social Capital and Civil Society', paper presented at the IMF Conference on Second Generation Reforms, Washington, DC, 8–9 November, 1999, Internet Website: http://www.imf.org/external/pubs/ft/seminar/1999/reforms/rodrik.htm.

Furman, Jason and Joseph E. Stiglitz (1998), 'Economic Crises: Evidence and Insights from East Asia', *Brookings Papers on Economic Activity*, 2:1998, pp. 1–135.

Furubotn, Eirik G. and Rudolf Richter (1997), *Institutions and Economic Theory – The Contribution of the New Institutional Economics*, Ann Arbor: University of Michigan Press.

Gershenkron, Alexander (1962), *Economic Backwardness: Historical Perspective*, Cambridge, MA: Harvard University Press.

Goldberg, V. (1976), 'Regulation and Administered Contracts', *Bell Journal of Economics*, 7, pp. 426–52.

Goldsmith, Arthur A. (1995), 'The State, the Market and Economic Development: A Second Look at Adam Smith in Theory and Practice', *Development and Change*, 26, pp. 633–50.

Goldstein, Morris (1998), *The Asian Financial Crisis: Causes, Cures, and Systemic Implications* (Policy Analyses in International Economics 55), Washington, DC: Institute for International Economics.

Götz, Roland (2000), 'Die russische Wirtschaft im Jahr der Präsidentenwahl. Abwertungsimpulse bestehen weiter, Wachstumserfolge sind ungewiss', *Aktuelle Analyse des BIOst*, No. 13/2000.

Granovetter, Mark (1973), 'The Strength of Weak Ties', *American Journal of Sociology*, 78(6), pp. 1360–80.

Granovetter, Mark (1978), 'Threshold Models of Collective Behavior', *American Journal of Sociology*, 83, pp. 1420–43.

Granovetter, Mark (1985), 'Economic Action and Social Structure: The Problem of Embeddedness', *American Journal of Sociology*, 91(3), pp. 481–510.

Greif, Avner (1997), 'Contracting, Enforcement, and Efficiency: Economics Beyond the Law', in: Michael Bruno and Boris Pleskovic (eds), *Annual World Bank Conference on Development Economics 1996*, Washington, DC: The World Bank, pp. 239–65.

Grindle, Merilee S. (1991), 'The New Political Economy: Positive Economics and Negative Politics', in: Gerald M. Meier (ed.), *Politics and Policy Making in Developing Countries. Perspectives on the New Political Economy*, San Francisco: ICS Press.

Grindle, Merilee S. (1996), *Challenging the state. Crisis and innovation in Latin America and Africa*, Cambridge: Cambridge University Press.

Grindle, Merilee S. (1999), 'In Quest of the Political: The Political Economy of Development Policy Making' (Center for International Development Working Paper No. 17), Cambridge, MA: Harvard University.

Grindle, Merilee S. and Mary E. Hilderbrand (1995), 'Building sustainable capacity in the public sector: what can be done?', *Public Administration and Development*, 15(5), pp. 441–63.

Grindle, Merilee S. and John W. Thomas (1989), 'Policy Makers, Policy Choices, and Policy Outcomes: The Political Economy of Reform in Developing Countries', *Policy Sciences*, 22, pp. 213–48.

Grindle, Merilee S. and John W. Thomas (1991), *Public Choices and Policy Change. The Political Economy of Reform in Developing Countries*, Baltimore and London: The Johns Hopkins University Press.

Groenewegen, John, Frans Kerstholt and Ad Nagelkerke (1995), 'On Integrating New and Old Institutionalism: Douglass North Building Bridges', *Journal of Economic Issues*, XXIX(2), pp. 467–75.

Haan, Jakob de and Clemens Siermann (1995), 'Luxury or Stimulus? The impact of democracy on economic growth', unpublished manuscript, University of Groningen.

Haber, Stephen, Armando Razo and Noel Maurer (1999), 'Political Instability, Credible Commitments, and Economic Growth: Evidence from Revolutionary Mexico', paper presented at the Conference of the International Society for New Institutional Economics, Washington, DC, 17 September, 1999.

Haggard, Stephan M. (1990), *Pathways from the Periphery: Politics of Growth in the Newly Industrializing Countries*, Ithaca, NY: Cornell University Press.

Haggard, Stephan M. (1998), 'Business, politics, and policy in East and Southeast Asia', in: Henry S. Rowen (ed.), *Behind East Asian Growth. The political and social foundations of prosperity*, London and New York: Routledge, pp. 78–104.

Haggard, Stephan M. (2000), *The Political Economy of the Asian Financial Crisis*, Washington, DC: Institute for International Economics.

Haggard, Stephan M. and Robert R. Kaufman (eds) (1992a), *The Politics of Economic Adjustment. International Constraints, Distributive Conflicts, and the State*, Princeton, NJ: Princeton University Press.

Haggard, Stephan and Robert R. Kaufman (1992b), 'Institutions and Economic Adjustment', in: Stephan Haggard and Robert R. Kaufman (eds), *The Politics of Economic Adjustment. International Constraints, Distributive Conflicts, and the State*, Princeton: Princeton University Press, pp. 3–37.

Haggard, Stephan M. and Robert R. Kaufman (1995), *The Political Economy of Democratic Transitions*, Princeton, NJ: Princeton University Press.

Haggard, Stephan M. and Chung-In Moon (1990), 'Institutions and Economic Policy: Theory and a Korean Case Study', *World Politics*, XLII(2), pp. 210–37.

Haggard, Stephan M. and Steven Webb (1993), 'What Do We Know About the Political Economy of Economic Policy Reform?', *The World Bank Research Observer*, 8(2), pp. 143–68.

Haggard, Stephan M. and Steven Webb (eds) (1994), *Voting for reform: Democracy, political liberalization, and economic adjustment,* New York: Oxford University Press.

Hall, P.A. and R.C.R. Taylor (1996) 'Political Science and the Three new Institutionalisms', *Political Studies,* 44, pp. 936–57.

Harberger, Arnold C. (1993), 'Secrets of Success: A Handful of Heroes', *American Economic Review,* 83(2), pp. 343–50.

Hardin, Russell (1982), *Collective Action,* Baltimore: Johns Hopkins University Press for Resources for the Future.

Hare, Paul G. (1997), 'The Distance between Eastern Europe and Brussels: Reform Deficits in Potential Member States', in Horst Siebert (ed.), *Quo Vadis Europe?* Tübingen: J.C.B. Mohr (Paul Siebeck), pp. 127–45.

Harriss, John, Janet Hunter and Colin M. Lewis (eds) (1995), *The New Institutional Economics and Third World Development,* London and New York: Routledge.

Havrylyshyn, Oleh, Ivailo Izvorski and Ron van Rooden (1998), 'Recovery and Growth in Transition Economies 1990–97: A Stylized Regression Analysis', IMF Working Paper WP/98/141. Washington, DC: International Monetary Fund.

Havrylyshyn, Oleh and Ron van Rooden (1999), 'Institutions Matter in Transition, But So Do Policies', paper prepared for the Fifth Dubrovnik Conference on Transition, Dubrovnik, Croatia, 23–5 June, 1999.

Hayami, Yujiro (1991), 'Land Reform', in: Gerald M. Meier (ed.), *Politics and Policy Making in Developing Countries. Perspectives on the New Political Economy,* San Francisco: ICS Press, pp. 155–71.

Hayek, Friedrich August von (1945), 'The Use of Knowledge in Society', *American Economic Review,* 35, pp. 519–30.

Hayek, Friedrich August von (1965), 'Arten des Rationalismus', in: *Freiburger Studien. Gesammelte Aufsätze von F.A. von Hayek,* Tübingen: Mohr 1969, pp. 75–89.

Hayek, Friedrich August von (1979), *Law, Legislation and Liberty. Volume 3: The Political Order of a Free People,* London: Routledge & Kegan Paul.

Hayek, Friedrich August von (1993/1976), *Law, Legislation and Liberty. Volume 2. The Mirage of Social Justice,* Padstow: T.J. Press Ltd.

Hellmann, Thomas, Kevin Murdock and Joseph E. Stiglitz (1997), 'Financial Restraint: Toward a New Paradigm', in: Masahiko Aoki, Hyung-Ki Kim and Masahiro Okuno-Fujiwara (eds), *The Role of Government in East Asian Economic Development. Comparative Institutional Analysis,* Oxford: Clarendon Press, pp. 163–207.

Herrmann-Pillath, Carsten (1993), 'Informal Constraints, Culture and Incremental Transition from Plan to Market', in: Hans-Jürgen Wagener (ed.), *On the Theory and Policy of Systemic Change*, Heidelberg: Springer, pp. 95–120.

Hesse, Helmut and Laura Auria (1998), 'Die Finanzkrise in Südostasien: Ursachen und Auswirkungen auf die Weltwirtschaft' (Vorträge am Ibero-Amerika Institut für Wirtschaftsforschung 1/1998), University of Göttingen.

Hiemenz, Ulrich (1989), 'Development Strategies and Foreign Aid Policies for Low Income Countries in the 1990s' (Kiel Discussion Papers 152), Kiel: Kiel Institute of World Economics.

Hirschman, Albert O. (1969), *Exit, Voice, and Loyalty. Responses to Decline in Firms, Organizations, and States*, Cambridge, MA: Harvard University Press.

Hirschman, Albert O. (1981), *Essays in Trespassing*, Cambridge: Cambridge University Press.

Hodgson, Geoffrey M. (1998), 'The Approach of Institutional Economics', *Journal of Economic Literature*, XXXVI(1), pp. 166–92.

Hoen, Herman W. (1996), 'Transformation in the Czech and Slovak Republics: Liberal Rhetoric versus Populist Disgrace', paper presented at the Fourth EACES Conference, Grenoble, 12–14 September, 1996.

Hoen, Herman W. (1998), *The Transformation of Economic Systems in Central Europe*, Cheltenham, UK and Lyme, US: Edward Elgar.

Homans, G.C. (1958), 'Social Behavior as Exchange', *American Journal of Sociology*, 62, pp. 606–27.

Horowitz, Donald L. (1985), *Ethnic Groups in Conflict*, Berkeley, CA: University of California Press.

Huff, W. Gregg (1995), 'The developmental state, government, and Singapore's economic development since 1960', *World Development*, 23(8), pp. 1421–38.

Huntington, Samuel P. (1968), *Political Order in Changing Societies*, New Haven: Yale University Press.

Huntington, Samuel P. (1991), *The Third Wave. Democratization in the Late Twentieth Century*, Norman and London: University of Oklahoma Press.

Huntington, Samuel P. and Jorge I. Dominguez (1975), 'Political Development', in: Fred I. Greenstein and Nelson Polsby (eds), *Handbook of Political Science*, Reading, MA: Addison-Wesley.

Hydén, Göran (1992), 'Governance and the Study of Politics', in: Göran Hydén and Michael Bratton (eds), *Governance and politics in Africa*, Boulder, CO: Lynne Rienner, pp. 1–26.

Hydén, Göran and Michael Bratton (eds) (1992), *Governance and politics in Africa*, Boulder, CO: Lynne Rienner.

Inglehart, Ronald (1994), *Codebook for World Values Surveys,* Ann Arbor, MI: Institute for Social Research.

Inman, Robert P. (1987), 'Markets, Governments, and the "New" Political Economy', in: Alan J. Auerbach and Martin Feldstein (eds), *Handbook of Public Economics. Vol. 2.* New York: Elsevier.

Inotai, András (1999), 'Benefits and Costs of EU Enlargement for present members, first-round candidates and other associated countries', paper presented at the Annual Bank Conference on Development Economics – Europe, Paris, 21–23 June, 1999, Internet Website: http://www. worldbank.org/research/abcde/eu_99/eu/inotai.pdf.

International Monetary Fund (1997), *Good Governance. The IMF's Role,* Washington, DC: International Monetary Fund.

International Monetary Fund (1998a), *World Economic Outlook. May 1998,* Washington, DC: International Monetary Fund.

International Monetary Fund (1998b), *World Economic Outlook. October 1998,* Washington, DC: International Monetary Fund.

Itoh, Motoshige and Shujiro Urata (1994), 'Small and Medium–Size Enterprise Support Policies in Japan', World Bank Policy Research Working Paper No. 1403. Washington, DC: The World Bank.

Jayawardena, Lal (1997), 'Sri Lanka: Reforming Public Administration', in: Asian Development Bank (ed.), *Governance. Promoting Sound Development Management,* Manila: The Asian Development Bank, pp. 79–99.

Jensen, Michael C. and William Meckling (1976), 'Theory of the Firm: Managerial Behavior, Agency Costs, and Ownership Structure', *Journal of Financial Economics,* 3, pp. 305–60.

Jin, Hehui, Yingyi Qian and Barry R. Weingast (1999), 'Regional Decentralization and Fiscal Incentives: Federalism, Chinese Style', unpublished manuscript, Stanford University.

Johnson, Chalmers (1982), *MITI and the Japanese Miracle. The Growth of Industrial Policy, 1925–75,* Stanford, CA: Stanford University Press.

Johnson, Chalmers (1987), 'Political institutions and economic performance: the government–business relationship in Japan, South Korea, and Taiwan', in: Frederic C. Doyo (ed.), *The Political Economy of the New Asian Industrialism,* Ithaca, NY: Cornell University Press, pp. 136–64.

Johnson, Chalmers (1999), 'The Developmental State: Odyssey of a Concept', in: Meredith Woo-Cumings (ed.), *The Developmental State,* Ithaca, NY and London: Cornell University Press, pp. 32–60.

Karnow, Stanley (1990), *In Our Image: America's Empire in the Philippines,* New York: Random House.

Kasper, Wolfgang and Manfred Streit (1998), *Institutional Economics. Social Order and Public Policy*, Cheltenham, UK and Lyme, US: Edward Elgar.

Kaufmann, Daniel, Aart Kraay and Pablo Zoido-Lobatón (1999), 'Governance Matters', World Bank Policy Research Working Paper No. 2196, Washington, DC: The World Bank.

Khaitun, S. (2000), 'Billions for Bureaucrats' Dictatorship', *Moscow News*, 26 January, 2000.

Kiewiet, D. Roderick and Mathew D. McCubbins (1991), *The Logic of Delegation*, Chicago: University of Chicago Press.

Killick, Tony (1989), *A Reaction Too Far. Economic Theory and the Role of the State in Developing Countries*, Boulder, CO: Westview Press.

Killick, Tony (1996), 'Principals, Agents and the Limitations of BWI Conditionality', *World Economy*, 19, pp. 211–29.

Kim, Linsu and Jeffrey B. Nugent (1994), 'The Republic of Korea's Small and Medium-Size Enterprises and Their Support Systems', World Bank Policy Research Working Paper No. 1404. Washington, DC: The World Bank.

Kiwit, Daniel and Stefan Voigt (1995), 'Überlegungen zum institutionellen Wandel unter Berücksichtigung des Verhältnisses interner und externer Institutionen', *ORDO. Jahrbuch für die Ordnung von Wirtschaft und Gesellschaft*, 46, pp. 117–48.

Kjær, Mette (1996), 'Governance – Making It Tangible', paper presented at the "Good Governance" working group at the EADI Conference, Vienna, 11–14 September, 1996.

Klein, Benjamin, Robert G. Crawford and Armen A. Alchian (1978), 'Vertical Integration, Appropriable Rents, and the Competitive Contracting Process', *Journal of Law and Economics*, 28, pp. 297–326.

Klein, Peter G. (1998), 'New Institutional Economics', unpublished manuscript, University of Georgia. Athens, GA.

Klitgaard, Robert (1991), *Adjusting to Reality. Beyond 'State versus Market' in Economic Development*, San Francisco: ICS Press.

Klitgaard, Robert (1994), 'Do Better Polities Have Higher Economic Growth?' (IRIS Working Paper No. 113), University of Maryland, College Park.

Knack, Stephen and Philip Keefer (1995), 'Institutions and Economic Performance: Cross-Country Tests Using Alternative Institutional Measures', *Economics & Politics*, 7(3), pp. 207–27.

Knack, Stephen and Philip Keefer (1997a), 'Does Social Capital Have an Economic Payoff? A Cross-Country Investigation', *Quarterly Journal of Economics*, CXII(4), pp. 1251–88.

Knack, Stephen and Philip Keefer (1997b), 'Why Don't Poor Countries Catch Up? A Cross-National Test of an Institutional Explanation', *Economic Inquiry*, 35(3), pp. 590–602.

Kohli, Atul (ed.) (1988), *India's Democracy. An Analysis of Changing State–Society Relations*, Princeton, NJ: Princeton University Press.

Kolodko, Grzegorz W. (1999), 'Ten Years of Postsocialist Transition: Lessons for Policy Reforms' (World Bank Policy Research Working Paper 2095), Washington, DC: The World Bank.

Kornai, Janos (1994), 'Transformational Recession: The Main Causes', *Journal of Comparative Economics*, 19(1), pp. 39–63.

Kralinski, Thomas (1999), 'Die russische Kommunalverwaltung im Wandel: Im Osten was Neues?', *Osteuropa-Wirtschaft*, 44(1), pp. 51–78.

Krehbiel, Keith (1991), *Information and Legislative Organization*, Ann Arbor: University of Michigan Press.

Kreps, David M. (1990), *A Course in Microeconomic Theory*, New York: Harvester Wheatsheaf.

Krishnaswamy, K.S., I.S. Gulati and A. Vaidyanathan (1992), 'Economic Aspects of Federalism in India', in: Nirval Mukarji and Balveer Arora (eds.), *Federalism in India. Origins and Development*, New Delhi: Vikas Publishing House.

Krueger, Anne O. (1974), 'The Political Economy of the Rent-Seeking Society', *American Economic Review*, 64(3), pp. 291–303.

Krueger, Anne O. (1988), *The Political Economy of Control: American Sugar*, NBER Working Paper, No. 2504.

Krueger, Anne O. (1993), *Political Economy of Policy Reform in Developing Countries*, Cambridge, MA and London: The MIT Press.

Krueger, Anne O. (1995), 'Policy Lessons from Development Experience since the Second World War', in: Jere Behrman and T.N. Srinivasan (eds) (1995), *Handbook of Development Economics, Vol. III B*, Amsterdam: Elsevier Science, pp. 2497–550.

Krugman, Paul (1991), *Geography and Trade*, Cambridge, MA: The MIT Press.

Krugman, Paul (1993), 'Toward a Counter-Counterrevolution in Development Theory', *Proceedings of the World Bank Annual Conference on Development Economics 1992*, pp. 15–38.

Krugman, Paul (1994), 'The Myth of Asia's Miracle', *Foreign Affairs*, 73(6), pp. 62–78.

Krugman, Paul (1998), 'What Happened to Asia?', Internet Website: http:// web.mit.edu/krugman/www/DISINTER.html.

Kuznets, Simon (1955), 'Economic Growth and Income Inequality', *American Economic Review*, 45(1), pp. 1–28.

Lal, Deepak (1999), 'Culture, Democracy and Development: The Impact of Formal and Informal Institutions on Development', paper prepared for delivery at the IMF Conference on Second Generation Reforms, Internet Website: http://www.imf.org/external/pubs/ft/seminar/1999/reforms/index.htm.

Lall, Sanjaya (1992), 'Technological Capabilities and Industrialization', *World Development*, 20(2), pp. 165–86.

Lall, Sanjaya (1995), 'Malaysia: Industrial Success and the Role of Government', *Journal of International Development*, 7(5), pp. 759–73.

Lall, Sanjaya (1997), 'Coping with New Technologies in Emerging Asia' (Centro Studi Luca d'Agliano – Queen Elisabeth House Development Studies Working Paper No. 112), Oxford University.

Lamb, Geoffrey (1987), 'Managing Economic Policy Change. Institutional Dimensions', World Bank Discussion Papers No. 14, Washington, DC.

Lancaster, Carol (1993), 'Governance and Development: The Views from Washington', *ids bulletin*, 24(1), pp. 9–15.

Landell-Mills, Pierre and Ismail Serageldin (1992), 'Governance and the External Factor', *Proceedings of the World Bank Annual Conference on Development Economics 1991*, pp. 303–20.

Lang, Kai-Olaf (2000), 'Slowakei: Rissiges Fundament der Orientierung auf NATO und EU', *Aktuelle Analyse des BIOst*, No. 23/2000.

Langlois, Richard N. (1986), *Economics as a Process: Essays in the New Institutional Economics*, Cambridge: Cambridge University Press.

La Porta, Rafael, Florencio Lopez-de-Silanes, Andrei Shleifer and Robert W. Vishny (1997a), 'Legal Determinants of External Finance', *Journal of Finance*, 52(3), pp. 1131–50.

La Porta, Rafael, Florencio Lopez-de-Silanes, Andrei Shleifer and Robert W. Vishny (1997b), 'Trust in Large Organizations', *American Economic Review (Papers and Proceedings)*, 87(2), pp. 333–8.

La Porta, Rafael, Florencio Lopez-de-Silanes, Andrei Shleifer and Robert W. Vishny (1998), 'Law and Finance', *Journal of Political Economy*, 106(6), pp. 1113–55.

La Porta, Rafael, Florencio Lopez-de-Silanes, Andrei Shleifer and Robert W. Vishny (1999), 'The Quality of Government', *Journal of Law, Economics, & Organization*, 15(1), pp. 222–79.

Lau, Lawrence J. (1997), 'The Role of Government in Economic Development: Some Observations from the Experience of China, Hong Kong, and Taiwan', in: Masahiko Aoki, Hyung-Ki Kim and Masahiro Okuno-Fujiwara (eds.), *The Role of Government in East Asian Economic Development. Comparative Institutional Analysis*, Oxford: Clarendon Press, pp. 41–73.

Lau, Lawrence J., Yingyi Qian and Gérard Roland (1997), 'Pareto-Improving Economic Reforms Through Dual-Track Liberalization', *Economics Letters*, 55(2), pp. 285–92.

Lau, Lawrence J., Yingyi Qian and Gérard Roland (2000), 'Reform without Losers: An Interpretation of China's Dual-Track Approach to Transition', *Journal of Political Economy*, 108(1), pp. 120–43.

Leftwich, Adrian (1993), 'Governance, democracy and development in the Third World', *Third World Quarterly*, 14(3), pp. 605–24.

Leftwich, Adrian (1994), 'Governance, the State and the Politics of Development', *Development and Change*, 25(2), pp. 363–86.

Leftwich, Adrian (1995), 'Bringing politics back in: towards a model of the developmental state', *Journal of Development Studies*, 31(3), pp. 400–27.

Leftwich, Adrian (ed.) (1996), *Democracy and Development: Theory and Practice*, Cambridge: Polity Press.

Leibenstein, Harvey (1950), 'Bandwagon, Snob and Veblen Effects in the Theory of Consumers' Demand', *Quarterly Journal of Economics*, 64, pp. 183–207.

Leipold, Helmut (1994), 'Interdependenz von wirtschaftlicher und politischer Ordnung', in: Carsten Herrmann-Pillath, Otto Schlecht and Horst Friedrich Wünsche (eds), *Marktwirtschaft als Aufgabe. Wirtschaft und Gesellschaft im Übergang vom Plan zum Markt*, Stuttgart: Gustav Fischer Verlag, pp. 723–38.

Leipold, Helmut (1996), 'Zur Pfadabhängigkeit der institutionellen Entwicklung. Erklärungsansätze des Wandels von Ordnungen', in: Dieter Cassel (ed.), *Entstehung und Wettbewerb von Systemen* (Schriften des Vereins für Socialpolitik, Neue Folge Band 246), Berlin: Duncker & Humblot, pp. 93–115.

Leisinger, Klaus M. (1995), 'Gouvernanz oder: "Zuhause muß beginnen, was leuchten soll im Vaterland"', in: Klaus M. Leisinger and Vittorio Hösle (eds), *Entwicklung mit menschlichem Antlitz. Die Dritte und die Erste Welt im Dialog*, Munich: C.H. Beck, pp. 114–72.

Levine, Ross (1997), 'Law, Finance, and Economic Growth', unpublished manuscript. Washington, DC: The World Bank.

Levine, Ross and David Renelt (1992), 'A Sensitivity Analysis of Cross-Country Growth Regressions', *American Economic Review*, 82(4), pp. 942–63.

Levy, Brian and Pablo Spiller (1994), 'The Institutional Foundations of Regulatory Commitment', *Journal of Law, Economics, and Organization*, 9, pp. 201–46.

Levy, Brian and Pablo Spiller (eds) (1996), *Regulations, Institutions, and Commitment: Comparative Studies of Telecommunications*, New York: Cambridge University Press.

Lewis, William A. (1955), *The Theory of Economic Growth*, London: George Allen & Unwin.

Li, Wei (1999), 'A Tale of Two Reforms', *RAND Journal of Economics*, 30(1), pp. 120–36.

Lin, Justin Yifu (1989a), 'An Economic Theory of Institutional Change: Induced and Imposed Change', *Cato Journal*, 9(1), pp. 1–33.

Lin, Justin Yifu (1989b), 'Rural Factor Market in China after the Household Responsibility Reform', in: B. Reynolds (ed.), *Chinese Economic Policy*, New York: Paragon, pp. 157–92.

Lin, Justin Yifu and Zhiqiang Liu (2000), 'Fiscal Decentralization and Economic Growth in China', *Economic Development and Cultural Change,* 49(1), pp. 1–22.

Lin, Justin Yifu and Jeffrey B. Nugent (1995), 'Institutions and Economic Development', in: Jere Behrman and T.N. Srinivasan (eds.), *Handbook of Development Economics, Vol. III A*, Amsterdam: Elsevier Science, pp. 2301–70.

Lindenberg, Marc M. (1993), *The Human Development Race: Improving the Quality of Life in Developing Countries,* San Francisco: ICS Press.

Lindenberg, Siegwart (1988), 'Contractual Relations and Weak Solidarity: The Behavioral Basis of Restraints on Gain-Maximization', *Journal of Institutional and Theoretical Economics*, 144(1), pp. 39–58.

Lipsey, Richard (2002), 'Some Implications of Endogenous Technological Change for Technology Policies in Developing Countries', *Economics of Innovation and New Technology*, 11(4-5), pp. 321–51.

Lupia, Arthur and Mathew D. McCubbins (1998a), 'Political Credibility and Economic Reform, Part 1: Do Politicians Intend to Keep the Promises They Make? A Report for the World Bank', Internet Website: http://mmccubbins.ucsd.edu/credibility.htm.

Lupia, Arthur and Mathew D. McCubbins (1998b), 'Conditions for the Stability of Political Agreements', unpublished manuscript, University of California at San Diego.

Macneil, I.R. (1974), 'The Many Futures of Contract', *Southern California Review*, 47, pp. 691–816.

Martimort, David (1996), 'The multiprinciple nature of government', *European Economic Review*, 40, pp. 673–85.

Martin, Denis-Constant (1992), 'The Cultural Dimensions of Governance', *Proceedings of the World Bank Annual Conference on Development Economics 1991*, pp. 325–41.

Martinelli, César and Mariano Tommasi (1997), 'Sequencing of Economic Reforms in the Presence of Political Constraints', *Economics and Politics*, 9(2), pp. 115–31.

Matthews, R.C.O. (1986). 'The Economics of Institutions and the Sources of Growth', *Economic Journal*, 96, pp. 903–18.

Mauro, Paolo (1995), 'Corruption and Growth', *Quarterly Journal of Economics*, CX(3), pp. 681–712.

McKelvey, Richard (1976), 'Intransitivities in Multidimensional Voting Models and Some Implications for Agenda Control', *Journal of Economic Theory*, 12, pp. 472–82.

McKinnon, Ronald I. (1991), 'Financial Control in the Transition From Classical Socialism to a Market Economy', *Journal of Economic Perspectives*, 5(4), pp. 107–22.

McKinnon, Ronald I. (1992), *The Order of Economic Liberalization. Financial Control in the Transition to a Market Economy*, Baltimore and London: Johns Hopkins University Press.

McKinnon, Ronald I. (1995), 'Market-Preserving Fiscal Federalism in the American Monetary Union', *Spectrum*, Summer 1995.

McNollgast (1989), 'Structure and Process, Politics and Policy', *Virginia Law Review*, Vol. 75, pp. 431–82.

Mehta, Pratap B. (1997), 'India: Fragmentation amid Consensus', *Journal of Democracy*, 8(1), pp. 56–69.

Meier, Gerald M. (ed.) (1991a), *Politics and Policy Making in Developing Countries. Perspectives on the New Political Economy*, San Francisco: ICS Press.

Meier, Gerald M. (1991b), 'Policy Lessons and Policy Formation', in: Gerald M. Meier (ed.) (1991a), *Politics and Policy Making in Developing Countries. Perspectives on the New Political Economy*, San Francisco: ICS Press.

Meier, Gerald M. (ed.) (1995), *Leading Issues in Economic Development* (6th edition), New York and Oxford: Oxford University Press.

Merkel, Wolfgang (1999), *Systemtransformation. Eine Einführung in die Theorie und Empire der Transformationsforschung*, Opladen: UTB Leske + Budrich.

Migdal, Joel S. (1988), *Strong Societies and Weak States: State–Society Relations and State Capabilities in the Third World*, Princeton, NJ: Princeton University Press.

Mody, A. (1998), 'Industrial policy after the East Asian crisis: From "outward-orientation" to new internal capabilities?', unpublished manuscript, Washington, DC: The World Bank.

Moe, Terry M. (1990), 'Political Institutions: The Neglected Side of the Story', *Journal of Law, Economics, and Organization*, 6, Special Issue, pp. 213–53.

Montinola, Gabriella, Yinyi Qian and Barry R. Weingast (1995), 'Federalism, Chinese Style. The Political Basis for Economic Success in China', *World Politics*, 48(1), pp. 50–81.

Moore, Mick (1993), 'Declining to Learn from the East? The World Bank on "Governance and Development"', *ids bulletin*, 24(1), pp. 39–50.

Morris, Cynthia Taft and Irma Adelman (1988), *Comparative Patterns of Economic Development, 1850–1914,* Baltimore: Johns Hopkins University Press.

Morris, Cynthia Taft and Irma Adelman (1989), 'Nineteenth-Century Development Experience and Lessons for Today', *World Development*, 17(9), pp. 1417–32.

Mueller, Dennis C. (ed.) (1983), *The Political Economy of Growth,* New Haven: Yale University Press.

Mueller, Dennis C. (1989), *Public Choice II,* a revised edition of *Public Choice,* Cambridge: Cambridge University Press.

Mukarji, Nirmal (1993), 'The Third Stratum', *Economic and Political Weekly*, 1 May, pp. 859–62.

Mukarji, Nirmal and Balveer Arora (eds.) (1992), *Federalism in India. Origins and Development,* New Delhi: Vikas Publishing House.

Mummert, Uwe (1995), *Informelle Institutionen in ökonomischen Transformationsprozessen,* Baden-Baden: Nomos.

Mummert, Uwe (1999a), 'Making institutions work: from *de jure* to *de facto* institutional reform', paper presented at the IAES conference, Vienna, 17–22 March, 1999.

Mummert, Uwe (1999b), 'Informal Institutions and Institutional Policy – Shedding Light on the Myth of Institutional Conflict', Diskussionsbeitrag 02–99, Max-Planck-Institute for Research into Economic Systems, Jena.

Mummert, Uwe and Michael Wohlgemuth (1998), 'Ordnungsökonomische Aspekte der Transformation und wirtschaftlichen Entwicklung Ostdeutschlands', Diskussionsbeitrag 03–98, Max-Planck-Institute for Research into Economic Systems, Jena.

Murrell, Peter (1991), 'Can Neoclassical Economics Underpin the Economic Reform of the Centrally-Planned Economies?' *Journal of Economic Perspectives*, 5(4), pp. 59–76.

Myrdal, Gunnar (1968), *Asian Drama,* New York: Random House.

Myrdal, Gunnar (1970), 'The "soft state" in underdeveloped countries', in: Paul Streeten (ed.), *Unfashionable Economics. Essays in Honour of Lord Balogh,* London: Weidenfeld and Nicolson, pp. 227–43.

Nabli, Mustapha K. and Jeffrey B. Nugent (1989a), 'The New Institutional Economics and Its Applicability to Development', *World Development*, 17(9), pp. 1333–47.

Nabli, Mustapha K. and Jeffrey B. Nugent (1989b), 'Collective Action, Institutions and Development', in: Mustapha K. Nabli and Jeffrey B. Nugent (eds), *The New Institutional Economics and Development. Theory and Applications to Tunisia,* Amsterdam: North-Holland, pp. 80–137.

Naìm, Moisès (1999), 'Fads and Fashion in Economic Reforms: Washington Consensus or Washington Confusion?', Paper presented at the IMF Conference on Second Generation Reforms, Washington, DC, 8–9 November, 1999, Internet Website: http://www.imf.org/external/pubs/ft/seminar/1999/reforms/Naim.HTM.

Nelson, Joan M. (1984), 'The Political Economy of Stabilization: Commitment, Capacity and Public Response', *World Development,* 12(10), pp. 983–1006.

Nelson, Joan M. (ed.) (1989), *Fragile Coalitions: The Politics of Economic Adjustment,* New Brunswick: Transaction Books.

Nelson, Joan M. (ed.) (1990), *Economic Crisis and Policy Choice. The Politics of Adjustment in the Third World,* Princeton, NJ: Princeton University Press.

Nishimoto, Shoji (1997), 'The Bank's Governance Policy', in: Asian Development Bank (ed.), *Governance. Promoting Sound Development Management,* Manila: The Asian Development Bank, pp. 7–11.

Niskanen, William A. (1971), *Bureaucracy and Representative Government,* Chicago: Aldine-Atherton.

North, Douglass C. (1981), *Structure and Change in Economic History,* New York and London: W.W. Norton and Company.

North, Douglass C. (1988), 'Ideology and Political/Economic Institutions', *Cato Journal,* 8(1), pp. 15–27.

North, Douglass C. (1989), 'A Transaction Cost Approach to the Historical Development of Polities and Economies', *Journal of Institutional and Theoretical Economics,* 145(4), pp. 661–8.

North, Douglass C. (1990a), *Institutions, Institutional Change and Economic Performance,* Cambridge: Cambridge University Press.

North, Douglass C. (1990b), 'A Transaction Cost Theory of Politics', *Journal of Theoretical Politics,* 2(4), pp. 355–67.

North, Douglass C. (1990c), 'Institutions and a transaction-cost theory of exchange', in: James E. Alt and Kenneth A. Shepsle (eds), *Perspectives on Positive Political Economy,* Cambridge: Cambridge University Press.

North, Douglass C. (1992), 'Institutions, Ideology, and Economic Performance', *Cato Journal,* 11(3), pp. 477–88.

North, Douglass C. (1993), 'What do we mean by rationality?', *Public Choice,* 77, pp. 159–62.

North, Douglass C. (1994a), 'Economic Performance Through Time', *American Economic Review,* 84(3), pp. 359–68.

North, Douglass C. (1994b), 'The Historical Evolution of Polities', *International Review of Law and Economics*, 14, pp. 381–91.

North, Douglass C. (1995a), 'Some Fundamental Puzzles in Economic History/Development', mimeo, St. Louis.

North, Douglass C. (1995b), 'The New Institutional Economics and Third World Development', in: John Harriss, Janet Hunter and Colin M. Lewis (eds.), *The New Institutional Economics and Third World Development*, London and New York: Routledge, pp. 17–26.

North, Douglass C. and Robert Paul Thomas (1973), *The Rise of the Western World. A New Economic History*, Cambridge: Cambridge University Press.

North, Douglass C. and Robert Paul Thomas (1977), 'The First Economic Revolution', *Economic History Review*, 30(2) (second series), pp. 229–41.

North, Douglass C. and Barry R. Weingast (1989), 'Constitutions and Commitment: The Evolution of Institutions Governing Public Choice in Seventeenth-Century England', *Journal of Economic History*, XLIX(4), pp. 803–32.

Nugent, Jeffrey B. (1998), 'Institutions, markets, and development outcomes', in: Robert Picciotto and Eduardo Wiesner (eds), *Evaluation & Development. The Institutional Dimension*, New Brunswick and London: Transaction Publishers, pp. 7–23.

Nunberg, Barbara (1999), *The State After Communism. Administrative Transitions in Central and Eastern Europe* (World Bank Regional and Sectoral Studies), Washington, DC: The World Bank.

Nunnenkamp, Peter (1995), 'What Donors Mean by Good Governance: Heroic Ends, Limited Means, and Traditional Dilemmas of Development Cooperation', *ids bulletin*, 26(2), pp. 9–16.

Oates, Wallace E. (1972), *Fiscal Federalism*, New York: Harcourt Brace Jovanovich.

Okimoto, Daniel I. (1989), *Between MITI and the Market: Japanese Industrial Policy for High Technology*, Stanford, CA: Stanford University Press.

Olson, Mancur (1965), *The Logic of Collective Action: Public Goods and the Theory of Groups* (edition reprinted in 1971 with an added appendix), Cambridge, MA: Harvard University Press.

Olson, Mancur (1969), 'The Principle of Fiscal Equivalence: The Division of Responsibilities among Different Levels of Government', *American Economic Review*, 59(2), pp. 479–87.

Olson, Mancur (1982), *The Rise and Decline of Nations*, New Haven: Yale University Press.

Olson, Mancur (1993), 'Dictatorship, Democracy, and Development', *American Political Science Review*, 87(3), pp. 567–76.

Olson, Mancur (1996), 'Big Bills Left on the Sidewalk: Why Some Nations are Rich, and Others Poor', *Journal of Economic Perspectives*, 10(2), pp. 3–24.

Olson, Mancur (1997), 'Why Some Nations are Rich and Others Poor' (Ernest Sturc Memorial Lecture), Johns Hopkins University, School for Advanced International Studies, Washington DC, 6 November, transcribed with the title 'Market Augmenting Government', IRIS manuscript, Department of Economics, University of Maryland.

Orchard, Lionel and Hugh Stretton (1997), 'Public Choice', *Cambridge Journal of Economics*, 21, pp. 409–30.

Ordeshook, Peter C. (1995), 'Russia, Federalism, and Political Stability' (IRIS working paper No. 156), University of Maryland at College Park, MD.

Ostrom, Elinor (1990), *Governing the Commons. The Evolution of Institutions for Collective Action,* Cambridge: Cambridge University Press.

Ostrom, Elinor, Larry Schroeder and Susan Wynne (1993), *Institutional Incentives and Sustainable Development. Infrastructure Policies in Perspective,* Boulder, CO: Westview Press.

Ostrom, Vincent, David Feeny and Hartmut Picht (eds) (1993), *Rethinking Institutional Analysis and Development,* San Francisco: ICS Press.

Overholt, William (1986), 'The Rise and Fall of Ferdinand Marcos', *Asian Survey*, 26(11), pp. 1137–63.

Overland, Jody and Michael Spagat (1996), 'Human Capital and Russia's Economic Transformation', *Transition. Events and Issues in the Former Soviet Union and East–Central and Southeastern Europe,* 2(13).

Pack, Howard and Larry E. Westphal (1986), 'Industrial Strategy and Technological Change', *Journal of Development Economics,* 22, pp. 87–128.

Panther, Stephan (1999), 'History, Informal Institutions and the Transition in Eastern Europe: Latin Winners. Orthodox Losers?', unpublished manuscript, University of Hamburg.

Parikh, Sunita and Barry R. Weingast (1997), 'A Comparative Theory of Federalism: India', *Virginia Law Review*, 83(7), pp. 1593–615.

Parsons, Talcott (1975), 'Social Structure and the Symbolic Media of Exchange', in: Peter M. Blau (ed.), *Approaches to the Study of Social Structure,* New York and London: Free Press, pp. 94–120.

Pedersen, Jørgen D. (1992), 'State, Bureaucracy and Change in India', *Journal of Development Studies,* 28(4), pp. 616–39.

Pejovich, Svetozar (1994), 'The Market for Institutions vs. Capitalism by Fiat: The Case of Eastern Europe', *Kyklos,* 47(4), pp. 519–29.

Pejovich, Svetozar (ed.) (1997a), *The Economic Foundations of Property Rights: Selected Readings,* Cheltenham, UK and Lyme, US: Edward Elgar.

Pejovich, Svetozar (1997b), 'Law, Tradition, and the Transition in Eastern Europe', *The Independent Review,* II(2), pp. 243–54.

Pelikan, Pavel (1985), 'Private Enterprise *vs.* Government Control: An Organizationally Dynamic Comparison', Working Paper No. 137, Industriens Utredningsinstitut, Stockholm.

Pelikan, Pavel (1987), 'The Formation of Incentive Mechanisms in Different Economic Systems', in: Stefan Hedlund (ed.), *Incentives and Economic Systems* (Proceedings of the Eighth Arne Ryde Symposium, Frostavallen, 26–27 August 1985), London & Sydney: Croom Helm, pp. 27–56.

Pempel, T.J. (1999a), 'The Developmental Regime in a Changing World Economy', in: Meredith Woo-Cumings (ed.), *The Developmental State,* Ithaca, NY and London: Cornell University Press, pp. 137–81.

Pempel, T.J. (ed.) (1999b), *The Politics of the Asian Economic Crisis,* Ithaca, NY and London: Cornell University Press.

Persson, Torsten and Guido E. Tabellini (1990), *Macroeconomic Policy, Credibility and Politics,* Chur: Harwood.

Persson, Torsten, Gérard Roland and Guido E. Tabellini (1997), 'Separation of Powers and Political Accountability', *Quarterly Journal of Economics,* CXII(4), pp. 1163–202.

Piazolo, Daniel (1998), 'Economic Growth through the Import of Credibility: The Importance of Institutional Integration for Eastern Europe' (unpublished manuscript), Kiel Institute of World Economics.

Polanyi, Karl (1995/1944), *The Great Transformation. Politische und ökonomische Ursprünge von Gesellschaften und Wirtschaftssystemen,* Frankfurt/Main: Suhrkamp.

Pou, Pedro (2000), 'Argentina's Structural Reforms of the 1990s', *Finance & Development,* 37(1).

Poznanski, Kazimierz Z. (ed.) (1995), *The Evolutionary Transition to Capitalism,* Boulder, CO: Westview Press.

Pradhan, Sanjay (1998), 'Reinvigorating state institutions', in: Robert Picciotto and Eduardo Wiesner (eds), *Evaluation & Development. The Institutional Dimension,* New Brunswick and London: Transaction Publishers, pp. 55–71.

Prud'homme, Rémy (1995), 'The Dangers of Decentralization', *World Bank Research Observer,* 10(2), pp. 201–20.

Przeworski, Adam (1991), *Democracy and the market. Political and economic reforms in Eastern Europe and Latin America,* Cambridge: Cambridge University Press.

Przeworski, Adam (1995), 'Reforming the State: Political Accountability and Economic Intervention', unpublished manuscript, New York University, New York.

Putnam, Robert D. (with Robert Leonardi and Raffaella Y. Nanetti) (1988), 'Institutional Performance and Political Culture: Some Puzzles about the Power of the Past', *Governance: An International Journal of Policy and Administration,* 1(3), pp. 221–42.

Putnam, Robert D. (1993), *Making Democracy Work: Civic Traditions in Modern Italy,* Princeton, NJ: Princeton University Press.

Putnam, Robert D. (1995), 'Comment on "The Institutions and Governance of Economic Development and Reform", by Williamson', in: Michael Bruno and Boris Pleskovic (eds), *Proceedings of the World Bank Annual Conference on Development Economics 1994,* Washington, DC: The World Bank, pp. 198–200.

Qian, Yingyi (1999), 'The Institutional Foundations of China's Market Transition', paper prepared for the World Bank's Annual Conference on Development Economics, Washington, DC, 28–30 April, 1999.

Qian, Yingyi and Barry R. Weingast (1996), 'China's Transition to Markets: Market-Preserving Federalism, Chinese Style', *Journal of Policy Reform,* 1(2), pp. 149–85.

Qian, Yingyi and Barry R. Weingast (1997a), 'Institutions, State Activism, and Economic Development: A Comparison of State-Owned and Township-Village Enterprises in China', in: Masahiko Aoki, Hyung-Ki Kim and Masahiro Okuno-Fujiwara (eds) (1997), *The Role of Government in East Asian Economic Development. Comparative Institutional Analysis,* Oxford: Clarendon Press, pp. 254–75.

Qian, Yingyi and Barry R. Weingast (1997b), 'Federalism as a Commitment to Preserving Market Incentives', *Journal of Economic Perspectives,* 11(4), pp. 83–92.

Qian, Yingyi and Chenggang Xu (1993), 'Why China's Economic Reforms Differ: The M-form Hierarchy and Entry/Expansion of the Non–State Sector', *Economics of Transition,* 1(2), pp. 135–70.

Radelet, Steven (1998), 'Indonesia's Implosion' (Harvard Institute for International Development), Internet Website: http://www.hiid.harvard.edu/pub/other/indimp.pdf.

Radelet, Steven and Jeffrey D. Sachs (1998a), 'The East Asian Financial Crisis: Diagnosis, Remedies, Prospects', *Brookings Papers on Economic Activity,* 1:1998, pp. 1–90.

Radelet, Steven and Jeffrey D. Sachs (1998b), 'The Onset of the East Asian Financial Crisis' (Harvard Institute for International Development), Internet Website: http://www.hiid.harvard.edu/pub/other/eaonset.pdf.

Radelet, Steven; Jeffrey D. Sachs and Jong-Wha Lee (1997), 'Economic Growth in Asia', HIID Development Discussion Paper No. 609. Cambridge, MA.

Raiser, Martin (1997), 'Informal institutions, social capital and economic transition: reflections on a neglected dimension', European Bank for Reconstruction and Development Working Paper No. 25.

Ranis, Gustav and Syed Akhtar Mahmood (1992), *The political economy of development policy change*, Cambridge, MA and Oxford: Basil Blackwell.

Reynolds, Lloyd G. (1983), 'The Spread of Economic Growth to the Third World: 1850–1980', *Journal of Economic Literature*, XXI(3), pp. 941–80.

Richter, Rudolf (1996), 'Bridging Old and New Institutional Economics: Gustav Schmoller, the Leader of the Younger German Historical School, Seen with Neoinstitutionalists' Eyes', *Journal of Institutional and Theoretical Economics*, 152, pp. 567–92.

Richter, Rudolf (1998), 'Neue Institutionenökonomik. Ideen und Möglichkeiten', in: Gerold Krause-Junk (ed.), *Steuersysteme der Zukunft* (Schriften des Vereins für Socialpolitik Neue Folge Band 256), Berlin: Duncker & Humblot, pp. 323–55.

Richter, Rudolf (1999), 'A Note on the Transformation of Economic Systems', contribution to a James Buchanan Festschrift; Internet Website: http://www.gmu.edu/jbc/fest/files/richter.htm.

Riker, William H. (1962), *The Theory of Political Coalition*, New Haven: Yale University Press.

Riker, William H. (1964), *Federalism: Origin, Operation, Significance*, Boston: Little, Brown and Company.

Riker, William H. (1976), 'Comments on Vincent Ostrom's Paper', *Public Choice*, 27, pp. 13–15.

Riker, William H. (1981), 'Implications from the Disequilibrium of Majority Rule for the Study of Institutions', *American Political Science Review*, 74, pp. 432–47.

Rodrik, Dani (1989), 'Promises, Promises: Credible Policy Reform Via Signalling', *The Economic Journal*, 99 (September), pp. 756–72.

Rodrik, Dani (1994), 'Comment', in: John Williamson (ed.), *The Political Economy of Policy Reform*, Washington, DC: Institute for International Economics, pp. 212–15.

Rodrik, Dani (1995), 'Getting interventions right: how South Korea and Taiwan grew rich', *Economic Policy. A European Forum*, 20, pp. 55–97.

Rodrik, Dani (1996), 'Understanding Economic Policy Reform', *Journal of Economic Literature*, XXXIV(1), pp. 9–41.

Rodrik, Dani (1997), 'TFPG Controversies, Institutions, and Economic Performance in East Asia', NBER Working Paper No. 5914, Cambridge, MA: National Bureau of Economic Research.

Rodrik, Dani (1998) 'Rethinking the World Economy', Internet Website: http://www.ksg.harvard.edu/rodrik/TNRpiece.html.

Rodrik, Dani (1999), 'Institutions For High-Quality Growth: What They Are and How to Acquire Them', paper presented at the IMF Conference on Second Generation Reforms, Washington, DC, 8–9 November, 1999, Internet Website: http://www.imf.org/external/pubs/ft/seminar/1999/reforms/rodrik.htm.

Roemer, Michael and Steven C. Radelet (1991), 'Macroeconomic Reform in Developing Countries', in: Dwight H. Perkins and Michael Roemer (eds) (1991), *Reforming Economic Systems in Developing Countries*, Cambridge, MA: Harvard Institute for International Development.

Roland, Gérard (1994), 'The Role of Political Constraints in Transition Strategies', *Economics of Transition*, 2(1), pp. 27–41.

Roland, Gérard (1997), 'Political constraints and the transition experience', in: Salvatore Zecchini (ed.), *Lessons from the Economic Transition. Central and Eastern Europe in the 1990s*, Dordrecht: Kluwer.

Roland, Gérard and Thierry Verdier (1999), 'Transition and the Output Fall', *Economics of Transition*, 7(1), pp. 1–28.

Root, Hilton L. (1994), *The Fountain of Privilege. Political Foundations of Markets in Old Regime France and England*, Berkeley, CA: University of California Press.

Root, Hilton L. (1996), *Small Countries, Big Lessons. Governance and the Rise of East Asia*, Hong Kong: Oxford University Press.

Root, Hilton L. (1998a), 'Distinctive institutions in the rise of East Asia', in: Henry S. Rowen (ed.), *Behind East Asian Growth. The political and social foundations of prosperity*, London and New York: Routledge, pp. 60–77.

Root, Hilton L. (1998b), 'India: Asia's Next Tiger?', unpublished manuscript, Hoover Institution/Stanford University.

Root, Hilton L., Mark Andrew Abdollahian, Greg Beier and Jacek Kugler (1999), 'The New Korea: Crisis Brings Opportunity', Internet Website: http://www.stern.nyu.edu/globalmacro/.

Root, Hilton L. and Barry R. Weingast (1996), 'The State's Role in East Asian Development', in Hilton L. Root, *Small Countries, Big Lessons. Governance and the Rise of East Asia*, Hong Kong: Oxford University Press.

Röpke, Wilhelm (1950), *The Social Crisis of Our Time*, Chicago: University of Chicago Press.

Rose-Ackerman, Susan (1978), *Corruption: A Study in Political Economy*, New York: Academic Press.

Rostow, Walt W. (1958), 'The Take-off into Self-sustained Growth', in: A.N. Agarwala and S.P. Singh (eds), *The Economics of Underdevelopment*, Oxford: Oxford University Press, pp. 154–86.

Roubini, Nouriel (1999), 'What Caused Asia's Economic and Currency Crisis and Its Global Contagion?', Internet Website: http://www.stern.nyu.edu/globalmacro/.

Rowen, Henry S. (1998), 'The political and social foundations of the rise of East Asia: an overview', in: Henry S. Rowen (ed.), *Behind East Asian Growth. The political and social foundations of prosperity*, London and New York: Routledge, pp. 1–36.

Rubinfeld, Daniel L. (1987), 'The Economics of the Local Public Sector', in: Alan J. Auerbach and Martin Feldstein (eds), *Handbook of Public Economics Vol. II*, Amsterdam: Elsevier Science Publishers BV (North-Holland), pp. 571–645.

Rueschemeyer, Dietrich (1986), *Power and the Division of Labour*, Cambridge: Polity Press.

Rutherford, Malcolm (1995), 'The Old and the New Institutionalism: Can Bridges Be Built?' *Journal of Economic Issues*, XXIX(2), pp. 443–51.

Ruttan, Vernon W. and Yujiro Hayami (1984), 'Toward a Theory of Induced Institutional Innovation', *Journal of Development Studies*, 20(4), pp. 203–23.

Sachs, Jeffrey and Andrew Warner (1995), 'Economic Convergence and Economic Policies', HIID Development Discussion Paper No. 502. Cambridge, MA: Harvard Institute for International Development.

Salmen, Lawrence (1990), 'Institutional Dimensions of Poverty Reduction', Policy, Research, and External Affairs Working Papers, Washington, DC: The World Bank.

Santiso, Carlos (1999), 'Towards Democratic Governance: Democracy and Good Governance in Latin America and the Contribution of the Multilateral Development Banks', unpublished manuscript, International Institute for Democracy and Electoral Assistance, Stockholm.

Sautter, Hermann (1990), *Ordnung, Moral und wirtschaftliche Entwicklung. Das Beispiel Taiwan*, München: Weltforum-Verlag.

Schleifer, Andrei and Daniel Treisman (1998), *The Economics and Politics of Transition to an Open Market Economy. Russia* (OECD Development Center Studies), Paris: The OECD.

Schmieding, Holger (1994), 'From Plan to Market: On the Nature of the Transformation Crisis', *Weltwirtschaftliches Archiv*, 129(2), pp. 216–53.

Schneider, Eberhard (1999), *Probleme des Föderalismus in Russland* (Bericht des BIOst No. 24/1999), Köln.

Schneider, Eleonora (1999), 'Machtwechsel in der Slowakei. Ergebnisse der Parlamentswahlen 1998', *Aktuelle Analyse des BIOst*, No. 10/1999.

Scholte, Jan A. (1998), 'The IMF Meets Civil Society', *Finance and Development*, 35(3).

Schumpeter, Joseph A. (1976/1942), *Capitalism, Socialism and Democracy*, New York: Harper and Row (Harper Colophon Edition).

Self, Peter (1993), *Government by the Market? The Politics of Public Choice*, London: Macmillan.

Sen, Amartya (1985), 'A Sociological Approach to the Measurement of Poverty: A Reply to Professor Peter Townsend', *Oxford Economic Papers* (December 1985), pp. 669–70.

Sender, John (1999), 'Africa's Economic Performance: Limitations of the Current Consensus', *Journal of Economic Perspectives*, 13(3), pp. 89–114.

Shah, Anwar (1994), *The Reform of Intergovernmental Fiscal Relations in Developing and Emerging Market Economies*, Washington, DC: World Bank Policy and Research Series 23.

Shepsle, Kenneth A. (1991), 'Discretion, Institutions, and the Problem of Government Commitment', in: Pierre Bourdieu and James S. Coleman (eds), *Social Theory for a Changing Society*, Boulder, CO: Westview Press, pp. 245–63.

Shepsle, Kenneth A. (1999), 'The Political Economy of State Reform – Political to the Core', paper presented at the Third Annual Conference of the International Society for New Institutional Economics, Washington, DC, 16–18 September, 1999.

Shirk, Susan L. (1993), *The Political Logic of Economic Reform in China*, Berkeley, CA: University of California Press.

Shleifer, Andrei (1997), 'Government in transition', *European Economic Review*, 41(3–5), pp. 385–410.

Shleifer, Andrei and Robert W. Vishny (1998), *The Grabbing Hand: Government Pathologies and Their Cures*, Cambridge, MA: Harvard University Press.

Siermann, Clemens L.J. (1998), *Politics, Institutions and the Economic Performance of Nations*, Cheltenham, UK and Lyme, US: Edward Elgar.

Simon, Herbert A. (1961), *Administrative Behavior*, 2nd edition, New York: Macmillan.

Simon, Herbert A. (1991), 'Organizations and Markets', *Journal of Economic Perspectives*, 5(2), pp. 25–44.

Sinn, Gerlinde and Hans-Werner Sinn (1993), *Kaltstart: volkswirtschaftliche Aspekte der deutschen Vereinigung*, 3rd edition, München: Deutscher Taschenbuch-Verlag.

Skocpol, Theda (1985), 'Bringing the State Back In: Strategies and Analysis in Current Research', in Peter Evans; Dietrich Rueschemeyer and Theda Skocpol (eds) (1985), *Bringing the State Back In*, New York: Cambridge University Press.

Smith, R.M. (1992), 'If Politics Matters: Implications for a "New Institutionalism"', *Studies in American Political Development*, 6, pp. 1–36.

Snow, David A., Louis A. Zurcher and Sheldon Ekland-Olson (1980), 'Social Networks and Social Movements: A Microstructural Approach to Differential Recruitment', *American Sociological Review*, 45, pp. 787–801.

Stevens, Mike and Shiro Gnanaselvam (1995), 'The World Bank and Governance', *ids bulletin*, 26(2), pp. 97–105.

Stigler, George (1971), 'The Theory of Economic Regulation', *Bell Journal of Economics and Management Science*, 2(3), pp. 3–21.

Stiglitz, Joseph E. (1974), 'Incentives and Risk Sharing in Sharecropping', *Review of Economic Studies*, 41, pp. 219–55.

Stiglitz, Joseph E. (1989), 'Sharecropping', in: John Eatwell, Murray Milgate and Peter Newman (eds), *The New Palgrave. Economic Development*, New York: W.W. Norton, pp. 308–15.

Stiglitz, Joseph E. (1996), 'Some Lessons From the East Asian Miracle', *The World Bank Research Observer*, 11(2), pp. 151–77.

Stiglitz, Joseph E. (1997), 'The Role of Government in Economic Development', in: Michael Bruno and Boris Pleskovic (eds), *Annual World Bank Conference on Development Economics 1996*, Washington, DC: The World Bank, pp. 11–23.

Stiglitz, Joseph E. (1998a), 'More Instruments and Broader Goals: Moving Toward the Post-Washington Consensus', 1998 WIDER Annual Lecture, Internet Website: http://www.wider.unu.edu/stiglitx.htm.

Stiglitz, Joseph E. (1998b), 'Redefining the role of the state: *What* should it do? *How* should it do it? And *how* should these decisions be made?', paper presented at the Tenth Anniversary of MITI Research Institute (Tokyo, Japan).

Stiglitz, Joseph E. (1998c), 'Development Based on Participation – A Strategy for Transforming Societies', *Transition. The Newsletter About Reforming Economies*, 9(6), pp. 1–3.

Stiglitz, Joseph E. (1999), 'Whither Reform? Ten Years of the Transition', paper prepared for the Annual Bank Conference on Development

Economics, Washington, DC, 28–30 April, 1999, Internet Website: http://www.worldbank.org/research/abcde/washington_11/pdfs/stiglitz.pdf.

Stiglitz, Joseph E. (2000), 'What I learned at the world economic crisis', *The New Republic Online,* Internet Website: http://www.thenewrepublic.com/041700/stiglitz041700.html.

Stiglitz, Joseph E. and Marilou Uy (1996), 'Financial Markets, Public Policy, and the East Asian Miracle', *The World Bank Research Observer,* 11(2), pp. 249–76.

Streeten, Paul (1993), 'Markets and States: Against Minimalism', *World Development,* 21(8), pp. 1281–98.

Streeten, Paul (1996), 'Governance', in: M.G. Quibria and J. Malcolm Dowling (eds), *Current Issues in Economic Development. An Asian Perspective,* Hong Kong: Oxford University Press, pp. 27–66.

Streeten, Paul (1997), 'Nongovernmental Organizations and Development', *ANNALS, AAPSS,* 554, pp. 193–210.

Sturzenegger, Frederico and Mariano Tommasi (eds) (1998), *The Political Economy of Reform,* Cambridge, MA: The MIT Press.

Sugden, Robert (1986), *The Economics of Rights, Cooperation, and Welfare,* Cambridge: Blackwell.

Summers, Lawrence H. and Lant H. Pritchett (1993), 'The Structural-Adjustment Debate', *American Economic Review Papers and Proceedings,* 83(2), pp. 383–9.

Tanzi, Vito (1996), 'Fiscal Federalism and Decentralization: A Review of Some Efficiency and Macroeconomic Aspects', in: Michael Bruno and Boris Pleskovic, Boris (eds), *Proceedings of the Annual World Bank Conference on Development Economics 1995,* Washington, DC: The World Bank, pp. 295–316.

Telser, L.G. (1980), 'A Theory of Self-Enforcing Agreements', *Journal of Business,* 53, pp. 27–44.

Thanner, Benedikt (1999), 'Systemtransformation: Ein Mythos verblaßt. Der tiefe Fall Rußlands: Von der Plan- zur Subsistenzwirtschaft', *Osteuropa-Wirtschaft,* 44(3), pp. 196–225.

Thomas, Alan (1996), 'What is Development Management?', *Journal of International Development,* 8(1), pp. 95–110.

Tiebout, Charles M. (1956), 'A Pure Theory of Local Expenditures', *Journal of Political Economy,* 64(5), pp. 416–24.

Tollison, Robert D. (1987), 'Is the Theory of Rent-Seeking Here to Stay'? in: Charles K. Rowley (ed.), *Democracy and Public Choice. Essays in Honor of Gordon Tullock,* Oxford and New York: Basil Blackwell, pp. 143–57.

Transparency International (1999), *1999 Corruption Perception Index,* Internet Website: http://www.gwdg.de/~uwvw/.

Treisman, Daniel (1996), 'The Politics of Intergovernmental Transfers in Post-Soviet Russia', *British Journal of Political Science*, 26, pp. 299–335.

Tullock, Gordon (1959), 'Some Problems of Majority Voting', *Journal of Political Economy*, 67, pp. 571–79.

UNDP (1996), *Human Development Report 1996. Economic Growth and Human Development*, Carey, NC: Oxford University Press.

UNDP (1997), *The Shrinking State. Governance & Sustainable Human Development*, New York: UNDP.

Unger, Roberto Mangabeira (1998), *Democracy Realized: The Progressive Alternative*, London and New York: Verso.

Vanberg, Viktor (1983), 'Der individualistische Ansatz zu einer Theorie der Entstehung und Entwicklung von Institutionen', in: E. Boettcher, P. Herder-Dorneich, and K.E. Schenk (eds), *Jahrbuch für Neue Politische Ökonomie, Vol. 2.* Tübingen: Mohr, pp. 50–69.

Vanberg, Viktor (1996), 'Korreferat zum Referat von *Helmut Leipold*', in: Dieter Cassel (ed.), *Entstehung und Wettbewerb von Systemen* (Schriften des Vereins für Socialpolitik, Neue Folge Band 246), Berlin: Duncker & Humblot, pp. 117–21.

Varshney, Ashutosh (1993), 'Self-Limited Empowerment: Democracy, Economic Development and Rural India', *Journal of Development Studies*, 29(4), pp. 177–215.

Verma, Ramesh Kumar (1994), *Regionalism and Sub-Regionalism in State Politics. Social, Economic and Political Bases*, New Delhi: Deep & Deep Publications.

Vogel, Heinrich (2000), 'The Russian Economy under Putin: Doomed to Boom?', contribution to the Colloquium 'Where is Russia heading?' organized by the Centre for Defense Studies in Brussels, 1 March, 2000, Internet Website: http://www.biost.de/preswahl/vogel.htm.

Voigt, Stefan and Daniel Kiwit (1995), 'Black Markets, Mafiosi and the Prospects for Economic Development in Russia – A Case Study on the Interplay of External and Internal Institutions', unpublished manuscript, Jena.

Voigt, Stefan and Daniel Kiwit (1998), 'The Role and Evolution of Beliefs, Habits, Moral Norms, and Institutions', in: Herbert Giersch (ed.), *The Merits and Limits of Markets*, Berlin: Springer, pp. 83–108.

Wade, Robert (1990), *Governing the Market: Economic Theory and the Role of Government in East Asian Industrialization*, Princeton, NJ: Princeton University Press.

Wade, Robert (1998), 'The Asian Debt-and-development Crisis of 1997–?: Causes and Consequences', *World Development*, 26(8), pp. 1535–53.

Wade, Robert (1999), 'Gestalt Shift. From "Miracle" to "Cronyism" in the Asian Crisis', *IDS Bulletin*, 30(1), pp. 134–50.

Wagener, Hans-Jürgen (1999), 'Rückkehr nach Europa' (Frankfurt Institute for Transformation Studies Discussion Paper No. 16/99), Frankfurt/Oder: Europa Universität Viadrina.

Wagener, Hans-Jürgen and Heiko Fritz (1998), 'Transformation – Integration – Vertiefung. Zur politischen Ökonomie der EU-Osterweiterung', in: Hans-Jürgen Wagener and Heiko Fritz (eds), *Im Osten was Neues. Aspekte der EU-Osterweiterung*, Bonn: Dietz, pp. 16–43.

Wallich, Christine I. (ed.) (1994), *Russia and the Challenge of Fiscal Federalism* (World Bank Regional and Sectoral Studies), Washington, DC: The World Bank.

Weber, Max (1972/1921), *Wirtschaft und Gesellschaft. Grundriss der verstehenden Soziologie*, Tübingen: J.C.B. Mohr (Paul Siebeck).

Weiner, Myron and Samuel P. Huntington (eds) (1987), *Understanding Political Development*, Boston: Little, Brown.

Weingast, Barry R. (1984), 'The Congressional-Bureaucratic System: A Principal–Agent Perspective (With Application to the SEC)', *Public Choice*, 44, pp. 147–92.

Weingast, Barry R. (1993), 'Constitutions as Governance Structures: The Political Foundations of Secure Markets', *Journal of Institutional and Theoretical Economics*, 149(1), pp. 286–311.

Weingast, Barry R. (1995), 'The Economic Role of Political Institutions: Market-Preserving Federalism and Economic Development', *Journal of Law, Economics & Organization*, 11(1), pp. 1–31.

Weingast, Barry R. (1996), 'Rational Choice Perspectives on Institutions', in: Robert E. Goodin and Hans-Dieter Klingemann (eds), *A New Handbook of Political Science*, New York: Oxford University Press.

Weingast, Barry R. (1997), 'The Political Foundations of Democracy and the Rule of Law', *American Political Science Review*, 91, pp. 245–63.

Weingast, Barry R. and William J. Marshall (1988), 'The Industrial Organization of Congress', *Journal of Political Economy*, 96, pp. 132–63.

Weiss, Linda (1998), *The Myth of the Powerless State*, Ithaca, NY: Cornell University Press.

Weiss, Linda and John M. Hobson (1995), *States and Economic Development. A Comparative Institutional Analysis*, Cambridge: Polity Press.

Werlin, Herbert (1991), 'Ghana and South Korea: Lessons from World Bank Case Studies', *Public Administration and Development*, 11(3), pp. 245–55.

Willgerodt, Hans (1994), '1948 und 1990: Zwei deutsche Wirtschaftsreformen im Vergleich', in: Carsten Herrmann-Pillath, Otto Schlecht and Horst Friedrich Wünsche (eds), *Marktwirtschaft als Aufgabe. Wirtschaft und Gesellschaft im Übergang vom Plan zum Markt,* Stuttgart: Gustav Fischer Verlag, pp. 65–78.

Williamson, John (1990), 'What Washington Means by Policy Reform', in: John Williamson (ed.), *Latin American Adjustment. How much has happened?* Washington, DC: Institute for International Economics, pp. 5–20.

Williamson, John (1993), 'Democracy and the "Washington Consensus"', *World Development,* 21(8), pp. 1329–36.

Williamson, John (ed.) (1994), *The Political Economy of Policy Reform,* Washington, DC: Institute for International Economics.

Williamson, John (1997), 'The Washington Consensus Revisited', in: Louis Emmerij (ed.), *Economic and Social Development into the XXI Century,* Washington, DC: Inter-American Development Bank.

Williamson, John and Stephan Haggard (1994), 'The Political Conditions for Economic Reform', in: John Williamson, (ed.), *The Political Economy of Policy Reform,* Washington, DC: Institute for International Economics, pp. 527–96.

Williamson, Oliver E. (1971), 'The Vertical Integration of Production: Market Failure Considerations', *American Economic Review, Papers and Proceedings,* 61, pp. 112–23.

Williamson, Oliver E. (1975), *Markets and Hierarchies: Analysis and Antitrust Implications,* New York: The Free Press.

Williamson, Oliver E. (1976), 'Franchise bidding for Natural Monopolies (in General and with Respect to CATV', *Bell Journal of Economics,* 7, pp. 73–104.

Williamson, Oliver E. (1979), 'Transaction-cost economics: The governance of contractual relations', *Journal of Law and Economics,* 22, pp. 233–61.

Williamson, Oliver E. (1985), *The Economic Institutions of Capitalism. Firms, Markets, Relational Contracting,* New York: The Free Press.

Williamson, Oliver E. (1991) 'Economic Institutions: Spontaneous and Intentional Governance', *Journal of Law, Economics, & Organization,* 7, Special Issue, pp. 159–87.

Williamson, Oliver E. (1995), 'The Institutions and Governance of Economic Development and Reform', in: Michael Bruno and Boris Pleskovic (eds), *Proceedings of the World Bank Annual Conference on Development Economics 1994,* Washington, DC: The World Bank, pp. 171–97.

Williamson, Oliver E. (1996a), 'Economic Institutions and Development: A View from the Bottom', paper presented at the All-India Distinguished

Speakers Conference: A New Institutional Approach to Development: Achieving India's Full Potential, New Delhi, Madras, and Calcutta, January 1996.

Williamson, Oliver E. (1996b), *The Mechanisms of Governance*, New York: Oxford University Press.

Williamson, Oliver E. (1999), 'Public and Private Bureaucracies: A Transaction Cost Economics Perspective', *Journal of Law, Economics, & Organization*, 15(1), pp. 306–42.

Wilson, James Q. (1989), *Bureaucracy. What Government Agencies Do and Why They Do It*, New York: Basic Books.

Winiecki, Jan (1990), 'Why economic reforms fail in the Soviet system: A property rights-based approach', *Economic Inquiry*, 28(2), pp. 195–221.

Wohlmuth, Karl (1998), 'Good Governance and Economic Development. New Foundations for Growth in Africa', Berichte aus dem Weltwirtschaftlichen Colloquium der Universität Bremen No. 59.

Wolf, Holger C. (1999), 'Transition Strategies: Choices and Outcomes' (Princeton Studies in International Finance No. 85), Princeton, NJ.

Wolfensohn, James D. (1999), 'Keynote Address', presented at the IMF Institute Conference on 'Second Generation Reforms: Reflections and New Challenges', Washington, DC, 8 November, 1999, Internet Website: http://www.imf.org/external/pubs/ft/seminar/1999/reforms/index.htm.

Woo-Cumings, Meredith (ed.) (1999), *The Developmental State*, Ithaca, NY and London: Cornell University Press.

World Bank (1989), *Sub-Saharan Africa. From Crisis to Sustainable Growth. A Long-Term Perspective Study*, Washington, DC: The World Bank.

World Bank (1990), *World Development Report 1990. Poverty.* Oxford et al.: Oxford University Press.

World Bank (1991), *World Development Report 1991. The Challenge of Development*, Oxford et al.: Oxford University Press.

World Bank (1992), *Governance and Development.* Washington, DC: The World Bank.

World Bank (1993), *The East Asian Miracle. Economic Growth and Public Policy*, Oxford: Oxford University Press.

World Bank (1994), *Governance. The World Bank's Experience*, Washington, DC: The World Bank.

World Bank (1995a), *Bureaucrats in Business: The Economics and Politics of Government Ownership*, New York: Oxford University Press.

World Bank (1995b), *China. Macroeconomic Stability in a Decentralized Economy* (A World Bank Country Study), Washington, DC: The World Bank.

World Bank (1995c), *Economic Developments in India. Achievements and Challenges* (A World Bank Country Study), Washington, DC: The World Bank.

World Bank (1996), *World Development Report 1996. From Plan to Market,* Oxford *et al.*: Oxford University Press.

World Bank (1997), *World Development Report 1997. The State in a Changing World,* Oxford *et al.*: Oxford University Press.

World Bank (1998), *Global Development Finance,* Washington, DC: The World Bank.

Yoshimoto, Masaru and Kenichi Ohno (1999), 'Capital-Account Crisis and Credit Contraction. The New Nature of Crisis Requires New Policy Responses' (Asian Development Bank Institute Working Paper No. 2), Internet Website: http://adbi.org/publications/wp/wp9905.htm.

Young, Alwyn (1995), 'The Tyranny of Numbers: Confronting the Statistical Realities of the East Asian Growth Experience', *Quarterly Journal of Economics,* CX(3), pp. 641–80.

Zak, Paul J. and Stephen Knack (1999), 'Trust and Growth', paper presented at the Third Annual Conference of the International Society for New Institutional Economics, Washington, DC, 16–18 September, 1999.

Zecchini, Salvatore (ed.) (1997), *Lessons from the Economic Transition. Central and Eastern Europe in the 1990s,* Dordrecht: Kluwer.

Zhuravskaya, Ekaterina V. (2000), 'Market-Hampering Federalism: Local Incentives for Reform in Russia', in: Jean-Jacques Dethier (ed.), *Governance, Decentralization and Reform in China, India and Russia,* Boston, MA: Kluwer Academic Publishers.

Index